ASSASSIN'S CREED
ORIGINS

Art by Li Ke Yi

TABLE OF CONTENTS

INTRODUCTION 5

THE ESSENTIALS. 6

MAIN QUESTS 18

SIDE QUESTS 78

ACTIVITIES. 200

   GLADIATOR ARENA. 202
   HIPPODROME. 210
   HUNTING GROUNDS 213
   PAPYRI PUZZLES. 216
   STONE CIRCLES 225
   TOMBS AND ANCIENT MECHANISMS 228
   WAR ELEPHANTS 237
   HERMIT LOCATIONS. 239
   PTOLEMY STATUES. 240
   OTHER ACTIVITIES 243
   MILITARY STRONGHOLDS 245

ATLAS OF ANCIENT EGYPT 260

REFERENCE AND ANALYSIS. 294

   THE HEROES. 296
   ENEMIES 300
   ABILITIES. 305
   GEAR 308
   INVENTORY 324
   CRAFTING 328
   ACHIEVEMENTS AND TROPHIES. 332

INTRODUCTION

THE FINAL PTOLEMAIC DYNASTY

THE BIRTH OF THE CREED

The year is 49 B.C.E., well into the 33rd dynasty of the Ptolemaic period and only two years since Cleopatra VII and Ptolemy XIII were named co-rulers of Egypt. It is a tumultuous time; after Cleopatra VII is forced into exile by her younger brother, she plots her return in an attempt to regain her rightful spot on the throne.

In *Assassin's Creed Origins*, you play the character Bayek. He is a proud Medjay on a mission of revenge against those he feels had a hand in his son's death.

This guide leads you through Bayek's campaign of retaliation with detailed maps and comprehensive strategies, as well as full coverage of every Medjay side quest.

There are also plenty of activities to keep Bayek busy beyond the campaign and side quests. These are all covered in the Activities chapter. This includes coverage of every tomb, stone circle, animal lair, war elephant, papyrus puzzle, hermit location, Ptolemy statue, gladiator arena boss, hippodrome race, and Phylake.

Turn to the Atlas of Ancient Egypt in this book to find every significant location plotted on meticulous maps of all 34 territories.

The Reference chapter offers lists of every inventory item, piece of gear, and ability along with achievements and trophies—providing you with everything you need to create the most lethal Assassin.

Upgrade the Medjay to his fullest potential and exact revenge against the corruption that has befallen Egypt.

THE ESSENTIALS

This chapter provides essential information to get you up and running in *Assassin's Creed Origins*. The game does a good job of teaching you the basics, so this coverage is limited to the following unique aspects of the game.

Those familiar with past *Assassin's Creed* games should be accustomed to the climbing and stealth gameplay. However, changes have been made to combat and a new loot system has been implemented.

PLAYER HEALTH AND SHIELD

The player's health is calculated based on current level, breastplate crafting level, and added Health Points from the equipped shield.

Your health regenerates anytime you are removed from conflict. In combat, your health regenerates once you own the Regeneration ability.

The health bar is made up of three equal sections. If your health dips into the middle section, it can rebuild to only two full sections. If it dips into the final segment, it may regenerate to only one full section. Therefore, for a prolonged battle, you really want to avoid losing more than one section of health—fleeing to safety before allowing it to dip that far. Keeping your health in the upper third can go a long way when battling tougher foes.

Shields make you more resistant to damage by increasing your Health Points. Hold up your shield by activating Shield Lock to negate all or part of an enemy's attack. The Shield Charge ability allows you to run at your target and bash with the shield. This consumes adrenaline, so use it sparingly.

When facing a soldier with a shield, you typically have to perform a shield break before attacking from the front. (Certain weapons can push shields out of the way.) With the Charge Heavy Attack ability, you can charge a heavy attack—allowing you to break any size shield, including a tower shield. This move leaves you briefly vulnerable, so time it well.

COMBAT

Combat comes in three varieties: ranged, melee, and stealth. Ranged combat consists mostly of bows and arrows. Four types of bows offer different attacks: hunter bows (standard),

predator bows (sniping), light bows (rapid fire), and warrior bows (spread fire). Note that headshots deal considerably more damage. You can also use a selection of tools from a distance.

You can perform melee attacks using bare fists or one of seven types of melee weapons, which range from the quick dual swords to the slow but deadly heavy blades.

Stealth attacks/assassinations are the simplest and quietest means to kill your rivals. Sneak up on or situate yourself above an unsuspecting foe and press the Interact button to attempt an assassination. The higher Bayek's level is in relation to the target, the more likely the assassination will succeed. The crafting level of the hidden blade also determines the amount of damage caused with a sneak attack. When a stealth attack is available, the enemy's health bar shows the amount of damage that will be caused with a successful attack.

HORSES IN COMBAT

Fighting on a horse presents extra challenges, as you control the mount while attempting to attack your rivals. This also gives a tactical advantage, since you are

harder to hit (if you stay on the move). Attacks are performed in the same manner, except that you are on a mobile horse.

When fighting a horseman, attacks against the horse damage the rider. Swipe at the moving target with light attacks and use your bow when farther away. It is possible to knock the enemy off the horse with enough damage.

FOCUS

Click the right stick to focus your attention on your target. Move the right stick in another enemy's direction to switch focus. This is extremely helpful when multiple foes are nearby. Try to target the biggest threats first and attempt to pull them away from packs, but be careful of ranged fire from your opponents. If possible, maneuver so that objects are situated between the archers and you.

DAMAGE

Damage caused is dependent on many factors, including the weapon and its level, Bayek's level, and the crafting level of certain gear (bracer, stabilizer, and hidden blade). A higher quality rating on a weapon typically indicates more damage.

ADRENALINE METER AND OVERPOWER MODE

An adrenaline meter appears at the bottom of your HUD, above the health bar. The bar builds with every successful hit with bonuses when certain attributes are attached to your weapon (such as Adrenaline on Hit). Once it is full, the Light Attack + Heavy Attack buttons appear on the bar, indicating that your Overpower ability is available. Pressing the two buttons releases the devastating attack, though be sure the timing is right. With an enemy targeted, wait for an opening and perform the ability.

The attack varies, depending on the type of melee weapon equipped. Regular swords, dual swords, spears, and heavy blades perform an overpower attack. Sickle

swords, heavy blunts, and scepters trigger a fury mode, which increases damage and speed for a few seconds.

TAGGING AN ENEMY

By aiming your bow at an enemy or moving the reticle over a foe in Senu's hover mode, you can tag the target, making them visible even when behind cover. A marked enemy's level is indicated above his head. A red background on an enemy's level indicates he is a higher level than you. A skull means he is at least four levels above yours, so consider retreating in this case.

A yellow crown above the enemy's tag signifies an objective. This includes captains and commanders at military strongholds and the primary target at animal lairs.

STEALTH

Stealth has been a staple throughout the *Assassin's Creed* series, and it doesn't stop with *Origins*. Use stealth whenever possible to improve odds of success.

Tall grass, hay/palm leaf piles, and booths offer hiding spots for Bayek—allowing you to perform assassinations on unsuspecting foes and escape an enemy pursuit. Hold

the Loot button next to a corpse to pick it up. Place it in inconspicuous locations or other guards will become alert when they find a corpse. These hiding locations are great spots to stow the bodies.

Press down on the D-pad to perform a short whistle. This gets the attention of a nearby enemy, and he may investigate the sound. Perform the whistle from a hiding spot and assassinate the foe when he's close enough.

MOUNTS AND VEHICLES

Running and climbing are great for getting around the immediate environment, but sometimes you need to travel long distances. This is where mounts and vehicles come in. You can use camels, horses, chariots, carts, and feluccas to traverse the world.

You can purchase a variety of camels, horses, and chariots (if you have the Chariot Owner ability) from the stables—though they can also be swiped. With the Hijack ability, simply approach an NPC riding a mount or vehicle and hold the Loot button to take it. You can also find mounts parked at various locations, such as stables and docks. They are free for the taking, but you may end up with an owner in pursuit. Horses, camels, and chariots that you own appear on the Gear screen. Select which one you wish to respond to your call and then hold down on the D-pad out in the world.

Press the Loot button to mount, and use the left stick to explore the overworld. The Dodge button slows the vehicle down. Holding the Grab Ledge button dismounts. Note that controlling a racing chariot at the hippodrome is completely different than driving out in the world. Refer to the Activities section for more details on the hippodrome.

Hold down the Parkour Interaction button to automatically follow the road. This works only when you are near a road and can't control where it goes. This allows you to sit back and enjoy the ride, though be careful you don't end up in a restricted area. Hold down the same button to cancel a follow command.

CART USAGE

You can use hay carts as a vehicle, but they also have other uses. Hop onto the back to hide in the hay and let the driver take you into restricted areas. You can

also set the hay on fire—a great distraction when attempting to sneak past guards.

FELUCCAS

A felucca is the ideal method for accessing ships or locations in the middle of a waterway. Feluccas do not require the Hijack ability, as Bayek can ask anyone to give up their boat by climbing on board and pressing the Loot button. Hold down the Heavy Attack button and the felucca will slowly build speed as the wind pushes it through the water. If you wish to take a ride on someone's felucca, hold the Loot button next to the mast and then sit back and relax.

ANIMUS PULSE

Animus Pulse allows you to detect nearby objectives and loot. Hold up on the D-pad to send out the pulse.

Items within range are marked as follows: white triangles signify loot, blue triangles indicate writings and yellow triangles indicate mission items.

Use this ability often to mark loot for easy identification. Treasure chests, jewelry boxes, and satchels also give off a sparkle.

Get accustomed to the sounds of Animus Pulse as it locates items. This allows you to quickly assess whether anything is nearby—especially helpful when searching enemy strongholds or dark tombs.

DISCOVERING LOCATIONS

Earn 25 XP simply by discovering locations. Moving close to any location—such as viewpoints, forts, tombs, Stone Circles, and treasures—displays the name on your HUD and rewards you with the XP. On your map, the site changes from a "?" to the appropriate icon. Entering a region for the first time earns 50 XP.

COMPLETING LOCATIONS

Besides cities, villages, gladiator arenas, and the hippodrome, every location can be completed to earn XP and other possible rewards. Treasure locations are noted on the map only as "treasure"; there are treasures littered throughout the country.

COMPLETE LOCATIONS

LOCATION TYPE	TOTAL ON MAP	HOW TO COMPLETE	REWARD
Ancient Mechanism	6	Activate mechanism	250 XP
Animal Lairs	40	Kill specific animal	150, 300, or 450 XP
Fort	10	Kill commander, kill captain, collect treasure	500, 1,000, or 1,500 XP
Hermit Location	5	Meditate at each location	1 AP
Medium Military	16	Kill captain, collect treasure	300, 600, or 900 XP
Papyrus Puzzle	25	Collect papyrus	150, 300, or 450 XP
Papyrus Reward	25	Find treasure	500 XP, 750 drachmas, piece of gear
Ptolemy Statue	19	Destroy statue	150, 300, or 450 XP
Small Military	78	Kill captain, collect treasure	200, 400, or 600 XP
Stone Circle	12	Align the stars	150, 300, or 450 XP
Tomb	14	Find ancient tablet	1 AP
Treasure	157	Find the indicated number of treasure	150, 300, or 450 XP
Viewpoint	58	Climb to the top and synchronize	100, 200, or 300 XP
War Elephant	4	Kill the elephant	1 AP, piece of gear

USING THE MAP

Access the map screen for an overhead view of the entire game world. Zoom out to see all 33 regions. At first only Siwa is visible, as the other regions are covered in fog. The city icon and viewpoints are displayed with question marks at every other site. These locations switch to the appropriate icons as you discover them. Press the Parkour Interaction button to place a custom marker.

FAST TRAVEL

Several locations offer a Fast Travel option—travel there immediately by highlighting the icon on the map screen and holding the indicated button. You can Fast Travel to cities, villages, gladiator arenas, and the hippodrome once you discover/unlock these areas. Viewpoints must be completed before you can Fast Travel to their locations.

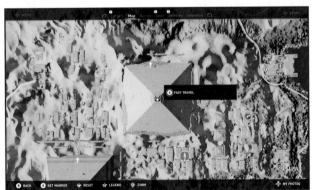

ABILITIES/ABILITY POINTS

The ability screen displays all available abilities as a skill tree. The player begins with three abilities: Eagle Tagging, Overpower, and Call Mount. As you earn Ability Points—by leveling up, completing a tomb, killing a war elephant, and meditating at the hermit locations—you may purchase skills. Refer to the Abilities section of the "Reference and Analysis" chapter for more information.

INVENTORY

The inventory screen shows how many of each item you currently possess. Highlight an item for more information. Refer to the Inventory section of the "Reference and Analysis" chapter for a full listing.

INVENTORY ITEMS

ITEM TYPE	DESCRIPTION
Animal Goods	Only good for selling to merchants. Loot from dead animals.
Arrows	Ammo for the four bow types. Refill at ammo stand or blacksmith. (Ammo stands take some time to refill after use.)
Resources	Gathered in the wild or swiped from military convoys. Used to upgrade gear.
Tools	Six tools used in combat. Corresponding abilities are required to acquire the tools. Refill at ammo stand or blacksmith.
Trinkets	Only good for selling to merchants. Loot from small-value containers.

INTRODUCTION

THE ESSENTIALS

MAIN QUESTS

SIDE QUESTS

ACTIVITIES

ATLAS

REFERENCE & ANALYSIS

EXPERIENCE AND LEVELING UP

In order to get stronger and take on tougher quests and activities, you need to earn experience (XP). To do so, find new locations, defeat enemies, complete quests and activities, and complete certain locations.

You accrue XP, and at certain levels, you moves up to the next player level. Each level also earns you an Ability Point (AP) that you can put toward new abilities. (See the table below for the specific amounts of XP required to reach each level.)

Bayek maxes out at Level 40, but you still earn XP. At this point, every 20,000 XP gets you another AP. You can do this indefinitely.

XP REQUIRED TO LEVEL UP

LEVEL	XP TO NEXT LEVEL	TOTAL XP	LEVEL	XP TO NEXT LEVEL	TOTAL XP	LEVEL	XP TO NEXT LEVEL	TOTAL XP
1	1,000	0	15	4,400	27,100	29	13,400	137,200
2	1,100	1,000	16	4,900	31,500	30	14,400	150,600
3	1,200	2,100	17	5,400	36,400	31	15,400	165,000
4	1,300	3,300	18	5,900	41,800	32	16,400	180,400
5	1,400	4,600	19	6,400	47,700	33	17,400	196,800
6	1,500	6,000	20	6,900	54,100	34	18,400	214,200
7	1,600	7,500	21	7,400	61,000	35	19,400	232,600
8	1,700	9,100	22	7,900	68,400	36	20,400	252,000
9	1,800	10,800	23	8,400	76,300	37	21,400	272,400
10	1,900	12,600	24	8,900	84,700	38	22,400	293,800
11	2,400	14,500	25	9,400	93,600	39	23,400	316,200
12	2,900	16,900	26	10,400	103,000	40	—	339,600
13	3,400	19,800	27	11,400	113,400			
14	3,900	23,200	28	12,400	124,800			

GEAR

WEAPON STATS

STAT	DESCRIPTION
Hidden Blade Damage	Upgrading your hidden blade increases your stealth attack damage.
Ranged Damage	Based on your character level, stabilizer crafting level, and damage of your equipped bow.
Melee Damage	Based on your character level, bracer crafting level, and damage of your equipped melee weapon.

OVERPOWER ATTACK AND MUTUAL ATTRIBUTES OF EACH WEAPON TYPE

WEAPON TYPE	DESCRIPTION	OVERPOWER	MUTUAL ATTRIBUTE
Dual Swords	Get more hits in with dual wielding. Great against one enemy, making it hard for your target to get a hit in. Which is good, since you cannot raise your shield. You can still use the Parry and Shield Charge abilities when using the left sword instead of a shield.	Jump attack with both swords extended	Adrenaline Regeneration
Heavy Blades	Heavy blades are very powerful but attack at an average speed. Its big swinging attacks cut right through an enemy, especially with successful combos, but they are relatively easy to avoid.	Vicious overhead swing at target.	Adrenaline on Hurt
Heavy Blunts	Incredibly powerful attacks but slow, leaving you vulnerable against quick opponents. Wind up your attack just as your rival finishes.	Fury mode (stronger and faster attacks) while meter drains. Be sure there are opponents around before releasing this special.	Adrenaline on Kill
Hunter Bows	Standard bow. Fires single shot; ideal for hunting. Enhanced hunter bow allows you to break a shield defense by holding the Heavy Attack button.	N/A	Charging Speed
Light Bows	The automatic bow. You remove 5 arrows from quiver and can shoot them off in quick succession. Hold down Heavy Attack to release them one after another. There is a pause before the next shot as Bayek grabs 5 more arrows from the quiver. Enhanced Light Bow increases the stability while shooting.	N/A	Rate of Fire
Predator Bows	Long-distance bow. Capable of hitting targets from farther away, allowing you to pick off guards from a safe locale. Enhanced Predator Bow ability allows you to control the arrow for more precise sniping.	N/A	Stealth Damage

WEAPON TYPE	DESCRIPTION	OVERPOWER	MUTUAL ATTRIBUTE
Regular Sword	Well-balanced weapon that is used in combination with your shield to throw enemies off guard. Follow up an evade with a light attack for a step-stab against vulnerable foes.	Vicious running stab. Be sure your target is stationary enough that your run attack will make contact.	Critical Hit Rate
Scepters	Scepters are long weapons with a blunt end and fast attacks. Open up your opponent with the long reach of a heavy attack and then strike with a flurry of light attacks.	Fury mode (stronger and faster attacks) while meter drains. Be sure there are opponents around before releasing this special.	Combo Multiplier
Shields	Adds to Bayek's HP. Use Shield Lock to deflect attacks. Parry and Shield Charge abilities allow you to use the shield to open up an opponent for attack.	N/A	Melee Resistance
Sickle Sword	The sickle sword's swings can flip an enemy around; great against soldiers carrying shields.	Fury mode (stronger and faster attacks) while meter drains. Be sure there are opponents around before releasing this special.	Bleeding on Hit
Spears	Long, pointed weapon that you can use in a swinging motion or a straight stab (heavy attack). It has a long reach and average power, allowing the player to stay outside the range of swords. Just after an opponent attacks, perform a lunge stab with the heavy attack and follow it up with a swinging light attack.	Two-step lunge and upward swing in an attempt to impale the target. Be sure your opponent is within range, as you take only a couple steps in.	Critical Hit Damage
Warrior Bows	The shotgun of bows. Fires 5 arrows at once, providing a spread effect, possibly hitting multiple targets. (Some bows, such as the Scales of Truth, fire more arrows at once.) Enhanced Warrior Bow ability reduces the dispersion zone; hold down the Heavy Attack button, concentrating the damage on a single target.	N/A	Precision

Bayek has a plethora of bows, melee weapons, and shields to choose from as he progresses through his adventures. Four types of bows and seven varieties of melee weapons allow for many different fighting styles, each with their own advantages and disadvantages.

At first you can equip a bow, melee weapon, and shield. Obtain the Weapon Bearer and Bow Bearer abilities to equip two melee weapons and two bows, respectively. Press left on the D-pad to change bows, and press right to switch to the alternate melee weapon. This allows you to be ready for multiple situations.

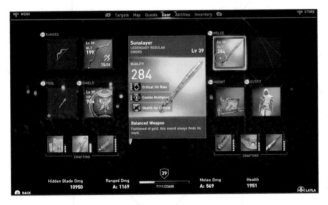

Besides increasing your weapon damage by purchasing or finding new items, you can also increase it by upgrading certain gear. Bow damage is improved with a higher-level stabilizer, while melee weapons see a boost with an upgraded bracer.

The level of weapons and shields you purchase from shops or loot from containers depends on your level. The level of gear dropped by enemies depends on their level, so if you kill a higher-level foe, you can end up with a more powerful weapon. However, you cannot equip the item until you reach its level.

At the Gear screen, you can see the "quality" of weapons and the HP of shields, along with an indication of how it compares to your equipped gear. While the quality/HP rating is the most important thing to consider when selecting your gear, you should also look at the attributes attached to each piece. Also remember that a blacksmith can upgrade your gear to your current level.

Each weapon and shield has at least one attribute attached; Rare gear possesses two attributes, and Legendary increases to three attributes. This makes the more uncommon items even more valuable beyond their increased quality. Seek out Legendary gear and upgrade it when it lags behind Bayek's level.

At any time you can dismantle weapons and shields at the Gear screen to receive bronze, cedarwood, and iron. Be careful you do not lose a favorite.

FIRE

Some weapons have the On Fire attribute, which can set a target ablaze with a successful hit. By touching an arrow to fire, especially prevalent at nighttime, you can use fire arrows from any bow. Fire can also be introduced by throwing your torch, though it doesn't travel very far.

Keep an eye out for the red oil jars that litter the landscape. It is highly flammable and can cause serious damage if fire is introduced to the element. If a fire sits next to a jar, simply bust it open with an arrow to create a hazard.

Refer to the Gear section of the "Reference and Analysis" chapter for more information on available weapons and shields, along with a full listing of their attributes.

INTRODUCTION

THE ESSENTIALS

MAIN QUESTS

SIDE QUESTS

ACTIVITIES

ATLAS

REFERENCE & ANALYSIS

TOOLS

Bayek carries a limited number of each tool, which can be increased by upgrading the tool pouch. The table displays the maximum number available at each level of the pouch. Tools can be refilled at any ammo stand or purchased from shops.

Six tools become available as you purchase the corresponding abilities: berserk, firebomb, flesh decay toxin, poison darts, sleep darts, and smoke screen. These abilities can be improved with other abilities on the Master Seer side of the skill tree. See Abilities in the "Reference and Analysis" chapter for more information.

AVAILABLE TOOLS

TOOL	MAX # (LV 0/1/2/3/4/5)	DESCRIPTION
Berserk	3/3/4/5/6/9	Use this substance on careless enemies to turn them against their allies.
Firebomb	3/3/4/5/6/9	Throw this bomb to set your enemies ablaze. While in game, hold left on D-pad to equip this tool.
Flesh Decay Toxin	5/6/7/8/10/15	Use this substance to infect a dead body and allow it to contaminate nearby enemies.
Poison Darts	3/3/4/5/6/9	Launch these darts to disable an enemy and spread poison to nearby enemies. While in game, hold left on D-pad to equip this tool.
Sleep Darts	3/3/4/5/6/9	Launch these darts to put lower-ranked enemies or animals to sleep and move past them without being detected. While in game, hold left on D-pad to equip this tool.
Smoke Screen	3/3/4/5/6/9	Use this powder in combat to blind nearby enemies.

FIREBOMB

USAGE:
Equip at Gear screen. Hold left on D-pad to switch to bombs. Aim and press Heavy Attack to toss it.

Firebombs set enemies and certain flammable objects on fire upon impact, causing extra elemental damage. Be careful, as Bayek can catch on fire just the same, so steer clear of the hazard. Fires are good for damaging your rivals, and they can create a barrier between enemies and yourself. Bayek can fling these a decent distance, so keep them in mind whenever infiltrating an enemy base. Be sure to aim above a distant target, as gravity brings the projectile to the ground.

SMOKE SCREEN

USAGE:
Press Loot button after performing melee attack or dodge roll.

Once you have the Smoke Screen ability, you can add a cloud of smoke to a fight after performing a successful melee attack or dodge roll. Quickly press the Loot button after these actions to use the powder, stunning nearby enemies and creating a smoke screen. With the Smoke Screen Damage ability, this tool becomes more valuable—damaging any enemy caught in the cloud.

The smoke breaks line of sight, allowing you to flee trouble, so it is best to have at least one available for fights that become overwhelming. Also note that you cannot target an enemy in a smoke screen.

Certain soldiers will use their own smoke bombs to create these clouds, so keep an eye out for incoming smoke—indicated by the yellow circle.

You can keep an enemy staggered by alternating melee attacks and smoke screens, though this will run through your supply quickly.

SLEEP DARTS

USAGE:
Equip at Gear screen. Hold left on D-pad to switch to darts. Aim and press Heavy Attack to throw it.

Sleep darts are incredibly useful in battle, especially when facing multiple foes. Enemies or animals at your level or lower will fall asleep with a successful hit. Use it on a lone rival and sneak past while he snoozes or hit one or two targets so that you can concentrate on another.

With the Animal Taming ability, you can use a sleep dart to get a companion. Put the animal to sleep and then hold the indicated button to make it your pet. Predators and defensive animals will fight by your side.

A meter counts down the time that the enemy or animal remains asleep. A slumbering foe will awaken with an arrow or melee attack, and you can assassinate them by pressing the Loot button. You can also apply Berserk to a sleeping enemy.

FLESH DECAY

USAGE:
After killing an enemy or animal, click the left stick next to any corpse to apply the toxin.

When standing next to any corpse, click the left stick to apply the Flesh Decay ability. These poisoned corpses contaminate nearby NPCs, staggering anyone caught in the gaseous cloud. When a group of enemies are incoming, infect a body between them and you—giving yourself extra time to get away or go in for easy kills.

BERSERK

USAGE:
Approach an enemy undetected and click the left stick.

Approach an enemy undetected and click the left stick to turn him berserk instead of assassinating him. This causes the foe to attack his nearest target. Note that this cannot be applied to captains and commanders at enemy bases.

Use this ability to cause chaos when infiltrating a stronghold. Note that you have a moment to apply berserk while being detected by a nearby guard. This is considered a hostile act, so if you use it on a soldier in an unrestricted area, they will come after you.

POISON DARTS

USAGE:
Equip at Gear. Hold left on D-pad to switch to darts. Aim and press Heavy Attack to throw it.

Hitting an enemy with a dart inflicts poison that periodically deals damage and contaminates nearby foes. This is a great way to begin a fight; hit a couple guards with the poison and let it spread to others. Bayek may not appreciate the smell, but the poison does not hurt him.

SENU

Senu is Bayek's pet and is an incredibly helpful asset for most aspects of the game. Press up on the D-pad to send your ally into the air. Hold the Heavy Attack button for faster flight, and hold the Aim button to enter hover mode, which allows Senu to mark enemies, animals, ballistae, underground entrances, and brazier alarms.

When tracking a quest, send Senu into the air when you near the next objective. A yellow arc points in that objective's direction. As the reticle gets closer, it becomes a circle and shrinks in size until the location is pinpointed and marked on the HUD. A similar white circle helps pinpoint the locations of enemies, ballistae, brazier alarms, and more.

Senu is unavailable when you are in a conflict, so survey a location before getting too close to hostiles. He also can't fly in a sandstorm, so wait it out if necessary.

A reward for completing each Viewpoint (synchronize at each location) is an increase in Senu's Perception. With a total of 58 Viewpoints, you can greatly improve the distance that your flying friend can sense objectives.

HUNT ASSISTANCE

Use Senu's hover mode to spot resources in the wild, whether on the animal or being transported by a military convoy. Mark the resource to create a custom waypoint for easier navigation. When the player hunts a prey animal (flamingo, gazelle, heron, ibex, ibis) in the world, Senu automatically starts attacking nearby prey and kills one of them.

SURVEY AND FIND TREASURE

Use Senu to survey locations. Enter hover mode by holding the Aim button and then look around the area. Hostiles are automatically tagged as the reticle gets close. The NPC's level is displayed above their head. Senu can also mark treasure,

ballistae, brazier alarms, and underground entrances—making your feathered friend invaluable when infiltrating enemy strongholds.

DISTANCE FINDER

Senu's hover mode is also useful for finding distance to a location that appears on your HUD. Place the reticle on an icon to display the distance (in meters) to that site. By pressing the Parkour Interaction button, you can set a custom marker, just as with the map.

ANIMALS

Animals, both wild and domesticated, played a big part in Ancient Egyptian culture, and they are prevalent in *Assassin's Creed Origins*. Hunt animals for valuable resources or tame them to gain a companion on your adventures.

ANIMALS OF ANCIENT EGYPT

ANIMAL	FULL NAME	TYPE	ANIMAL GOODS	CRAFTING RESOURCE	CAN BAYEK TAME?
Cat	Cat	Domestic	No	No	Yes
Cattle	Sanga Cattle	Domestic	No	No	Yes
Chicken	Chicken	Domestic	No	No	No
Cobra	Egyptian Cobra	Defensive	Cobras Venom	No	No
Crocodile	Nile Crocodile	Defensive	Crocodile egg	Hard Leather	Yes
Dog	Pharaoh Hound	Domestic	No	No	Yes
Donkey	African Wild Donkey	Domestic	No	No	Yes
Flamingo	Great Flamingo	Prey	Flamingo Tongue	No	No

ANIMAL	FULL NAME	TYPE	ANIMAL GOODS	CRAFTING RESOURCE	CAN BAYEK TAME?
Gazelle	Soemmerring's Gazelle	Prey	Gazelle Hooves	Soft Leather	Yes
Heron	Gray Heron	Prey	Heron Feather	No	No
Hippo	Hippopotamus	Defensive	Hippo Meat	Hard Leather	Yes
Hyena	Spotted Hyena	Predator	Hyena Ears	Soft Leather	Yes
Ibex	Nubian Ibex	Prey	Ibex Horn	Soft Leather	Yes
Ibis	African Sacred Ibis	Prey	Ibis Beak	No	No
Leopard	African Leopard	Predator	Leopard Fur	Pelt	Yes
Lion	Lion	Predator	Lion Claw	Pelt	Yes
Lioness	Lioness	Predator	Lion Claw	Pelt	Yes
Sheep	Sheep	Domestic	No	No	Yes
Vulture	Griffon Vulture	Defensive	Vulture Skull	No	No

HUNTING ANIMALS

Any animal that provides animal goods and/or resources is worth hunting when the opportunity arises. All of these items can be sold to merchants, while the resources are required to upgrade certain gear. The animals range from easy kills, such as ibex and gazelle, to tougher opponents, like lions and crocodile.

PREY

Use Senu to spot a desired resource and then head to that location to hunt the animal. Simple prey can be taken down with one arrow, but they will flee if they detect your presence. Senu joins in, occasionally taking down an animal too. You also find dead prey in the wild that have been killed by nearby predators. Be sure to loot their corpses.

PREDATORS

Predators attack Bayek as soon as they detect his presence. They are ferocious opponents at similar or higher levels. Limit fights with predators to one or two. Better yet, find a high point, inaccessible to the animals, where you can pick them off with your bow. If possible, use Flesh Decay after killing a member of a group for added damage.

Hyenas go down fairly easy but are often in big packs. Pick them off from afar if possible, but if you must take them on up close, do not allow yourself to become surrounded.

Lions and lionesses are the toughest predators to kill due to their strong exterior. Combine that with a ferocious claw attack and they are best avoided or taken down from a safe distance. If Senu spots a higher-level lion or worse, a pride of lions, steer clear of the site.

Leopards are easier to kill than lions, but their speed makes it tough to hit them. Up close, target the leopard, keeping it in front if possible. Leopards can ascend easy climbs, so when facing a group, find a vantage point that is more out of reach and pelt them with a volley of arrows.

DEFENSIVE

Cobras can be found almost anywhere, even inside big jars, so stay on your toes when exploring tombs and other tight quarters. They lunge at their target when within range in an attempt to poison but are easily taken out with an arrow or two. One sleep dart kills any cobra. A melee weapon can wipe out snakes with ease, though you do risk getting bitten in the process. Do not underestimate these guys in battle.

Hippos and crocodiles are the strongest defensive animals with their vicious attacks and tough exteriors. They are unable to climb anything more than a short step up, so take advantage of this and pelt them with arrows from a safe location.

Use a sleep dart on hippos to limit their attacks, since they often require numerous hits to take down. Watch out for their charge attack, dodging to the side to avoid the hit.

The crocodile's biggest attack is the tail whip, so be ready to step back when within range. Hack once or twice and immediately evade away to avoid taking the big hit.

TAMING ANIMALS

The Animal Taming ability allows Bayek to have a companion, though only a select few attack your target. Predators and defensive animals will fight alongside you, while prey and domestics simply follow. Birds cannot be tamed.

Hit an animal of similar or lower level with a sleep dart to put it to sleep. Approach the slumbering creature and hold the Grab Ledge button to tame it. Release the animal by holding this same button.

BEYOND THE QUESTS

There is plenty to keep the player busy beyond the main story and the numerous side quests. The following table lists activities along with the section of the guide in which we cover them.

ACTIVITIES

ACTIVITY	DESCRIPTION	CHAPTER COVERED
Ancient Mechanisms	Inside several tombs, find the mysterious Ancient Mechanism and activate it.	Activities
Gladiator Arenas	Arenas in Krokodilopolis and Cyrene offer the opportunity to fight against waves of soldiers, followed by one of seven bosses.	Activities
Hermit Locations	Meditate at five locations to earn 1 Ability Point for each.	Atlas of Ancient Egypt
Hippodrome	Race chariots at the hippodrome in Kanopos.	Activities
Military Strongholds	Forts, medium military, and small military locations are noted on the map with the following objectives: kill the captain(s), kill the commander, and collect the treasure.	Throughout quest chapters and activities
Papyrus Puzzles	Find Papyri within temples around Ancient Egypt, solve the riddle contained on the scroll, and collect the hidden treasure.	Activities
Phylakes	These bounty hunters hunt Bayek from the start of the game (ranging from Lv. 20-40). There are 10 of these foes that can be dispatched for specific rewards.	Activities
Ptolemy Statues	Destroy the statues of Ptolemy that have been erected in order to instill fear in the public.	Atlas of Ancient Egypt
Stone Circles	Find the Stone Circles and align the stars in the sky.	Activities
Tombs	Explore dark corridors, plunder treasure, and find the ancient tablet inside each tomb.	Activities
Treasures	There are many treasures scattered throughout Ancient Egypt, but completion XP is earned by collecting them at the locations noted as "Treasure."	Atlas of Ancient Egypt
War Elephants	Kill the powerful elephants at four locations.	Activities

CRAFTING

Use Senu to spot resources in the wild, collect the loot, and use them to upgrade some of your equipment. Refer to the Crafting section of the "Reference and Analysis" chapter for more information.

LOOT

We show locations for treasures found at "Treasure" locations, tombs, and enemy strongholds, but there are more to be found in the world. Use the Animus Pulse to sense nearby loot.

SHOPS

Blacksmiths, stables, and weavers are located in many cities and villages around Ancient Egypt. Their stock changes every time you return to the region and visit them. Level of weapons and shields are based on the player's level.

SHOP INVENTORY

SHOP	INVENTORY
Blacksmith	Weapons, shields, and arrows/tools refill as well as upgrade weapons and shields. With the Buy Materials ability, the blacksmith sells bronze, cedarwood, and iron.
Stables	Camels, horses, chariots (with Chariot Owner ability).
Weaver	Outfits. With the Buy Materials ability, the weaver sells hard leather, pelts, and soft leather.

A blacksmith can upgrade any piece of equipment that is below your current level. New weapons and shields come fairly often, but if you have a favorite, spend drachmas to bring it up to your level.

Nomad's Bazaar moves around 15 different locations, offering a limited number of carbon crystals and mystery gear. Reda also offers a daily quest.

ASSASSIN BUREAU (BUREAU OF THE HIDDEN ONES)

After the **final quest, Birth of the Creed**, the Bureau of the Hidden Ones becomes available in Memphis. Here you read documents that provide backstory, and an Assassin NPC sells special items. He carries Legendary gear along with the items in the following table.

BUREAU SHOP

LEGENDARY QUEST ITEM	DESCRIPTION	COST (DRACHMAS)
Tablet of Knowledge	This tablet holds the secrets of an ancient civilization. Reading it gives you 1,000 additional experience points. The Tablet of Knowledge can be purchased repeatedly to progress even more.	1,000

VIEWPOINTS

There are 58 Viewpoints located at high points around the world map, often requiring a lot of climbing to access. Once you reach a Viewpoint, hold the Loot button to synchronize the location—providing a great view of the area around you. Each Viewpoint rewards you with 100 XP. Also, the location becomes available for Fast Travel, nearby sites are discovered, and Senu's perception is increased—allowing the bird to detect farther away.

Every viewpoint has a safe spot to land below, into which Bayek can make a leap of faith.

SANDSTORMS

In any desert territory, a sandstorm can whip up at just about any time. A cloud of sand disrupts vision for you and for NPCs in the game. If you know enemy positions, take advantage of the situation and attack. Otherwise, retreat to safety and wait it out. Senu is unavailable during a sandstorm.

TAKING PHOTOS

If enabled in Gameplay Options, click the left and right analog sticks to snap a photo of your current view. These photos are then accessible at the map screen. Snap a picture within all 33 regions to earn the Reporter achievement/trophy.

AVENGE QUEST

When an online friend is killed in his game, you can find his corpse where he died. Interact with it to receive a new objective to defeat what killed your friend. You must be online for Avenge Quests to appear.

THE ESSENTIALS

MAIN QUESTS

SIDE QUESTS

ACTIVITIES

ATLAS

REFERENCE & ANALYSIS

MAIN QUESTS

WHAT'S INSIDE

When playing the main quests, you enter regions with gradually increasing, suggested playing levels. That's how this guide is organized. The intended path of the main quests is followed in this chapter. The side quests and activities that are encountered along the way are all covered in their own sections of the book.

While it is possible to reach the end of the main quests playing only the minimum required side quests, this is discouraged. It's best to clear each region of all the quests, side quests, and activities. Without the experience, weapons, and shields found during these side quests, the main quest becomes very difficult, as you would take on high-level challenges at a very low level and you would be ill equipped. The guide is arranged by the suggested participation level of each quest. The only exception is when a lower-level quest is unlocked after completing a higher-level quest; in this case it will come after the quest(s) that unlocks it.

SAQQARA PYRAMID

THE HERON ASSASSINATION

Bayek confronts his first target, Rudjek (known as the Heron) at the Saqqara Pyramid. By the appearance of the plump man's lavish wardrobe, it seems he is wealthy and holds a high position in Egypt's hierarchy. However, by the swiftness of his execution, and his inability to defend himself against Bayek's fueled rage, it's also obvious that Rudjek was not prepared to cross paths with Bayek, paying the ultimate price for his transgressions. The reason for this first of many targeted assassinations is not yet known.

SIWA

HOMECOMING

Prerequisite: Start the game

SUGGESTED LEVEL: 0	**UNLOCKS:** *The Oasis*	**DETAILS:** A weathered Bayek confronts the bodyguard of a man he killed.

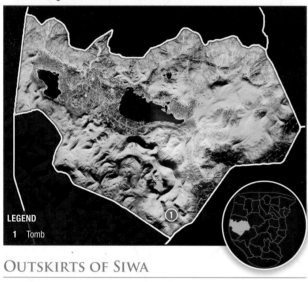

LEGEND

1 Tomb

OUTSKIRTS OF SIWA

A BATTLE TUTORIAL

You begin in the outskirts of Siwa **(1)** one month after assassinating the Heron. You are engaged in battle with a very large adversary. You're armed with a Level 1 Medjay shield and bronze sword. Hypatos is a Level 2 brute wielding a large heavy blunt mace seeking to avenge his fallen master. The battle begins with half his health depleted, as indicated by the gauge over his head.

During the battle with Rudjek's bodyguard, you learn how to lock on to your enemy and how to perform a block and light attack, following the onscreen prompts. If he picks you up and throws you on the ground, then you also learn how to recover. You have total freedom of movement during battle, and your positioning is very important while fighting.

Wait for Hypatos to swing and miss before you quickly move in for an attack. Then quickly move away as he draws back for another swing. Run behind your opponent after dodging an attack and hit him from behind repeatedly. Hypatos smashes the ground with his mace, breaking the ground below you. Both of you fall through the crumbling foundation.

The battle continues after the fall. Once you regain your stance, you are instructed on how to use Shield Break (which is the strong yet slower weapon attack). Then you are instructed on how to dodge—press the Dodge button while moving in any direction. This is a great way to quickly move away from an attack as it's happening.

A blue adrenaline gauge appears above your health meter. This gauge fills with each successful attack on your enemy.

ADRENALINE QUICK FILL

It's always faster to fill the adrenaline gauge using light attacks as opposed to the slower heavy attack. You accumulate adrenaline in equal amounts, regardless of whether it's a light or heavy hit; therefore, the more hits you can accumulate in the shorter amount of time, the faster the adrenaline gauge fills.

Once the adrenaline gauge is full, release the special attack. The controls to initiate the attack always appear on the gauge when it is full and ready to release. To release the attack, simultaneously press and hold both the Light and Heavy Attack buttons. Always select your target just before releasing a special attack. The actual attack that you perform depends on the weapon you're holding when the special attack is engaged.

Loot the body to acquire a mace and a few drachma. The mace is heavy and slow but does twice the damage of your sword. It has faster adrenaline regeneration and gives additional adrenaline on each kill. Consider using it for the next battle.

Leave the Battle Arena

ANIMUS PULSE

You can tag items of interest in a large radius surrounding you. A sound effect is heard and a pulse wave emanates from your position outward, tagging all items of interest in your vicinity. Items are only temporarily marked. Investigate each marker for collectibles. If the markers disappear before you find all the items, simply press the Animus Pulse button again to retag the remaining items.

Now it's time to start your adventure. Use Animus Pulse to mark a wall block covered in scrambling scarabs. Approach this area and press the Pass Through Crack button to push the

movable slab up, revealing a secret entrance that allows you inside the temple.

Temple Interior

ANTEROOM

Once inside, you learn how to use the torch for lighting. Press and hold the Torch button to raise and light a torch. You can throw your torch as a projectile using the Free Aim button in conjunction with the Throw Object button or just drop it by pressing the Drop Object button. The torch can also be used as an effective weapon—the fire that leaps onto an enemy continues to do damage even after the initial attack. Use Animus Pulse in the first room to locate some coins and other items on a high ledge above you.

TREASURES GALORE

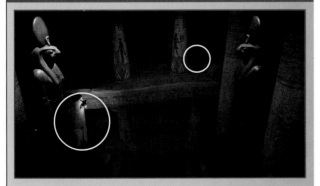

This first room in the temple exemplifies the treasure-hunting element in the game. Pulse the room again and look up to the ledge behind the entrance. A few markers light up. Use the cracked pillar on the right to reach the high ledge and loot the many containers.

LOOT CONTAINERS

On the high ledge above the entrance in the first room you'll find your first loot container. Unlike all the vases you can loot by simply pressing the Pick Up Object button, the loot containers appear with a "Loot" prompt gauge. To get the contents inside, press and hold the Pick Up Object button until the loot gauge fills. Loot containers often contain weapons or shields.

WHY YOU SHOULD LOOT

Even if you're not a collectionist, you should still pick up loot. Looting is the fastest way to make money, which you can use to upgrade and buy weapons and shields, clothing, crafting items, and mounts. There's a blacksmith in your hometown of Siwa. With the right amount of money, you can start out with a serious advantage over your enemies by upgrading your most powerful weapons and shield.

After looting the first chamber, vault over the fallen columns in the pathway, run up the stairs, and enter the second chamber.

THE SECOND CHAMBER

Fully explore the second chamber for loot. Use Animus Pulse to mark treasures located in almost every corner and then return to the fallen column **(A)** on the left. Use this column to climb to the high left ledge **(B)**. Access a network of tunnels through an opening here. There is also an open hallway in the back-left corner on the lower level near a stash of loot that connects to the tunnels above.

The left tunnel system has much more loot than you'll find on the right-side chambers **(C)**.

After you completely pillage the entire second chamber and connecting tunnels, return to the left upper ledge **(B)**. Climb over the large slab to reach a fallen column that allows you to jump to the back ledge **(D)**. From there, head to the final interior chamber.

FINAL CHAMBER

At the top, you are instructed on how to drop an item (the torch in this case). Climb either of the tall statues to the top of the head and then leap down to the ledge.

Approach the wall that's covered in crawling scarabs and perform either a light or heavy attack on the cracked wall to break through, allowing you to exit the tomb.

EXTERIOR HALL BATTLE

In the distance, you can see men fighting as you stand perched on a high ledge in a large exterior hall.

Rush into battle to help an old friend. Use the techniques learned in the introductory battle with Hypatos. There are four Level 1 soldiers that you can beat rather easily compared to your first competitor. You should be able to use your special adrenaline attack at least once during this fight.

HEPZEFA ESCORTS YOU HOME

After the battle, you reunite with your old friend Hepzefa. It's been a year since you've seen him. Bayek tells him that he's defeated one of the masked ones, the Heron. Hepzefa replies, "Four more!" It's apparent that your good friend is privy to your quest to assassinate those who have wronged you. He mounts his camel and invites you to rest at home.

BAYEK'S TATTOOS

When Bayek says, "No, no rest. Not until all the masked one's guts lie baking in the sand," he directs your attention to his tattooed arm. The masked ones are tattooed on his arm, and each time he assassinates one, he marks through their image with a sharp object.

THE OASIS

Prerequisite: Complete Main Quest: Homecoming

SUGGESTED LEVEL: 1	REWARD: 1,000 XP	UNLOCKS: Senu; Side Quest: Gear Up; Main Quest: The False Oracle	DETAILS: Bayek returns to Siwa. His close friend Hepzefa helps him prepare to battle the false Oracle, Medunamun.

WHISTLE TYPES

There are two different types of whistles available by pressing down on the D-pad. A quick press gives you an attention-getting whistle used to attract enemies to your location. Use this when you are hiding and they are unaware of your position. The second whistle is a longer one used to call your mount. Just hold down on the D-pad longer.

FOLLOW HEPZEFA

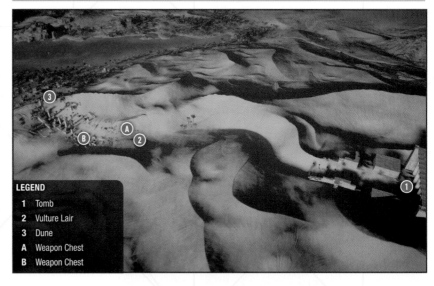

LEGEND

1. Tomb
2. Vulture Lair
3. Dune
A. Weapon Chest
B. Weapon Chest

At the Temple buried in the sand **(1)**, press and hold the Call Mount button to summon a camel. Mount it and follow Hepzefa back to Siwa. See Mount Controls in The Essentials chapter for riding help. During the ride, Hepzefa tells you about the conditions at Siwa since you left, focusing on the garrisons the soldiers set up to oppress the people.

VULTURE LAIR

The first area you come to is a small village **(2)** in ruins. This later becomes a Vulture Lair challenge covered in the Activities section of the guide. Use the Animus Pulse throughout this village to find all the loot. You'll be able to find weapon chests **(A)** and **(B)** inside the ruined structures.

Follow Hepzefa to the top of the dune **(3)** where Siwa's name is presented. Notice that 25 XP is given each time you discover a new area. Continue to follow Hepzefa down the dune and into your hometown.

SIWA

LEGEND
3   Dune (Siwa Intro)
4   Hepzefa's Home

Travel through Siwa and follow Hepzefa to his home **(4)**. Dismount and enter his home through the open doorway. It is a good idea to keep a low profile and avoid fights with Ptolemaic guards.

Hepzefa encourages you to rest, but you have no interest in that now. Rabiah enters the house in a panic about the local soldiers. While reuniting with Rabiah, she patches up your wounds as she has always done for you and your wife, Aya. She encourages you into a deep, much needed sleep.

PRACTICE USING THE BOW

BOW LESSON

After you wake up, Hepzefa hands you a bow outside and tells you to practice on the two target dummies in his backyard. Raise the bow, aim, and shoot the heads off the two dummies. The dummy on the right requires two shots to the head. This is because it is Level 3 and you are Level 1. If you need more arrows, take them from the supply next to you. When you finish with bow practice, a girl runs up and warns Hepzefa that soldiers are coming for him.

KILL THE SOLDIERS

A LESSON IN STEALTH

LEGEND
5   Tall Grass Assassination
6   Arrow Assassination/Front Door
7   Takedown Assassination
8   Takedown Assassination
9   Tall Grass
10   Whistle & Assassination
11   Last Soldier

As the two of you hide in nearby bushes **(5)**, you overhear the soldiers announcing that they are looking for the Medjay who killed Nomarch Rudjek.

DETECTION

The soldiers surround the house. Before control returns to you, the nearest soldier spots you in the tall grass. A white directional meter appears, pointing in his direction. This means you've been spotted. You are prompted to press the Crouch button to enter a stealth state by crouching in the tall grass around you. Your character will glow with a white light. This means you are hidden.

ASSASSINATION

As the soldier gets closer to you, the Awareness meter turns from a suspicious white to a cautious yellow and finally to an engaging battle red. You can perform a stealth attack when the meter displays any of these colors, including the last one (red) if you strike quickly enough. During this first trial kill, you always perform a successful stealth assassination, but be aware of those warning signs for all future attacks. Always try to strike before the Awareness meter turns red.

ASSASSINATED VS. KNOCKED OUT

Until you receive your hidden wrist blade, all stealth kills performed by hand result in an unconscious enemy lying on the ground and an extra step is required to assassinate them (use the Assassinate button to kill them). Once the enemy is dead, you can loot or move the body to hide it from others. This first body is in the tall grass and does not need to be hidden.

BOW TAGGING

The next closest soldier **(6)** is standing with his back to you at Hepzefa's front door. Pull out the bow and aim at the soldier. Notice that aiming the bow at the enemy tags them (the soldier's level appears in a marker over his head). Tagged enemies are visible through walls. The full orange meter above the enemy's head means that one shot will kill him. If you don't see a full orange gauge, then aim at the head to kill him. Release the arrow and assassinate your target while remaining in stealth.

Note that with enemies at levels higher than yours, you may not be able to kill them with one shot to the head. Therefore, it is important to do everything you can to always be above the enemies' levels. Achieve this by playing all the side quests and activities in a region before moving on to the next.

When you shoot the soldier near the door, Hepzefa picks up the body, moves it into the tall grass, and warns you to not leave bodies in the open. If another enemy sees the dead body, he leaves his patrol route and searches the area for you. Sometimes you may leave dead bodies where they lie as a strategy to lure enemies closer to your hiding place.

TAKEDOWN ASSASSINATION

Climb up the side of the house near the front door. Avoid passing in front of the open doorway on the second level (the patrolling soldier inside the house may spot you). Continue up the next wall to reach the second-floor balcony. Move directly to the west side, and perch on the short wall and look down. When the patrolling second-floor soldier **(7)** comes into view, you can perform a dropping takedown assassination. You can perform these from insane heights that would normally kill you if you weren't landing on an enemy. You can successfully execute this move only if the assassination prompt appears when the enemy is directly below you.

Climb back to the top balcony and move to the north side short wall. Wait for the soldier **(8)** patrolling below to walk into your dropping assassination range. Pounce on him.

WHISTLE TO ATTRACT ENEMIES

Crouch down and sneak into the tall weeds in the backyard **(9)**. Here you can spot your next target. A soldier **(10)** searches through the tall weeds. Move closer to him and then whistle. Do not hold down the Whistle button or you'll call your mount. Assassinate the soldier as he moves closer to inspect the sound.

Follow the tall weeds around to the house's east side. Remain crouched as you slowly and silently exit the weeds to come up behind the last patrolling soldier **(11)** and assassinate him.

RETURN TO HEPZEFA

Return to Hepzefa, who is going into his house **(6)**. He invites you upstairs and presents you a couple jobs that were given to him from the people of Siwa. He says that the real problem is with the next man on your hit list, Medunamun. Hepzefa suggests you become tougher and upgrade your armor before you take him on. This is a tip to level up, explore, and do some side quests before tackling an enemy with a higher level than yours.

He suggests you visit Benipe, the blacksmith, or use Senu's help finding better weapons. You believed your old friend Senu was dead, but Rabiah nursed him back to health. Senu is Bayek's falcon and sidekick. He is like an ancient drone that does reconnaissance for you. A cheerful reunion between you and your feathered friend occurs and the first quest ends successfully, earning you 1,000 XP and pushing you to Level 2.

ABILITY POINTS

Each time you level up, you earn an Ability Point (AP). Spend APs on new abilities in the Ability menu. Consider making your first purchase be the Master Warrior ability Regeneration; this allows you to regenerate life during combat. For more information on abilities, see "Abilities" in the Reference chapter.

LEVELING UP: WHAT TO DO NEXT

Walk over to the table where Hepzefa is standing (on his rooftop balcony) and accept the side quests Water Rats and Family Reunion. This gives you three available side quests. Consider playing them in the order of the suggested level. Open your map and explore every location marked on the map in Siwa. There are three viewpoints (one on Hepzefa's property). Synchronizing with all three reveals every point of interest in and around Siwa. There are hunting opportunities, a fort to overthrow, and a stone circle to align with the stars. Do everything you can in Siwa before continuing the main quests. This keeps you at a higher level than your enemies, giving you the advantage in battle and ensuring that stealthy takedowns become one-hit kills.

PAGE OVER TO SIDE QUESTS

You are currently in the Main Quest section, which covers only main quests. Do everything that Siwa has to offer before continuing to the next main quest. See the Side Quests section for help leveling up.

THE FALSE ORACLE

Prerequisite: Complete Main Quest: The Oasis

SUGGESTED LEVEL: 5	**REWARD: 1,250 XP**	**UNLOCKS: Main Quest: May Amun Walk Beside You**	**DETAILS: Bayek is determined to kill Medunamun, the false oracle with surprising strength who is rigorously protected.**

INFILTRATION STRATEGY COVERED IN FAMILY REUNION

This quest and a few others can be completed while inside the Temple of Amun. See the Side Quests section.

FIND AND KILL MEDUNAMUN

TEMPLE OF AMUN

LEGEND

1. West Tunnel Entrance
2. Tall Grass/West Approach
3. Hiding Spot
4. Rooftop with Arrows
5. Rope for crossing
6. Vantage Point 1
7. Medunamun's House
8. Route Stop
9. Vantage Point 2

LEGEND

- 🏹 Arrow Supply
- 🌾 Haystack
- 🛖 Hiding Booth
- 🔥 Brazier
- ↑ Ballista
- ▥ In Captivity
- 🏳 Fortress Flaw
- 🗄 Treasure

Medunamun has been installed as the new oracle of Siwa. He is traversing the village, brutally interrogating the inhabitants. Bayek prepares to battle the powerful priest, then tracks him down for assassination.

HIGHER-LEVEL ENEMIES

Medunamun and his bodyguards are Level 5. If you try to assassinate him during Side Quest: Family Reunion, your level may be too low to do this easily. When it is possible one-hit kills won't work, the level marker above the enemy's head will be red. When you are within range of executing a stealth attack, their health meter should be all orange for a successful kill. If any white is showing, then you will end up in a fight if you attempt a stealth kill.

ARROW KILL?

To defeat Medunamun with a stealth kill, you should wait until you are Level 4 or 5 and partaking in many Siwa's side quests and activities. Even an arrow to the head while at Level 3 will not be enough to take him down with one shot.

Medunamun walks around the temple grounds with his two Level 5 bodyguards. Given time, he takes many paths and may even be spotted walking through the city. But if you select the quest and send Senu to the temple to scout, you'll likely find him starting from his rooftop balcony at his home **(7)** and then heading to the east yard **(8)**, where he will stop for a while. This gives you time to mount a ride and head into the temple through the west entrance as described in Side Quest: Family Reunion.

Kill the guard at the entrance and climb to the top of the building on your left **(3)**. Continue to the next building with the arrow supply **(4)**. Collect arrows if you need them. Walk across the rope **(5)** between this building and the temple. Crouch and wait on the temple's southwest rooftop edge **(6)** (above the main entrance). Medunamun and his men eventually walk up the stairs and enter the temple below you. If you are Level 4 or higher, you can perform a Stealth Strike here by jumping down on top of him. Confirm the kill and a cinematic begins.

RANDOM CITY STROLL AND DAWN & DUSK

Instead of walking from his house to the temple, sometimes Medunamun leaves the fort for a stroll through Siwa's streets, passing in front of the weaver's and then Hepzefa's home before finally returning to the temple through the tunnel entrance **(1)**. If you see his silhouette through the floor of the temple when looking down through the skylight **(9)**, then he has stopped in the tunnel and will turn back and retrace his steps through the city. Either find another vantage point in the city to take him out or use Dawn & Dusk to speed up his route to get him back inside the fort. This ability can be unlocked in the Seer skill tree and now would be a good time to put an Ability Point into this skill to use it.

INTRODUCTION

THE ESSENTIALS

MAIN QUESTS

SIDE QUESTS

ACTIVITIES

ATLAS

REFERENCE & ANALYSIS

If you miss your opportunity at the temple entrance, wait until he enters the temple. Stand on the edge of the skylight **(9)** and perform the stealth attack from there. If it is taking too long from him to reach the temple, then find any other high vantage point along his route to attack. Use arrows to eliminate his bodyguards; then kill him with a combination of arrows or a stealth attack jump. Approach Medunamun's body and press the Interact button to fill the Confirm Kill meter.

After confirming the kill, you enter a cutscene in which Bayek and Medunamun speak in the Animus White Room. Medunamun is angry that you ended his life before he could finish his life's work—to usher in the perpetual rule of the strong and "virtuous." He mentions the price of one life a boy paid. That boy was Bayek's son, which set him off on this journey of assassinations. The cutscene ends by taking you back to the day Medunamun killed Bayek's son.

SIWA OASIS

ONE YEAR AGO

Bayek and his son, Khemu **(10)**, are doing some target practice when Chenzira runs up and asks Khemu to check out a hyena cave. Khemu, not as brave as Chenzira, declines the invitation. Bayek decides to take them on a real hunting expedition.

BRING KHEMU TO THE IBEX PACK

LEGEND

10 Starting Position
11 Hunting Location
12 Halma Point

Run north to the hunting area **(11)**. Along the way, Chenzira turns to go home, leaving you and your boy alone. When you get close to the pond, send Senu up to spot the ibex. Crouch down and sneak up to the ibex until you are within range to put an arrow in its heart. If you scare the ibex off, then you'll have to chase it down and try again.

FIND AND GET THE IBEX PACK LEADER'S PELT

Once the ibex is down, step up to it and claim the pelt.

REACH THE TEMPLE OF AMUN WITH KHEMU

Now run with Khemu southwest to the marker in the distance. Bayek decides to detour to Halma Point to give Khemu a test in bravery. He explains along the way that his father had taken him this way when he was a boy.

BRING KHEMU TO HALMA POINT

Bayek says his father told him one word that helped him get over fear, and he intends to share this with his son once they reach Halma Point **(12)**. Climb up the side of the hill and walk to the ledge overlooking the lake, standing in the marker.

The word is **jump**, but standing on the edge of the high cliff has Khemu thinking twice about jumping into the water below. A little frustrated, Bayek allows him to back out of this lesson, citing that he is not yet ready. Just then, Chenzira's screams are heard. Bayek commands his son to run straight home while he investigates.

You regain control, facing the cave at Halma Point. Pass through the cave to confront the soldiers holding Chenzira captive. Initiate the battle with the soldiers, whose levels are higher than yours. You don't have to fight if you don't want to. There's only one outcome of this battle—you being knocked out. There's no changing the past.

FOLLOW THE MASKED MAN

You enter the Temple of Amun and are instructed to follow the man in the mask. The man mentions that it is of great importance that they get into the vault.

When you reach your destination on the lower floor, the guards reunite you with your son. Because you are Medjay to the pharaoh, they think you know some key or clue to getting into the vault using the orb in their possession (the same orb you've seen Medunamun carrying). They threaten your son to get this information from you. Eventually they take Khemu's life. All the men in that room are now on your hit list.

Bayek gets kicked in the head and is knocked unconscious. While he is out, he returns to the white room with Medunamun still alive. That is, until you smash his head with his orb, sending him to the next realm where Duat waits. When you return to the "real world," you are sitting with Hepzefa, telling him you need to get to Alexandria to see Aya, your wife.

INTRODUCTION

THE ESSENTIALS

MAIN QUESTS

SIDE QUESTS

ACTIVITIES

ATLAS

REFERENCE & ANALYSIS

MAY AMUN WALK BESIDE YOU

Prerequisite: Complete Main Quest: The False Oracle

SUGGESTED LEVEL: 5	REWARD: NA	UNLOCKS: Main Quest: Aya	DETAILS: Bayek is ready to continue his pursuit of the Snake.

WHEN READY TO LEAVE SIWA, SPEAK TO HEPZEFA

HEPZEFA'S HOME

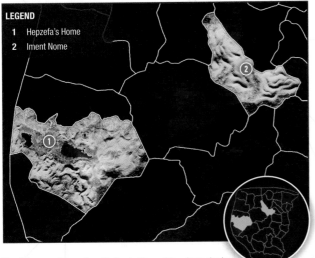

LEGEND
1 Hepzefa's Home
2 Iment Nome

Bayek is eager to reunite with Aya in Alexandria, where she has been researching the others responsible for their son's death. Visit the Atlas and Side Quests sections to do everything you can in Siwa before leaving. That way you are at the highest level possible before entering Alexandria. When you are ready to leave, visit Hepzefa at home **(1)** and speak to him.

You must confirm that you are ready to leave Siwa—you can easily return later. After your choice, Hepzefa bids you farewell and gives you an idea where to start looking for Aya in Alexandria…and suggests you cut your beard.

LAYLA HASSAN, HTT

CURRENT TIME

While Bayek travels to Iment Nome on his way to Alexandria, the game switches to his controller, Layla, in present time. She awakes from the Portable Animus, which is hooked into his body in a tomb where Layla operates from.

You need to take some cyclosporine, as suggested by your medical officer, Deanna Geary, communicating with you from her hotel room over air-con. The Animus was rejecting you, and you need a 10-minute break before you go back in. Layla is trying to impress Abstergo with this off-the-grid Animus assignment while trying to get a position on the Animus Project and hopes that finding Bayek secures that position.

FIND AND TAKE CYCLOSPORINE

Head to the marked cyclosporine in the red medkit. Before returning to the Animus, you can explore some of the area. Follow the cords from the Animus down a sloped tunnel to find the mummified body of Bayek inside an open crypt, all wired up and connected to the Animus.

THE PAUSE MENU

Explore Layla's Pause menu. It's chock-full of information, Abstergo Documentation, Animus Design docs, e-mails, pictures, and audio. Spend some time exploring the files and learning about the Abstergo Historical Research Division and the Animus.

Reading her e-mails from top to bottom puts in perspective what's going on and why they are in a cave with a Portable Animus hooked to a mummy (see e-mail "Subject: What if").

ALEXANDRIA

AYA

Prerequisite: Complete Main Quest: May Amun Walk Beside You

| SUGGESTED LEVEL: 10 | UNLOCKS: Main Quest: Egypt's Medjay | DETAILS: Bayek travels to Alexandria to search for his wife. |

TRAVEL TO ALEXANDRIA

BACK TO BAYEK

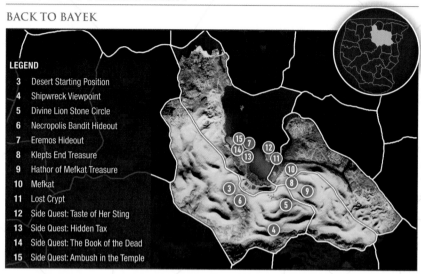

LEGEND

3   Desert Starting Position
4   Shipwreck Viewpoint
5   Divine Lion Stone Circle
6   Necropolis Bandit Hideout
7   Eremos Hideout
8   Klepts End Treasure
9   Hathor of Mefkat Treasure
10   Mefkat
11   Lost Crypt
12   Side Quest: Taste of Her Sting
13   Side Quest: Hidden Tax
14   Side Quest: The Book of the Dead
15   Side Quest: Ambush in the Temple

Bayek is now in the middle of the Iment Nome desert **(3)**. The quest you were on, May Amun Walk Beside You, is now complete and you are prompted to select Main Quest: Aya.

But before you do, sweep new areas of all challenges that are within your current level range. You should be around a Level 8 if you have employed this strategy. So instead of heading directly to the Aya quest, consider doing the following (covered in the Side Quests section):

TO-DO LIST

- Synchronize with the desert shipwreck Viewpoint **(4)** to the southeast

- Complete the Divine Lion Stone Circle **(5)**

- Conquer the Necropolis Bandit Hideout **(6)** (Level 5 and 6 enemies); can be done during Side Quest: The Book of the Dead

- Conquer the Eremos Hideout **(7)** (Level 5 and 6 enemies); can be done during Side Quest: Ambush in the Temple

- Loot the Klepts End treasure **(8)** in Khensu Nome (kill cobras)

- Loot the treasure of Hathor of Mefkat **(9)** in Khensu Nome (Level 7 enemies)

- Loot the treasure in Mefkat **(10)**

- Synchronize Viewpoints in Lake Mareotis

- Loot the Lost Crypt **(11)** treasure

- Beat these side quests in Lake Mareotis: Hidden Tax **(13)**; The Book of the Dead **(14)**; Ambush in the Temple **(15)** (unlocked when Lake Mareotis is discovered) and the quests it unlocks (Ulterior Votive, Lady of Slaughter, and Birthright); Taste of Her Sting **(12)**

MEET AYA AT THE LIBRARY

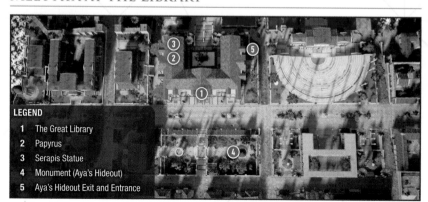

LEGEND

1   The Great Library
2   Papyrus
3   Serapis Statue
4   Monument (Aya's Hideout)
5   Aya's Hideout Exit and Entrance

LAKE MAREOTIS ACTIVITIES

As you work your way from the desert of Iment Nome and head north through the Lake Mareotis area to reach Alexandria to the north, do every activity available within your level range. This excludes anything on the lake's east side; we will cover this later as the story takes us there. Continue synchronizing with all the Viewpoints in the lake and around Alexandria before reaching the library.

AYA'S HOUSE

Two blocks east of the Sarapeion is Aya's house. Get in and out of her home without confrontation by entering through her courtyard via the rooftops. Investigating her house (a loot activity) explains why she is in hiding.

Follow the marker to the north docks area to find the great library **(1)**.

LOCATION OBJECTIVE: FIND PAPYRUS PUZZLE

The Papyrus **(2)** is in the library, located on a table at the bottom of the stairs that lead to the Serapis Statue **(3)**. For more information on this puzzle, see the Activities chapter of this guide.

Upon entering the Great Library **(1)**, run down the left hallway and then turn right and head to the stairway. You can find the large Serapis statue **(3)** on the landing. Interact with it to meet a bearded scholar who asks you to follow him to find Aya.

FOLLOW PHANOS

As you walk with Phanos, he explains he is Aya's cousin and what happened at her house. Gennadios, the head of the phylakitai (police) of Alexandria, is searching for her to beat information out of her. Phanos leads you out of the library, across the street, and to the monument **(4)** in the garden. He tells you she is in the monument.

EXPLORE THE WELL

Climb up the side of the monument to the base of the second set of support columns. Take a leap-of-faith dive into the well inside the monument.

Find the shallow end of the water. A tunnel leads to Aya's hideout. The happily married husband and wife reunite. Bayek tells Aya that he took pleasure in the assassination of Medunamun. She shaves his beard off while explaining how she killed Actaeon and how another masked one tracked her to her home. They both believe there is one more masked one to kill in order to finally avenge their son.

Her contact, Apollodorus, who works closely with Cleopatra, helps her uncover that the Snake is in Ptolemy's court. This is their last target. Cleopatra wants the Snake dead as well and even gave Aya a weapon to slit his throat. Aya hands it to Bayek, and he now wears it on his wrist to instantly assassinate anyone when he performs a stealthy takedown.

HIDDEN WRIST DAGGER

Aya gives Bayek the hidden wrist dagger in this cinematic. From here on, when you perform a stealthy takedown, you will stab the victim in the throat, killing them instantly. (As long as you match their level, or have upgraded your blade enough.) You no longer will have the assassinate option after a takedown. You can turn this off by choosing "Unarmed" in the Gear/Melee menu.

END OF THE SNAKE & GENNADIOS THE PHYLAKITAI

The main quests End of the Snake and Gennadios the Phylakitai unlock after the cinematic in which Aya gives you the wrist dagger.

ASSASSINATE YOUR TARGET

Complete Main Quest: End of the Snake
Complete Main Quest: Gennadios the Phylakitai

After the cinematic, Aya tells you she must stay hidden until Gennadios is dealt with. Two new main quests unlock: End of the Snake and Gennadios the Phylakitai. Aya says she will meet you at the Paneion Viewpoint after you complete these quests.

The Paneion Viewpoint is within Main Quest: Aya, but you cannot continue this until you kill the Snake and Gennadios (the first objective in Main Quest: Aya).

Use Animus Pulse to locate her weapon chest; then use the gate in the chamber's north corner to exit Aya's hideout. This places you outside in some bushes on the northeast corner **(5)** of the Great Library.

WRATH OF THE POETS

After the cinematic in which Aya gives you the wrist blade, Side Quest: Wrath of the Poets (Level 20) unlocks. Find this next door to her hideout in the amphitheater. Talk to Phanos to begin. He offers you a good-sized quest strand.

AYA CONTINUES

You must assassinate the Snake and Gennadios as part of the next objective in Main Quest: Aya. After you kill those two targets, select the Aya quest to keep the main quest progressing.

END OF THE SNAKE

Prerequisite: Find Aya in Main Quest: Aya

SUGGESTED LEVEL: 12	REWARD: 1,000 XP, bathhouse towel outfit	UNLOCKS: One of two prerequisites for continuing Main Quest: Aya	DETAILS: To assassinate the Snake, Bayek must discover his identity.

FIND THE ROYAL SCRIBE'S OFFICE

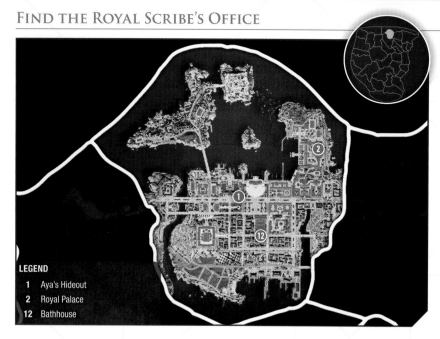

LEGEND

1. Aya's Hideout
2. Royal Palace
12. Bathhouse

Once reunited with Aya **(1)** (in Main Quest: May Amun Walk Beside You), Bayek learns that the Snake is someone on the Royal Council. He must search the palace for the seal with the sign of the Snake to discover his target's identity. Then he must assassinate that target.

Instead of trying to go back up out of the well to exit Aya's hideout, simply use the door in the north corner. This places you in a flowerbed outside the great library. Mount a horse and follow the marker to the Royal Palace **(2)** while avoiding hostile territory.

ROYAL PALACE

Prerequisite: Approach the palace

SUGGESTED LEVEL: 12 or higher

LOCATION OBJECTIVES: Loot three treasures

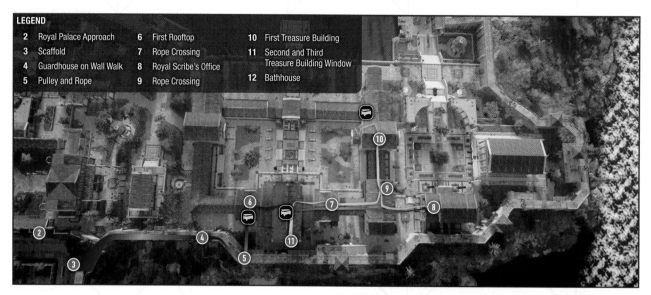

LEGEND

2	Royal Palace Approach	6	First Rooftop	10	First Treasure Building
3	Scaffold	7	Rope Crossing	11	Second and Third Treasure Building Window
4	Guardhouse on Wall Walk	8	Royal Scribe's Office		
5	Pulley and Rope	9	Rope Crossing	12	Bathhouse

ROYAL PALACE: APPROACH

Although the Royal Palace **(2)** is one of the largest forts you've seen, it's not actually an activity with captains; however, there are three treasures inside and more soldiers than you have arrows. So, we will show you the quickest way in and out to get the Snake's whereabouts while still obtaining the three treasures. Start by using this scaffold **(3)** to reach the walkway on the battlement on the palace's southeast side.

The long battlement makes it hard to know where the restricted area of the Royal Palace actually starts. You may want to stay out of the first guardhouse **(4)** until you have sent Senu up to mark all the soldiers. There are many. You don't need to mark them all, but it helps. Do mark the ones around the

buildings covered in this strategy and definitely mark the ones along this wall walk. Mark the treasures as well (check the map for help finding them).

ROYAL PALACE: CLEAR THE ROUTE

Clear the inside of the first guardhouse **(4)** and then get on its roof to put arrows in anyone who looks like they may get close. Cross the pulley and rope **(5)** that stretches from the wall to a building **(6)** on the left that houses two treasures. You can get the treasures on the way out.

ROYAL PALACE: ROOFTOP PATH

Head north along the rooftop, watching for any soldiers patrolling the wall walk, which is now on your right. At the end of the building, you can cross a rope **(7)** to navigate over the covered walkway below. Take this to the north end of the next rooftop and cross one more rope to reach the Royal Scribe's office building **(8)**. While walking along the rope, notice the open window on the right, below where the rope attaches to the building you're heading to. This is the window entry to get inside.

ROYAL SCRIBE'S OFFICE WINDOW ENTRY

Stand on the rooftop's edge, above the open window. None of the soldiers

patrolling below will see you. Just be sure there are no soldiers patrolling nearby on the wall walk. Drop from grip point to grip point until you drop through the open window.

INVESTIGATE THE ROYAL SCRIBE'S OFFICE

The scribe's office is the second room on the left as you enter through the second-story window. There are four investigation items: the locked chest, scrolls, a ladder on the floor, and a key to the chest on top of the corner wardrobe. Reach the key by climbing up the statue between the two shelves and shimmying over to a hanging position just below the key. Interact with it to take it; then drop to the floor and open the chest.

You find a scroll in a hidden compartment on the bottom of the chest. The scroll talks about the assassinated members of their group that he and Aya have already killed and also implicates Eudoros as the Snake.

REACH THE BATHHOUSE

FIND THREE TREASURES

Before you leave the Royal Palace, you should get the three treasures there to complete an activity. Head out the same window you entered and return to the rooftops. Cross the rope **(9)** over the covered walkway to the west and head across the next building **(10)**. Use Senu to make sure all the soldiers in the area are marked and then move down the side of the building on the south side (the courtyard side). When the coast is clear, enter the first floor through the main doorway (the guard will walk away or you can assassinate him).

Enter the first room on the left and use Animus Pulse to find the treasure in the back-left corner.

INTRODUCTION

THE ESSENTIALS

MAIN QUESTS

SIDE QUESTS

ACTIVITIES

ATLAS

REFERENCE & ANALYSIS

Return the way you came. Return to the rooftops and work your way south **(7)**. Scale down the west side of the tallest building along the route and enter the building through one of the large open windows **(11)**.

Get to the floor and find the second treasure in the middle of the room next to a lion rug. Loot the entire building.

Find the last treasure in the room to the south. It's in a red chest in the left corner.

TO THE BATHHOUSE

If you have synchronized the Paneion Viewpoint one block west of the bathhouse **(12)**, then use that to Fast Travel close to your next destination. Otherwise, backtrack along the route used to enter the Royal Palace grounds and ride to the bathhouse now. Synchronize the Paneion Viewpoint on your way. Enter the bathhouse through the marked door on the north side.

ASSASSINATE EUDOROS

BATHHOUSE INTERIOR

Once inside the bathhouse, you find yourself in a towel, standing on the raised stairway entrance. Without moving, look to your left and right. There are ladders in nooks on both sides that lead to a network of rafter pathways.

You only have the hidden blade, so the easiest way to assassinate Eudoros is to perform a takedown assassination from above. Climb the ladder on the right since you'll have to access that side of the rafters to reach your target anyhow.

Once you have reached the rafters, run to the building's south side. Look for the T-intersection that leads to the east side of the bathhouse, where your target is located.

Take a right at the path's end. You'll be just above your target's room. Stand at the edge of the window and look for him in the small room below. When he moves into position, drop down and assassinate him with a jump take down. If you make a mistake and end up fighting him hand-to-hand, then you must deal with his bodyguards and then confirm your kill. In a cinematic, you struggle with Eudoros but you overpower him and eliminate him in the white room.

ESCAPE THE BATHHOUSE

If you didn't kill Eurodos's guards, then you must deal with them after the assassination. The easiest thing to do is avoid them by quickly scaling the wall to return to the rafters. Run back to the ladder in the front of the room. Slide down and sprint to the exit. The quest is complete once you are outside the bathhouse. You earn XP and the bathhouse towel outfit.

BAYEK LOSES HIS FINGER

The first time using the hidden blade does not go so well for Bayek, as it removes part of his finger. In the returning cinematic, you can see him cauterize the wound with fire. Notice that you are now missing part of a finger when control returns to you.

GENNADIOS THE PHYLAKITAI

Prerequisite: Complete Main Quest: May Amun Walk Beside You (find Aya)

SUGGESTED LEVEL: 11	REWARD: 500 XP	UNLOCKS: One of two prerequisites for continuing Main Quest: Aya	DETAILS: Aya must stay hidden until Gennadios is dealt with.

FIND AND ASSASSINATE GENNADIOS

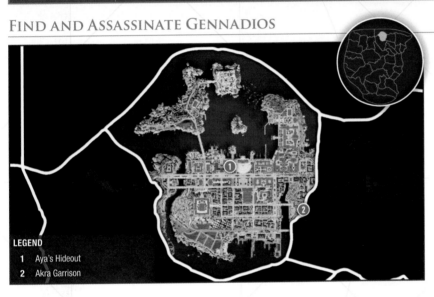

LEGEND

1 Aya's Hideout
2 Akra Garrison

The Phylakitai of Alexandria, Gennadios, has expended every effort to track down the killer of Acteon. Aya has eluded him by remaining hidden. Gennadios is known to roam the Akra Garrison. From time to time, he takes several men to search for Aya in the district outside the garrison. For Aya to walk freely, you must kill Gennadios.

You receive this quest in Aya's hideout **(1)** in Main Quest: May Amun Walk Beside You, but you may want to beat Main Quest: End of the Snake first, as it has a lower-level prerequisite. The first objective is approaching Akra Garrison **(2)**.

AKRA GARRISON

Prerequisite: Approach the Garrison

SUGGESTED LEVEL: 10 or higher   **LOCATION REWARD: 900 XP**   **LOCATION OBJECTIVES: Kill two captains and one commander; loot four treasures**

LEGEND

2 Garrison Approach
3 West Entrance (Loot Rooms)
4 Main West Entrance
5 Treasure (First Floor)
6 Treasure (Second Floor)
7 Ballista
8 Captain Patrol Area
9 Central Guardhouse
10 Treasure Room
11 Treasure Room

AKRA GARRISON: APPROACH

Use Senu to mark all the soldiers in the garrison, including the captain and the commander. They range in level from 8 to 11. Mark the treasures using our map as a guide to their locations. There is one unguarded entrance into the garrison and that's through the lower west doorway **(3)**, found below the main west entrance.

Although it's always best to begin your infiltration from above, we wanted to mention this entrance because there are a couple rooms and a floor above full of loot. Grab all the good stuff and then get to the top of the garrison's wall walk.

WAIT AND GENNADIOS MAY COME TO YOU

We had Bayek sitting in this lower-level loot room **(3)** for about five minutes, and Gennadios eventually investigated this room. We killed him when he arrived. If you aren't planning to sweep the entire garrison for treasures and assassinating the location objective targets, then you could try the same approach to see if it works for you.

We suggest going up the west wall and shimmying along the top until you are above the main entrance **(4)** and looking at the brazier (trap) and a ballista. Look for nearby patrolling guards before pulling up onto the wall walk. Set the trap and man the ballista. Look through the sights and see if you can take down any patrolling soldiers from this position.

Move south or north along the wall walk that encompasses the garrison. Assassinate every target that comes into view using arrows or ballistae. Use

our map to find arrow supplies and hiding places, keeping in mind some callouts are inside buildings (like the treasures).

Discover the easternmost treasure by entering the large guardhouse through the wall walk entrance and heading down the ladder inside to the second floor (where a hiding booth is located). Use the stairs to reach the first floor. Be careful, as one of the captains patrols this house; if you have not dealt with him already, expect to see him around here. Use Animus Pulse to locate the treasure **(5)** along the west wall.

Head back up the stairs to the room with the hiding booth. Notice there is a second room on the second floor. Investigate this room to find the other treasure **(6)** in this guardhouse.

Head to the rooftop of the same guardhouse and use the ballista **(7)** to take out patrolling guards on the garrison's northwest side. You may be able to get the second captain **(8)** under the tent from this position as well.

Use connecting ropes to cross rooftops, heading west to the central guardhouse **(9)**. Use arrows to stealthily remove guards from the area. Enter this house through the top doorway. Drop down to the next level through the ladder hole Find the third treasure on a table in a small box **(10)**.

You can often find a couple soldiers on the first floor. Head down the stairs and kill them. Use the booth near the exit to hide from any guards that may hear the commotion and come in to investigate. This is often a good way to kill the commander who patrols this area.

Head north across the rooftops and drop down on the north side of the central guardhouse complex. Enter the first-floor entryway and find the last treasure (11) on the ground in a narrow side room.

ASSASSINATING GENNADIOS

You may want to save this guy for last. If Gennadios travels outside the garrison he will be out of the Restricted Area and will be easier to assassinate. When most of the soldiers in the fort are dead, locate Gennadios (3), get on a nearby rooftop, and put an arrow through his bodyguards and then through his skull. Confirm your kill and you'll meet Gennadios in the land of the dead, place a feather on him, and send him off to where he belongs.

AYA

Prerequisite: Complete Main Quests: End of the Snake and Gennadios the Phylakitai

| SUGGESTED LEVEL: 9 | UNLOCKS: Main Quest: Egypt's Medjay | DETAILS: Return to Aya after killing the Snake and Gennadios. |

SPEAK TO AYA AT THE PANEION

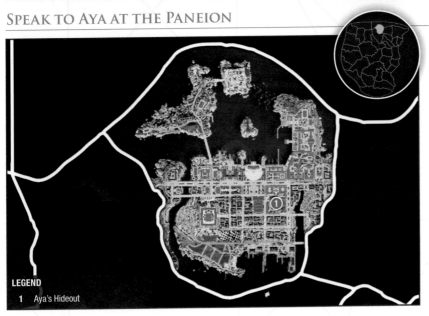

LEGEND
1 Aya's Hideout

When you return to Bayek and Aya at the Paneion, Bayek gets a feeling that the last two targets assassinated were not all the men involved in their son's death. Aya tells him to meet with Apollodorus to find out if this is true. She says he's with Cleopatra at the hippodrome. This unlocks Main Quest: Egypt's Medjay and takes you out of Alexandria and into the neighboring region of Kanopos Nome.

Travel to the Paneion Viewpoint (1) and climb up to reunite with your wife. She is now safe to be seen in public, as Gennadios, the Phylakitai hunting her down, is now dead. After a passionate reunion, you are pulled back into modern time with Layla in the Portable Animus in the cave.

PRESENT TIME: LAYLA

FOLLOW THE BLEEDING EFFECT TO FIND AYA'S MUMMY

Layla, roused by the Assassins' reunion, disconnects herself from the Animus and explains to Dee that she is certain that Aya's mummy is also in the cave. Follow Aya's ghost (the Bleeding Effect) through the narrow passageway, past Bayek's mummy, and to the edge of a subterranean chasm's edge.

Take a leap of faith off the edge and Layla dives into a shallow pool below. As you exit the water, Layla finds Aya's mummy. Her hidden blade lies next to her mummy. Layla uses it to extract some DNA from Aya. With this DNA, Layla will be able to access Aya's past through the Animus.

RETURN TO THE ANIMUS

Begin your ascent out of the chasm by scaling the wall with the fallen ladder below it. On top of the first ledge is a narrow crevice with light shining through ahead. Squeeze through the crevice. Follow the path and slide under the low opening in a cave wall. Now just keep heading upward when it's an option. She can scale walls as well as Bayek.

Continue through the spider webbed passage until you reach a large cavern. Drop down off your ledge and head to the cavern's right side, following the power cables connecting the construction lights. The tunnel entrance to the lab is on the right side. Reenter the Animus to return to Bayek. Before you return, a rush of Aya's memories floods Layla's brain, just as Dee warned.

PLAY ALEXANDRIA SIDE QUESTS

The main quests are now leading you out of Alexandria and into the neighboring region of Kanopos Nome. We strongly suggest playing all the side quests associated with Alexandria close to your level before leaving so you continue to find nice gear and gain more XP to keep your level above that of your opponents. See the Side Quest section for assistance.

INTRODUCTION
THE ESSENTIALS
MAIN QUESTS
SIDE QUESTS
ACTIVITIES
ATLAS
REFERENCE & ANALYSIS

KANOPOS NOME

EGYPT'S MEDJAY

Prerequisite: Complete Main Quest: Aya

SUGGESTED LEVEL: 12	REWARDS: 900 XP, Golden Medjay Badge	UNLOCKS: Main Quests: The Scarab's Sting; The Lizard's Mask; The Hyena; and The Crocodile's Scales	DETAILS: Bayek seeks Apollodorus in order to meet the exiled Queen of the Nile.

FIND APOLLODORUS'S CONTACT NEAR THE HIPPODROME

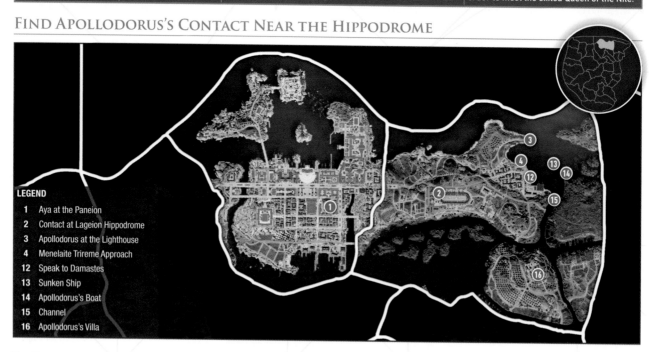

LEGEND

1. Aya at the Paneion
2. Contact at Lageion Hippodrome
3. Apollodorus at the Lighthouse
4. Menelaite Trireme Approach
12. Speak to Damastes
13. Sunken Ship
14. Apollodorus's Boat
15. Channel
16. Apollodorus's Villa

Beset by concerns that he has not, in fact, killed the Snake, Bayek parts with Aya and sets out to Kanopos in search of Apollodorus, who is said to be all knowing and should be able to tell Bayek the real identity of the Snake.

Leave the Paneion **(1)** and travel east into Kanopos Nome. Head toward the massive Lageion Hippodrome **(2)**. There you can find a young man standing on its outer northwest corner; he tells you that you can find Apollodorus at the lighthouse at night.

OLD TIMES

Before you leave the hippodrome, you can start Side Quest: Old Times by talking to Claridas, who is also located in front of the hippodrome.

SPEAK TO APOLLODORUS AT THE LIGHTHOUSE IN KANOPOS

Do not meditate and turn the day into night until you have synchronized the lighthouse **(3)** Viewpoint in northeast Kanopos. (If you do not have this skill yet, now might be a good time to spend an Ability Point on it.) Once you have done so, meditate in that location and a cinematic begins. In it, Bayek meets Apollodorus, who is helping some injured man to safety. Apollodurus recognizes you from your name as being Aya's Medjay. Bayek asks him for the real identity of the Snake, but before Apollodurus will answer that question, he asks Bayek to complete a task to prove himself trustworthy.

MENELAITE TRIREME

Prerequisite: Approach the Menelaite Trireme (ship)

Suggested Level: 11 or higher   Location Reward: 300 XP   Location Objective: Loot one treasure

LEGEND

4. Kanopos Harbor
5. Menelaite Trireme
6. Bulkhead Approach
7. Harbor Shelter
8. Pier Hoist
9. Bowsprit
10. Soldier Camp
11. Damastes Caged

MENELAITE TRIREME APPROACH

There are countless ways to approach this challenge, since it is so open with no castle walls to deal with. The main advantage is all the water in the harbor, which provides instant hiding space all around the battlefield. Although not a prerequisite, we strongly suggest you defeat all the soldiers in the area since

Damastes will want to fight any soldier he sees as soon as you break him out of the crate **(11)**. Doing this allows you to control the chaos.

One approach to consider is leaping from your boat **(4)** and swimming underwater (to stay undetected) up to the bulkhead **(6)** on the docks' east side. You can get onto the rooftop of the nearby shelter **(7)** and shoot soldiers around the Menelaite Trireme **(5)**; you are within range, yet immediately undetectable by others. Cross the rope from the rooftop to the hoist on the pier **(8)** while shooting more soldiers within your range on either side.

From the top of the bowsprit **(9)** of the middle ship (or from the high crow's nest), you can shoot all the remaining soldiers to the west, including those on the pier with the cage **(11)**, those in the camp **(10)**, and any who might be on the westernmost ship at the pier's end.

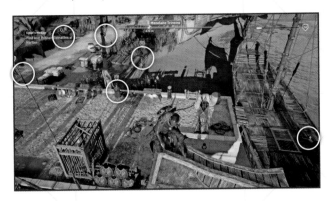

Once everyone is dead, grab the treasure from under the tent on the Menelaite Trireme **(5)** and then free Damastes **(11)**.

ESCORT DAMASTES TO SAFETY

Follow Damastes as he runs around in a rage, looking for a soldier to kill. He runs southeast. Follow him closely, as he may or may not run into random soldier traffic on the road. He's looking for a fight and will start one given the opportunity. He stops near a pier **(12)** on the harbor's east side.

SPEAK TO DAMASTES

Deal with all the soldiers, then talk to Damastes. He has come to rest on the east pier **(12)**. You ask for the scroll and he says he hid it on their ship, which is now at the bottom of the lake.

FIND AND RETRIEVE THE SCROLL IN KANOPOS LAKE

While standing next to Damastes, send Senu up in the air and east over the lake to spot the location of his sunken ship **(13)**. It's only 200 meters out. Take the nearby boat to the location, dive in, and retrieve the scroll from below.

SUNKEN TEMPLE OF SARAPEION

If you continue to swim underwater toward the Apollodorus marker, you will come across the Sunken Temple of Sarapeion. There's no time constraint during this quest, so you can go find the three hidden treasures there now. For location details, see the Activities section.

GIVE THE SCROLL TO APOLLODORUS

Apollodorus has come to you to retrieve the scroll. You can now find him near **(14)**, to the southeast of the sunken ship. Get to him and hand over the scroll. He tells you now that he may be able to trust you.

BRING APOLLODORUS TO HIS VILLA

Take control of Apollodorus's boat and paddle it southwest into the channel **(15)** to reach his villa. He is about to introduce you to Cleopatra. Along the way, you tell him about taking out Gennadios. He tells you that act may cause you problems ahead. He says the Phylakes are a tight group and will come looking for you. This unlocks the Phylakes activity and these are covered in the Activities chapter of this strategy guide. Head to the villa **(17)**. Apollodorus will follow you there and lead you inside.

FOLLOW APOLLODORUS TO MEET WITH CLEOPATRA

Talk with Apollodorus as he leads you up an inclining dirt road to the villa. Along the way, he tells you how Aya got thrown into their circle of trusted allies and then how to present yourself around Cleopatra—how to speak to her correctly. A cinematic takes over once you reach the villa's inner courtyard.

In the cinematic, Apollodorus becomes distressed that you did not kneel before Cleopatra as he instructed before the meeting. Aya makes an appearance and stands

by your side the entire time. Cleopatra says that Eudoros (the man you killed) was a member of the Order of Ancients, which was responsible for her exile, tearing her from her throne.

You learn that the Snake has many heads and those heads make up the Order of Ancients. One called the Scarab rules in the Nile Delta, and a shadowy figure called the Hyena controls Giza. There's also one that calls himself the Lizard. Eudoros was known as the Hippo, and the Crocodile oppresses Faiyum.

Cleopatra names you her Medjay, and you agree to assassinate all these targets—anything to get to the one that killed your son.

MAIN QUESTS UNLOCKED

Completing this quest unlocks the following Main Quests: The Scarab's Sting, The Liard's Mask, The Hyena, and The Crocodile's Scales. We cover these in order of their suggested level. But now that you're new to Kanopos, we suggest synching its Viewpoints and partaking in its side quests to level up before taking on the main targets. Start with Side Quest: Old Times.

SAPI-RES NOME

THE SCARAB'S STING

Prerequisite: Complete Main Quest: Egypt's Medjay

SUGGESTED LEVEL: 15	REWARDS: 1,125 XP	UNLOCKS: Main Quest: The Scarab's Lies	DETAILS: Bayek travels to Sais to meet the informant Harkhuf to learn about one of his targets: the Scarab.

TRAVEL TO SAIS

SAPI-RES NOME: SAIS

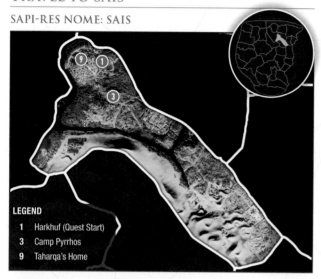

LEGEND

1 Harkhuf (Quest Start)
3 Camp Pyrrhos
9 Taharqa's Home

LEGEND

1 Harkhuf (Quest Start)
2 Harkhuf's Home
7 Taharqa's Estate

Apollodorus sends Bayek to Sais to track down a member of the Order of Ancients named the Scarab, a cruel shadow terrorizing the region. The brewery closes at night, but Harkhuf can be found at his home. Meditate it to daytime to meet him at the brewery. The brewer **(1)** is too scared to talk about the Scarab in public and asks you to retire with him at his home.

Shh! Please! That is an evil name to speak aloud!

FOLLOW HARKHUF TO HIS HOME

Follow Harkhuf across the street and into his home **(2)**. He tells you horrific stories about what the Scarab does to people, namely burying them up to their necks in the desert sand. He almost believes that the Scarab is a myth and says there's real villains in Sais. He moves a large vase from a large crack in the back wall of his home. This reveals a room secret; access it by squeezing through the crack.

LOOK AT HARKHUF'S INFORMANT TABLE

Inside the secret room are arrow supplies and an informant table that contains a **Story of the Scarab** letter. Read it. It concerns evidence that the Scarab may be real after all.

SIDE QUESTS

From the secret room, you can access a menu of four side quests, which we recommend playing as soon as this quest is complete.

MEET HARKHUF OUTSIDE

When you squeeze back out of the room, Harkhuf tells you about Ghupa, an old man who had his tongue cut out when he asked questions about the Scarab. Ghupa is the father-in-law of Taharqa, the most powerful man in the region who was mentioned in the letter you just read. His grandson, Kawab—playing outside—tells you where you can begin to look for Ghupa.

FIND AND RESCUE GHUPA FROM CAMP PYRRHOS

CAMP PYRRHOS

Prerequisite: Speak to Harkhuf

SUGGESTED LEVEL: 16 or higher   **LOCATION REWARD: 400 XP**   **LOCATION OBJECTIVE: Kill one captain, loot one treasure**

LEGEND

3 Camp Pyrrhos (Approach)

4 Captain Assassination in Tall Grass

5 Brazier (Alarm Trap)

6 East Gate Soldiers

7 Treasure

8 Ghupa (Captive)

INTRODUCTION

THE ESSENTIALS

MAIN QUESTS

SIDE QUESTS

ACTIVITIES

ATLAS

REFERENCE & ANALYSIS

CAMP PYRRHOS APPROACH

The first objective in this quest is to free an old man from a small military camp in Sapi-Res Nome. This is a small military outpost lightly guarded by Level 15 to 17 soldiers. Six of the soldiers patrol in pairs, so it's a little difficult to quickly take them out stealthily with arrows. Two soldiers guard each of the main entrances on either

side of the camp. But the captain seems to hang out around the south fence, where you can find a hole **(3)** to slide under. You can hide in the tall grass just on the other side of the fence.

Whistle to get the captain's attention if he wandered away a bit. Execute him **(4)** stealthily and then carefully make your way to the brazier **(5)** to set a trap. To avoid being spotted by the two soldiers in the treasure tent **(7)**, follow the tall grass along the inner fence before the brazier platform.

The east **(6)** or west gate soldiers may spot you, but once you set the brazier trap, you can easily take on the weaker soldiers all at once if you must. If needed, escape outside the fence and hide in tall grass; when things clear up, get up into a tower and shoot the remaining soldiers. This camp has a crazy amount of arrow supply areas and animal cages that can be used to cause chaos.

Find the treasure **(7)** in the largest tent to complete the location objective and then free Ghupa **(8)** from the cage. Open the prison and pick him up.

CARRY GHUPA BACK TO HIS HOME

Call your mount or use one of the horses in the camp. Drop Ghupa on the horse and take him back to his home in Sais **(9)**. You can use the "follow road" option if you have the destination marker selected. This commands the horse to take you right to Taharqa's estate without you having to do the "driving."

Once you stop in the marker at his front door, Kawab runs up to welcome his grandfather home. Taharqa's wife enters and dismisses the old man's quest for the Scarab as a silly waste of time, but Kawab hands you a letter that his grandfather took from the camp. It says that the Scarab is summoning warriors to the city of Letopolis. Oddly enough, that is where Taharqa has been spending a lot of his time. His son hands you a toy to give to his father when you meet him.

SIDE QUESTS UNLOCKED

Side Quests: Conflicts of Interest, Smoke Over Water, All Eyes on Use , and Lost Happiness are all available from inside Harkhuf's secret room in his house **(2)**. You can also play The Tax Master, Abuse of Power, and The Ostrich before heading to the other side of the region to continue the main quest in Letopolis.

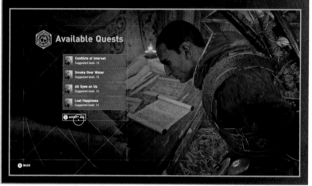

THE SCARAB'S LIES

Prerequisite: Complete Main Quest: The Scarab's Sting

SUGGESTED LEVEL: 18	**REWARDS:** NA	**UNLOCKS:** Main Quest: Pompeius Magnus	**DETAILS:** Bayek meets with Letopolis's leader, Taharqa, to discuss a plan to find the Scarab once and for all.

SPEAK TO TAHARQA IN LETOPOLIS

SAPI-RES NOME: LETOPOLIS

LEGEND
1 Letopolis Blacksmith
2 Letopolis Viewpoint
3 Taharqa (Quest Start)

Sandstorms risk to take all of Letopolis, but they are nothing compared to the constant threat of the Scarab, who has transformed the desert into a graveyard. When you enter the sandy city, you should first visit the Letopolis blacksmith **(1)** to upgrade your favorite weapons and shield. You are thrown into battle as soon as you meet Taharqa, so it's best to be prepared. Next, scale the Temple of Horus to synchronize the Letopolis Viewpoint **(2)**.

Follow the marker to find Taharqa **(3)** wandering somewhere in the Temple of Horus. You introduce yourself and he replies with announcing his title: grand

planner of Sais and steward of Letopolis. You tell him you met his family and that he may know how to find the Scarab. He asks you to speak in private.

FOLLOW TAHARQA

Follow him a short distance into a building (4) to the north. Inside, Bayek hands him the wooden toy Taharqa's son gave him. You press him for information on the Scarab, but Taharqa says he preys on the weak, so he is no threat to him. Bayek is startled that he is not upset with what the Scarab did to his father-in-law. A servant rushes in and disrupts the conversation to announce that bandits are attacking the ruins again. Taharqa asks you to come fight with him.

ESCORT TAHARQA

LEGEND

4	Taharqa's Temple Home
5	First Bandit Battle Site
6	Second Battle Site
7	Intersection Battle
8	Temple Entrance (South)
9	South Exit
10	Taharqa's Horses and Soldiers

Follow Taharqa back out the door and into a brutal sandstorm. Visibility is at a minimum. This also makes Senu unavailable. You turn north and head for the first confrontation with bandits on the northern steps (5). Consider using a heavy blunt weapon to damage multiple enemies attacking you at once. These are Level 18

bandits and you should be pushing Level 22 by now. It should be rather easy to take them out. Taharqa moves west after taking out about five enemies here.

The next battle site (6) is to the west, where you will find three of Taharqa's men fighting three bandits. Help them finish off these foes. Switch between the heavy blunt and a fast sword or dual swords to see which works best for you in this situation. After you kill them, follow Taharqa through the nearby building heading south to an intersection (7), where a large fight occurs.

Here you battle around nine bandits, assisting Taharqa's men. Taharqa may circle a nearby building looking for a tenth bandit, but the next major battle lies back toward the Temple of Horus by entering the west hall (8). You'll battle around six or seven bandits in the west hall. The one arriving late to the battle carries a shield, so be prepared for dodging and shield break moves.

Next, Taharqa hunts for the bandits outside the south exit (9). Here you battle a group of six bandits; two have shields. Finish off the soft targets quickly and then concentrate on the bandit with the shield. This is the last of the ruin battles.

SPEAK TO TAHARQA

Speak to Taharqa after winning the five bandit battles. He's impressed by your fighting skills and asks you to help finish them off for good by attacking their camp. You are reluctant to help at first, but he insists that he will not share any info he has about the Scarab until you help him.

FOLLOW TAHARQA

Follow Taharqa south to his five soldiers and seven horses (10). You can call your own ride if you are that attached. Follow Taharqa southeast to Plesionhudor Hideout (11) on the northern tip of the new region, Ineb-Hedjet Nome.

INTRODUCTION
THE ESSENTIALS
MAIN QUESTS
SIDE QUESTS
ACTIVITIES
ATLAS
REFERENCE & ANALYSIS

KILL ALL THE BANDITS INSIDE THE CAMP

PLESIONHUDOR HIDEOUT

Prerequisite: Approach the hideout

SUGGESTED LEVEL: 18 or higher   **LOCATION REWARD: 400 XP**   **LOCATION OBJECTIVE: Kill one captain, loot one treasure**

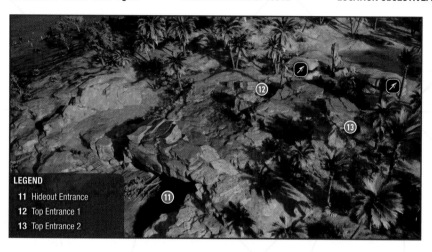

LEGEND

11 Hideout Entrance
12 Top Entrance 1
13 Top Entrance 2

The bandits in this hideout are Levels 17 to 19. There's one captain and about eight other bandits. Taharqa will just march in through the main, watery entrance **(11)** to this cave hideout. There's no need to go stealthy here; just follow him in and take out the enemies as a group. Use the warrior bow for the infiltration and then switch

to your favorite weapon. The objective is to kill all the bandits so yellow markers appear above the remaining stragglers. Hunt them down. They may be out somewhere scouting for enemies outside the camp.

Notice there are two rooftop entrances into the cave: Dropping down into hole **(12)** places you in the first cave you reached if you stormed in through the front entrance **(11)**. The rooftop hole **(13)** drops you into a room with a haystack cart and the treasure.

There's a third cave that branches off from the first **(12)**, where you can find cages. A Memphis priest is captive there. Free him when the bloodshed is over. The connecting room is the treasure room, so collect that and ensure that the captain is dead to collect the location objective reward.

SPEAK TO TAHARQA

After you kill all the bandits, speak to Taharqa in the prison cave. You grill him about who the bandits were to him and if they have anything to do with the Scarab. He says no and that he will bring the freed priest back to the city and wants you to meet him at his house. There he will tell you anything you need to know over food and wine.

MEET TAHARQA AT HIS HOME

Return to Letopolis and enter Taharqa's temple home **(3)** to have food, drinks, and conversation. His family, whom you've already met, made the trek from Sais for dinner. You raise glasses to honor the savior of Letopolis (Bayek). Suddenly Bayek becomes dizzy and passes out. Have you already guessed the identity of the Scarab?

LOCKED IN

Once you begin this step, you will be locked into completing it.

FREE YOURSELF FROM THE SANDS

KHENSU NOME

The next thing you know, you wake up in the desert buried up to your neck in sand… like the horror stories of the Scarab you've heard about. Whistle for your horse to pull you out. The horse stops short of you being able to grab its reins, but Senu comes to the rescue and scares the horse closer to you. You grab the reins and get pulled out of what would have been your grave. The desert heat has you seeing and hearing the ghosts of your past. Besides other bodies in the nearby sand craters, you can find one Silica in one of them.

FIND AND RETRIEVE YOUR GEAR

Mount your horse and ride toward the marker to find your gear.

Continue following the marker for another 120 meters to reach Camp Achlys. This is where your gear is stored. Send Senu up in the air to locate the building holding your gear while also marking what few soldiers are in the camp.

CAMP ACHLYS

Prerequisite: Approach the camp
SUGGESTED LEVEL: 19 or higher
LOCATION REWARD: 400 XP
LOCATION OBJECTIVE: Kill one captain, loot one treasure

LEGEND

14	Desert Burial
15	Ruins
16	Camp Achlys Approach
17	Captain's Tent
18	Treasure Tent
19	Bayek's Gear
20	Temple of Horus in Letopolis

Approach the south side of the brazier tower **(16)** and climb to the top. Set the trap just in case. On the tower's west side are birds and bird poop, symbolizing a possible eagle dive. Jump from the railing down into the haystack cart below and immediately assassinate the soldier standing next to it.

Now look north to the two tents in front of you. Each has a soldier standing at the entrance. There are small access flaps in the back you can slide under and then stealthily come up behind each soldier and assassinate him. Perform this move on both soldiers at both tents. The soldier at tent **(17)** is the captain. Steal the treasure from the second tent **(18)**. This completes the location objective for the camp.

Head west into the small yard and free the captive from the corner cage; then enter the building to retrieve your gear from the chest inside **(19)**. You obtain a letter to Sefetu. Your gear was supposed to be payment for him from Taharqa.

RELEASED

Once you complete this step, you are no longer locked into this quest.

FIND AND ASSASSINATE THE SCARAB

TEMPLE OF HORUS

If you feel resentful, get to the rooftop and take out any remaining soldiers using the ballista. Call your mount and follow the marker back to the Temple of Horus in Letopolis **(20)**.

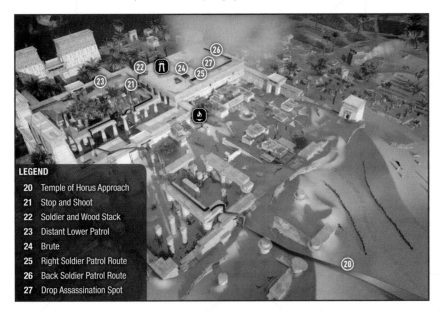

LEGEND

20	Temple of Horus Approach
21	Stop and Shoot
22	Soldier and Wood Stack
23	Distant Lower Patrol
24	Brute
25	Right Soldier Patrol Route
26	Back Soldier Patrol Route
27	Drop Assassination Spot

Now jump to the rooftop behind the stack of lumber the soldier was standing near **(22)** so the other rooftop soldiers won't see you. Wait for a minute to see if the soldier **(23)** patrolling the lower platform accesses the rooftop. If so, put an arrow between his eyes.

Now shoot the patrolling soldier **(25)** if he is on your end of the rooftop. Next, use the hiding booth to lure and assassinate the brute **(24)**. If he will not be lured, shoot him in the face and run into the booth before he sees you if he doesn't die.

When you return to the temple from the desert, you will reach the southwest side first. This is a great way to approach this next challenge. Send Senu up to mark Taharqa's position and all the soldiers on the temple rooftop and around the temple. Most of the soldiers on the ground are concentrated around the southwest side.

Follow our platform jumping and climbing pathway we mapped out from **(20)** to **(21)** to avoid all the ground troops. Stop on top of the pillars before the temple rooftop at position **(21)**, as this is just about as close as you can get without being spotted by the corner roof guard **(22)**. Shoot him in the face with a predator arrow. The large brute soldier **(24)** will not spot you from this distance.

That leaves one more soldier **(26)** on the rooftop that patrols the back edge. Take him out and then get on the right side **(27)** of the rooftop skylight

opening and look down. Position yourself over the kneeling and praying Scarab on the temple floor below. Perform a jump assassination on him.

Make sure it's him and not one of his guards. You do not need to confirm the kill. You enter the white room after the assassination and do not have to battle the guards left alive when you return to this world.

Taharqa's family enters the temple to see you over their family member's body. Obviously they are all upset even after you explain who he really was.

WHERE TO NEXT?

After assassinating the Scarab, Layla begins connecting with Aya's memories and you get automatically drawn into Aya's first quest, Pompeius Magnus.

POMPEIUS MAGNUS

Prerequisite: Complete Main Quest: The Scarab's Lies

SUGGESTED LEVEL: 12	REWARDS: NA	UNLOCKS: Main Quest: Ambush at Sea	DETAILS: Aya and Phoxidas sail the Aegean Sea to rendezvous with Pompey the Great in a bid to ally him with Cleopatra's cause. A great naval battle ensues against rival forces.

SAIL TO THE AEGEAN COAST

AEGEAN SEA

Aya and Phoxidas sail the Aegean Sea to rendezvous with Pompey Magnus and offer him gold, in a bid to ally him to Cleopatra's cause. But Ptolemy has other ideas, sending waves of ships against them. Phoxidas and Aya beat back the attacks.

Watch the on-screen prompts closely for the controls needed to navigate and achieve battle speed. Sail toward the marker in the south. Navigate around large rocks in the sea and then you'll be introduced to the Triple Arrow Volley. Give it a try before you are facing enemy ships. Shoot a volley of arrows into the water and play with the arrow aiming arc while maintaining the ship's speed and the direction.

YOUR SHIP'S HUD

Your ship's heads-up display (HUD) is in the screen's bottom right corner. The top bar is your ramming speed readiness gauge; the bar below that is your ship's health. Let it drain and you're sunk. The first circle gauge to the right of the bars is your firebombs readiness gauge and beside that is a catapult readiness that you will not use in this battle.

SINK THE PTOLEMY FLEET

BRACING FOR IMPACT

You spot and engage with an enemy ship in similar size to your own at 142 meters from the destination marker. The enemy ship quickly fires at you; at that moment you are introduced to bracing for an attack. You brace when arrows are flying toward you or when an enemy ship is about to ram your own. If you release the brace command immediately after the enemy arrows hit your crew's raised shields, then an automatic bonus return fire occurs. The return fire is also automatically aimed back at the enemy ship.

DESTROYING SHIPS

Aim your arrow arc so that it touches the enemy ship's weak points, which appear as glowing sections across the sides of enemy ships. Hitting ships in other areas (even the sails) does damage, but repeatedly hitting these weak points sinks a ship more quickly. Your aiming arc turns red when you have successfully aimed at a weak spot. That's when you send the triple arrow volley repeatedly. The enemies' health appears next to the ship. Drain it and it sinks.

RAMMING SHIPS

After sinking the first ship, turn north to find two more, some distance away. You can use ramming acceleration to get there more quickly. Get into a position where you are sailing by them side by side. You need to avoid being in front of an enemy ship where they can ram you. If a ship heads for the side of your ship, use ram speed to get out of the way; if it's already too close, brace for impact.

Alternatively, if you position your ship to head directly for the side of an enemy ship, then engage ram speed and plow into the ship's side to inflict your ultimate damage capability. Finishing an enemy ship with a ram move reduces weapon reload times.

MEET POMPEY THE GREAT IN THE AEGEAN COAST

After destroying three enemy ships, your next objective marker appears in the distant west. Use ramming speed to get there more quickly. When you reach the west marker, another appears to the south some 1,700 meters away. This marks Pompey's location. Use ramming speed to reach his ship. At about 400 meters away, you clearly see Pompey battling three enemy ships.

DEFEND POMPEY'S OCTAREME

Now Pompey's ship's health appears in the screen's top left corner. You must help defend his ship. You fail if that health gauge drains. Head south to get beside the enemy ships and attempt a ram while they're aiming at and focused on Pompey's ship—for the time being. A successful ram to a healthy ship can drain more than half its health with one hit. Quickly send firebombs and arrows to finish it off before it can execute a counterattack.

Circle single ships to attack the weak spots on both sides of the ship. And the most important thing: keep moving. If you stop, you're a sitting duck. Destroy the four enemy ships to be victorious. After you win the battle, sail toward Pompey's ship.

During the closing cinematic, Pompey the Great asks why a mercenary ship came to his aid. Aya tells him that Cleopatra sent her and offers friendship and gold for his alliance and to call Caesar her king. He agrees to the offer and says his fleet will be ready for Egypt.

WHERE TO NEXT?

Upon completing this quest, we return to Bayek in the Temple of Horus, where he just killed the Scarab. We suggest finishing the Letopolis side quests and then playing Main Quest: The Hyena, as it is closer to Sapi-Res Nome than The Lizard's Mask quest start location. The Hyena will have you traveling southeast to Giza.

GIZA

THE HYENA

Prerequisite: Complete Main Quest: "Aya"

SUGGESTED LEVEL: 20	REWARDS: 2,250 XP	UNLOCKS: One of three quests that unlocks Main Quest: Way of the Gabiniani	DETAILS: Bayek travels to Giza to meet the informant Mered to learn about one of his targets: the Hyena.

TRAVEL TO GIZA

GIZA

LEGEND
1 Mered (Quest Start)
2 Depleted Quarry Hideout
10 Khaliset's Lair
18 Tomb of Khufu

Bayek travels to Giza, where one of his targets, known as the Hyena, comes to the market in search of something precise to fulfill her mysterious agenda. Apollodorus's contact is Mered, a merchant who has kept tabs on the Hyena's activity.

SPEAK TO APOLLODORUS'S CONTACT IN THE GIZA MARKET

LEGEND
1 Mered (Quest Start)
2 Depleted Quarry Hideout
10 Khaliset's Lair

Mered **(1)** is at his wares booth at the market south of the Great Sphinx. Speak to him and he tries to sell you some of his junk. Bayek asks for information on the Hyena. The salesman says that's the most expensive thing at the store.

PAY MERED TO LEARN MORE ABOUT THE HYENA

Pay Mered 100 drachmas to get information. If you don't have it, sell something. You learn that the Hyena's real name is Khaliset. He will tell you where to find her if you go retrieve his stolen horse from a camp south of the market.

FIND AND BRING MERED'S HORSE BACK TO THE MARKET

DEPLETED QUARRY HIDEOUT

Prerequisite: Approach the hideout
SUGGESTED LEVEL: 20 or higher
LOCATION REWARD: 600 XP
LOCATION OBJECTIVE: Kill one captain, kill one commander, loot two treasures

LEGEND					
2	Depleted Quarry Hideout	5	Captain	8	Main Camp (Commander's Tent)
3	Tunnel Exit (Hideout Entrance)	6	Mountainside Climb	9	Mered's Horse
4	Tall Grass	7	Mountainside Climb Down		

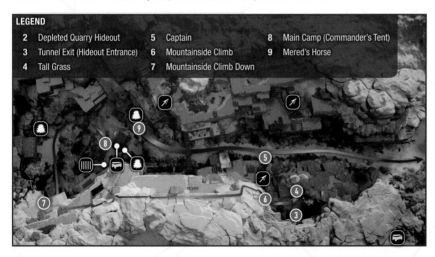

Mered gives you three men to assist you. Let them follow you even if you don't need them (they won't disrupt your stealth approach). Mount your ride and head south around the lake to the Depleted Quarry Hideout **(2)**. Use the secret tunnel on the mountain's north side to enter the base. Send Senu up to mark the location of the horse, the enemies, and the treasures.

DEPLETED QUARRY SECRET TUNNEL ENTRANCE

Head into the tunnel until you reach a fire-lit clearing where a ladder allows access to ledges above. Use Animus Pulse to locate all the loot around. Before climbing the ladder, explore the tunnel to the right (west). At the tunnel's end is the first of two hideout treasures.

Head back to the cave with the ladders and climb three sets of ladders and platforms to reach the cave exit. This exit **(3)** places you in a small gully with lots of tall grass. If you wait for a short while, the captain **(5)** inspects the gully area. Lure him into the tall grass **(4)** and assassinate him.

Use the gully to climb up the mountainside **(6)** to the south. Reach the highest ground above all the lower hideout rock platforms. Begin shooting everyone in range with predator or hunting arrows (you always have better range and damage with a predator bow). The hideout is large, and most of the bandits are alone, making this slaughter nice and stealthy. You can easily take out the Level 20 enemies on the ravine's opposite side, on the rock platforms and guard towers from your side of the hideout.

Grab the arrow supply and continue along the mountaintop to the south end **(7)**. Walk the edge, shooting bandits on the different levels below and even in the main camp **(8)** on the ground level. By the time you climb down into the camp **(7)**, you should have killed most of the bandits. If the commander remains, you can find him around the main tent **(8)** with the last treasure. Use the haystack behind the tent or any obstruction to hide behind and come up behind him and assassinate him. Or use arrows. You can get a legendary weapon from this commander.

You can release the prisoner near the main tent for more XP. Find the horse **(9)** on a higher ledge near the main tent. Ride it out of the hideout and head back to the Giza market to return it to Mered **(1)**, who is now waiting just outside the walls of the market.

Find Khaliset's Lair in the Hills West of the Pyramids

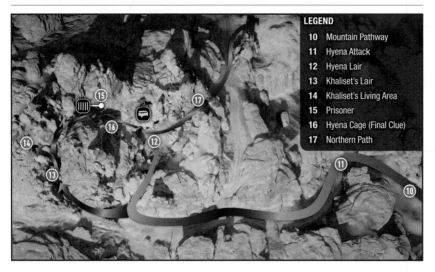

LEGEND

10	Mountain Pathway
11	Hyena Attack
12	Hyena Lair
13	Khaliset's Lair
14	Khaliset's Living Area
15	Prisoner
16	Hyena Cage (Final Clue)
17	Northern Path

It turns out that the horse you returned was not even Mered's, but he does come through on his word and tells you where you can find the Hyena. He points you to the hills west of the pyramids. Ride west to the marker.

When you get close to the mountain pathway **(10)**, call Senu to do some recon and locate Khaliset's Lair. You also discover the Giza Hyena lair nearby. The enemies you tag in that location are Level 17 and 18 hyenas.

Going up the mountain path, expect a hyena attack around the first bend **(11)**. Equip a heavy blunt or a spear so you can attack them without getting off your horse. If you just keep riding, you can outrun them.

When "New Location Discovered: Hyena Lair" appears on-screen, you'll find a narrow pathway to the right that leads to the hyena lair. You do not have to go there to complete the task, as the leader of the pack often patrols Khaliset's Lair, which is where you are headed. There is a treasure at the hyena lair **(12)** in a small outpost building.

Continue along the main pathway to reach a ridge, where you'll have to leave the horse. This is the back entrance to Khaliset's Lair **(13)**. Climb the short ladder up the side of the canyon wall and notice the left passage. It leads to Khaliset's living area. She's gone. You may encounter hyenas now. The leader from the hyena lair is somewhere here too; defeat him to get the 300 XP Location Objective award.

Investigate Khaliset's Lair to Uncover Her Whereabouts

Investigate the blanket on the ground where she sleeps. "A Message to Khaliset" is on the ledge opposite the bedding. It's from the Snake. Exit this area and explore the rest of the lair (head left down the pathway).

Free the prisoner **(15)** from the small cage and speak to him. He does not have the Hyena's location.

Head to the pathway's other side and unlock the hyena cage **(16)**. Kill the hyena and then interact with the large rock in the corner. Behind the rock is the final clue: **Khaliset's Drawing**. It's a detailed map of Khufu's tomb. This must be where she is located.

REACH THE PYRAMID OF KHUFU

Call your mount and ride through the hyena lair and down the side exit to the north **(17)**. Taking this path to the pyramid runs you through some serious hunting opportunities. Do some ibex hunting for crafting materials. Follow the next marker to the north side of Khufu's pyramid. Climb the pyramid now or when you finish this quest to synchronize the Viewpoint on top. Have fun sliding down (hold the Drop Object button so you don't automatically grab on to handgrips on way down).

EXPLORE THE PYRAMID IN SEARCH OF KHALISET

KHUFU'S TOMB

Enter the small tunnel entrance about five pyramid block layers from the ground. Be careful of the hyenas in this area. Light a torch and explore the interior. The Hyena screams at you from somewhere inside the tomb when you breach the entrance. At the top of the first slope, you reach an intersection...

ANCIENT TABLET AND MAIN QUEST INTERSECTION

When you reach the first intersection, you must make a choice: take the large tunnel running off to the left or head through a crack in the wall on the right. Slipping through the crack **(20)** leads to the continuation of this main quest, but exploring the left tunnel **(19)** leads you to the Ancient Tablet in the Tomb of Khufu. The path to the tablet is explained in detail in the Activities section of this guide. If you go for the tablet, we suggest lighting the torch in the intersection so you don't pass the crack in the wall on your way back.

Slip through the crack and follow the tunnel to an open cave, where a torch marks the location of a large hole in the ground. Drop carefully down into the hole to continue. Khaliset screams a warning at you once you reach the tunnel at the bottom of the hole. Follow the lower tunnel to a humongous open tomb.

INVESTIGATE KHALISET'S PURPOSE IN THE MYSTERIOUS TOMB

Collect Silica from all over the large chamber **(21)**. There's also a platform **(22)** that beams you out of the pyramid. Don't use this device. You have also entered an investigation area **(23)**. There are four clues near the mysterious monolith. Check out the drawings, the offerings, and the warm, dead sacrificial corpse on the floor. Lastly, inspect the sarcophagus. Bayek will put the clues together and walk you through what happened.

OPEN THE SARCOPHAGUS

After Bayek's walkthrough of the ritual site, you are prompted to open the sarcophagus. A female child's body is inside. Khaliset shows herself and explains that the body is her deceased child. She throws a smoke bomb and escapes the pyramid in a cloud of white smoke.

KILL KHALISET

Run out of the tomb. Follow the objective marker down the long passage. Push through the pyramid block to enter a pitch-black room. Light your torch, vault over the obstruction, and immediately raise your shield to block Khaliset's fire arrows.

Don't stop; keep pressing forward or Khaliset will keep firing at you. At the top of the tunnel incline is a left turn. Stop there. Khaliset sets some oil vases on fire and the entire floor burns. Avoid running through it. Let the fire die out before continuing. Climb the wall at the tunnel's end to reach the outside.

Use the arrow supply in the next area to refill your arrows. Climb out of the ruins above the arrow supply to begin the real battle.

THE RUINS BATTLEGROUND

The battlegrounds are dark, and a small sandstorm has rolled through. Visibility is low. You should be around Level 23; Khaliset's hyena bodyguards are Level 26. Khaliset is Level 20 and her health gauge is at the top of the screen.

THE HYENAS

Her hyenas are tough to beat but it just takes a little more time than usual. Consider using a very powerful sword. A heavy weapon is too slow, giving the hyenas time to knock you to the ground. Drop down off the ruins (where you begin the battle) to avoid Khaliset's fire arrows. She keeps her distance and shoots arrows while you try to find her and deal with her hyenas. If you stay off the ruins platforms, you'll be relatively safe from her flaming arrows.

FINDING AND DEFEATING KHALISET

Once you've dealt with her hyenas (if you come across them before you find her), start looking for Khaliset. Just raise your shield and walk toward the direction the flaming arrows are coming from. Once you find her, climb up to her ruin platform, rush her with your shield raised, and start hitting her with your most powerful weapon. Alternatively, you can use a good warrior bow to do the damage. She will escape in a puff of white smoke from a smoke bomb.

Now you repeat the same process a few times; fight hyenas while staying low. Look for the direction of the fire arrows and chase them with the shield raised. Do some rolls and dodges as you get near and then attack her again. Save your built-up adrenaline for a close-contact battle with Khaliset instead of wasting it on hyenas. You should be able to take her out about the fourth time you run into her. Once she is on the ground, confirm the kill to complete the quest.

WHAT'S NEXT?

Now that you are in Giza, go ahead and sweep the area of activities and side quests to help level up. When you're done, play Main Quest: The Lizard's Mask, where you will explore the southern region of Memphis.

INTRODUCTION

THE ESSENTIALS

MAIN QUESTS

SIDE QUESTS

ACTIVITIES

ATLAS

REFERENCE & ANALYSIS

THE LIZARD'S MASK

Prerequisite: Complete Main Quest: Aya

SUGGESTED LEVEL: 20	REWARDS: NA	UNLOCKS: Main Quest: The Lizard's Face	DETAILS: Bayek travels to Memphis to meet with the High Priest Pasherenptah to learn about one of his targets: the Lizard.

SPEAK TO PASHERENPTAH IN THE GREAT TEMPLE OF PTAH

MEMPHIS: TEMPLE OF PTAH

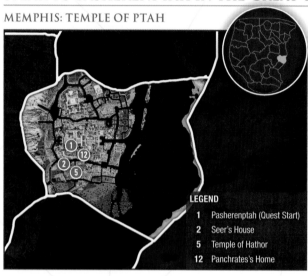

LEGEND
1   Pasherenptah (Quest Start)
2   Seer's House
5   Temple of Hathor
12   Panchrates's Home

LEGEND
1   Pasherenptah (Quest Start)
2   Seer's House
3   Boat
4   Temple Dock
12   Panchrates's Home

Bayek must work with Pasherenptah **(1)** to uncover the whereabouts of the Lizard, who is believed to be behind the curses that are plaguing the city of Memphis. Before you leave the Great Temple of Ptah after speaking with Pasherenptah, synchronize with the Viewpoint on the southeast tower.

REACH THE SEER'S HOUSE AND SPEAK TO TAIMHOTEP

Travel southwest to the marker to find the Seer **(2)** and Pasherenptah's wife, Taimhotep. She is inside a small home performing a ritual to help prevent her child from being stillborn like her past pregnancies.

BRING THE CAULDRON INTO THE RITUAL CIRCLE

Follow the marker 9 meters away to find the small cauldron on the floor. Pick it up and take it to the fire the participants are gathered around. During the excitement of the ritual, Taimhotep forces out some of the liquid from the cauldron meant for her. Bayek passes out from the drug.

You awaken in a drug-induced dream world. The Seer and Taimhotep are there with you. Walk through the raging sandstorm down the nearby dune slope. Continue along a pathway lined with ominous statues.

Continue into a large, dark tomb. Keep running straight through a brightly lit, narrow hallway. A cinematic shows Bayek's doppelganger standing in front of the scale of justice just as a giant serpent (Apep, the Soul Eater) breaks through and eats your glowing heart, which the Bayek doppelganger throws into the air. A bow materializes in your hand. Magic, glowing arrows fall from above, forming a perfect circle around you.

DEFEAT THE SOUL EATER

The glowing bow has an unlimited number of arrows. The large snake rises out of the water and wraps itself around distant columns. Its health gauge appears at the top of the screen. The snake also spits damaging, poisonous, green acid that you should avoid. Dodge the projectile acid as well as the pool of acid that forms on the platform you fight from.

Hitting the snake anywhere on its body is damaging, but it is most damaging to shoot the snake in the weaks spots that are indicated with light. Aim for the body as it crawls up columns. As it slithers back down into the water below, keep hitting the exposed body with arrows.

The snake switches sides of the ship, so keep an eye on the ripples in the water to track its submerged position. Finally, dodge to avoid its lunging attack. It will come right at you and lunge across the platform where you are fighting. When the snake is down to half of its health, it destroys the ship. The fight continues in an arena where the snake is much more aggressive. At this point, the snake shoots even more poison and breaks the floor when it strikes. As the beast nears death, it shoots poison everywhere around the stage until it finally dies.

After the battle, you are knocked into a dark pool with floating lily pads. Swim to the stone crypt. A cinematic plays in which Bayek opens it and retrieves his heart. He grips it tightly in his hand and suddenly hears his son's voice calling. He turns to look and he finds himself in a wheat field with Khemu. They approach each other, and Khemu whispers something in Bayek's ear just before he wakes up.

The Seer translates what you've experienced and concludes that your enemy and Taimhotep's enemy is the same and that someone is poisoning the temple food, which is killing Taimhotep's unborn children.

SPEAK TO PASHERENPTAH ABOUT TAIMHOTEP

When leaving to head back to the temple, you run into Aya outside the Seer's house. You tell her about the dreams of your son and how the Seer claims whoever is poisoning Taimhotep is your enemy.

FOLLOW AYA

From the Seer's **(2)**, Aya heads to the stream and enters a boat **(3)**. Get in and drive west. Turn right at the watery intersection to head north to the temple dock **(4)**. Along the way, Bayek and Aya catch up and share what happened in each other's lives while they were separated.

FOLLOW AYA TO THE APIS BULL'S QUARTERS

Exit the boat and follow Aya as she runs north up the temple stairs and into the temple. She heads to the Apis Bull **(1)**. When you reach the destination, Aya tells you to check on the bull while she talks to the priestesses.

INVESTIGATE THE SICK APIS BULL'S QUARTERS

You need to find the cause of the bull's (and Taimhotep's) illness. Activate Animus Pulse to locate the clues around the bull pen. Pivot to your left and investigate the pile of bull dung. Bayek reaches deep into the large pile and pulls out a handful of peach pits.

Speak to the man in the bull pen. He says the priestesses feed the bull and the fodder is in a shed that has been shut up since the bull got sick. Enter the bull's chambers and investigate the water bowl, the Apis Bull, and the offerings on the table behind the bull.

Exit the bull's chambers. Head left and leave the bull pen. Interact with the food for the bull near the shed. Break through the sealed doorway to the right of the bull food to enter the shed. Investigate the peach pits inside to the left. These are the poison causing all the illness. Lying beside the peach pits is one of the priestesses' necklace.

FAI-JON LAMENTU CRYPT: TREASURE

Follow the shaft inside the shed downward. You'll reach a ledge overlooking a small chamber of treasure and cobras. You can use fire and arrows found on the ledge to eliminate the cobras below, grab the treasure, and return to the shed to continue the main quest.

SPEAK TO AYA AND THE TWINS TO REPORT YOUR FINDINGS

Aya is talking to the priestess twins in front of the food shed. Approach them to present your condemning evidence. The twin with the missing neckless takes off running but is quickly captured. They admit to the poisoning but they did it because they were being pressured by bandits who have kidnapped their brother. They present his severed finger in a box.

FIND AND RESCUE THE TWINS' BROTHER, PANCHRATES

TEMPLE OF HATHOR

Prerequisite: Approach the temple
SUGGESTED LEVEL: 22 or higher
LOCATION REWARD: 400 XP
LOCATION OBJECTIVE: Kill one captain, loot one treasure

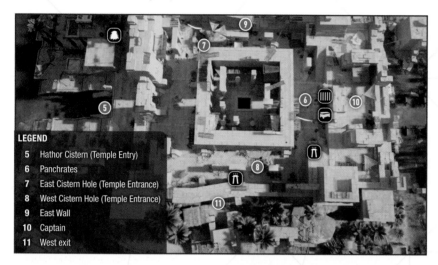

LEGEND

5	Hathor Cistern (Temple Entry)
6	Panchrates
7	East Cistern Hole (Temple Entrance)
8	West Cistern Hole (Temple Entrance)
9	East Wall
10	Captain
11	West exit

Aya watches over the twins while you go off to find the bandits at the temple of Hathor **(5)**. Send Senu over the temple to locate Panchrates **(6)** and to mark all the bandits and treasure. Enter the temple via the north entrance **(5)** and the channel that runs underneath it.

Swim into the underbelly of the temple and execute the two guards below. This is the Hathor Cistern. There are east and west passages that lead to exits up into the temple above. The east passage has you entering through the east hole **(7)** and the west cavern has you popping up through the west hole **(8)**.

HATHOR CISTERN: TREASURE

Swim through the west passage in the Hathor Cistern under the Temple of Hathor to find a small cavern with one of two treasures and a cobra. Dive deep into the pool near this treasure. Swim through a watery tunnel to reach a dry cavern containing the second treasure guarded by two protective crocodiles. Collect the treasure to complete the location objective.

We suggest climbing up the east passage's cavern wall to enter the temple through the east hole **(7)**. Hang on to the edge of the hole. Pull the nearby patrolling bandit down into the hole to his death. Call any other nearby bandits

to the same death trap. Once you are safely standing in the northeast corner, plan your next move. We suggest getting to higher ground.

Climb the nearby east wall ladder **(9)** to reach the wall's top. Begin moving around the temple's top level, shooting arrows into the heads of any bandits who can spot you up here. This includes the captain **(10)** who patrols the upper platform above the south gate.

CARRY PANCHRATES BACK HOME

Eliminate all the bandits in the camp and approach Panchrates **(6)**. Free the captives near him for an extra 100 XP, and take the treasure near the captive cage to complete the location objective. Carry Panchrates west to a small exit **(11)** near a hiding booth. Call your mount, place him on it, and ride to his house **(12)** to the left across the bridge.

After you drop Panchrates off at home, he reveals that his abduction was ordered by a priest of Anubis at the Great Temple—a priest in Pasherenptah's circle. He says he wears a blue scarf and has a terrible cough. You rejoin Aya outside his home. This quest ends here and continues in Main Quest: The Lizard's Face.

THE LIZARD'S FACE

Prerequisite: Complete Main Quest: The Lizard's Mask

Suggested Level: 23	REWARDS: NA	UNLOCKS: One of three quests that unlocks Main Quest: Way of the Gabiniani	DETAILS: Bayek must help the High Priest finally rip the Order of Ancients out of Memphis.

FOLLOW AYA

MEMPHIS

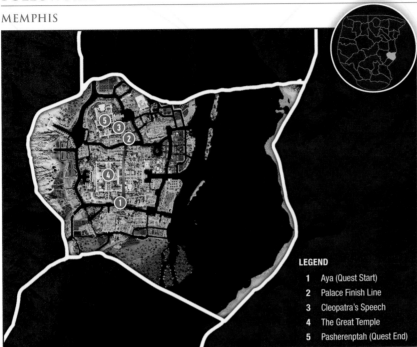

LEGEND

1 Aya (Quest Start)
2 Palace Finish Line
3 Cleopatra's Speech
4 The Great Temple
5 Pasherenptah (Quest End)

Shall we race, like we did in Siwa?

If you have been following the guide and sweeping up side quests as suggested, you should be around Level 29. Start this quest when you are at least Level 23. Find Aya **(1)** waiting for you south of the Temple of Ptah.

Memphis's curses are lifted, but the source still remains in the Great Temple: the Lizard. With Cleopatra arriving to rally the Egyptians to her name and rightful throne, Bayek and Aya must take out the Lizard, a rotten priest at the core of Memphis. With the Lizard out of the way, joy and festivities may occur without an oppressive cloud overhead.

REACH THE ROYAL PALACE BEFORE AYA DOES

The race is on. Both you and Aya mount horses of equal speed and head north past the temple to the Palace of Apries **(2)** to hear Cleopatra's speech. We suggest letting your wife win. If you're married, you'll know why.

FOLLOW AYA TO THE ROYAL PALACE

Head north on foot. Turn left at the intersection to discover Cleopatra's speech **(3)**. After the presentation, Aya reports to Cleopatra and tells her the Apis bull was poisoned. You continue to get the twins who poisoned it out of hot water and point the blame at the priest of Anubis with the blue scarf and a cough. Pasherenptah is shocked that it is a priest in his circle but gives you the location of where he will be and when.

FIND HETEPI AMONG ANUBIS'S PRIESTS AND ASSASSINATE HIM

Send Senu up and over the Great Temple **(4)**. Locate the five priests walking around (some together, some not). After you mark them all, fly to get a closer look at each of the priests' hood colors. You are looking for the blue one. Fly as low as you can and wait for priests inside to walk into a clearing so you can find Hetepi. When you spot him, use Senu to mark him so that it's easier to find him when you return to Bayek.

You can march right into the Great Temple with no fear of being attacked by soldiers. Walk right up to Hetepi and assassinate him. Confirm the kill to enter the between world.

DON'T KILL THE WRONG PRIESTS

If you kill the wrong priests and there are guards around, they will attack you. Also, if any of the priests witnesses the death of a wrong priest, Hetepi will run away to a nearby military fortress. This will make it more difficult to kill him.

SPEAK TO PASHERENPTAH TO REPORT HETEPI'S DEATH

Return to the Palace of Apries **(3)** and report the news to Pasherenptah and Cleopatra. She again thanks you and promises to get to the matter of Khemu's death. A festival is thrown, but afterward, Aya breaks the news to Bayek that she will be parting ways to continue her duty to Cleopatra.

WHAT'S NEXT?

You should now be completely done with Memphis, having killed the Lizard and finished all the side quests here and in Saqqara Nome as suggested. You should now be headed to Soknopaiou Nesos in Faiyum to get the Crocodile in Main Quest: The Crocodile's Scales.

FAIYUM

THE CROCODILE'S SCALES

Prerequisite: Complete Main Quest: Aya

SUGGESTED LEVEL: 25	REWARDS: NA	UNLOCKS: Main Quest: The Crocodile's Jaws; Side Quests: Fires of Dionysias; The Sickness; Demons in the Desert	DETAILS: Bayek travels to Faiyum to hunt his next target, the member of the Order of the Ancients known as the Crocodile.

TRAVEL TO FAIYUM

FAIYUM: SOKNOPAIOU NESOS

LEGEND

1. Soknopaiou Village, Faiyum
2. Beached Trireme Camp
7. Hotephres' Ship
8. Euhemeria's Viewpoint
9. Khenut in Euhemeria

Travel to Soknopaiou Village in Faiyum and synchronize with the Viewpoint **(1)**, if you have not done so during your side quest travels. Bayek must find Apollodorus's informant in Faiyum in order to discover the identity of his next target, the Crocodile. Use Senu to locate the informant's house. You can easily see it while atop the Viewpoint.

FIND AND MEET HOTEPHRES, THE FAIYUM INFORMANT

You enter the informant's home that Senu identified, only to find no one is home.

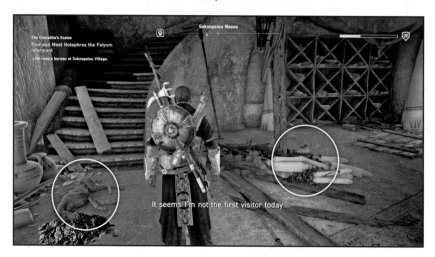

INVESTIGATE THE DISAPPEARANCE OF HOTEPHRES

Use Animus Pulse to locate the clues on the first floor. Inspect the broken vase, piles of scrolls, and the dead pet at the stairs. Head upstairs and examine the doll pierced with a spear, then enter the sunroom to inspect the scrolls on the table. You find a feather of a messenger pigeon beside the scrolls.

Climb the ladder in the room to the top of the carrier pigeon house to find the final clue: the **Letter Left Behind by Hotephres**. The letter says that the Crocodile knows his identity.

FIND AND RESCUE HOTEPHRES'S SERVANT

Access the map and spot the next location west of Soknopaiou. The servant is being held in the Beached Trireme Camp **(2)**.

BEEN THERE, DONE THAT

If you've been following our strategy of completing side quests in the suggested level order, then you may have already completed the location objective at Beached Trireme Camp. If you need help with that, see Side Quest: Rebel Strike.

BEACHED TRIREME CAMP

Prerequisite: Approach the camp

SUGGESTED LEVEL: 26 or higher

LOCATION REWARD: 600 XP

LOCATION REWARD: Kill one captain, loot one treasure

LEGEND

2 Beached Trireme Camp (Approach)
3 West Gate Guard
4 Patrolling Soldier
5 Servant (in Captivity)
6 Prison Guard
7 Hotephres's Ship

There are Level 25 to Level 27 (the captain) soldiers in the camp. We suggest getting in and out with the least amount of disturbance. The captain and treasure will be in the camp only if you have not already completed the location objective in Side Quest: Rebel Strike.

Approach the camp from the hilltop (2) above the west gate. Put an arrow through the gate guard's head; then move east along the hillside to look for the next closest soldier (4). One patrols the area near the same gate. Take him out with an arrow.

Continue east on the ledges and get into the grass on the low ledge west of the prisoner (5). Make sure no one on the ships is looking your way. Drop down and sneak up behind the prison guard (6) and execute him. Free the injured prisoner and pick him up.

Now walk around the short wall in front of the prison with the servant on your shoulders. Crouch-walk through the tall grass, hugging the right walls. Head out the west gate. Continue until you get the prompt to set him down.

SPEAK TO HOTEPHRES'S SERVANT

Talk to the servant to learn that Hotephres took a trader's ship to Lake Moeris and that the Crocodile has hired mercenaries to find him.

FIND AND MEET HOTEPHRES THE INFORMANT

From the servant, head south to the water. Find a boat to sail southeast toward the marker, which is 850 meters away. When you get close to the large ships, send Senu up to pinpoint Hotephres's ship (7). Board the ship and speak with Hotephres.

At first, Hotephres wants to kill you—that is, until you show him the Golden Medjay badge. Once he sees you share a common interest, he lowers his guard and explains what he knows about the Crocodile. But he does not know his true identity. However, he says he has a ledger that could have his name on it, but he gave it to his wife, Khenut, to hide. He gives you a doll to give to his daughter Shadya when you meet his family.

SIDE QUESTS UNLOCK

Side Quests: The Sickness; Fires of Dionysias; and Demons in the Desert all unlock after you meet Hotephres. If you do not accept these quests while on his ship, then their start location moves inland to various areas around Euhemeria—the village where you are headed now to meet Hotephres's family.

MEET KHENUT, THE INFORMANT'S WIFE

EUHEMERIA

LEGEND

2 Euhemeria's Viewpoint
3 Khenut in Euhemeria
4 Shadya's vantage point
5 Khenut's villa
6 Euhemeria Lighthouse Camp

Get a boat and sail south to Euhemeria, avoiding the Okteres Blockade offshore. Synchronize the Viewpoint (8) east of the city; then head to the alms kitchen (9) to meet Khenut and Shadya.

She tells you ever since her husband got that ledger, the town has been on edge. Soldiers with torches patrol every night. She says she gave the ledger to their most trusted servant to hide it in their villa. She has Shadya show you the way.

FOLLOW SHADYA TO KHENUT'S VILLA

Run east after Shadya as she takes off and starts climbing ladders almost as quickly as you can scale the wall beside her. She stops on a small rooftop **(10)** across the street from her villa.

FIND AND GET THE LEDGER FROM KHENUT'S VILLA

KHENUT'S VILLA

Send Senu up to mark all the Level 25 soldiers around the villa. Locate the ledger **(11)** on the first floor of the main structure.

From the east end of the last rooftop connected to the building where Shadya stopped, shoot the soldier out of the nearest rooftop pergola. Enter the villa grounds through the broken wall below the pergola. Climb to the rooftop under the pergola.

Drop to the lower rooftop on the right and drop-assassinate the soldier standing near the gate entry.

Head up the nearby stairs, and climb the walls to reach the top balcony of the main building **(11)**. Enter the building through the open doorway.

Jump from the railing to drop-assassinate the soldier with the large shield on the floor below. Head down to the ground level and come up behind the brute standing guard at the back door and assassinate him.

Reenter the house and use Animus Pulse to locate the ledger. Unfortunately, what you find is one of Shadya's dolls near **Shadya's Diary**. The diary reveals that her mother was hiding scrolls for Hotephres and that she's going to keep the ledgers so her daddy doesn't have to worry anymore. This means the soldiers just found out where the ledger is and you just left Shadya unattended.

REACH THE EUHEMERIA ALMS KITCHEN

Exit the villa grounds using a route that you have cleared and rush back to the alms kitchen **(9)**. The man at the kitchen tells you that soldiers just came and took Khenut and Shadya to the lighthouse.

FIND AND RESCUE KHENUT

Call your mount and ride to the Euhemeria Lighthouse, but stop short of entering the soldier camp **(12)** unless you are ready to battle five soldiers (including a brute) all at once.

EUHEMERIA LIGHTHOUSE CAMP

Prerequisite: Approach the camp
SUGGESTED LEVEL: 26 or higher
LOCATION REWARD: 600 XP
LOCATION OBJECTIVES: Kill one captain, loot one treasure

LEGEND

12	Euhemeria Lighthouse Camp Approach
13	Tall Grass Vantage Point
14	Tall Grass Vantage Point
15	Khenut
16	Shadya's pier

Creep in near the south entrance **(12)** through the tall grass. There's a low hole in the wooden fence here that allows you to creep over to the west entrance **(13)**. Whistle to separate the guards; then use the fence and grass to hide assassinations from nearby guards on the other side of the fence. Move from the west to the east side of the fence **(14)** to keep the hiding game going. Try to at least take out the Level 27 brute with the large shield; then you can eliminate the remaining, lesser enemies.

Grab the treasure from the tent to complete the location objective and then rush to the lighthouse pier to talk to Khenut **(15)**.

FIND SHADYA

Shadya is not with her mother! Send Senu up to search to the south just off the coast near the next pier. She's 120 meters away. Cut back through the camp. Use the south exit **(12)** and turn left to reach the next pier **(16)**. Dive into the water and swim underwater. Prognosis is gloom. There are many dead people tied down to large rocks here. Sadly, Shadya is one of them. Interact with her to pull her out of the water and present her to her heartbroken mother.

Hotephres meets you on the pier. He is defeated. The ledger, lost. His daughter… the Crocodile has taken everything from him. He vows to do anything he can to help get revenge. He points you to the gladiator arena in Krokodilopolis. That's where you can begin the hunt. The Crocodile uses his gladiators to do his bidding.

WHAT'S NEXT?

Before you head off to kill that dirty, no good Crocodile, we suggest completing all the side quests in Faiyum, except Fires of Dionysias (Level 37) and Demons in the Desert (Level 39), as those suggested levels are out of your range right now. You should be around Level 29 at this point.

INTRODUCTION

THE ESSENTIALS

MAIN QUESTS

SIDE QUESTS

ACTIVITIES

ATLAS

REFERENCE & ANALYSIS

FAIYUM OASIS

THE CROCODILE'S JAWS

Prerequisite: Complete Main Quest: The Crocodile's Scales

SUGGESTED LEVEL: 28	REWARDS: NA	UNLOCKS: Shadya's Rest; Legendary Light Bow; and one of three quests that unlocks Main Quest: Way of the Gabiniani	DETAILS: Bayek remains on the trail of the Crocodile, who is clearly using gladiators to carry out their dirty work.

REACH THE KROKODILOPOLIS ARENA

FAIYUM OASIS: KROKODILOPOLIS

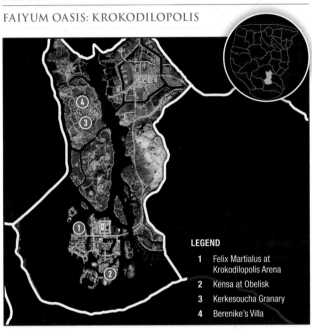

LEGEND
1 Felix Martialus at Krokodilopolis Arena
2 Kensa at Obelisk
3 Kerkesoucha Granary
4 Berenike's Villa

Faiyum's populace is enthralled by the gladiatorial ring **(1)**, but the stars of the arena are busy in the shadows, and Bayek must drive headfirst into the world of warriors and corruption.

INVESTIGATE THE ENTRANCE OF THE ARENA

We suggest synchronizing with the Viewpoint on the Schena Wab and then approach the arena. To learn more about the arena, inspect these clues: talk to the old lady near the statues, talk to the man sitting at the table between fighter statues, check out the two scrolls next to the Diovicos and Veridovix fighter statues, and speak to the arena owner, Felix Martialus, on the steps of the arena.

You ask him about fighting in the arena. He brushes you off and tells you that you have to prove yourself on the streets before you will be considered for fighting in the arena. The man beside him points you to another fighter from Siwa. She hangs around the obelisk **(2)** in the east end.

FIND THE SIWAN GLADIATOR

KROKODILOPOLIS: EAST END

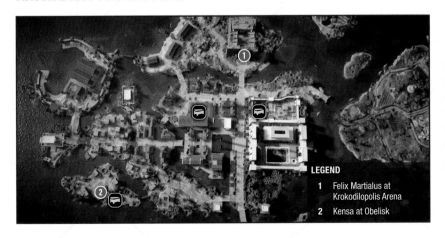

LEGEND
1 Felix Martialus at Krokodilopolis Arena
2 Kensa at Obelisk

Head to the obelisk **(2)** on the east side near the Confiscated Stathmos. Here you discover an old friend from Siwa on her knees praying before the obelisk. You go off to have drinks and catch up. Afterward, you tell her you were turned away at the arena doors. She tells you that she can get you in and that the two of you can fight side by side on the same team.

ENTER THE KROKODILOPOLIS ARENA WHEN YOU ARE READY

KROKODILOPOLIS ARENA

Now head back to the arena and talk to Felix **(1)**. With Kensa at your side vouching for you, you get in with no problems.

FOLLOW FELIX MARTIALIS

Now Felix introduces you to the inside of the arena and lays out the rules, most important being that you will fight with the weapons that he gives you.

SPAR WITH KENSA

He leads you over to where Kensa is training and tells you to spar with her so he can study your form. Start by selecting her as your target and start dodging to get beside or behind her to land hits behind her shield. Take her health down to a quarter and the fight ends. The fight also ends if she takes your health down close to zero. In either case, the quest continues.

After the sparring session, Felix agrees to let you be Kensa's fighting partner. As you exit the field, you run into the Gallic brothers. They are the reigning champion gladiators you believe were responsible for Shadya's death.

SPEAK TO FELIX TO START THE MATCH

Next you find yourself inside the arena hall. You can exit at any time by interacting with the main doors. You can speak with Felix now to start the games, but to learn more about the politics around the games, speak to Kensa, Horus (ex-champion-turned trainer), and the Ptolemy soldier sitting in one of the side rooms. When you are ready to fight, speak to Felix. He says he'll start you out against a few novices.

ENTER THE ARENA GROUNDS

Walk into the arena with Kensa to begin the first round.

WIN THE FIRST ROUND OF THE GAMES

FIRST TEAM

Senu, climbing, and your weapon selection are not available in the arena. The arena changes hazard props for each event. In this first event, there are spinning spike pillars. Don't get pushed into them while fighting. However, you can use them to your advantage by pushing someone into them.

In the first round, you go up against four Level 27 soldiers, all of whom have only swords. An easy fight. Let Kensa do her thing while you fight others. This keeps a couple soldiers preoccupied while you reduce their numbers. It won't take long to fill up your adrenaline in this round.

SECOND TEAM

The next team consists of four soldiers with swords and an archer who quickly switches to his spear (an option you do not have). If you get surrounded, perform heavy attacks to do more damage to nearby opponents and push them back at the same time. Use fast light attacks when you can single out enemies. This helps build up your adrenaline and then focuses the special attack on whoever has the most health remaining.

THIRD TEAM

The final team consists of four soldiers: one with a spear, another with a sword, one with a sword and shield, and the last with a spear and shield. Keep your eye on the guys with the shields. Avoid them until you have built up an adrenaline special and then unleash it on one of the guys with the shield. Finally, you and Kensa can gang up on the last guy with a shield.

After the round ends successfully, Felix congratulates you but knocks your ego down a notch when he says you are not ready for the Gallic brothers just yet. He says your next round will be with gladiators and a lion!

SPEAK TO KENSA

Back in the hall, check out the letter to Felix from "C," which could stand for Crocodile. It talks about his gladiators doing side jobs. Speak to Horus again. This time it's about the mercenary jobs. Speak to the soldier in the side room again. Lastly, speak to Kensa about the mercenary jobs.

SPEAK TO FELIX TO START THE MATCH

Now it's time for round two. You inquire about the mercenary jobs he's assigning to gladiators, but he'll have no jobs for you until you prove yourself further in the arena. Enter the arena when you are ready to fight again.

WIN THE SECOND ROUND OF THE GAMES

FIRST TEAM

The environment has changed. Now there is a lion cage in the middle of the grounds, and the rotating spike columns are in new locations. Fire pits have been uncovered and lit. Lastly, there's a pressure-sensitive spike platform in the back-right corner. Don't stand on it, but do push opponents onto it for added damage. The lion stays caged during the first team bout. However, you can break the door (accidentally or on purpose) freeing the lion.

You are equipped with a spear in this round. This gives you the ability to do more damage to gladiators crowding around you. There are four Level 27 soldiers with swords and one with a shield and spear. Avoid the guy with the shield until you have built up an adrenaline special on the others to use on him.

SECOND TEAM

In the second bout, you face two brutes with maces and one soldier with a sword. Save the brute for last and try to lead opponents into hazards to help diminish their health. Use the adrenaline special on the brutes.

INTRODUCTION
THE ESSENTIALS
MAIN QUESTS
SIDE QUESTS
ACTIVITIES
ATLAS
REFERENCE & ANALYSIS

THIRD TEAM

In the third bout, you face two soldiers with spears and shields and a brute with a mace. A lion has also been released from one of the side gates. Move away from the lion so it focuses on the enemy and helps take the attention off your team. Do more running in this round to single out enemies and separate them from the group. Also, try to lure them into the hazards. Use more dodging to get behind shields. Try to use the adrenaline special on the brute.

Felix goes nuts up in the stands when you win this one. He's really starting to pull for your team now.

The Guardians of Siwa are victorious once again!

SPEAK TO FELIX TO START THE MATCH

You find yourself back in the arena hall again after the match. Kensa is gone; she's off on a special mercenary job. Speak to Felix to start the next round without her but not with the Gallic Brothers quite yet. You can also speak to Horus and learn that Kallistos was killed on a job he was sent on by Felix. Learning this prior to speaking to Felix will slightly alter his conversation.

Another errand for the unknown patron?

WIN THE THIRD ROUND OF THE GAMES

FIRST TEAM

You're going it alone this time. Don't worry, you'll be okay. The environment has changed again. The spinning spike columns are present; the two on the sides are rolling and spinning on a track. There is now a pit of spikes where the lion cage used to be. Falling in means instant death. Walk around the pit of death to help divide the opponents; they'll have to pick a direction to reach you and then you can circle it to keep an opponent away from you.

The first team consists of three soldiers with swords and a brute with a large shield and spear. Avoid the brute while you build up adrenaline on the soldiers. As soon as the special is ready, target the brute and unleash it on him.

SECOND TEAM

During this phase, you face two soldiers, one with a sword and the other with a sword and shield. They're accompanied by a brute with large shield and a heavy blade (bronze axe). Fight as close to the hazards as possible without getting knocked into one. Target the brute when you have an adrenaline special ready.

THIRD TEAM

In this round you face an elite soldier with a sword and shield. He's an accomplished fighter with skills. Save this guy for last or when your special attack is filled up. With him are two

soldiers with swords—or you could call them "adrenaline fuel."

Back in the arena hall, after the battle, Kensa shows up and slaps you on the butt. She apologizes for leaving you alone. When you press her about the job she was on, she changes the subject.

Bayek. This is the moment we've longed for. Our chance to seize the mantle of champions. Felix awaits!

SPEAK TO FELIX TO START THE MATCH

Speak to Horus again and he'll give you tips on fighting the Gallic Brothers: separate them and fight them individually.

Speak to Felix to start the final round. He's counting on you to make the fight entertaining and begs you not to kill them since they are two of his top four fighters.

DEFEAT BROTHERS DIOVICOS AND VIRIDOVIX

Diovicos is the crazy brother in chains. He has a back-breaking special move. Don't fight up close for too long or he will show you how that works. Viridovix displays his amazing skills with his extremely long heavy blade (scythe) that can hook you, swing you around in the air, and then fling you to the ground. This is a very damaging move, so avoid him and make Diovicos your first target.

Keep moving to avoid attacks. Keep Diovicos selected as your primary target. After he attempts to strike you, dodge and strike him using only heavy attacks. Follow

heavy attacks with a chain of light attacks to build up adrenaline. It will take more than one adrenaline special attack to defeat Diovicos.

With Diovicos out of the picture, you and Kensa can concentrate on Viridovix. Two against one is very helpful. While he is attacking Kensa, dodge behind him and attack him, but get out quickly and far enough away that his wide weapon swing will not make contact. Move in for an attack as soon as he fails to make contact.

THE AFTERMATH

After you defeat both brothers, Felix looks shocked and Bayek is about to kill the brothers over the death of Shadya. The wounded and beaten brothers say they had nothing to do with it but points fingers at the Crocodile, whose name is

Berenike—the old lady they keep showing in the crowd near Felix. They say she is the one who drowned the child and took the ledger from her. She gets nervous and whispers in Felix's ear before she leaves.

Kensa gets upset when she sees what's unfolding in front of her. She's mad that you did not confide in her, admitting that she would have tried to help you if you had asked her.

SPEAK TO HOTEPHRES

After the battle, you find yourself outside the arena. Hotephres is standing nearby. Talk to him. He has learned, like many others now, that Berenike is the Crocodile. He tells you where her estate is located and that every night she retires to her villa.

INTRODUCTION

THE ESSENTIALS

MAIN QUESTS

SIDE QUESTS

ACTIVITIES

ATLAS

REFERENCE & ANALYSIS

KERKESOUCHA GRANARY

Prerequisite: Approach the Hideout

SUGGESTED LEVEL: 28 or higher   **LOCATION REWARD: 1,500 XP**   **LOCATION OBJECTIVES: Kill two captains, kill one commander, loot four treasures**

LEGEND	
3	Kerkesoucha Fort
4	South Villa Gate
5	Garden Statue
6	Villa Courtyard
7	Villa Approach
8	Balcony Soldier
9	North Villa Gate
10	Drop Assassination Location Option 1
11	Drop Assassination Location Option 2
12	Commander's Office
13	Possible Captain Location
14	Possible Captain Location
15	Possible Captain Location

Mount a horse and ride north to the indicated area on the map. When you get close, send Senu up to locate Berenike. During the daytime, she can be found walking around the Kerkesoucha Granary **(3)**, a very large fort in northern Faiyum Oasis. However, at nighttime it is much easier to get at her without all the soldiers around. She walks around her villa at night, which is technically part of the fort but is very lightly guarded. Meditate to change it to nighttime.

At night, you can find her and her bodyguard Kensa (yes, your dear friend from Siwa and gladiator partner) near the front gate **(4)** of the villa. Two Level 28 brutes stand guard at this entrance. You may also find her near the statue **(5)** in the garden. No matter where she is in the villa, she eventually walks closely under rooftops or the ropes stretched across the villa courtyard **(6)**. So we suggest an approach from the extremely, unguarded northeast wall **(7)**. Hop the fence and get to the rooftops. The only guard you should be wary of is the one on the balcony **(8)** under the pergola. If things go badly and you are chasing the Crocodile, then there will be a couple guards at the north gate **(10)** as well.

At night, reach the villa rooftops and get as close to Kensa and the Crocodile as possible. You won't get a damage report from aiming a bow at the Crocodile's head, so an arrow kill will likely

set her scrambling for the nearest guards and Kensa will be hot on the trail for you.

WHAT NOT TO TRY ON KENSA

If you think you can quietly crouch-walk up behind Kensa (who is Level 29) and assassinate her, you got another think coming. If you attempt this, she will leap out of the way at the last second and attack.

DROP ASSASSINATION LOCATION OPTION 1

If you see that her nighttime walk route takes her to the southwest corner of the villa grounds, then drop off the edge of the roof **(10)** over her to achieve a drop assassination. Make sure that you target the Crocodile and not Kensa, or the

Crocodile will run to the guards and you'll have to try to take her out with arrows before she alerts any. The Crocodile has an objective marker over her head.

DROP ASSASSINATION LOCATION OPTION 2

If you meditate the time to night and the Crocodile and Kensa appear near the south villa entrance **(4)**, then their nighttime walk likely has them heading straight for the villa courtyard **(6)**. In this case, get to the low rooftop at the courtyard entrance, or use the suspended ropes **(11)** to get over your target as she passes under.

SLEEP DARTS

Sleep darts are very useful in this situation. You can shoot Kensa with one, creating more separation between her and the Crocodile. You can also just hit them both with darts to make assassinating them very easy. Just don't do it while face-to-face from a low-level perch; Kensa has very good vision.

LAYLA UNPLUGGED

You enter the kill room and Bayek gets in the final word with the Crocodile.

But you are pulled into the present after returning from the kill room. Dee pulls the plug, wakes you up, and is screaming about Abstergo having discovered her. She gets cut off. Layla gets sick all over the ground and realizes that Abstergo has found her as well.

Layla has many of the skills Bayek and Aya have but without all the fancy weapons and Animus Pulse. So you can take out the Abstergo intruders with stealthy takedowns. Crouch and sneak up the stairs to the main cave where they are searching for you.

Sneak into the tall grass to the right of the stairway exit. Wait for the nearest guard to approach the stairway and then silently assassinate him from the tall grass. Layla has the hidden wrist blade that she found on Aya's mummy, so a takedown kills the intruders.

Let the next closest guard (to the left) see you for just a moment as you work your way into the tall grass on the left side of the stairway exit. As long as you hide before his meter goes red, then you'll stay hidden and he'll come investigate. Take him out when he gets close.

Two more to go. Head deeper into the cave and creep up behind the intruder near the construction light.

Lastly, head outside the cave and get the last one with his back to the entrance. A sandstorm kicks up, making visibility even worse for him. Take him out and you hear Dee getting murdered over the radio that he drops. Return to the Mobile Animus. This unlocks Main Quest: Way of the Gabiniani.

BACK TO BAYEK

When you return to Bayek, you must complete the location objective for the fort. See our map for the four treasure locations: two in the villa and two at the commander's office **(12)** in the fort. You can find captains in locations **(13)** or **(14)** and **(15)**.

HERAKLEION NOME

WAY OF THE GABINIANI

Prerequisite: Complete Main Quests: The Crocodile's Jaws; The Lizard's Face; The Hyena; The Scarab's Lies

SUGGESTED LEVEL: 31	REWARDS: NA	UNLOCKS: Main Quest: Aya: Blade of the Goddess	DETAILS: Bayek meets with Cleopatra to confirm this hunt is complete, yet he remains determined to find the man who actually killed his son.

SPEAK WITH CLEOPATRA IN HERAKLEION

HERAKLEION

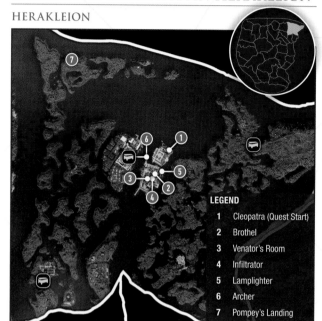

LEGEND

1. Cleopatra (Quest Start)
2. Brothel
3. Venator's Room
4. Infiltrator
5. Lamplighter
6. Archer
7. Pompey's Landing

If this is your first time in Herakleion Nome, you should synchronize the Viewpoints, at least the one near Cleopatra's Palace **(1)**. Apollodorus greets you as you enter the palace and hands you some drink. You leave him and talk to Cleopatra about finding the men who killed your son. Bayek and Cleopatra have a light argument, each fighting for control over the other. Cleopatra reminds him of the duties associated with the golden Medjay badge. She says she has a gift for you. Follow her.

FOLLOW CLEOPATRA

While following Cleopatra, Bayek asks about Aya and learns that she is still defending the seas and will be back any day. As you head down the hallway and back outside, claim your share from the palace's loot opportunities. Along the way, Cleopatra reveals that two new names on your list—the Jackal and the Scorpion—are within her brother's circle.

Cleopatra says Septimius sent a Gabiniani named Venator to try to assassinate her. Then Apollodorus shows up with a captive and throws him at your feet. He says he caught him snooping around and thinks the spy knows who killed your son. Bayek strangles information out of him. He says that Septimius killed your son.

Apollodorus and Cleopatra send you on an assignment to dig up more information on the plot against her. Septimius is in town; his main Phylakes is a man named Venator. There are rumors he's lurking around the brothel.

SPEAK WITH THE BROTHEL OWNER

Head south into the city and enter the brothel **(2)**. When you meet the brothel owner, she offers you a discount if you aren't with the Gabinianis. You tell her you are a Medjay and would like to speak to the legendary twins the spy had mentioned. She tells you it will cost you to see the twins.

PAY THE BROTHEL KEEPER

To continue, pay the brothel keeper 200 drachmas. She tells you to make yourself comfortable upstairs and the twins will come for you.

WAIT FOR THE TWINS UPSTAIRS

Head upstairs and meditate in the objective marker location. The male and female twins arrive. You tell them you are looking for Venator. They immediately get scared and tell you not to say that name out loud. They say everyone is scared of him and that you *should* kill him. They tell you he's staying at the top of the square.

REACH VENATOR'S ROOM

Leave the twins and head southwest to Venator's room **(3)**. Travel by rooftops and drop onto his balcony.

INVESTIGATE VENATOR'S ROOM

The room is unoccupied. Use Animus Pulse to find clues to see what occurred there. There is blood on the walls and broken dishes on the floor, but the clues that count are downstairs.

Downstairs are these clues: arrows shot at a Cleopatra bust (target practice); lutes; lipstick; scented oils on a chair; a crate of wine casks filled with oil—enough to burn down an entire city; and a letter from Septimius in a vase that you need to break (beware of the cobra inside). The letter mentions multiple assassins assigned to killing Cleopatra.

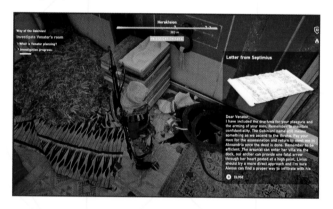

Bayek deduces that one of the assassins is posing as a woman to infiltrate the palace. Another is leading a group posing as wine merchants that will dock and set a fire to cause panic. Then, in the confusion, an archer will pick off the queen from somewhere high.

FIND AND KILL THE MERCENARIES

There are three targets you must hit: the infiltrator **(4)**, the lamplighter **(5)**, the archer **(6)**. Send Senu up to locate these three targets around the palace.

INFILTRATOR ASSASSINATION

Start your assassinations with the nearest target to you: the infiltrator **(4)**, posing as a woman. Run up behind him and assassinate him in the crowd. Beware the Romans enjoying the bath area as they will attack if they see you killing the infiltrator.

LAMPLIGHTER ASSASSINATION

Next, run from soldiers, heading northeast as you chase the lamplighter **(5)**. If you want, hide in safety and send Senu up to find the lamplighter. He is surrounded by several Level 30 to 31 soldiers. Now you may have some collateral damage.

Reach the rooftop and drop down into the yard near the shoreline. Throw sleep darts at everyone (or at least throw the amount of darts you have), including the lamplighter. Now run up and assassinate the sleeping lamplighter. You can leave the others alive or just send them to Duat.

ARCHER ASSASSINATION

To avoid the Romans at the foot of tower, jump into water and swim around to the back north side of the lighthouse tower. Ledge assassinate the lower guard and run northwest toward the

viewpoint lighthouse tower. The archer **(6)** is perched high on the topmost platform near the large flame. There is a guard on the lower platform as well. You can either put an arrow through the archer (which is poetic justice) or you can fight through the Level 31 bandits at the base of the lighthouse, climb up, and kill him close. Be cautious of the bandit bodyguard on the platform below him.

RETURN TO CLEOPATRA

Before you head back to Cleopatra, equip yourself with weapons that you'd be comfortable with in an ambush. Select your favorite bows and your most powerful weapons. Head back to Cleopatra's palace to reunite with Aya, who jumps on you and kisses you like she hasn't seen you in a year.

But the threat is not over yet! She pushes you out of the way of another archer coming up behind you from the shore. Aya defects the arrow with her sword and the rumble begins.

DEFEND THE QUEEN

Where you thought you were going to report the good news of thwarting an assassination attempt, here you are in the middle of another attempt you did not know about. You are up against five mercenaries. Pull out your hunter bow and pick off the advancing gang with multiple headshots.

Six Level 31 mercenaries are marching toward you. You should be able to eliminate all but the large brute before they're on top of you.

Use a special adrenaline move on the brute and finish off any stragglers to complete the objective. When you do clear the warm-up band, Raging Axes "Venator" arrives.

KILL VENATOR

Venator is a Level 31 massive brute wielding twin heavy blades. He comes from the docks (the same direction as the previous gang), so there's plenty of space to put distance between you. Begin with long-range arrow attacks to the face. When you have built up adrenaline, release it on him. Target-select him so your dodge moves become more effective and send you behind him instead of out of hit range.

After he swings and misses, hit his side or back with your most powerful fast weapon. He's relentless and doesn't get knocked down easily, so be vigilant. Keep moving, dodging, and striking; when possible, back up and get some arrow shots to his head. Eventually he goes down.

After the battle, Cleopatra is fed up with her brother's antics and expresses her desire to have a throne. She tells Apollodorus to instruct Phoxidas to prepare a ship. She plans to meet Pompey. Aya tells Bayek that if they don't get to Pompey first, Septimius might.

BRING AYA TO WHERE POMPEY IS LANDING

Take a boat from the nearby pier and allow Aya aboard. Sail toward the marker **(7)** on the north shore of the small island in the northeast.

Aya and Bayek have time to catch up along the way.

When you reach the camp area, you find many dead and rotting Roman soldiers scattered about. When you reach the marker, you find the skewered, headless corpse of Pompey sitting upright on the beach. Septimius beat you here. Cleopatra and Apollodorus arrive soon after your discovery. She demands that Aya escort her to Caesar.

INTRODUCTION

THE ESSENTIALS

MAIN QUESTS

SIDE QUESTS

ACTIVITIES

ATLAS

REFERENCE & ANALYSIS

AYA: BLADE OF THE GODDESS

Prerequisite: Complete Main Quest: Way of the Gabiniani

SUGGESTED LEVEL: 31	REWARDS: NA	UNLOCKS: Main Quest: The Battle for the Nile	DETAILS: Caesar's arrival in Alexandria has complicated Cleopatra's precarious journey.

SPEAK TO AYA

HERAKLEION

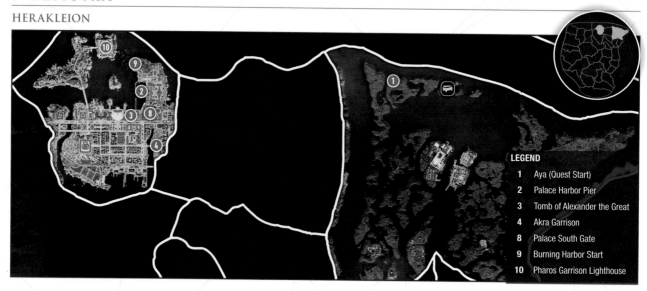

LEGEND

1. Aya (Quest Start)
2. Palace Harbor Pier
3. Tomb of Alexander the Great
4. Akra Garrison
8. Palace South Gate
9. Burning Harbor Start
10. Pharos Garrison Lighthouse

Speak to Aya **(1)**. She's where you left her at the end of Main Quest: Way of the Gabiniani. She warns you that once they board the ship, there's no turning back. You finish with either the queen on the throne or each of your heads on a pike. Choose to "Sail to Alexandria" if you are ready to leave.

SINK THE FLEET

MEDITERRANEAN COAST

Cleopatra and Apollodorus are aboard Phoxidas's ship with Bayek and Aya. You travel with four other warships and encounter trouble in the beginning of the voyage.

There are two enemy ships dead ahead. Position yourself to avoid a ram maneuver, which one of the enemy ships attempts from the start. Sink the two ships and head for Alexandria, close to 3,000 meters away.

CATAPULTS

At about 2,560 meters, you encounter enemy warships. You have access to the catapults in this sea battle. Activate the catapult aiming. Aim the reticle over a ship (you know your aim is true when the reticle turns red) and execute a catapult call. When you fire catapults, all the ships in your fleet also fire catapults on the targeted ship. This is a great way to do some serious damage to the enemy. The catapult takes time to recharge; use it strategically.

After destroying one of the four ships in the second wave, a cutscene displays how oil in the water (spilled from the sinking ship) is used as a weapon. An enemy shoots a flaming arrow into the spill and creates a large fire hazard. Two of your ally ships sink from this attack. Now you and two ally ships face a couple small ships and a large warship. Be cautious of the new hazard. Fight the remaining ships while avoiding patches of floating fire.

Fire catapults at the big ship while continually moving into position to attack the smaller ships. Put the smaller ships between you and the large warship. After you take out the two smaller ones, concentrate on the large one. And don't forget about the catapults; they do a great deal of damage.

After you win the battle, a celebration occurs just before arrows rain down on your ship. Phoxidas tells you to get on the small reed boats and use the fog to hide your escape.

DELIVER CLEOPATRA

ALEXANDRIA: ROYAL PALACE

You disembark in the Royal Palace's harbor. While on the bulkhead **(2)**, the party contemplates how they will enter the palace unnoticed, especially with Cleopatra accompanying you. They decide to wrap her in a roll of carpet and have Apollodorus carry her in as a gift. Aya and Bayek carry a vase and gift basket.

Follow Apollodorus to the first checkpoint, where he explains to the guards that they have gifts for Caesar from the nomarch of Heliopolis (Apollodorus) and local merchants. He explains that the you and Aya are his Phylakitai. He not only lets you pass but also escorts you through multiple checkpoints.

At the next checkpoint, the escort asks if he can carry the rug. Apollodorus dissuades him by saying it's sacred. At the next checkpoint, one of the guards recognizes Bayek from the hippodrome races but allows him to pass. Once inside the palace, the big reveal occurs. Pompey's head is in a box on Caesar's desk. Cleopatra's brother Ptolemy stands nearby in council with the ruler. Just before they discuss an alliance, your party barges in with Cleopatra.

Caesar lends an open ear as Cleopatra offers her hand in marriage, something her brother cannot do. Ptolemy runs off in a tizzy and Caesar dismisses everyone from the room so he and Cleopatra can discuss their new arrangement.

Outside, Bayek and Aya discuss their disappointment at missing Pothinus and Septimius. Apollodorus says once Cleopatra is queen, they can act from within and crush the network. Apollodorus says he'll meet you at the gardens tomorrow.

REACH THE TOMB ENTRANCE

THE TOMB OF ALEXANDER THE GREAT

Cleopatra wants to invite Caesar to visit the tomb of Alexander the Great. The tomb is sealed, but not by royal decree. She tells Aya that an earthquake in the early years of her father's reign blocked the door. Aya suggests getting to it from underground and finding an easy way in for everyone else.

You find yourself at the entrance to the tomb of Alexander the Great **(3)**. Enter the building and follow the marker down the stairs. You find a set of open double doors. This is the tomb entrance.

INVESTIGATE THE TOMB ENTRANCE

Head through the double doors and down the stairs. Use Animus Pulse to discover a cracked wall on the left side. There's also the sealed main entrance and blood on the floor to inspect. Use a weapon to break through the crack in the wall. Push through and both you and Bayek will enter the tomb behind the wall.

EXPLORE THE TUNNELS

Begin exploring the tunnels. Head down the slope and slide under the small hole below a boarded-up doorway.

In the new area are metal bars on a passage to the left and a few large vases on the right. Smash the vases to reveal another small hole. Slide through it to reach the next hallway.

In the next hall, leap off the edge of the path. There's water below, so you'll live. Swim downward to find a passage to the next area.

You enter a very large water-filled chamber. The way out is through a high tunnel on the west wall. Follow the tunnel as it bends north. Keep swimming upward to find the surface and catch a breath. Run up along the wooden scaffold to the next hallway. Run to the northwest corner to find the next tunnel.

You reach a T-intersection. There is a large crack in the wall to the left, a barred window straight ahead, and a dead-end hallway to the right. Go through the crack in the wall.

On the other side, Aya and Bayek find the tomb of Alexander the Great. Bayek reads inscriptions and Aya feels it's time to let the others in.

OPEN THE GATE

Head up the red-carpeted staircase. Interact with the ornate doors to let the others in. While they ogle the tomb, Bayek asks Aya when Cleopatra might give them leads to their son's killers. Flavius rushes into the tomb to announce that Caesar's emissaries have been captured at the southern garrison of Alexandria. Seems Cleopatra's brother kept his promise of revenge. Aya and Bayek volunteer to take care of this predicament.

RESCUE CAESAR'S EMISSARIES

On your way out of the tomb, Bayek offers to distract the garrisons while you (Aya) procure the emissaries. Call for your mount and chase the objective marker to the Akra Garrison in the southeast.

AKRA GARRISON

Prerequisite: Approach the Garrison
SUGGESTED LEVEL: 10 or higher
LOCATION REWARD: 500 XP
LOCATION OBJECTIVES: Kill two captains and one commander, loot four treasures

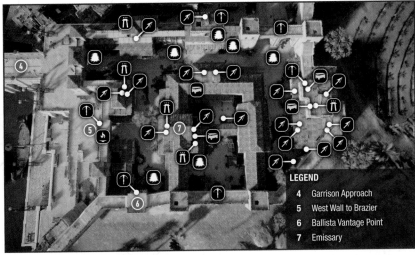

LEGEND
4 Garrison Approach
5 West Wall to Brazier
6 Ballista Vantage Point
7 Emissary

You've been to this garrison a few times already during your adventure, so you should've already taken its treasures and killed its commander and captains. You assassinated Gennadios the Phylakitai and freed an actor from there during Side Quest: Wrath of the Poets. We suggest a similar approach, as the brazier will be lit as soon as the soldiers within spot you.

Cross the bridge **(4)**, climb up the west wall **(5)**, and set the brazier trap to keep reinforcements from arriving. Many of the soldiers occupying this fort are at the same levels they were when you were last there. You're facing Level 8 soldiers mixed with Level 31 newcomers.

Reach the ballista and take out soldiers who may try to stop the rescue. Enter the third floor of the central building **(7)** to find a bloodied emissary on the floor. The wounded man tells you to warn Caesar. Septimius is preparing a siege of the harbor and wants to take the palace. He passes out before you learn their current location.

EXTRACT THE EMISSARY

Pick him up and drop down the hole in the floor (where a ladder is located) to reach the second floor. Take the stairs to the first floor. Run out of the building, avoiding any soldiers who still live. Place the emissary on a horse (there's some near the stables at the main west gate). Ride out of the fort, follow the marker north, and get him back to Caesar's palace. You enter the palace from the south road entrance **(8)**, near the Tomb of Alexander the Great.

Aya gets news to Caesar that Septimius plans on trapping him in the palace. Caesar orders Flavius to attack in the harbor while he joins the battle by chariot. Apollodorus decides to defend the queen as she remains at the palace on the throne. Caesar has Bayek put powder into the brazier of the Pharos to let the fleet know what's happening onshore. Before Aya leaves, Cleopatra gives her the okay to assassinate her brother.

Once outside **(9)**, Aya asks Bayek to give her the powder, as Caesar thinks a woman can't do the job and she aims to prove him wrong. Bayek complies and throws her the powder.

REACH THE TOP OF THE PHAROS

The harbor is burning, just as Caesar ordered. You need to reach the top of the Pharos Garrison **(10)** and put the powder in the flames to signal the fleet. Climb the dead tree at your starting position, and leap to the top of the ship mast. Leap from burning ship mast to ship mast until you reach one that breaks under your weight. Aya safely falls into the water below.

Now swim directly west for the marker and the shore of the garrison. Defeat the soldier on the walkway near the water. Follow the stairs up to the interior, where you find a bloody massacre. Avoid confrontation or help allies fight near the base of the tower.

PHAROS GARRISON

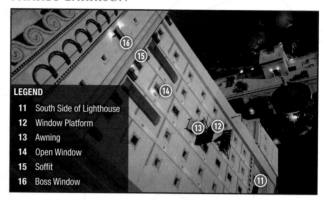

LEGEND

11	South Side of Lighthouse
12	Window Platform
13	Awning
14	Open Window
15	Soffit
16	Boss Window

Run to the lighthouse's south side **(11)** (left as you enter the garrison) and start scaling the wall. Continue to the platform **(12)** below an open window.

If you want to fight through more soldiers inside the lighthouse, then enter this window. If you want to skip right to the boss fight, then climb atop the awning (using the south side of the poles holding it up) and continue to scale the wall.

Keep climbing past the second open window **(14)**. Negotiate past the large soffit **(15)** and into the open boss window **(16)**. The brute reaches through the window and pulls you in and throws you on the floor.

KILL THE GUARDIAN

Now you face a Level 31 brute with a large hammer. You're equipped with a quick bow and a hunter's bow. There are multiple arrow supplies around the chamber, so if you need arrows, you got 'em. Start with the quick bow to the brute's face, and don't let up until you are out of arrows. You can easily put him down this way without ever laying a finger on him. If he still stands, this attack builds up enough adrenaline that you can release a special move on him to finish him off.

If you want to fight through more soldiers inside the lighthouse, then enter this window. If you want to skip right to the boss fight, then climb atop the awning (using the south side of the poles holding it up) and continue to scale the wall.

Keep climbing past the second open window **(14)**. Negotiate past the large soffit **(15)** and into the open boss window **(16)**. The brute reaches through the window and pulls you in and throws you on the floor.

LIGHT THE PHAROS

Interact with the large doors on the northeast side of the boss chamber. Aya eventually muscles them open. Once outside, climb up the rest of the tower. You can uncover one of the garrison's treasures in the room below the fire.

Climb up the ladder in the small room to reach the fire. Walk around it until you locate and activate the interact prompt. One more soldier will challenge you. He's upset about you killing his captain. Back on the ground, Caesar grows impatient, especially now that he's learned that Bayek has passed this critical mission to a woman. Just before he blows a gasket, Aya comes through and gets the powder in the fire, turning it green to signal the fleet. Mission accomplished. The mission now transitions into Main Quest: The Battle for the Nile as Caesar and Bayek ride off together in a chariot.

INTRODUCTION

THE ESSENTIALS

MAIN QUESTS

SIDE QUESTS

ACTIVITIES

ATLAS

REFERENCE & ANALYSIS

ALEXANDRIA

THE BATTLE FOR THE NILE

Prerequisite: Complete Main Quest: Aya: Blade of the Goddess

| SUGGESTED LEVEL: 31 | REWARDS: NA | UNLOCKS: Main Quest: The Aftermath | DETAILS: Bayek must get Caesar to the battlefield to direct his forces and defeat the forces of King Ptolemy. |

DEFEND CAESAR

ALEXANDRIA

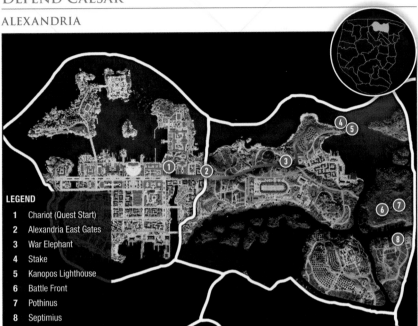

LEGEND

1 Chariot (Quest Start)
2 Alexandria East Gates
3 War Elephant
4 Stake
5 Kanopos Lighthouse
6 Battle Front
7 Pothinus
8 Septimius

Don't worry too much about shooting soldiers in the streets; they pose no threat and cannot follow you on foot. The real challenge starts when you pass the first couple soldiers on horseback. This begins near the gates **(2)** of Alexandria. Try for only headshots to take them down quickly.

Horseback and chariot offenders remain in hot pursuit until the war elephant tramples through a hut **(3)** and onto the road behind you. There's no killing it yet, but if you stop shooting arrows at it, it will run you over and send you back to the start.

Just before you reach the lighthouse **(5)**, Bayek grabs a stake **(4)** from the ground and throws it into the elephant's eye. This kills it and throws everyone to the ground. But the trip was a success; everyone lived but the elephant and its passenger. Caesar and Bayek successfully board with the fleet.

Aya lights the Pharos green to signal the fleet. Now you and Caesar have to make it across Kanopos to reach them at the lighthouse in the northeast. Caesar yells at you to cover the retreat. Keep your eyes behind the chariot and shoot anything that gives chase.

The die is cast. Come, we go to the battlefield! Medjay, cover the retreat.

You begin the wild ride leaving the south gate **(1)** out of the Royal Palace. Pivot around so you are looking behind the chariot. Let Caesar worry about the driving. You have unlimited arrows for the quick bow you are wielding. You cannot switch to any other weapons; you do not have access to Senu or the map.

NILE DELTA

THREE DAYS LATER

The next scene starts three days later in the Nile Delta. The battle rages on with the forces of King Ptolemy. You watch as your comrades continue a bloody battle on the frontlines **(6)**. Caesar is holding his own, fighting alongside Bayek and Aya. Caesar reports that Pothinus leads the charge. Bayek tells Caesar to keep the soldiers distracted while he deals with Pothinus.

KILL POTHINUS

This is your chance to reconfigure your weaponry choices and add any new abilities to your profile. Select your strongest weapons, as you are preparing for a boss battle with Pothinus **(7)**. If you have found Raneb's Hammer and Mustapha's Blade (legendary weapons), then you are more than ready to do battle with this adversary.

Run to the marker to find many allies battling the enemy in the fog of war. Enter the large fenced arena, and the doors shut behind you. There's no turning back now. Inside, Pothinus introduces you to his war elephant, Yugr Tn.

Begin by volleying arrows at the large beast with a strong, Legendary hunting bow. Dodge the elephant's charge attacks and use your Legendary sword on his body just after his charge; he has a moment of recovery after the charge attack. This is your window of opportunity to inflict more damage than the arrows are capable of.

Use the adrenaline special attack to inflict almost 2,000 points of damage, compared to an arrow attack of only 380 points. Aim for the area of trunk that is exposed just below his face armor—this is a weak spot. His rear is also a sensitive area. An arrow there can do around 1,200 points of damage. Arrow supplies are located around the perimeter of the battle arena.

When you knock the elephant over, Pothinus is finished and you meet him in the kill room. When you return to reality, Caesar tells you that Septimius is in the nearby village. He will distract his men while you capture him.

REACH THE VILLAGE

Battle your way through the frontlines on your way to the village **(8)** to the south, across the river.

Once in the village, fight your way to another battle arena. Short wood spikes comprise the fence. Use the upright cart next to the fence to run and jump into the ring.

KILL SEPTIMIUS

The Level 31 Septimius steps out of his tent and is ready to fight. If your Legendary weapon has full adrenaline at the start of conflict, then begin the battle with a special attack. Otherwise, soften him up with arrows to the face.

Follow up the arrows with a long heavy blunt or spear, knock him to the ground, and keep pummeling him.

Switch to your Legendary warrior bow. When Septimius starts his fancy twirling blade attack, hold him back with a volley of simultaneous arrows to the cranium. That'll knock him back when he tries to advance on you. Finish him off with a special attack.

When you go to confirm the kill, you realize he's not dead. He grabs your head and slams you to the ground. When you start to get the upper hand in the struggle and are seconds away from ending him with the hidden blade, Caesar yells at you to stop. His reasoning: Septimius is a Roman and they deal with him under their laws.

Two soldiers restrain Bayek from killing the man who murdered his son. The focus switches to Aya, who is about to kill Ptolemy, but just before she puts an arrow through him, his boat overturns and he's eaten by crocodiles. Septimius then knocks Bayek unconscious.

THE AFTERMATH

Prerequisite: Complete Main Quest: The Battle of the Nile

SUGGESTED LEVEL: 31	REWARDS: 6,000 XP	UNLOCKS: Main Quest: Last of the Medjay	DETAILS: Aya and Bayek believe they've been betrayed by the Romans. They go to investigate Alexander's Tomb to figure out what their enemies are planning.

ALEXANDRIA, SARAPEION

TWO WEEKS LATER

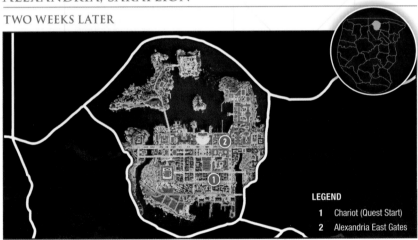

LEGEND

1 Chariot (Quest Start)
2 Alexandria East Gates

Two weeks later, Apollodorus, Cleopatra, and Caesar are celebrating their victory with the people of Alexandria. Standing between them is none other than Septimius. This won't sit well with Bayek and Aya.

LATER THAT DAY

Aya corners Apollodorus outside the palace. She screams at him for standing with Septimius and for being banned from the palace. Cleopatra released them as Medjays and paid them off in gold. Caesar is now protecting the Order and not judging Septimius. The man who killed their son is now Apollodorus's ally, and they'll do anything to kill Septimius. Caesar is upset that Aya killed Ptolemy, yet Cleopatra gave her the order. Apollodorus asks them to wait things out, but that doesn't sit well with our betrayed husband and wife team.

SPEAK TO AYA

That night, Bayek and Aya meet at Phanos's house with their true friends, who form a brotherhood and develop a creed. They swear to stand and fight together to fix what they have mistakenly created and to eradicate corruption. Aya walks out of the meeting feeling guilty for defending Cleopatra. Bayek and Aya discuss why Septimius and Flavius have so much interest in Alexander's Tomb.

REACH THE TOMB OF ALEXANDER THE GREAT

Speak to Aya **(1)** after the cutscene. You and Aya head to the Tomb of Alexander the Great **(2)**. Aya runs off her frustration instead of taking a horse to the tomb. It gives the two of you more time to catch up and share your feelings about the latest developments.

Caesar's Roman soldiers stand guard, four strong, at the gates of the tomb. Follow Aya up the wall to avoid them. Or you can drop down in the middle of them and take them on.

DEFEND APOLLODORUS

Enter the tomb. The doors are now open (Aya opened them earlier). Descend the stairs to the lower level. Roman soldiers are attacking Apollodorus around Alexander's tomb. There are three Level 31 soldiers to defeat before you can check on Apollodorus, who is lying on the ground before the tomb. Watch your back, as another soldier will enter the tomb behind you.

Apollodorus, bleeding heavily, tells you that Flavius killed your son and that they took the orb from him and headed for Siwa. With his dying breath, he urges you go to Siwa to save your people. They are in danger.

SIWA

THE FINAL WEIGHING

Prerequisite: Complete Main Quest: The Aftermath

SUGGESTED LEVEL: 32	REWARDS: 4,500 XP	UNLOCKS: Main Quest: The Aftermath and Side Quests: Playing with Fire and One Bad Apple	DETAILS: Bayek and Aya journey to Siwa on the trail of Flavius and the Oracle's Relic.

REACH THE VAULT

SIWA

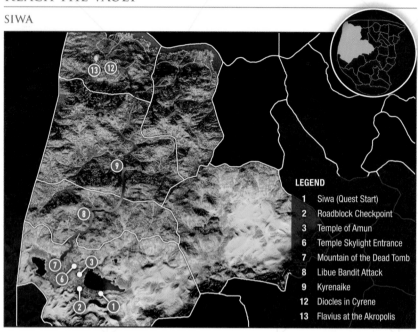

LEGEND

1	Siwa (Quest Start)
2	Roadblock Checkpoint
3	Temple of Amun
6	Temple Skylight Entrance
7	Mountain of the Dead Tomb
8	Libue Bandit Attack
9	Kyrenaike
12	Diocles in Cyrene
13	Flavius at the Akropolis

This mission starts automatically after you complete Main Quest: The Aftermath, where, with his dying breath, Apollodorus tells you to go to Siwa to help your people. Flavius has stolen the orb and is headed to your hometown.

SUGGESTED LEVEL: 38

Although the suggested level of this quest is 32, near the quest's end you face the Level 35 Flavius. If you want to complete the Roman Akropolis fort location objectives in Cyrene, then you should wait until you are Level 38 or above to take or complete this quest. Or, have the Legendary gear, abilities, and crafting levels needed to fight enemies a few levels above your own.

You begin on the eastern road **(1)** into Siwa. You are on horseback with Aya by your side. Devastation is immediately seen. If you follow the main road heading toward the first objective marker **(2)**, you'll discover a well-guarded roadblock.

You must fight through Level 31 and 32 soldiers and brute soldiers. This is not the only troop you'll face between here and the vault. If you wish to avoid the heavy resistance between here and the Temple of Amun, head north to the lake. Follow the shoreline to reach the Temple of Amun **(3)**.

TEMPLE OF AMUN

LEGEND

1	Temple of Amun Approach
2	South Temple Wall
3	Parkour Up Pulley System
6	Temple Rooftop Entrance

When you reach the area south of the Temple of Amun **(3)**, send Senu up to mark Roman soldiers. A good-sized force guards all the major entrances, but they didn't bring enough to patrol the temple grounds. To avoid all confrontation before entering the vault, scale the south wall **(4)** just west of the southeast gate entrance.

Use the wall walk and suspended ropes to quickly travel across the temple grounds. You can climb and leap up the pulley system **(5)** on the temple's northwest corner to quickly reach the rooftop (or scale the walls). Drop down into the northeast skylight **(6)** to enter the temple.

When you reach the vault, you notice two guards facing the vault entrance with their backs to you. Throw sleep darts at them and then assassinate them, or keep them alive and unconscious while you enter the vault.

Head down the stairs to discover a glowing, spherical map of Earth. It perplexes Bayek and Aya; they believe it's the work of gods. Bayek sadly discovers the dead body of his dear friend Hepzefa. Aya is ready to fight back to avenge your friend, but Bayek puts your plans on hold to take care of Hepzefa's body and give him a proper burial.

CARRY HEPZEFA'S BODY OUT OF THE VAULT

When you exit the vault with Hepzefa's body, you discover that all the Roman soldiers are gone and the tunnel has filled with the people of Siwa, including your dear friend Rabiah, the healer.

Rabiah explains that before you arrived, Septimius and Flavius entered the vault with the orb and it activated it. Hepzefa tried to stop them but they rendered him helpless. A blue fire emerged from the vault and the entire village fell to the ground like dolls.

SPEAK TO RABIAH

MOUNTAIN OF THE DEAD TOMB

Next you find yourself with all your Siwan friends in the Mountain of the Dead Tomb **(7)**, laying Hepzefa to rest. You can interact with Hepzefa's mummy, the skeleton on the ground, and your grandfather's mummy, but to progress the story, speak to Rabiah (she's

in the tomb with you). Rabiah gives you Hepzefa's Sword. This is quite a gift! It's a Legendary sword with a Level 3 critical hit rate and a Level 2 Adrenaline on Hurt, and it is on fire. That's right, when you wield the sword, flames shoot from it, setting your target on fire.

SPEAK TO AYA

Find Aya in a side room inside the Mountain of the Dead Tomb. She tells you that the villagers interrogated a Roman soldier. He said Flavius is headed for Cyrene and Septimius for Alexandria. You volunteer to kill Flavius, while Aya chooses to kill Septimius. Aya stands at your son's sarcophagus. After speaking with her, you can pay tribute.

TRAVEL TO KYRENAIKE

LIBUE

If you need to upgrade weapons before you leave, use the Siwa blacksmith. Kyrenaike is a village in the Green Mountains. If you have not been there yet, then you'll have to ride north through the Siwan mountains and pass through Libue. If you have been there, you can travel to an active Viewpoint. Along the road through Libue, you are likely to meet mounted bandits who are Level 31 to 33 **(8)**. Finish them off or they will follow you relentlessly.

GREEN MOUNTAINS

Not far north into the Green Mountains region is the small farm village of Kyrenaike **(9)**. Send Senu up to locate someone who might have seen Flavius travel through.

When you visit the farm on the west side of the main road, you catch a horrific scene. A man named Mereruka is beheading people in captivity, but a brave, beautiful young lady rushes to their aid, risking her own life to set the rest free before they are slaughtered next. With some obvious sword skill, she runs Mereruka through, stopping the madness.

Bayek stops Praxilla just in time from making him her next victim of her blade. She calms down and you exchange formalities; then Bayek offers to help her look for survivors at the farm.

LOOK FOR SURVIVORS AROUND THE FARM

PRAXILLA'S FARM

Head to the north side of the large farmhouse. There you discover a group of Level 32 Roman soldiers. Try to take them out stealthily or just go in loud and proud with Praxilla by your side. It's best to defeat these soldiers before you enter the farmhouse or you'll just have to do it later.

Try out Hepzefa's sword on the brute with the large shield and spear. Just be careful not to stand too close to the burning bodies after an attack or you will also feel the wrath of the burning blade.

Head to the house's second-floor balcony **(11)** to find a survivor, Nenet, sitting and shaking. The half-blind lady's cryptic story of the events that happened sounds like what happened to the people of Siwa—people fell to the ground under the orb's power.

LEGEND
9 Praxilla
10 Roman Soldiers
11 Survivor

ESCORT PRAXILLA AND NENET TO THE CART

I pray you get the justice you seek, Bayek

This is why you killed the soldiers before you rescued Nenet. Now you must escort her through the house and out to the cart **(9)** in the road. If you had not killed the soldiers, you'd be fighting to protect the ladies now. Once at the cart, Praxilla tells you to look for her trusted friend and magistrate in Cyrene named Diocles. She gives you a ring to present to him to prove you are a friend.

Praxilla is also a side quest giver. She says she will take Nenet to her clinic in Balagrae, south of the Temple of Asclepius. Bayek picks up on the hint and tells her he will find her if he can. This unlocks Side Quests: Playing with Fire and One Bad Apple. You can do those side quests before you end this quest, as they do not take you too far out of the way. Otherwise, continue your mission.

FIND FLAVIUS

Travel north to Cyrene, Kyrenaika, and send Senu up to locate Diocles **(12)** in the Agora in the middle of Cyrene. Give him the ring from Praxilla to prove that you are a friend. He tells you that Flavius is in the Akropolis, which is crawling with Romans.

Find and Assassinate Flavius

ROMAN AKROPOLIS

Prerequisite: Approach the hideout

SUGGESTED LEVEL: 35 or higher   **LOCATION REWARD: 1,500 XP**   **LOCATION OBJECTIVES: Kill two captains and one commander, loot four treasures**

LEGEND

13	Flavius
14	Northeast Waterfall Pond
15	Northeast Guard Tower
16	Captain Kill Opportunity
17	Suspended Rope Start
18	Suspended Rope End
19	Parkour Up Hoist
20	Open Window

Travel west to the Roman Akropolis and send Senu up to locate Flavius, who is in the Acropolis building **(13)**. Scope out the open windows just below the rooftop. Mark enemies in the fort's northeast section. The following walkthrough is a way to reach Flavius quickly, stealthily, and with the least number of Roman soldiers dying.

LOCATION OBJECTIVE

For help with finding treasures and details about this fort, see "Roman Akropolis" in the Activities section of this guide.

Find the waterfall pool **(14)** in the fort's northeast corner. Climb the canyon wall above and continue up the side of the fort walls. Stop at the window of the northeast guard tower **(15)**. Whistle to lure a guard to the window. Pull him through and throw him to the rocks below.

Get to the rooftop of the guard tower. Head northwest, traveling parallel with the wall walk. Find the suspended rope above where a captain **(16)** often sits in a tent below. If he's there and no one can see you, drop-assassinate him (to count toward the location objective).

Get back to the rooftop and find the suspension rope **(17)** connected to the west building's rooftop **(18)**. Cross that and then cross the rooftop to reach the large stair landing with the parkour hoist **(19)**. Use it to reach the base of the Akropolis building.

Watch out for the brute soldier behind the pillars. Climb one of the nearby pillars and stop just before reaching the overhang. Jump to the next pillar or to the inside wall and then enter

through the high open window **(20)** to begin the boss battle.

FLAVIUS BATTLE

The battle begins as soon as you enter the building. Flavius senses you sneaking up on him—no doubt an enhancement from the orb's power. He's a Level 35 combatant with the ability to cloak and spawn decoy apparitions.

If you have a weapon that gives you full adrenaline at the start of conflict, then begin with a special attack; otherwise you can put arrows in his head from a distance to build up adrenaline. When you've knocked off about 20 percent of his health (his health bar appears at the top of the screen), he begins his cloaking move and sends ghosts of those you've murdered from the Order of Ancients to attack you.

You can slice through and defeat the ghosts with one hit. After you make all the ghosts disappear, Flavius shows himself again. You get to taste a bit of what victims in Siwa felt from the power of the

orb. Flavius can send you into a state of paralysis; there's nothing you can do but suffer damage from the attack he follows up with.

With about 30 percent of his health remaining, Flavius cloaks and sends the ghosts after you once again. Defeat them all to force Flavius to show himself once more. You do not earn adrenaline off the ghosts, so you must earn any adrenaline specials needed by attacking Flavius. There is a single arrow supply on the side of the room. Use this only when you run completely out of arrows to get the most out of the one-time supply. If Flavius is hanging on by a thread, use arrows to finish him off from a safe distance.

Confirm the kill to enter the kill room where your son gets the pleasure of sending Flavius to Hades. This completes the quest and unlocks the Main Quest: Last of the Medjay.

ALEXANDRIA

THE LAST MEDJAY

Prerequisite: Complete Main Quest: The Final Weighing

SUGGESTED LEVEL: 35	REWARDS: 3,000 XP	UNLOCKS: Main Quest: Fall of an Empire, Rise of Another	DETAILS: Bayek returns to the den and meets Aya along with her Roman allies.

SPEAK TO AYA IN ALEXANDRIA

ALEXANDRIA

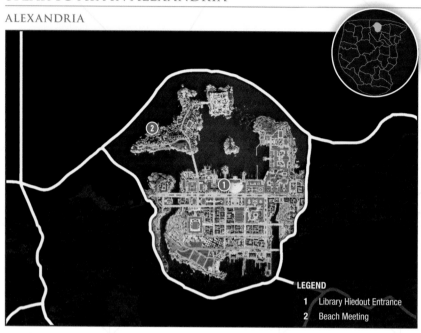

LEGEND

1   Library Hiedout Entrance
2   Beach Meeting

Enter Aya's hideout passage on the Great Library's northeast corner **(1)**. Bayek reunites with Aya and gives her the good news that Flavius is dead. She tells Bayek that she's heading to Rome now.

Aya has kept herself busy while Bayek was in Cyrene. Brutus and Cassius are two Romans who have found a common enemy with Aya. Phanos the Younger and Phoxidas are preparing to send scrolls across Egypt and toward Rome and Greece to inform their trusted allies of the new brotherhood fighting against the Order of the Ancients.

SPEAK TO AYA ONE LAST TIME

It seems the couple's hard journey is splitting them apart. Bayek does not want to let Aya go so easily now that he feels his quest is complete. He locks the orb in a box to keep it from anyone else's hands. Exit the hideout the way you entered. Head northwest to the marker **(2)** on Alexandria's north shoreline to find Aya.

On the beach, Aya and Bayek face the truth of what their relationship has suffered. Aya pushes Bayek away when he hopes to let the gods decide the fate of their relationship. But with a little more contemplation, he agrees to the separation, as they sacrifice their personal lives for the greater good. They develop an Assassin's creed: to kill only in the shadows and to eliminate only those who deserve it. (Notice the shape of the bird skull imprint in the sand when Aya lifts it off the beach.)

CURRENT TIME

LAYLA

After witnessing the sad breakup of Bayek and Aya on the Alexandria beach, Layla wakes up from the Animus with a man sitting and staring at her. Layla jumps up in shock and threatens him with the wrist blade duct-taped to her arm. William Miles, the Assassin, calmly introduces himself and emphasizes his occupation by revealing his own hidden wrist blade.

He tells you that the Assassins have been watching her and are curious why an Abstergo employee is taking interest in a country's revolution. He reminds her of how she was deceived by the company she works for. He offers to get her out of the cave and to Alexandria safely. He also offers her a job with the Assassins working on her version of the Animus and doing things her way—giving her an out from under Abstergo. She agrees and reenters the Animus to complete unfished business.

TYRRHENIAN SEA

FALL OF AN EMPIRE, RISE OF ANOTHER

Prerequisite: Complete Main Quest: Last of the Medjay

SUGGESTED LEVEL: 35	REWARDS: NA	UNLOCKS: Birth of the Creed	DETAILS: Aya heads to Rome to finish her task.

SAIL TO ROME

Aya, edgy from her recent breakup, nearly kills a teasing crewmember. Phoxidas tries to comfort her and get her mind off Bayek. She tosses the golden Medjay badge into the sea.

Brutus and Cassius have met with Aya to discuss the removal of Julius Caesar, who has declared himself dictator in perpetuity. The seas are aflame with change and battle as Aya attempts to find solace in dealing with the Romans.

You sail west with three ally warships. Your first destination is marked some 1,700 meters away. At around 800 meters from the destination, you see a flare in the sky. You've been spotted. An enemy fleet will confront you shortly.

SINK THE ROMAN FLEET

To the east is a fleet of six ships. Begin with catapults and then steer to the side of a ship on the outside of their line so you don't get caught in the middle.

SINK THE FIRE SHIPS

After destroying the last ship in the first wave, Phoxidas spots small ships set on fire. Do not let the small fire ships hit yours. Keep moving and destroy the little ships as soon as possible. Consider using your catapults on the fire ships from a safe distance.

After destroying the fleet of fire ships, more fire ships and two enemy ships appear to the north. Sail east to keep the enemy battleships between you and the small fire ships. Use catapults on the large ships. You can stop the fire ships by taking out their sails if hitting their low-profile hulls proves difficult.

SINK THE TWIN ROMAN OCTAREMES

The next wave of the battle is with two large octaremes. Sail west to find them before they find you. Use catapults on the nearest one as soon as it's in range. With your ally ships chipping in with catapults, a direct hit can shave off a quarter of an octareme's health. So let those loose each time they charge up. Ram the ships to get quicker weapon charges. Circle the ships, keep your speed up, and use your allies as cover (sounds awful doesn't it). Destroy the two octaremes and you find shore in Rome on the Ides of March.

Men! Don't fear this beast. She's a great and girthy whale, but we'll dance around her bulk like minnows in a pond!

44 BCE, IDES OF MARCH

ASSASSINATE SEPTIMIUS

Aya enters the Roman Coliseum and finds Caesar with Septimius by his side. Septimius begs Caesar to let him be his right-hand man. Caesar agrees. When Caesar leaves, Septimius catches Aya's glare an entire coliseum's length away… and it's on!

Both Aya and Septimius jump into the arena and the battle begins. Both Aya and Septimius are Level 35 fighters. Aya does not have any arrows, so you cannot cheat your way to an easy kill. You must use your dual blades and fighting finesse. Target-select your opponent and begin strafing and dodging as he goes in for attacks. As soon as he swings and misses, go in for a series of quick attacks to fill up your adrenaline gauge as fast as possible.

Take advantage of knock-downs and move in quickly for a flurry of quick attacks. If you get knocked down, get up and move before he hits you with a debilitating move where you glow and become paralyzed. Once this occurs, there's nothing to do but wait for the hurt. Avoid getting caught in his special attack by continually moving and dodging. Advance only when he has just finished with a combo attempt.

You should be able to fill up your adrenaline gauge after four successful rounds of hits on Septimius. Release the special move on him as soon as you get an opening. Follow up the special with a series of quick attacks to start filling the gauge again.

After three special attacks and a little bit more hacking, you can take Septimius down for good. No need to confirm the kill. Next you get to gloat in the kill room. Septimius continues to taunt Aya, but she gets the last word and the final attack.

REACH THE CURIA

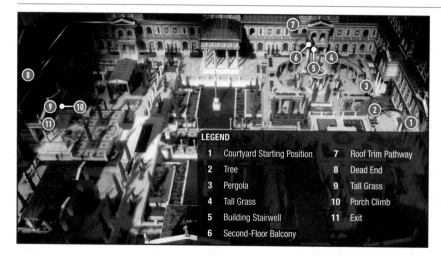

LEGEND

1	Courtyard Starting Position	7	Roof Trim Pathway
2	Tree	8	Dead End
3	Pergola	9	Tall Grass
4	Tall Grass	10	Porch Climb
5	Building Stairwell	11	Exit
6	Second-Floor Balcony		

Exit the Coliseum. Follow the objective marker west out of the arena and into a large hall. Run to the top floor. Exit the building onto a balcony with an arrow supply at a railing. Fill up on arrows. Hop onto the railing **(1)** and look at what you are up against in the courtyard below.

There's about 50 soldiers of every type possible. Their levels are closely matched to yours, so stealthy assassinations are not guaranteed on most of the tougher soldiers. Of course, you want to avoid going up against them, as they would immediately outnumber you. Your goal is to get to the doors **(11)** on the courtyard's opposite side and open them while you are not in conflict. This means you can't just sprint through chaos and open the doors. You must reach the doors and then open them without being noticed.

Here's how to do it. Jump from the balcony **(1)** to the right tree **(2)**. Run through the tree branches and leap to the top of the pergola **(3)**. Run and jump to the next pergola and then leap down into the tall grass **(4)** in the corner near the stairs. Duck down.

Duck into the building and take the stairs **(5)** to the second-level balcony **(6)**. Begin scaling the north wall and get up above the windows. Start shimmying along the roof trim **(7)**. Continue shimmying around the courtyard until you reach the corner **(8)**, where you must drop down because metal spikes keep you from going any farther. Drop into tall grass **(9)** and duck down.

There's a very good chance a nearby guard will spot you. Throw a sleep dart at him and get to the top of the destination porch **(10)**. Dash for the exit doors **(11)** and open them while in stealth.

ASSASSINATE CAESAR

Once inside, Aya finds a robe to disguise her identity. Caesar is entertaining guests in the next room. Simply walk up to him and assassinate him in front of everyone. Aya walks away as Casca, Decimus Junius Brutus, and Marcus Junius Brutus continue to stab him 22 more times until he is dead. Aya sends him off to eternity in the kill room

OUTSKIRTS OF ROME

TWO DAYS LATER

Aya pays a visit to Cleopatra to verbally settle the score with her. Aya threatens to kill her if she does not become the ruler the people deserve.

BIRTH OF THE CREED
ROME, PANTHEON DISTRICT

43 BCE

Prerequisite: Complete Main Quest: Fall of an Empire, Rise of Another

Rewards: 9,600 XP   **Unlocks: Hidden Ones Bureau**   **Details: Bayek has established the first bureau of Hidden Ones in Memphis, and Amunet has done the same in Rome.**

Aya writes a letter to Bayek informing him that Caesar has been assassinated. Septimius is also dead. She has founded a bureau in the middle of Rome, yet no one knows of its existence. Like Amun, they are the Hidden Ones. She tells him they are free of each other but she feels no happiness. She says she is no longer who she was; she has renounced all love she once had and has renounced Aya. She has killed Aya and is now the Hidden One known as Amunet (the female name for Amun).

During this ending cinematic, there's a touching scene where Bayek frees young children from ruthless abductors. When told to run home, one little boy says he is scared to go alone. Instead of repeating his painful past with his son, he opts to escort the child home.

INTRODUCTION

THE ESSENTIALS

MAIN QUESTS

SIDE QUESTS

ACTIVITIES

ATLAS

REFERENCE & ANALYSIS

SIDE QUESTS

SIWA

GEAR UP

Prerequisite: Complete Main Quest: The Oasis

SUGGESTED LEVEL: 2

REWARD: 500 XP

CRAFT A BREASTPLATE

A breastplate requires soft leather, which you can obtain from hunting hyena, gazelle, and ibex. Use Senu to mark these animals traveling in herds around Siwa. Return to Bayek, mount a camel or horse, and track down the targeted animal. Shoot it with arrows. You can do this on foot or from your mount.

You can also loot the animal while remaining on your mount. If you run out of arrows (which can be retrieved from your victims), then use a long spear.

Hunting from a mount is much easier, as you can chase down the herd when they scatter after the first kill. Get behind the herd and keep picking them off.

SENU: YOUR HUNTING PARTNER

Sometimes when you target animals and do not fire at it, a bird's-eye icon may appear above the animal. Senu will then dive-bomb-kill the animal for you.

To complete this quest, you need only five pieces of soft leather. Enter the Gear tab in the menu and select the breastplate. Hover over the box and the crafting interface appears. Press the Craft button and hold it until the gauge fills to craft the breastplate.

Continuing to craft your breastplate raises your health. Each time you level it up, a new number of various resources are required to craft up to the next level.

PIN A CRAFTING ITEM

There is a pin option in the lower right crafting box of each crafting item. If you pin an item, a reminder of the crafting objective appears at the top

left portion of the screen while flying Senu. It's a good reminder to have while exploring from above.

To the left of the breastplate, you'll see that you can also increase your melee damage by crafting the bracer; farther left is a stabilizer glove for increasing range damage; and a quiver for increasing arrow capacity. Two other crafting categories are currently locked, but you can learn more about these in our Crafting section in the "Reference and Analysis" chapter.

FAMILY REUNION

Prerequisite: Complete Main Quest: The Oasis

SUGGESTED LEVEL: 2

REWARD: 750 XP

FIND AND RESCUE TEREMUN AND THE FARMERS

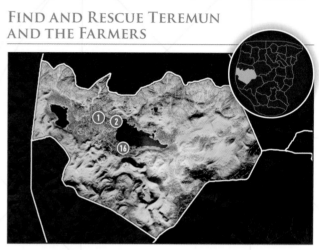

This quest is started by accepting it from Hepzefa's informant table **(1)**. Teremun, and a group of local farmers have been arrested for protesting onerous tax increases. His wife asks you to free him along with all the other farmers.

Select the quest in the Quests menu. A marker **(2)** appears to the northeast, near the lake. Mount a ride and head to that area. When close, switch to Senu and fly over the temple. Press the Free Aim button to enter first-person view and to acquire targeting guidance. The yellow line indicates the direction of your target. When it becomes a circle, it directs you to your target. When you are far off from the target, an arrow will appear in a quarter yellow circle. Move in that direction. The closer you get to the target, the smaller the circle becomes until you have zeroed in on the target and it becomes marked.

TEMPLE OF AMUN

Prerequisite: Approach the Temple

SUGGESTED LEVEL: 5   LOCATION REWARD: 150 XP   LOCATION OBJECTIVE: Loot three treasures

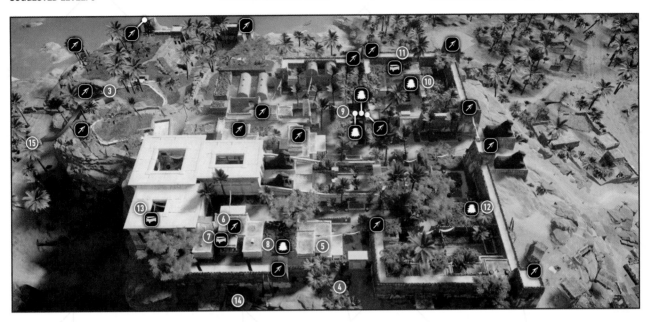

When scanning for soldiers from above, always look for guards at fort entries as well as doorways into buildings. After finding the stationary guards, start looking closely at the pathways for patrolling guards. After Senu locates and marks Teremun **(3)** and every soldier in the Temple of Amun, find the best point of entry.

HIGHER-LEVEL ENEMIES

The soldiers in Temple of Amun are Level 4 and 5, so you can't expect successful stealthy one-hit kills by hand if you are Level 2. If they're a higher level, they'll break your hold and enter a very aware battle mode, which also alerts nearby enemies. Enemies that can break a stealth grip are marked red in the level indicator above their heads. If you want to complete everything there is to do in this temple, then take part in more activities around Siwa to match their level or get it at least one level below so you can perform stealth kills.

ARROW KILLS

If you want to tackle enemies at higher levels, then watch for a full orange damage meter above their head when you aim. An arrow to the head kills them and you retain your stealth. There're enough arrow supplies in the temple to allow you to take each enemy out this way.

Use the tall grass **(4)** along the northwest side to slump down and whistle for the Level 4 entry guard to join you. You can perform a stealthy takedown on him if he is one level above yours; otherwise, put an arrow in his head. Enter the temple and climb to the top of the structure on the immediate left.

Notice the small booth **(5)** on the balcony. You can dash inside to hide and remain in stealth if no one sees you enter. There are a few of these at the temple. Use them if you get into trouble and find yourself retreating.

Continue heading north up and over the rooftop, across the vine-covered pergola, and up to a high rooftop **(6)**, where you will find an arrow supply. Look for all the soldiers that enter your range from this rooftop and take them down with arrows. Replenish lost arrows and move into the interior of the same building.

LOOT TREASURES 1 OF 3

Loot the treasure chest **(7)** on the floor. This is the first of three treasures needed to complete the Temple of Amun activity. If it's a weapon or shield greater than one you carry, equip it.

THREE CAPTIVE PRIESTS: PRISONERS IN THE TEMPLE

Head back south along the outer wall walkway. Look under the pergola you crossed earlier to find one **(8)** of five captive priests for the Side Quest: Prisoners in the Temple. You can select that quest and have Senu hone in on the remaining four captives to mark them on the map.

Use the rooftops and tall grass to travel south to the two imprisoned priests locked inside a wooden cage **(9)**. Defeat any soldiers in the area, then open the cage to free them.

Get to high ground and continue using the many arrow perches marked on the map to take out the soldiers below. Head to the building in the east. Defeat the guards before you enter, then free the fourth priest **(10)**.

LOOT TREASURES 2 OF 3

Head upstairs in the same building to find the second **treasure (11)**. It's in a red chest near the open balcony doorway.

THE LAST CAPTIVE PRIEST: PRISONERS IN THE TEMPLE

Traverse the top of the fortress wall or stay mostly in the tall grass as you head west, stealthily killing any soldiers that remain. Reach the last priest prisoner **(12)** under a

pergola in the fort's southwest corner. This completes Side Quest: Prisoners in the Temple, earning you 500 XP!

LOOT TREASURES 3 OF 3

Use the rooftops and fortress walls with arrow supplies to continue clearing the fort of soldiers, keeping Medunamun alive (until you want to begin The False Oracle quest). This is critical if you want to get the last **treasure (13)**, which is in the temple's side room on an altar. Medunamun is often located in the temple, so you can either drop in through the rooftop skylight or enter through the tunnel **(14)**, which may have guards if you have not defeated them already.

TEREMUN AND THE FARMERS

Head to the fort's northwestern branch. Use the same tactics to clear the enemies from this area. You find Teremun and the farmers together in a single cage **(3)**.

BRING TEREMUN'S BODY TO HIS FARM

Unfortunately, it's too late for Teremun, who died in captivity. Retrieve his body from the cage. Carry him east until you reach a ravine that leads west out of the fort. Once out of the fort, whistle for your mount **(15)**. Lay the body on the animal's back. Now mount your ride and take Teremun home **(16)**.

Once at his farm, follow the marker to a man standing in the burning cinders. This used to be a farmhouse. Dismount and carry Teremun to the man. He explains that Teremun's entire family perished and instructs you to lay the body with the rest of his family.

LAY TEREMUN TO REST WITH HIS FAMILY

Carry Teremun a few meters south, where you will find the rest of his family in a tent. Drop him next to them to complete the quest.

WATER RATS

Prerequisite: Complete Main Quest: The Oasis

SUGGESTED LEVEL: 3	Reward: 750 XP

FIND THE AMANAI CAVE IN THE MOUNTAINS

KILL THE BANDITS OCCUPYING THE CAVE

Climb to the top of the hill, crouch down, and shoot enemies below through the cave hole **(4)**. Drop below and enter the tall grass. Look around to make sure no more bandits are around before you move to the ledge's edge to continue investigating.

There are Level 3 and 4 bandits patrolling the cave's lower levels. Use arrows to take them out from afar. There's a quiver of arrows on the second-level balcony below. Use Animus Pulse to help locate them. If enemies begin seeking you out, then use the tall grass to hide and create stealth kill opportunities.

THREE TREASURES OF AMANAI CAVE

This cave is also a treasure-hunt activity. One **treasure** is located on the second-level ledge on the cave's southwest side.

The Amanai Cave **(2)** is hidden in the mountains north of Hepzefa's house **(1)**. The quest starts via the documents on Hepzefa's informant table. Send Senu over the hills to spot a rooftop entry hole **(4)**. Mark as many enemies inside the cave as you can. Notice that there's also a northwest **(5)** and a southeast **(3)** cave entrance. We prefer dropping in from above; higher ground is always tactically better.

The last two **treasures** are on the cave's lower level. Use Animus Pulse to help locate these. When you exit the cave, an old man (who would have greeted you if you had chosen the northwest entrance **(5)**) thanks you for saving the town's water supply. While in the area, look west to take on Side Quest: Hideaway.

HIDEAWAY

Prerequisite: Complete Main Quest: The Oasis

SUGGESTED LEVEL: 3

REWARD: 500 XP

EXPLORE THE TOMB AND REACH CHENZIRA

Enter the cave **(1)**. Light a torch and head through the narrow tunnels, using Animus Pulse along the way; this is a treasure-hunt location as well.

When you reach the end of the first tunnel, find a note on the floor and a hole in the wall on the right. The wall to the left can be smashed. Take the coins from the right room and then smash through the wall to continue.

Pass through the first room. When you start walking down a slope, notice there's an open passage on the right and a room just ahead. Enter the passage to the right.

You'll reach a web-covered stairway at the hall's end and an open room with loot on the left. Smash the vase in the corner for a rare find. The stairs are a dead end, but there are coins up there.

LOOT CRATE

Continue through the left room to reach a chamber with two shelves on adjacent walls separated by a collection of large vases. Smash the vases in the corner so you can move

the shelf on the left; it's blocking the hallway. Before you move into that hallway, push the shelf on the right into the hallway and find a chest in a small mummified cat tomb on the right. Return to the room with the two movable shelves. Enter the unexplored hallway to reach Chenzira on a lower floor. Jump down and talk to him.

LOCATION OBJECTIVE: ANCIENT TABLET

Inspect the hieroglyphs on the tablet Chenzira stands beside. This unlocks a Ubisoft Club Action. This is the **Ancient Tablet** needed to complete the Mountain of the Dead treasure hunt. You earn one Ability Point for each Ancient Tablet you discover.

ESCORT CHENZIRA OUT OF THE TOMB

After speaking to Chenzira and before you leave the room, raid the three chests in the chamber. Check the upper ledge if you can only find two chests.

Descend the tunnel where it drops and then slide under the wall where sunlight spills into the cave. You emerge at the exit and face three Level 2 to 4 hyenas. You can burn them with a torch, and this does continual but minimal damage to them until the fire burns out. Use a weapon to finish off the hyenas to complete the quest. Chenzira runs home to safety. Loot the hyenas before calling your mount to leave. You can seek out Chenzira at his brother's place to speak with him in the future.

STRIKING THE ANVIL

Prerequisite: Discover Siwa

SUGGESTED LEVEL: 3

REWARD: 500 XP

Bayek's blacksmith friend Benipe **(1)** could help him improve his weaponry.

INTRODUCTION

THE ESSENTIALS

MAIN QUESTS

SIDE QUESTS

ACTIVITIES

ATLAS

REFERENCE & ANALYSIS

FIND AND KILL THE CAPTAIN

CAMP SHETJEH

Prerequisite: Approach the camp
SUGGESTED LEVEL: 2 or higher
LOCATION REWARD: 200 XP
LOCATION OBJECTIVES: Kill one captain, loot one treasure

Fly Senu southwest over Camp Shetjeh **(2)**. Mark all the soldiers; don't neglect the one on the high ledge **(4)** overlooking the camp. Mark the camp captain and the **treasure** in his tent **(3)**.

Enter through the front "door." Creep up the stairs **(5)** with your bow raised. Sometimes you can find the captain or another soldier at this door. Take him out.

Once inside, there's plenty of tall grass to cover your approach to the main road that runs through the camp. From here **(6)** you can perform stealth attacks by hand or more arrows. Wait here, crouched in the grass, for the captain to return to his tent (if you didn't get him when you entered). Put an arrow in his head.

FIND AND GET BENIPE'S TOOLS

Follow the tall grass around the tents to get behind soldiers or to find better vantage points to get them in your sights with the bow. Eliminate the soldiers that can spot you when you enter the captain's tent **(3)**

where you find the **treasure** and **Benipe's tool bag**. We suggest clearing the camp of soldiers and using Animus Pulse to raid all their loot.

RETURN TO BENIPE

With the tool bag in your inventory, exit the camp, call your mount, and ride back to the blacksmith's **(1)**. He thanks you by allowing you to choose a free weapon for yourself. Head to the area to his right and look at what he has to offer: a shield, a bow, a spear, and a mace. Study your inventory and see what you need most. We chose the Phalanx Shield and then used the blacksmith's services to upgrade all our favorite weapons and the shield we just received for free.

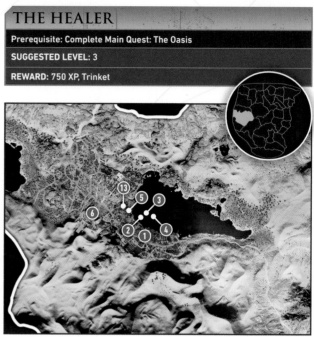

Find Rabiah **(1)** at her house on the lake's south side. Some of her medicines have been prevented from entering Siwa. Bayek offers to help recover them to thank her for nursing him and Senu back to health.

FIND AND GET THE JARS FROM THE SUNKEN SHIP

Send Senu to scout over the lake. You'll spot three search areas—**(2)**, **(3)**, **(4)**. If you have any Ability Points, spend them on the Breath Holding Champion ability. This allows you to

remain underwater for longer periods of time.

THREE JARS FROM THE SUNKEN SHIP

Dive underwater and find a jar near the temple stairs. Find this very small jar wedged between a crack in some shipwreck wood.

Head northeast from the stairs to find the next jar lying on a side section of the ship.

Now head due north and find the last jar in the middle of a small sunken boat. Loot the remaining loot markers before leaving the area.

BRING THE JARS BACK TO RABIAH

Sail the boat to the shore **(5)** in the direction of the House of Life **(6)**. Run the boat ashore and call for your mount. Ride to the House of Life, where you can find Rabiah.

HOUSE OF LIFE

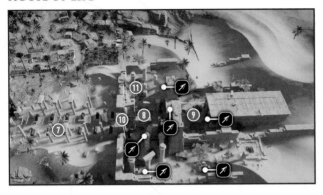

Speak to Rabiah **(7)** and she'll explain that the soldiers ran her and her patients out of the temple ruins that they were using as a hospital.

KILL THE SOLDIERS PILLAGING THE HOUSE OF LIFE

Send Senu to mark around eight Level 2 soldiers around the tents **(8)**. Scan through tents like this one **(11)** to see if there's anyone inside. There are a couple soldiers in the main temple area **(9)** beyond the entryway.

Put an arrow in the guard's head at the main entrance **(10)**; then climb the walls and get to higher ground. Use the many pillars around to stay out of sight as you place arrows precisely in the heads of the troublesome soldiers.

HOUSE OF LIFE: PAPYRUS PUZZLE

The Papyrus is in the tent just south of the main temple area **(9)**. These puzzles are covered in more detail in the Activities chapter of this strategy guide.

RETURN TO RABIAH

Now head back to Rabiah **(7)** to give her the jars you found.

PAPYRUS PUZZLE SOLVED: LEGENDARY SHIELD

There is a large round well **(13)** near the lake. Stand on the edge, use Animus Pulse to mark the item below, and then jump in and retrieve a shield from the open crypt at the bottom of the "bowl."

PRISONERS IN THE TEMPLE

Prerequisite: Complete Main Quest: The Oasis

SUGGESTED LEVEL: 5

REWARD: 500 XP

THIS QUEST IS COVERED IN FAMILY REUNION

There are four activities you can complete when you take on the Temple of Amun. We have covered this Side Quest in full detail on a previous page. Find "Family Reunion" for help with this quest.

BAYEK'S PROMISE

Prerequisite: Complete Main Quest: The Oasis

SUGGESTED LEVEL: 5

REWARD: 150 XP, Miscellaneous

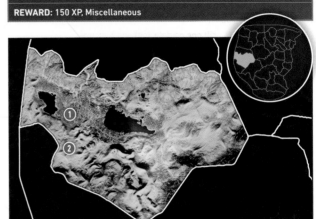

Bayek spots this location far south of Siwa when synchronizing the Viewpoint **(1)** near Camp Shetjeh. He comments on the Stone Circle **(2)** after synchronization. Call a mount and examine the Stone Circle.

AMUN STONE CIRCLE

There are 12 of these circles dedicated to ancient gods and their constellations. This personal pilgrimage will open the way to a long-hidden secret in the heart of Egypt. Interact with this first circle and study the shape of the four-star alignment known as Aries. When the star alignment appears in the sky, move it all the way right, past a couple star clusters, until you see the same star group all by themselves. Turn the stars to match the alignment to the real ones in the sky and overlap them. When they align, the image of the ancient god will appear.

Yes, my son. We have not forgotten who we are. We will endure no matter our origin.

BAYEK'S PROMISE

For information on finding all the Amun Stone Circles and how to solve them, see the Activities section in this guide.

INTRODUCTION

THE ESSENTIALS

MAIN QUESTS

SIDE QUESTS

ACTIVITIES

ATLAS

REFERENCE & ANALYSIS

LAKE MAREOTIS

HIDDEN TAX

Prerequisite: Discover Lake Mareotis
SUGGESTED LEVEL: 6
REWARD: 600 XP

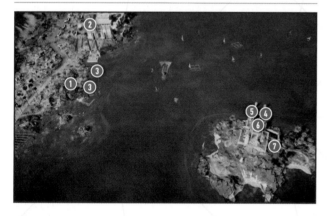

FIND KLAUDIOS, THE MISSING HUSBAND

A woman **(1)** by the lakeside is begging passersby to help search for her husband, Klaudios, who was last seen taking a boat toward the ruins **(4)** on Lake Mareotis.

Synchronize with the Temple of Sekhmet's Viewpoint **(2)**. Head east and find a small boat **(3)** near the shore. Use the boat to reach Klaudios **(4)** at the island ruins. Use Senu to locate the missing husband on a broken column in the water surrounded by snapping crocs.

KILL THE CROCODILES THREATENING KLAUDIOS

Shoot the crocodiles using a bow. If you are out of arrows, try a long weapon while swimming next to them. Collect their loot (crocodile eggs) and speak to Klaudios.

ISLAND RUINS ACTIVITIES

Before you talk to Klaudios, you can synchronize with the island ruins' Viewpoint **(5)**; complete the first phase of Side Quest: Taste of her Sting by interacting with the scene of death near the sheet and burning candles **(6)**; and find the Lost Crypt's **(7)** two hidden treasures (see the Activities section). Lastly, there is a weapon chest underwater near the pillar where you find Klaudios. Use Animus Pulse to find it.

SPEAK TO KLAUDIOS TO MAKE SURE HE'S SAFE

Talk to Klaudios and with a drunken sway, he'll explain how he got there. He seems confused about having a wife when you explain that you'll be escorting him back to her.

BRING KLAUDIOS BACK TO HIS WIFE

Commandeer a boat and head back to the mainland **(1)** with Klaudios aboard. Dock it near a pier and follow the marker back to Klaudios's wife.

DEFEND KLAUDIOS FROM THE BANDITS

When you finally reunite Klaudios and his wife, he suddenly remembers that this woman is the reason he escaped to the island. Her two brothers walk up and begin a brawl. Start by filling them with arrows and if that doesn't kill them move in with your favorite weapon.

SPEAK TO KLAUDIOS TO MAKE SURE HE'S SAFE

In the background you can hear Klaudios's wife screaming that you killed her brothers. Speak to Klaudios after the fight to complete the quest.

THE BOOK OF THE DEAD

Prerequisite: Discover Lake Mareotis
SUGGESTED LEVEL: 8
REWARD: 600 XP

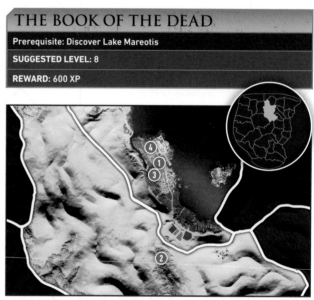

FIND THE BOOK OF THE DEAD

An old man **(1)** sits in the midst of the Yamu market, mourning for his lost Book of the Dead. He asks Bayek to help him find it while directing him toward the Necropolis, where the thieves were last seen.

NECROPOLIS BANDIT HIDEOUT

Enemy Levels: 6—8

LOCATION REWARD: 200 XP

LOCATION OBJECTIVES: One captain, one treasure

Head to the Necropolis Bandit Hideout **(2)**. Use Senu to locate the book inside the cave. There are five bandits and a captain patrolling the area. Use either the bushes on the ledges beside **(A)** or above **(B)** the cave to hide and set up for a bow-and-arrow attack on the enemies below or using the tall grass **(C)** around the area to sneak up behind the enemies for stealthy takedowns. There's a haystack hiding place **(D)** you can use as well.

After you kill everyone, move into the cave entrance **(E)**. Use Animus Pulse to find loot and the Book of the Dead on a broken barrel of grain. Loot the treasure chest as well.

BRING THE BOOK TO THE OLD MAN

A bandit on a horse is quickly closing in on your position. It's easier to defeat him using arrows before getting on a horse. Otherwise you'll meet this guy on your journey home and must deal with him while riding.

Follow the marker back to Yamu. You find his sobbing daughter on the balcony of the old man's house. The old man died while you were retrieving his book.

Head northwest to the mummification temple **(4)** and enter the gated area. Follow the marker to old man's body, lying on a table. Interact with him to return the book to him.

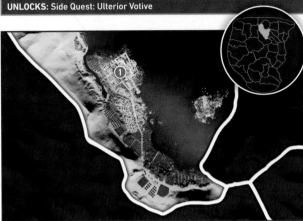

MEET MENEHET THE PRIEST AT THE TEMPLE OF SEKHMET

Arriving in the village of Yamu, Bayek visits his old friend Menehet **(1)** at the temple where he serves as a priest.

SPEAK TO MENEHET TO START THE TOUR

Menehet tells you that his rank has changed, as has the temple. He wants to give you a tour of it. Talk to him a second time to start the tour.

FOLLOW MENEHET INTO THE TEMPLE

The tour is short and leads only to the reflecting pool **(2)** area, where you are attacked by his play-fighting kids.

FIND MENEHET'S CHILDREN

The four children scatter and hide. Send Senu up to find Soris, Hasina, Nailah, and Keba. From the pool, head back the way you came to find Nailah **(3)** running around in the temple atrium.

Ride southeast into the Iment Nome desert and the Eremos Hideout **(3)**. Send Senu to mark enemies. In this location, you also must deal with the possibility of traveling bandits entering the base, so keep an eye to the dunes while you infiltrate.

Start your approach using the tall grass for cover on the camp's northwest side. If you are in range to get one-hit kills with arrow headshots, then pick off a few of the lone bandits. The predator bow is the most powerful bow for this purpose. If you can't acquire a full damage meter for a one-hit kill, then move closer, using the tall grass **(A)** that surrounds the camp.

Lure bandits to you so you can kill them with a stealthy takedown in the tall grass. Once everyone is dead, loot the treasure **(C)** in the tent. Resupply your arrows **(B)** and begin destroying the religious icons.

DESTROY THE CACHES OF FALSE RELIGIOUS ICONS

There are five large vases full of false religious icons around the camp **(blue dots)**. Smash them with a weapon, shoot them with an arrow or light them on fire to complete the objective.

SPEAK TO MENEHET AT THE TEMPLE OF SEKHMET

Ride back to the Temple of Sekhmet. Talk to Menehet **(4)**. He tells you about the fight tonight, which is a spectacle where their goddess Sekhmet defends the people against Isfet's chaos. This unlocks Side Quest: Lady of Slaughter.

LADY OF SLAUGHTER

Prerequisite: Complete Side Quest: Ulterior Votive

SUGGESTED LEVEL: 8

REWARD: 800 XP, Sekhmet Costume

FIND AND BRING PAMU TO MENEHET

This mission starts when you talk to Menehet **(1)** to complete Side Quest: Ulterior Votive. Menehet is in trouble again. The fighter playing Sekhmet has gone missing. Bayek is enlisted to track him down.

Send Senu into the air to search for Pamu **(2)**. You find him near a wooden fence in the market. Pick him up; he's drunk. It's not far from the temple. Just carry him to Menehet **(1)**.

Drop him at Menehet's feet. Menehet is upset about the state of this fighter. Bayek volunteers to fight in his place. Menehet thanks you and tells you to speak to the high priest in the temple courtyard.

SPEAK TO THE HIGH PRIEST ABOUT REPLACING PAMU

Head back toward the temple exit, speak to the high priest **(3),** and he leads you to the fighting event.

ENTER THE RING TO FACE ISFET'S FIGHTER

Isfet is a Level 7 fighter but you're only armed with a spear and a shield. Dodge away from swings and then hit your opponent with many quick light attacks to fill your adrenaline gauge. Once filled, hit 'em hard with the special attack to finish him off.

After the battle, you say goodbye to your friend Menehet and wish good will for his children. You earn the Sekhmet Costume worn during the battle.

BIRTHRIGHT

Prerequisite: Complete Side Quest: Lady of Slaughter

SUGGESTED LEVEL: 9

REWARD: 600 XP

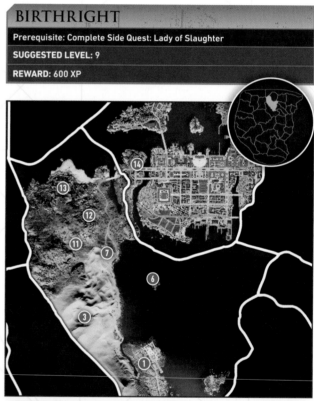

LEGEND

○ Papyrus

LOCATION OBJECTIVE: PAPYRUS PUZZLE

Run up a column in the pool room and stop on the second-level balcony. Find the **Fertile Lands** Papyrus Puzzle on a table on the east wall.

Run back into the reflecting pool room and climb up one of the large columns to reach the rooftop. Run north across the rooftop and drop down a level to find Hasina **(4)** standing near the rooftop's edge.

Drop down off the rooftop's edge where Hasina was standing. A hyena bursts through its cage and attacks while Soris **(5)** drops down from the top of the cage. Defeat the hyena and loot it for its ears.

Finally, drop into the shallow well to the east to find Keba **(6)** safely inside. To leave the well, use a weapon to break open the wooden gate and head through the tunnel to exit **(7)** in the lake on the temple's east side.

SPEAK TO MENEHET AT THE TEMPLE OF SEKHMET

Return to Menehet **(1)**, who is standing in the same area where you started the quest. Talk to him to complete the current quest and unlock Side Quest: Ulterior Votive.

ULTERIOR VOTIVE

Prerequisite: Complete Side Quest: Ambush in the Temple

SUGGESTED LEVEL: 7

REWARD: 600 XP

UNLOCKS: Side Quest: Lady of Slaughter

MEET THE MERCHANTS IN THE YAMU MARKET

Menehet is worried about the false religious icons sold in Yamu's market, sullying the reputation of both the priesthood and the Festival of Sekhmet.

You enter an investigation area when you reach the market **(1)**. Use Animus Pulse to identify three merchants—**(A)**, **(B)**, and **(C)**—to talk to at their stands. You can just talk to the farthest merchant **(C)**, who says he can help you with what you seek. But he asks you to meet him at night.

SPEAK TO THE MERCHANT OUTSIDE YAMU AT NIGHT

After the conversation, meditate the time to night. A marker appears to the southeast.

Speak to the merchant **(2)**. Bayek grows impatient with his stalling attempts and justly so; his bandit friends show up and attempt to silence you.

Three Level 6 bandits come running around from the other side of the hut and attack. Back away as you soften them up with arrows. Attempt headshots for a quick kill. Build up your adrenaline with light sword attacks and then unleash your special move on the surviving bandit.

SPEAK TO THE TREACHEROUS MERCHANT

After you kill his friends, he tells you the fake mummies are made in a camp among the dunes southeast of there.

FIND THE BANDIT CAMP

EREMOS HIDEOUT

Prerequisite: Approach the bandit camp

SUGGESTED LEVEL: 7

LOCATION REWARD: 200 XP

LOCATION OBJECTIVES: Kill one captain, loot one treasure

LEGEND
● Religious Icons

INSPECT THE CORPSES IN THE MUMMIFICATION TEMPLE

Find the three corpses **(1)** laid out carelessly in Yamu's mummification temple.

LOCATION OBJECTIVE: PAPYRUS PUZZLE

As suggested during Side Quest: Ambush in the Temple, obtain the **Fertile Lands** Papyrus Puzzle. The clue leads you to the date farm where you'll visit on this quest.

SPEAK TO THE EMBALMER ABOUT THE CORPSES

Follow the marker to the next building to the north. The temple's head embalmer **(2)** explains that Iras, the young woman who brought them in, lives on a small farm half buried in the desert. On learning that her family was slaughtered, Bayek decides to help her.

TRAVEL TO IRAS'S FAMILY FARM

LEGEND
● Animus Pulse

Travel to the date farm **(3)**. Have Senu mark all the soldiers occupying the farm before you enter. There are about five Level 8 and 9 soldiers scattered throughout the area. Try vaulting over the stone wall and entering the bushes **(4)** on the farm's southwest edge, as most of the soldiers patrol the other side of the property.

Hop fences and use the tall grass around the farm to stealthily move around. Whistle to attract the guards to you; then perform silent takedowns. For the guards who can't be lured, shoot them with arrows.

SPEAK TO IRAS AT THE FARM

After ridding the farm of soldiers, approach the well **(5)** and Iras crawls out and tells you that a soldier came by and said his master held a deed of sale to her family's farm. Her family fought to the death to keep it.

FERTILE LANDS PAPYRUS PUZZLE TREASURE

The papyrus clue leads you to the rock fence on the farm that has no pass-through. Use Animus Pulse **(blue dot)** to mark the treasure and then obtain the rare or better equipment. No loot will appear if you have not first obtained the temple papyrus puzzle.

GET INFORMATION FROM THE MASTER'S VILLA

A marker now appears north of the date farm. This is the soldier's master's villa **(7)**. Heading north to the Lakeside Villa Outpost.

SYNCHRONIZE VIEWPOINT AND DEAD MEN TELL NO TALES

Synchronize the northwest Viewpoint on the small island **(6)** in Lake Mareotis where Dead Men Tell No Tales (treasure) is located. The treasure is underwater near the shoreline and the hungry crocodiles.

LAKESIDE VILLA OUTPOST
Prerequisite: Approach the outpost
SUGGESTED LEVEL: 8
LOCATION REWARD: 200 XP
LOCATION OBJECTIVES: Kill one captain, loot one treasure

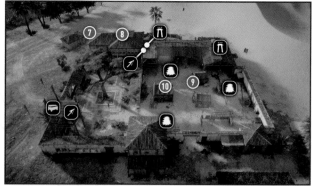

Approach the south side of the Lakeside Villa Outpost **(7)**. Send Senu over it to tag all the soldiers and the Letter from Sophronios **(9)**. You face about ten soldiers and a captain. You should be around Level 11 now, so their lower levels should be no issue.

Climb the south wall and take command of the ballista **(8)** on the rooftop. This weapon can kill any of these guards with one hit, except the captain, who can withstand a few bolts, so leave him for last. You have 20 bolts, more than enough to clear the outpost. If soldiers are grouped together, then shoot them in quick succession so they don't alert others, spot you, and come at you.

From the roof, perform jump assassinations on the remaining enemies below.

Read the Letter from Sophronios **(9)** on the table in front of a tent. Take the treasure **(10)** from the adjacent tent to complete the location objective. Loot the many containers in the camp and replenish your arrow supply before you leave.

FIND AND ASSASSINATE SOPHRONIOS

ANOIA CAVE, VIEWPOINT, AND ABANDONED TEMPLE HIDEOUT

Find the treasure at Anoia Cave **(11)**, synchronize the ruins Viewpoint **(12)**, and conquer the Abandoned Temple Hideout **(13)**. They provide good leveling-up opportunities.

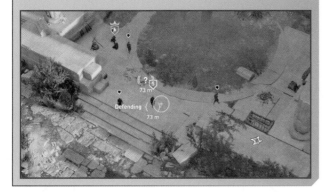

ALEXANDRIA

Travel to Alexandria to locate Sophronios **(14)** behind the tall city walls. Send Senu toward the marker to locate Sophronios and two Level 6 bodyguards.

Climb the city walls to reach the rooftops above Sophronios. Either perform a drop assassination or hit him with arrows. Kill the guards around him. If you perform a takedown, assassinate him with your hands since you do not yet have the hidden blade. Once you kill him, the quest is complete.

TASTE OF HER STING

Prerequisite: Discover Lake Mareotis

SUGGESTED LEVEL: 17

REWARD: 3,000 XP

RITUAL SITE: LOST CRYPT

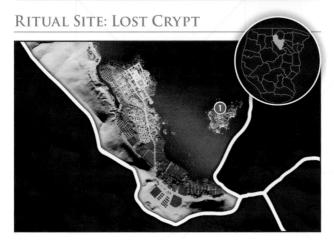

LEARN MORE ABOUT THE MURDER

Bayek discovers signs of a gruesome killing **(1)** on the small Lost Crypt island in Lake Mareotis.

When you synchronize with the Viewpoint **(1)** on the small southern island in Lake Mareotis, you stumble across this crime scene near the base of the Viewpoint pillar. Investigate the blood **(2)** near the blanket surrounded by candles.

FIVE CLUES

Use Animus Pulse to mark the five clues in the area. Investigate the bloody blanket **(3)**. Inspect the Prayer Scroll to Serqet **(4)** at the top of the stairs.

Investigate the statue of Sekhmet **(5)** at the bottom of the stairs. Inspect the sarcophagus **(6)** on the blocks below the stairs and then the lid of the sarcophagus **(7)** in the bloody water. Look for all of the Side Quests in this chapter named Taste of Her Sting to begin and complete this quest. Any of these locations can begin this quest line.

INTRODUCTION

THE ESSENTIALS

MAIN QUESTS

SIDE QUESTS

ACTIVITIES

ATLAS

REFERENCE & ANALYSIS

THE ACCIDENTAL PHILOSOPHER

Prerequisite: Discover Alexandria

SUGGESTED LEVEL: 20

REWARD: 1,500 XP, Miscellaneous Item (+75 Drachmas)

UNLOCKS: Side Quest: Higher Education

REACH THE BEACH

Tjepu, an Egyptian mother **(1)**, is in south Alexandria, near Lake Mareotis. She asks you to find her son Tefibi. He went to the beach and has not returned in quite some time.

INVESTIGATE THE BEACH

Run west to the marker on the beach to investigate the shoreline **(2)**. Torn clothing here is the first clue. Inspect it. Enter the water and swim to the middle of the blood cloud; investigate it.

Use Animus Pulse in the water to find the next clue on the lighthouse island shore. Investigate the blood on the rocks. The blood leads around the lighthouse. Investigate the small hut beside the lighthouse.

SPEAK TO TEFIBI

Smash in the hut's door and you'll find Tefibi inside. Speak to him.

ESCORT TEFIBI TO SAFETY

Follow Tefibi out of the hut and back to the beach, where his clothes are. He heads farther north up the beach, where a few Level 20 soldiers are out for blood. Finish them off.

ESCORT TEFIBI TO SAFETY

Defeat all the enemies and then speak to Tefibi to complete the quest. Loot the fallen.

THE LAST BODYGUARD

Prerequisite: Discover Alexandria

SUGGESTED LEVEL: 15

REWARD: 800 XP, 500 Drachmas

FOLLOW THE MERCHANT

Bayek runs into a merchant **(1)** on the docks of northern Alexandria, begging for someone to guard his precious cargo.

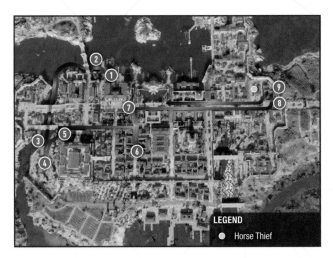

LEGEND
● Horse Thief

Follow the merchant north to the docks, where you meet his cargo, his spoiled daughter Kara **(2)**. You become her bodyguard while she shops for tonight's reception.

BRING KARA TO THE DOCKS IN THE EGYPTIAN DISTRICT

Enter and take control of the nearby boat. Allow Kara to get aboard. Follow the canal west and take the first left (south) passage around the Kibotos Arsenal.

FOLLOW KARA

Stop at the dock **(3)** at the marker on the canal's east side. Kara jumps out and heads to her horse, Pegasus **(4)**.

SPEAK TO THE HORSEMASTER

Speak to the horsemaster, who wants payment for the horse. Bayek and Kara tell him to take it up with her father.

BRING KARA TO THE EASTERN MARKET

Remount Pegasus with Kara. Ride north up the same road and take a right **(7)** at the largest street in Alexandria. Head east toward the Great Synagogue, and stop in the marker at the eastern market **(8)**.

FOLLOW KARA

Follow Kara into the eastern market until she stops at a bundle of linens **(9)**.

CARRY THE BUNDLE

Equip a light or warrior bow and then pick up the crate for Kara; however, drop it immediately, as a horse thief just took off with Pegasus.

GET PEGASUS FROM THE THIEF

The horse thief is a soldier who rides east on the main road that you just traveled. Run out the east exit in the direction of the horse thief, and shoot a flurry of arrows at him. Hit him before he gets too far and you have to call your mount; otherwise this becomes a drawn-out chase. If you hit him with an arrow and he lives, then he stops to fight. Continue to attack him until he falls from Pegasus.

BRING PEGASUS TO KARA

Mount Pegasus and ride him back to the eastern market **(8)** in the Great Synagogue, where you find Kara and her father. Dismount in the marker **(9)** in the market.

SPEAK TO KARA'S FATHER

Kara's father rewards you for being a hero bodyguard for the day.

HIGHER EDUCATION

Prerequisite: Complete Side Quests: The Accidental Philosopher

SUGGESTED LEVEL: 21

REWARD: 1,500 XP

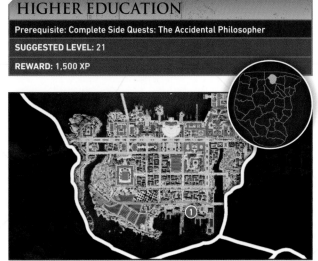

THE ESSENTIALS
MAIN QUESTS
SIDE QUESTS
ACTIVITIES
ATLAS
REFERENCE & ANALYSIS

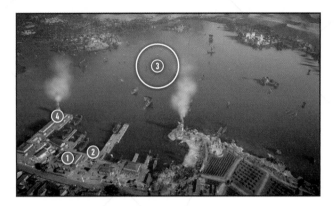

You can either drive into the enemy boat **(3)** and make them stumble while you board their boat and engage in a swordfight or you can take them out from afar with arrows. Boats come with burning lanterns; use these to set your arrows on fire if you wish.

FIND AND RECOVER THE PAPYRUS

Tefibi **(1)** has gotten into trouble again and has lost his precious papyrus.

Head south to the boat docks and commandeer a nice boat **(2)**. Drive it toward the marker out in Lake Mareotis. Immediately send Senu up in the air to find the correct felucca to avoid steering in the wrong direction.

RETURN THE PAPYRUS

Confirm the kill of the marked soldier to collect Tefibi's Notes. Now drive the boat back to Tjepu, who is to the north at the lighthouse **(4)**.

SERAPIS UNITES

Prerequisite: Discover Alexandria	
SUGGESTED LEVEL: 10	Reward: 800 XP

FIND AND RESCUE THE DRUMMER

Bayek, in a moment of piety, prays to Serapis in the Sarapeion **(1)** for help on his journey. The local priest wants Bayek to look into a situation with his drummers who have been arrested unjustly.

Follow the marker to Kibotos Arsenal **(2)**. Send Senu for reconnaissance. Have her mark the captive drummer, all the enemies, and the treasure. Enemies in this fort are Levels 8 to 11.

KIBOTOS ARSENAL

Prerequisite: Approach the Arsenal

SUGGESTED LEVEL: 9 or higher   **LOCATION REWARD: 300 XP**   **LOCATION OBJECTIVES: Kill one captain and one commander, loot two treasures**

Scale the column on the fort's southeast corner. Pull up to the wall walk and make sure no soldiers are in sight. Climb to the top of the southeast guard tower **(3)**. Look down and north to the front gate **(4)** below the brazier. If there is a solider near the brazier, shoot him in the head with an arrow. The captain may be guarding the front gate as well. Shoot him in the head with an arrow if one or two shots take him out. Replenish your arrows using the supply atop the tower.

Jump down onto the west wall walk. Hop over the parapet and down onto the keep's roof **(5)**. Look for soldiers from the roof's edge. Shoot arrows into any within range of a one-shot kill. Cross the rope and head to the guard tower rooftop to the north **(6)**. Look over the north edge down onto the southernmost wall walk, and drop-assassinate any soldier patrolling there.

Move west along the wall walk, eliminating soldiers who patrol nearby. There are plenty of areas to freshen your arrow supply along the way. Use the northwest guard tower rooftop **(7)** as a vantage point for defeating remaining patrols on the wall walk. Drop down and head south to the arrow supply and fire pit. Just beyond is the end of the parapet; use this vantage point **(8)** to shoot arrows down at the soldiers patrolling the bailey (around the captive drummer) and those who exit the keep and enter the kill zone (the bailey).

Flee to the top of the previous guard tower **(7)** if you need to escape aware soldiers. The commander also hangs out in the keep and will be one of the last ones out. Defeat them all and then loot the entire arsenal. Find both treasures at the keep—one on the exterior balcony and one on a table on the second floor. Raid the entire fort when all the soldiers are dead.

EXIT THE RESTRICTED ZONE

Unlock the cage door and pick up the drummer **(9)** inside. Carry him out the east gate **(4)**. After you step out of the restricted zone **(10)**, drop him onto the sidewalk near the main road.

SPEAK TO THE DRUMMER

Speak to the drummer now. He tells you that a bandit stole the lion skin the moment he turned away from it.

FIND AND RETURN THE LION SKIN

Ride into the Egyptian district **(11)** to find the bandit who stole the drummer's lion skin. Send Senu out to search for the bandit. Mark multiple Level 10 bandits in the area. Take to the rooftops to avoid running into them on the streets. As you head to the marked bandit with the skin, take out the individual bandits you encounter to avoid a battle with all of them at once.

RETURN TO THE PRIEST

You can use the Viewpoint atop the Sarapeion to return quickly to the priest **(1)**; otherwise, scale the mountainside from the Egyptian District to reach him without using a horse and the roads (which would take longer). Return the skin to the priest in the Sarapeion, completing the quest. Talk to him afterward and you can unlock Side Quest: A Tithe by Any Other Name.

A TITHE BY ANY OTHER NAME

Prerequisite: Complete Side Quest: Serapis Unites

SUGGESTED LEVEL: 10

REWARD: 800 XP

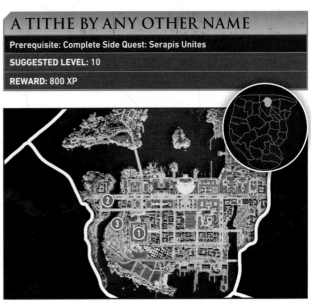

FIND AND STEAL THE CART

Bayek returns to the priest **(1)** of Serapis to see if he needs any more help in the moral quagmire of Alexandria.

Run north to the main road. Call for your horse and send Senu into the air to track the stolen cart and the soldiers who march behind it. The cart **(2)** appears near the road bridge leading into Alexandria.

Race east along the parallel road; then work your way north to reach the same road ahead of the cart. Get onto the tall median walls or find a rope that stretches across the road and get on top of that. When the cart passes by, jump down into the haystack in the cart. Stealthily attack the driver from the hay. Take ahold of the reins.

BRING THE CART TO THE PRIEST

Follow the quickest and easiest path to the priest, who waits in the Egyptian District **(3)**.

SPEAK TO THE PRIEST

Speak to the priest **(2)** to complete the objective.

THE SHIFTY SCRIBE

Prerequisite: Complete Main Quest: End of the Snake

SUGGESTED LEVEL: 11

REWARD: 750 XP

FIND AND RESCUE ARISTO

Aristo's wife, Callista **(1)**, asks Bayek to help her husband escape the city. Bayek, moved by her story, agrees to help free the man.

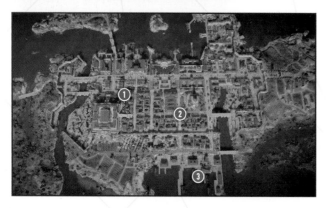

Exit Callista's home, near the Sarapeion. Send Senu up to find Aristo. He is in a jail cart **(2)** driven by a soldier who is escorted by several Level 11 soldiers. You can find them on the main road in central Alexandria near Aya's home.

It does no good to just commandeer the jail cart, as you need to carry Aristo to safety and you can't do that with an entire platoon after you. So come up behind the caravan on your horse and begin stealthily picking off guards with arrows to the head.

SLEEP DARTS

You can also use sleep darts on the driver, which would stop the cart. You can use sleep darts on horses too.

BRING ARISTO TO THE PORT

Carry Aristo out of the cage and put him on a horse. Carry Aristo to the port to the south. As you near, you'll see a marker on a boat **(3)** where Callista is waiting. Ride the horse on board. Take Aristo off the horse and put him on the boat in the marker.

SPEAK TO ARISTO

Speak to Aristo to complete the quest.

THE ODYSSEY

Prerequisite: Complete Side Quests: A Tithe by Any Other Name (three hours of game time later—meditate to skip that time.)

SUGGESTED LEVEL: 10

REWARD: 800 XP

ESCORT THE PRIEST TO THE NORTHERN TEMPLE

Bayek finds the priest **(1)** cowering in fear, pacing the easternmost road in the Egyptian District. The priest begs for assistance in fleeing the city.

Take the most direct path west to the channel and board a boat **(2)**, avoiding any soldiers wandering the streets. Allow the priest to board with you and then paddle the boat north, following the marker.

You'll run into a couple small boats with soldiers as you near Kibotos Arsenal **(3)** on the corner to your right (when you enter the larger channel). They aren't much of a threat if you paddle fast and stay as far away from them as possible.

You head east. Once you pass under the bridge, you should be in the clear. Paddle north quickly to the marker **(4)** on your left along the coast. The priest will jump out of the boat and make for the beach.

SPEAK TO THE PRIEST

Once onshore, exit the boat and speak to the priest to complete the quest.

WRATH OF THE POETS

Prerequisite: Meet Aya in the den during Main Quest: Aya

SUGGESTED LEVEL: 20

REWARD: 1,500 XP

UNLOCKS: Side Quest: Symposiasts

FIND AND RESCUE THE ACTORS

Bayek discovers Phanos at the amphitheater **(1)**, railing against the regime. Guards stole Phanos's play and jailed his actors.

They say if I attempt to put on the play, I will be put to death.

AKRA GARRISON

Prerequisite: Approach the Garrison

SUGGESTED LEVEL: 10   **LOCATION REWARD:** 500 XP   **LOCATION OBJECTIVES:** Kill two captains and one commander, loot four treasures

Approach the garrison from the west bridge **(2)**. Senu up to mark as many enemies as you wish, but concentrate on those around the west entrance **(3)** and the south courts around the guard tower **(4)** and ballista **(5)**. You just need to clear a path of enemies from the gate to the actor in the cage **(6)**. Use the same approach as discussed during Main Quest: Gennadios the Phylakitai. This time, shoot the guard at the gate **(3)** and then scale the west wall.

INTRODUCTION
THE ESSENTIALS
MAIN QUESTS
SIDE QUESTS
ACTIVITIES
ATLAS
REFERENCE & ANALYSIS

Work your way along the west wall walk, killing guards in the courtyard with arrows to the head. Head to the top of the south tower **(4)**. Shoot the guards on the wall walk, especially the one guarding the ballista **(5)**. Use the ballista to clear the courtyard below of all soldiers.

When the courtyard is free of soldiers, jump down and free the actor from the wooden cage **(6)**. Pick him up and carry him west, out the west gate **(3)**. Walk to the stairs farther west to leave the restricted zone. Set him down and talk to him.

SPEAK TO THE ACTOR

The actor tells you that there are two other actors to find. They fled for their lives. Soldiers took Phanos's script with them to the palace. They were headed toward the palace.

RESCUE THE ACTORS

Now two blips appear on the map. One in some small neighborhood to the northwest **(7)** and another **(12)** south of the Great Synagogue. Head to the northwest neighborhood.

Stop in the street **(7)** and send Senu to investigate around the actor's house **(10)**. You can mark nearby patrols. Knowing their movement is key to getting in and out with the actor without a fight.

Start by scaling the house at the street **(8)** and getting to the rooftops. Leap from the rooftop to the next house **(9)** and then again to the top of the actor's house **(10)**. Look for the soldiers in the alleys below. When the coast is clear, drop down to his balcony and enter the house through the second-story open doorway **(11)**.

The actor is in a corner on the second floor of his house. Talk to him. You discover there is one more actor who was supposed to be with him but he fled.

ESCORT THE ACTOR

Watch for the patrolling soldiers in the alleys below and then retrace your steps back to the street. Head out to the second-level balcony, scale the wall, and get to the roof. Jump from rooftop **(10)** to rooftop **(9)**, **(8)** and then drop to the street. The actor is very agile and should follow you without being caught.

SPEAK TO THE ACTOR

Once out of harm's way, speak to the actor and he'll return to the theater. This leaves retrieving the script.

FIND AND RECOVER THE SCRIPT

Now head toward the final marker **(12)**, which is to your northeast and north of the Akra Garrison's large north gate. Send Senu to find the exact location of the script.

Get on the rooftop of the building across the street from the soldiers guarding the script. One soldier holds the script. From the rooftop, use a predator bow to take the marked soldier with one shot. If you can't kill him with one hit, then you'll have to chase him down the street as he runs away. Once he is down, you must confirm the kill to obtain the Politics of the Gods script.

RETURN TO PHANOS

Ride or use a nearby Viewpoint to return to Phanos, who is with his actors at the amphitheater **(1)**.

SYMPOSIASTS

Prerequisite: Complete Side Quest: Wrath of the Poets

SUGGESTED LEVEL: 21

REWARD: 1,500 XP

UNLOCKS: Side Quest: Phylakitai in the Eye

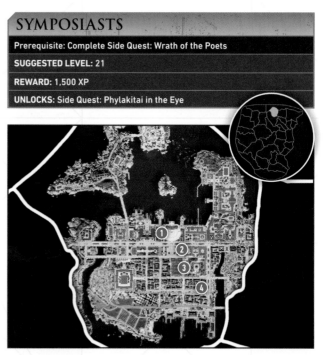

ESCORT PHANOS

Make sure you have arrows before you begin this quest. This time you can find Phanos **(1)** sitting on a bench on the amphitheater's southwest corner. Phanos invites Bayek to his home to celebrate and plan the next steps in their plan to unite the masses.

Walk with him to the street. Mount a horse and follow Phanos as he rides east. Take the first right **(2)** and head south. Stop near the next intersection when Bayek mentions Senu seeing something.

Ahead on the right are four Level 20 soldiers **(3)** on foot and horseback. They attack on sight. Phanos leads the charge, so there's no avoiding the conflict; if you try, Phanos is still caught up in the battle until you deal with the soldiers. If you aren't comfortable fighting on horseback, then dismount and fight on your own two feet. This allows you to more easily escape battle if you are getting hurt and then reenter the fray from higher ground. This area is heavily trafficked by soldiers, so expect this battle to escalate.

After you win the battle,
loot the soldiers' bodies,
remount your horse,
and follow Phanos. He
continues south and
then east to his home
(4). Follow him into his
house (notice the stairs
that lead to the second level) and into his backyard.

CELEBRATE WITH PHANOS

Make sure you have correct weapons selected for an ambush. We suggest
equipping a heavy blunt weapon like a mace or using a spear. Prepare for a brutal
fight after the conversation with Phanos in his backyard.

DEFEND PHANOS

There's no sneaking around here. After the conversation in the backyard, Level 21
soldiers come jumping, one by one, over his backyard fence to attack. Instead of
getting surrounded by soldiers, back into Phanos's house, get to his second-level
balcony, and hit the fence jumpers with arrows. But be aware that the soldiers will
also come into the house.

Being inside helps funnel the enemy toward you. And, of course, use your special
adrenaline attack once it's powered up. This will help you lay waste to several
soldiers fairly quickly.

SPEAK TO PHANOS

Speak to Phanos after you win the fight.

PHYLAKITAI IN THE EYE

Prerequisite: Complete Phanos's Side Quest: Symposiasts

SUGGESTED LEVEL: 22	Reward: 1,500 XP, Rare Mount

TALK TO PHANOS

You can now
find Phanos
(1) standing
or wandering
around his home.
Phanos sends
Bayek to deal
with those who
dared attack him.

Three objectives become active at once: Find and kill the charioteer; find and kill
the soldiers; find and attack the armory. We like to start with the Armory.

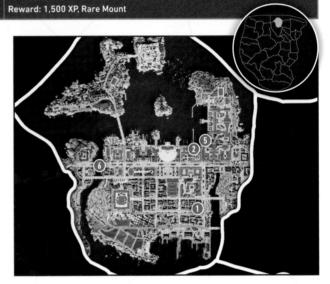

FIND AND ATTACK THE ARMORY

ARMORY

Prerequisite: Approach the Armory

SUGGESTED LEVEL: 9	LOCATION REWARD: 150 XP	LOCATION OBJECTIVE: Loot one treasure

INTRODUCTION

THE ESSENTIALS

MAIN QUESTS

SIDE QUESTS

ACTIVITIES

ATLAS

REFERENCE & ANALYSIS

The armory activity objective is only to steal its one treasure; however, for this quest you must kill all the soldiers occupying the armory. To do this, we suggest stopping on the lawn **(2)** of the Tomb of Alexander the Great (see the Activities section for acquiring the Papyrus Puzzle inside) and sending Senu over the wall to mark all the soldiers in the armory. Scale the wall and use the rooftops to shoot arrows down at the soldiers.

You can use the flagpole on the roof **(3)** to leap into the haystack below. When aiming to shoot arrows from a haystack, you automatically pop up and enter aim view but then hide back in the hay when you exit from aiming mode. This is a very effective way to defeat the soldiers in this area. You can also whistle to lure one to the hay (or to the nearby hiding booth) and pull him in and kill him. Find the treasure along the south wall under the covered area.

When only a few soldiers remain, they appear with yellow markers above their heads, so you know where they are and how many are left. After defeating them all, loot the armory, refill your arrow supply, and head to the next closest target.

FIND AND KILL THE SOLDIERS

The soldiers are in the channel tunnel under the Royal Palace next to the armory **(5)**. Dive into the water in front of the armory and swim to the tunnel. Dive underwater. Swim as close to the nearest marker without coming up for air (to remain stealthy).

Exit the water behind the soldier as he stands at the edge of the platform facing the channel. He may be accompanied by another soldier; if so, forget stealth and just finish them off quickly before more soldiers in the tunnel join the fight. Kill the marked soldier, dive back in the water to enter stealth, and swim back out the way you came.

FIND AND KILL CHARIOTEER

The Charioteer **(6)** by now has made his way to the western side of Alexandria on the main (northern) two-lane road. Ride up to 25 meters away then shoot the marked soldier in the chariot before you scare him off. There is a second soldier in the chariot; you don't have to kill him, so don't accidentally target him first, as this will waste arrows and possibly give the marked soldier a chance to escape.

RETURN TO PHANOS

Ride back to Phanos's to find him walking around his home. Speak to him to complete the quest. You receive a Rare Mount upon completion of the quest.

KANOPOS NOME

OLD TIMES

Prerequisite: Discover Kanopos Nome

SUGGESTED LEVEL: 12

REWARD: 1,000 XP

UNLOCKS: Side Quest: Wild Ride

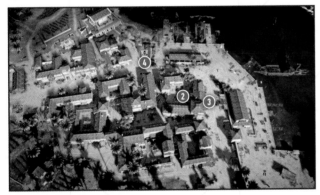

SPEAK TO CLARIDAS AT THE TAVERN

Bayek and Claridas **(1)**, were boyhood friends and competitors in Siwa. Claridas asks him to come drink with him to catch up. A marker appears in town. Ride there to meet Claridas at the tavern **(2)**.

KANOPOS

FOLLOW CLARIDAS

When control returns, you are completely drunk and must follow Claridas. Follow Claridas downstairs and into the street **(3)**.

Eventually Claridas leads you near the Icarus Memorial **(4)** and starts a drunken, yet friendly fistfight. He teases that Aya would have been his had he stayed in Siwa.

FIGHT CLARIDAS

The fight is a friendly one, so no weapons are available. You can't block, but it doesn't matter; the fight is quick and easy. Hit him with a heavy attack and follow it with a series of quick punches. Claridas goes down before you even have enough adrenaline built up to perform a special.

You both pass out and wake up sober in a pile of hay, still friends.

WILD RIDE

Prerequisite: Complete Side Quest: Old Times

SUGGESTED LEVEL: 12

REWARD: 1,000 XP, Rare Mount

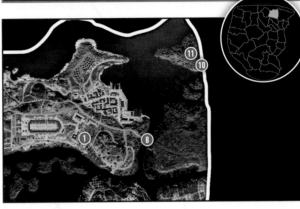

SPEAK TO NIKIAS

LEGEND
● Checkpoint

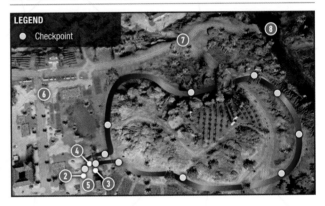

Bayek needs to speak to Nikias **(2)** at his father's estate to learn more about the green team.

ZEPHYROS STABLES: PAPYRUS PUZZLE

You can find the Dead End Papyrus Puzzle **(3)** on a table in the stable's southwest corner. The stables are a rock's throw from where you meet Nikias.

MOUNT THE CHARIOT WITH NIKIAS

Follow Nikias back toward the stables and mount the chariot **(4)** with Nikias as your passenger.

RACE THE COURSE

You must race a course around the estate. There are 12 checkpoints, yet no time limit. Follow the markers on the course and pass through all the checkpoints while you carry on a conversation with Nikias.

SPEAK TO PHILOCRATES

Dismount the chariot and approach Philocrates **(5)** in the corral. He says horse thieves stole his winningest horse. They strongly suspect the blue team is behind this.

FOLLOW NIKIAS TO THE BANDIT HIDEOUT

Nikias and three of his friends from the green team mount nearby horses and take off to find the bandits who stole the prize horse. Call your mount and ride after them. Before you even leave the estate, you may encounter a soldier **(6)** or two before accessing the main road. The team will stop and attack any bandits or soldiers (if you attack them) along the way, so prepare to use many arrows. If more soldiers are just randomly passing by on the road, then this battle with a single soldier could escalate (if you choose to fight them).

On the north end of the small island (beyond the river crossing) you'll encounter a band of bandits on horseback near the second shallow river crossing **(9)**. Defeat them with arrows and heavy weapon attacks.

FIND AND BRING BACK SAGANAKI TO THE ESTATE

With the bandits eliminated, follow the marker due north to the bandit camp.

SHRINE OF SEREPIS: LOOT TREASURE

On your way to the bandit camp, you can stop at the nearby Shrine of Serepis **(10)**. The treasure is in a small cave with a narrow opening below the shrine.

Elements of Side Quest: Taste of Her Sting are also located around the shrine, so page ahead if you need help with that.

A random encounter with a large group of soldiers on horseback could occur at the intersection **(7)** to the east (if you attack them). Use the warrior bow first and then switch to another bow if you run out of arrows. You may lose some of the company here, but it doesn't matter. Jump down, collect arrows, and then remount. Follow Nikias across the river **(8)**. Nikias turns sharply left and heads north across the river.

ALS HIDEOUT

Prerequisite: Approach the Hideout

SUGGESTED LEVEL: 11	**LOCATION REWARD: 400 XP**	**LOCATION OBJECTIVES: Kill one captain, loot one treasure**

Send Senu over the hideout to mark the bandits. The large rock hill **(12)** at the back of the camp offers some fun opportunities. Climb up the rock hill and crouch down.

Spot Saganaki **(13)** below to your left and near a Y-shaped tree. You can jump into the Y in the tree and then leap to the next tree before dropping into a haystack. From the haystack, you can hit many of the bandits in the camp with arrows while remaining in stealth.

Find the treasure in the open tent under the central tree. Defeat all the bandits to win the location objective. Loot all the containers and mount Saganaki **(13)**. Ride her back to Philocrates **(5)** at the estate. Follow a path similar to the one you used to reach the bandit camp so that you cross the rivers in the shallow areas. Philocrates thanks you by rewarding you with a Rare Mount.

TASTE OF HER STING

Prerequisite: Discover Kanopos Nome	
SUGGESTED LEVEL: 17	
REWARD: 3,000 XP	

RITUAL SITE: SHRINE OF SERAPIS

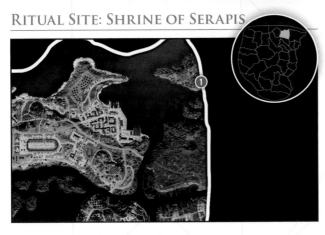

SHRINE OF SERAPIS INVESTIGATION

Bayek discovers even more signs of a gruesome killing **(1)** in northeast Kanopos.

Investigate the scorpion drawing **(2)** on the front side of the statue's base. Find the scroll **(3)** on the cliff's edge. Leap down to the lower

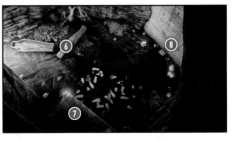

ground and investigate the devoured body **(4)**. Push through the crack in the wall to access a small cave **(5)**.

Once inside the cave, investigate the sarcophagus on the ground for the symbol of the Goddess of Magic **(6)**. Also check the bloodstains on the table **(7)**, where it looks like someone prepared a body. Finally, to complete the location objective, collect the treasure **(8)** from the floor. Bayek concludes that the deaths seem like a ritual against the gods.

LOCATION OBJECTIVE: SHRINE OF SERAPIS

While investigating the Taste of Her Sting area, loot the treasure **(8)** in the cave to complete the Shrine of Serapis's location objective and collect the treasure.

BLUE HOOLIGANS

Prerequisite: Discover Kanopos Nome	
SUGGESTED LEVEL: 12	
REWARD: 1,000 XP	

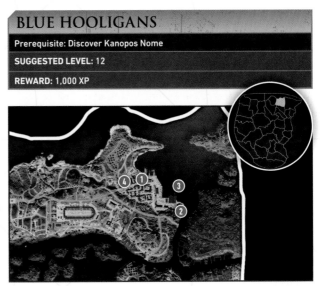

FIND AND RESCUE ICARIUS

Selene **(1)**, begs Bayek to save her remaining boy.

Ride east toward the marker near the river. When you get close, send Senu up to find Icarius's **(2)** exact position. Notice the many blue hooligans guarding him. They're extremely easy to defeat and really require no stealth. They have weak weapons and no armor. Untie Icarius and then speak to him.

FIND AND RETRIEVE THE BUST

Icarius says he needs to retrieve the bust of his brother Icarus and threw it in the river. He wants you to retrieve it for him. Ride or run to the water. Use Senu to pinpoint the bust's location **(3)** and

then dive in and retrieve it from the riverbed.

BRING THE BUST TO SELENE

Now return to Selene, who is in her house **(4)** not far from the memorial.

THE WEASEL

Prerequisite: Discover Kanopos Nome

SUGGESTED LEVEL: 14

REWARD: 1,000 XP

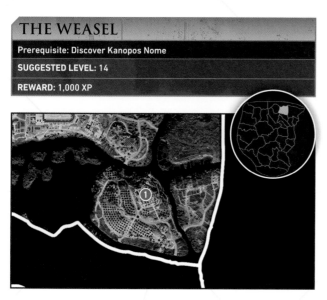

REACH THE PIGEON TOWER

At Apollodorus's farm, the Steward Pelias **(1)** sends Bayek to fetch the letter from the Pigeon Tower for him.

INVESTIGATE THE DISTURBANCE

From the south end of Apollodorus's estate, follow the nearby marker to the north to find the Pigeon Tower **(2)**. Activate Animus Pulse to mark the investigation points. The single

investigation point on the tower's south side is a pile of spilled charcoal.

Climb the side of the wall above the charcoal to see where it spilled from. Use Animus Pulse again to mark the clues. On the balcony, you find an overturned grill **(3)**, a pool of blood **(4)**, and blood on broken boards **(5)**. Drop to the ground and inspect the blood there **(6)**. Follow the cart tracks down the hill to the hay cart. Inspect the cart to find Ruia's dead body hidden inside.

CARRY RUIA BACK TO PELIAS

Carry Ruia out of the hay and call for your mount. Place her body on the horse and ride back to her father Pelias **(1)** to break the bad news. You explain she was thrown to her death from the Pigeon Tower. You retrieve the letter from her body as well as a badge worn by Dymnos, the master of arms.

SPEAK TO DYMNOS, THE MASTER OF ARMS

Head to the armory **(7)**, which is the next large structure to the west. Select a long weapon such as a spear. You find Dymnos sitting inside. You confront him about Ruia and he has no remorse whatsoever. A fight to the death breaks out.

KILL DYMNOS

Dymnos is a Level 14 enemy with a very large mace. Fight smart. Dodge and roll away from his attacks. He wields a large weapon, so he has slow but strong swinging attacks. Roll out of the way and come up behind him just as he swings and misses. Hit him with a hard attack and follow it with a few light, fast attacks to build up adrenaline until you can release a special attack to finish him off.

SPEAK TO PELIAS

After killing Dymnos, you retrieve a letter from his body that Alcandros wrote. Head back to Pelias **(1)** to complete the mission.

THE HUNGRY RIVER

Prerequisite: Discover Kanopos Nome

SUGGESTED LEVEL: 14

REWARD: 1,500 XP

BRING THE DEAD BACK TO THE CART

A farmer asks Bayek for help collecting the dead.

Look for the dead bodies in the field to the south near the river full of hungry hippos. You can find arrows at Apollodorus's Estate **(2)**.

We suggest taking out all the hippos first to reap the rewards of their hard leather crafting materials. Higher ground is always a good escape plan if needed—hippos don't climb walls.

After you kill all the hippos, pick up each body and drop it at the cart near the farmer **(1)**. The farmer is looking for his protector, Meketre.

SPEAK TO THE FARMER

Speak to the farmer. He'll tell you that Meketre would keep them safe from the bandits to the north.

FIND AND RESCUE MEKETRE IN THE CANYON BANDITS' CAMP

Sap-Meh Nome has yet to be discovered. This is where the bandit camp is located. Ride toward the marker. Take a detour to synchronize the nearby Viewpoint **(3)**. Check the world map to see more side quests appear in the area (In Protest, Thick Skin, Fair Trade) and another to the west, still in the fog (Abuse of Power). This is the direction we'll be headed in the side quest section.

POTAMOS HIDEOUT
Prerequisite: Approach the Hideout
SUGGESTED LEVEL: 13
LOCATION REWARD: 400 XP
LOCATION OBJECTIVES: Kill one captain, loot one treasure

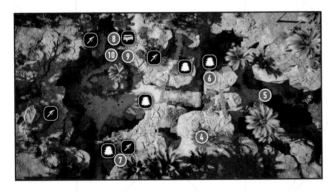

Send Senu up to locate Potamos Hideout **(4)** and mark all the enemies within. You have the higher ground all around their crevasse hideout. Remove the bandits along the northern creek exit **(5)**. Use the high ground and put arrows in them from above.

There are plenty of haystacks around the camp to hide in and shoot arrows from (or lure bandits to you). From the rock pillar **(6)** you can jump into two different haystacks at different levels. Haystack **(7)** is also a great place to start eliminating the bandits in the main base area. There's an arrow supply next to it, making it easy to replenish and get back to cover.

Work your way around the base, along the high ledges, eliminating the bandits and their captain below. Loot the treasure **(8)** and free Meketre from his cage **(9)**. Read the note posted on the beam **(10)**. It points you to the smuggler's dock treasure **(11)** behind a tree in the water and next to a fallen tree in the water. This wouldn't be a bad place to raid after leaving this hideout.

DEFEND THEN SPEAK TO MEKETRE

If you eliminated every bandit in the camp, then defending Meketre after busting him out of prison is easy. There'll be no resistance. Loot everything in the camp, replenish your arrows, and then find and talk to Meketre **(11)** at the southeast exit. He wants you to help him save everyone.

KILL ALL THE BANDITS AT MEKETRE'S VILLAGE

Race to the marker in the east **(13)** to find Meketre's village. Fly Senu over to mark the enemies and to assess the situation. There are around eight Level 12 to 14 bandits raiding the village. Race in and slaughter them using your most damaging weapons.

SPEAK TO MEKETRE

Follow the marker to speak with Meketre in the village. After stroking each other's ego, the quest ends successfully.

TASTE OF HER STING
Prerequisite: Discover Kanopos Nome
SUGGESTED LEVEL: 17
REWARD: 3,000 XP

RITUAL SITE: CROCODILE LAIR

CROCODILE LAIR INVESTIGATION

Bayek discovers yet even more signs of a gruesome killing **(1)** in southeast Kanopos. You may not run into this crime scene until you start hunting down lairs during side activates. Defeat the crocodiles around the ruins in the river. Defeating the crowned croc completes the location objective.

There are four clues here. Investigate the Prayer to Serqet **(2)** parchment on the ruins' west side. Inspect the Sobek Statue **(3)** contained within a symbol that invokes Serqet, the scorpion goddess of magic. Take the treasure from the chest next to it as well. Check out the corpse **(4)** on the ruins block. The lungs have been removed. Finally, investigate the embalming tools left on the felucca **(5)**. That wraps up this part of the investigation. You don't find the next site until you explore the ruins in Sapi-Res Nome.

SAP-MEH NOME

IN PROTEST

Prerequisite: Discover Sap-Meh Nome

SUGGESTED LEVEL: 13	REWARDS: 1,000 XP

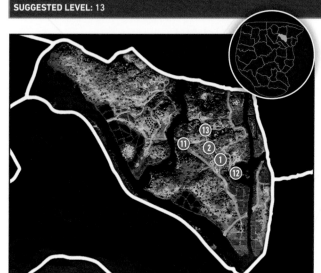

FIND AND DESTROY THE WAR CHARIOT AT ANTHYLLA OUTPOST

While exploring Mareia Port, you'll find a widow **(1)** looking for help. This is Eryx's widow, Europa, and she asks you to find a stolen war chariot and destroy it.

LOCATION OBJECTIVE: VALUABLES

You can read the note at the merchant stand (near **(1)** on our map) and have Senu look toward point **(A)** on the map below. There are hippos and valuables left behind.

Send Senu over Anthylla Outpost **(2)** to find the chariot and to mark all the enemies.

ANTHYLLA OUTPOST

Prerequisite: Approach the Hideout

SUGGESTED LEVEL: 14	LOCATION REWARD: 400 XP	LOCATION OBECTIVES: Kill one captain, loot one treasure

Enter the fort at the first wall break **(2)** to the left of the main gate. This puts you in tall grass and near the open window you go through to access the building where the commander is. He sits at his desk with his back to you. There's also a treasure **(3)** and a hiding booth inside.

Enter the window. Kill the commander and take the treasure from the table. If a soldier is near the doorway, enter the hiding booth. Lure him to the booth and stealthily kill him.

Exit the room through the same window and hide in the tall grass **(4)** until the soldier patrolling this area comes close. Assassinate him. Move along the tall grass by the west wall and stop **(5)** at the pathway between the groups of storage buildings.

Whistle for the soldier patrolling on the rooftops and assassinate him in the tall grass. Head up the storage building stairs and hide behind the sandbags near the arrow supply **(6)**. Study the archer **(7)** in the guard tower to the northeast and put a predator arrow in his head.

Head east off the storage buildings, climb the brazier tower, and set the trap **(8)**. You don't want the Phylake, Ptolemy's Fist, responding to a distress signal. Jump from the end of the extension beam on the tower's east side and get to the next structure **(9)**. Turn north, vault over the wall, and look for the captain. He patrols this area but could be inspecting the dead commander instead. Leap down to the ground inside the court if there are no soldiers in sight. Enter the building and take the treasure **(10)** from the floor.

Slide under the small opening in the west wall of this building and crouch down in the tall grass.

You can enter the small window on the north side of the commander's quarters. If the captain is in checking on the Commander, sneak up behind him and take him out in the same location **(3)**. This captain can move around.

Exit the outpost the way you entered and find the chariot on the nearby road **(11)**. Use a warrior bow to kill the driver and passenger and take the chariot.

GULLY ENTRANCE

You can also enter the outpost through a secret tunnel that contains a treasure. The tunnel entrance is located north of base in the gully beside the large rock bridge. Follow the tunnel up into the north building **(14)** inside the outpost.

DESTROYING THE CHARIOT

The easiest and quickest way to destroy the chariot is to drive it east into the deep lake **(12)** behind Mareia Port until it is submerged.

SPEAK TO EUROPA

Speak to Europa **(1)** to finish the quest. Next, travel to Sau Village to the west.

THICK SKIN

Prerequisite: Discover Sap-Meh Nome

SUGGESTED LEVEL: 13	REWARDS: 1,000 XP, Miscellaneous

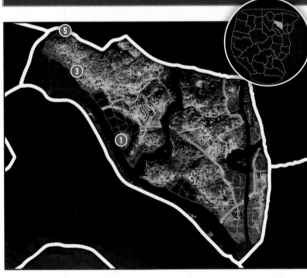

Bayek meets a woman **(1)** in Sau Village who is wife to the local tanner. She tells Bayek to seek the tanner out in his hunting camp.

Climb up the crumbled west wall beside the tanner's wife. Climb and jump to the westernmost columns to find the scented oils **(2)** with other loot.

Travel northwest to the tanner's hunting camp **(3)**.

DEFEND THE TANNER

You find the tanner wrestling with some crocodiles. Help him eliminate them and then loot the croc bodies.

SPEAK TO THE TANNER

Follow the tanner into his camp and speak with him. You tell him his wife sent you to help him hunt. He accepts your help and tells you that he needs hyena ears, crocodile eggs, and vulture skulls.

FIND THE TANNER IN HIS HUNTING CAMP

INTRODUCTION

THE ESSENTIALS

MAIN QUESTS

SIDE QUESTS

ACTIVITIES

ATLAS

REFERENCE & ANALYSIS

HUNT ANIMALS FOR THE TANNER AND BRING BACK THE ANIMAL PARTS HE NEEDS

You need two vulture skulls, two crocodile eggs, and two hyena ears. Travel north from the camp to find the hyena lair **(5)**. There is a high rock platform with a large branch hanging out over the water **(4)**. Use a predator or hunting bow to shoot the 12 or so vultures to get more than the two skulls needed.

While standing on the vulture rock, look down over the west edge to find the hyena lair below. Shoot the hyena and take out as many as you can for soft leather crafting and trading.

LOCATION OBJECTIVE: HYENA LAIR

Use Senu or your bow to locate the Level 14 leader of the pack in the hyena lair. Kill it to complete the location objective and earn 300 XP.

Loot the treasure and other containers on the vulture rock's west side. If you need crocodile eggs, try the croc lair **(6)** below the vulture nesting grounds or along the coastline.

Continue hunting on the way back to the tanner's camp **(3)** and clear his camp of wild animals. Give him the products he requested and the scented oils his wife wanted him to use. You earn a small amount of money for the scented oil gift.

FAIR TRADE

Prerequisite: Discover Sap-Meh Nome	
SUGGESTED LEVEL: 13	
REWARD: 1,000 XP	

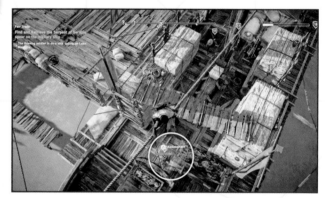

FIND AND RETRIEVE THE SERPENT OF SERAPIS SPEAR ON THE MILITARY SHIP

Read the note on the table to the left of the blacksmith **(1)** in Sau Village. This strikes up a conversation with the blacksmith; you learn that one of Sefetu's men stole a spear.

Travel to the nearest Viewpoint **(2)**. You should end up on the island with the Dead Men Tell No Tales treasure.

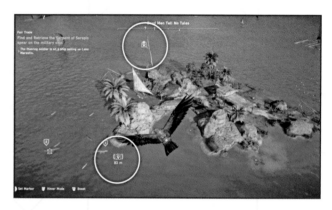

Use Senu to pinpoint the location of the roman military ship **(3)**. Take a boat from the shoreline or just start swimming and one will come rescue you.

You'll find four Level 11 soldiers onboard. The soldier with the spear is marked. Climb up to and cross the sail rope suspended above the length of the ship. Wait for the marked soldier to pass below you; perform a drop assassination, then just jump ship and leave. If you have the Assassination Loot ability, then a drop assassination will put the spear in your position automatically. Otherwise, confirm the kill to get the spear. The quest ends successfully once you have the spear.

SAPI-RES NOME

CONFLICTS OF INTEREST

Prerequisite: Complete Main Quest: The Scarab's Sting

SUGGESTED LEVEL: 15 | **REWARDS: 1,000 XP, Miscellaneous**

ACCEPT ALL SIDE QUESTS

SAIS VILLAGE: HARKHUF'S SECRET ROOM

Enter Harkhuf's home **(1)** and go into the secret room in the back via the crack in the wall (available upon completion of Main Quest: The Scarab's Sting). Interact with the side quests list on the back table. Accept all the quests.

SPEAK WITH THE MERCHANTS OF SAIS ABOUT ZERVOS

SAIS VILLAGE: MARKET

Bayek needs to find Zervos before Sefetu can. Talk to local merchants to see who is loyal to the harbormaster.

At the market **(2)**, use Animus Pulse to identify the clues. Three of the merchants are key to the investigation: **(3)**, **(4)**, and **(5)**. Talk to these merchants to complete the investigation phase. You conclude that they must be hiding something. Meditate day into night; this is when the merchants leave their jobs.

FOLLOW THE SUSPICIOUS MERCHANTS

Use Senu to mark the three wandering merchants. Some are spotted to the west **(6)**, but they all eventually wander to the building in the southeast **(7)**. You can find Zervos hiding out and very much alive inside this building. He explains why he is in hiding and asks for your help recovering his confiscated boat.

STEAL OR DESTROY THE BOAT

Send Senu up to locate his boat at Sap-Meh Warehouse **(8)**.

SAP-MEH WAREHOUSE

Prerequisite: Approach the warehouse
SUGGESTED LEVEL: 15
LOCATION REWARD: 300 XP
LOCATION OBJECTIVES: Loot one treasure

There are eight to ten soldiers in this very small warehouse. Climb the front wall to the rooftop. Silently take out the patrolling archer; then start shooting lone soldiers with arrows.

Jump down and use the ballista on the remaining enemies. Once they're all gone, take the treasure **(9)** from inside the warehouse and then deal with the boat **(10)**.

You can find the boat **(10)** docked at the end of the long north pier. You could destroy it with fire arrows, but if you return the boat in working condition, Zervos rewards you. Sail it to a dock in the south **(11)** in one piece for the maximum reward.

SPEAK TO ZERVOS

Follow the marker back to Zervos's hideout, where he bravely stands outside **(7)**. Talk to him to complete the quest.

INTRODUCTION

THE ESSENTIALS

MAIN QUESTS

SIDE QUESTS

ACTIVITIES

ATLAS

REFERENCE & ANALYSIS

SMOKE OVER WATER

Prerequisite: Complete Main Quest: The Scarab's Sting

SUGGESTED LEVEL: 15

REWARD: 1,500 XP

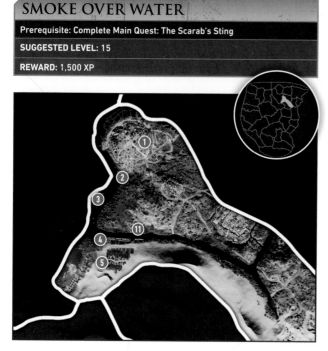

FIND AMOSIS NEAR THE DOCKS

Enter Harkhuf's **(1)** secret room through the crack in the wall (accessible when you complete Main Quest: The Scarab's Sting). Accept the quest from the back table. You must find Jeska's friend Amosis, the fish merchant, and see if she'll step up to help the cause.

Talk to Amosis **(2)**, who works on the western shore. She informs you that Jeska is not dead and is currently at the hippo lair.

FIND JESKA

Take a boat from the shoreline and fly Senu south to locate Jeska. You'll find her battling hippos at the hippo lair **(3)**.

KILL THE HIPPOS AROUND THE ISLAND

Assist her in killing the Level 15 beasts. Use the small dead tree to escape and heal if needed. After taking out a couple hippos, yellow markers appear above the remaining hippos to help you locate them.

> **LOCATION OBJECTIVE: HIPPO LAIR**
>
> Defeat the alpha hippo (it's marked yellow) to complete the hippo lair objective and to earn 150 XP.
>
>

SPEAK TO JESKA

Speak to Jeska after the battle. You tell her that Harkhuf thought she was dead and needs her back. She agrees but needs your help getting supplies to her village first.

ESCORT JESKA

Enter her felucca and let her do the sailing. She sails southeast and tells you how she barely escaped Sefetu. She stops at a pier **(4)** at the mouth of the connecting river.

FOLLOW JESKA TO HER VILLAGE

Exit the boat and walk into the tall grass outside her village **(5)**. You soon come upon the horrific sight of the burned-out village. Jeska rushes to the village, which is full of Level 16 soldiers. Send Senu up to mark all the soldiers and the treasures. Approach Jeska to trigger the next objective.

KILL THE LOOTERS

MEFKAT

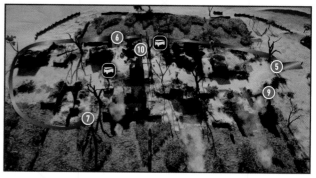

You can approach this stealthily by walking along the south side of the burned-out village, using smoke and tall grass as cover **(6)**.

Look for opportunities to put arrows in nearby soldiers between the burned-out buildings. Continue working your way to the east end of the village while eliminating only the soldiers you can kill while remaining in stealth.

We recommend stealthily taking out the brute with the large shield before blowing your cover. When only a few remain, run in and assist Jeska. If you become overrun, take to the rooftops to battle the soldiers.

SPEAK TO JESKA

Talk to Jeska **(8)**, who is standing next to the tree with a man hanging from it. Grab a treasure from this hanged man.

> **LOCATION OBJECTIVE: MEFKAT**
>
> Collect the treasure from the cart in the middle of the village. To reach the treasure above the man hanging from a tree, climb the thinner tree next to it and then leap to the treasure tree.
>
>

Jeska goes on the hunt for survivors. She finds a conscious man named Pentu. He is badly burned. She needs you to carry him to a friend's farm nearby.

DESTROY STATUE OF KING PTOLEMY

Destroy the statue of King Ptolemy at the west entrance **(9)**.

CARRY PENTU TO THE FARM

Pick up Pentu **(10)** and place him on a soldier's horse in the village. You can also exit the village and call your own mount. Ride north across the river and deliver him to the farm **(11)**.

Jeska thanks you for your help and tells you she'll help Harkhuf find a way to stop Sefetu. You agree to help her again.

ALL EYES ON US

Prerequisite: Complete Main Quest: The Scarab's Sting

SUGGESTED LEVEL: 16

REWARD: 1,000 XP

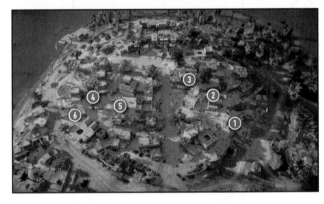

KILL SEFETU'S ARCHERS

Enter Harkhuf's **(1)** secret room in the back of his home through the crack in the wall. Accept the quest from the back table and resupply your arrows from this room.

Sefetu the Firebrand has stationed archers on the rooftops in Sais. You must eliminate his eyes to bring safety to Sais.

There are six archers stationed in groups of two on three rooftops. Fly Senu to mark all the soldiers and then kill them.

Get on the house's rooftop **(2)** west of Harkhuf's home and shoot the archers on the rooftop to the west **(3)**. Use a predator bow or a hunting bow for one-shot-kill head shots.

Resupply arrows from their rooftop and then move south to the next rooftop **(4)**, where you can eliminate the remaining rooftop archers on top of the other buildings **(5)** and **(6)**.

INTRODUCTION

THE ESSENTIALS

MAIN QUESTS

SIDE QUESTS

ACTIVITIES

ATLAS

REFERENCE & ANALYSIS

LOST HAPPINESS

Prerequisite: Complete Main Quest: The Scarab's Sting

SUGGESTED LEVEL: 16

REWARD: 1,000 XP

SPEAK WITH THE BREWERY WORKER ABOUT THE MISSING ASSISTANT

Enter Harkhuf's home **(1)** and enter the secret room in the back through the crack in the wall. Accept the quest from the menu accessed from the back table. Fill up on arrows before you leave.

Start by talking to the brewery worker **(2)** on the job site. She only knows that he headed down the south road. Send Senu up to find him in captivity at Psenemphaia Hideout **(4)**. Ride south and synchronize with the Viewpoint **(3)** where the dead man hangs. Loot his belongings near the burned horse to obtain a weapon.

FIND NESSAMUN

PSENEMPHAIA HIDEOUT

Prerequisite: Approach the hideout

SUGGESTED LEVEL: 15

LOCATION REWARD: 400 XP

LOCATION OBJECTIVES: Kill one captain, loot one treasure

Get close to the camp by hiding in the nearby haystack **(4)**. Watch the soldiers' movements. Use the tall grass around the crocodile cage **(5)** to lure soldiers to their death. Free the crocodile for some real fun; just clear out quickly so he doesn't focus on you. Stealthily kill the captain before resorting to an all-out brawl, which is not too dangerous since there are only five soldiers in the hideout. Free Nessamun from his bindings in the tent **(6)** and loot the treasure to complete the location objective.

SPEAK WITH NESSAMUN

Talk to Nessamun to learn that they smashed and drank all his beer. You send him back to Sais to prepare the next delivery.

ABUSE OF POWER

Prerequisite: Complete Main Quest: The Scarab's Sting		
SUGGESTED LEVEL: 16	REWARD: 1,000 XP	UNLOCKS: *Side Quest: The Tax Master*

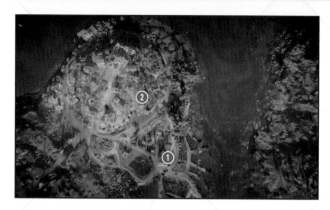

CARRY THE FARMER'S CROPS TO THE CART

Cruel tax collectors are abusing the people of Sais, threatening to kill them or burn their homes if they don't pay up. You must help a farmer **(1)** and his son deal with the farm, and then with the tax collectors.

Walk into the hay-baling circle in front of the farmer's house. Grab the three bundles of hay individually and place them in the cart beside his house.

FIND AND KILL THE TAX COLLECTOR

Send Senu up over Sais to locate the tax collector **(2)**. Head into town and access the rooftops. Work your way over to the brute tax collector (he has the objective marker over his head). Kill him with a drop assassination and confirm the kill. He has two Level 17 bodyguards but they're no match for you.

THE TAX MASTER

Prerequisite: Complete Harkhuf's four side quests	
SUGGESTED LEVEL: 17	Reward: 1,000 XP

FIND AND RESCUE HARKHUF FROM NIKIOU FORT

This quest becomes active after completing all four of Harkhuf's quests. In his home **(1)**, Jeska tells Bayek that Sefetu's force has raided Sais and taken Harkhuf prisoner. He'll be tortured and killed. You must find a way into Nikiou Fort to free him.

NIKIOU FORT

Prerequisite: Approach the hideout

SUGGESTED LEVEL: 18 or higher	LOCATION REWARD: 1,000 XP	LOCATION OBJECTIVES: Kill two captains and one commander, loot four treasures

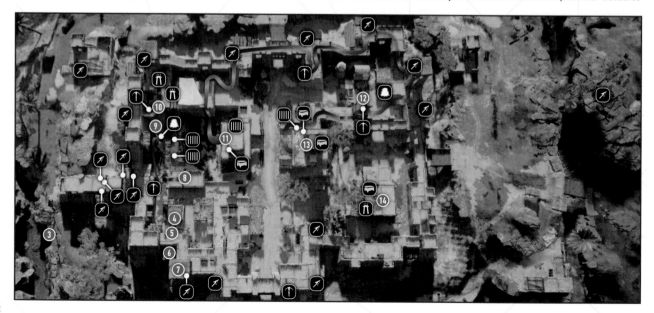

Use a boat to reach the fort **(2)**. Move in on foot through the water to access the connecting river (it's barricaded by large wooden spears that keep

boats out). Use Senu to mark all the enemies and locate Harkhuf and the east tunnel entrance **(3)**.

UNDERGROUND ENTRANCE

Squeeze through the narrow cave entrance on the fort's east side. Expect to battle a crocodile at the pool midway through. Head for the light at the end of the tunnel to reach the well **(4)**. Climb up the bloodstained walls to reach the exit above.

FORT INFILTRATION

Quickly enter the tall grass **(5)** next to the well exit. Whistle so nearby enemies come to investigate; assassinate them so you can move a little more freely in the area.

Crawl up the wall to reach the wall walk and drop down to the wooden platform **(6)** near the guard tower. Eliminate anyone on the field below so they won't see you climb the

tower **(7)**. If there's a guard in the tower, stealthily eliminate him. Use a predator or hunting bow to eliminate every lone patrolling soldier you can.

Use the rope on the tower's south side to repel down to the rooftop of the building **(8)** near the prisoners. A Level 13 captain guards the prisoners and a Level 16 brute patrols the upper walkway. Use single arrows to take out any guards you can see on the wall walk around this area.

KILL THE CAPTAIN PRISONER GUARD

Jump off the south end of the rooftop into the tall grass below. Crouch and head to the tall grass behind the haystack cart **(9)**. Call the Level 16 brute to you and assassinate him from the hay. You can attempt to take out the captain the same way but you may not be successful, depending on your level. If no other soldiers are around, you can finish him off with combat. If this draws attention, escape over a wall, get into tall grass, and then return to try again.

If you don't defeat the soldiers in this quadrant of the fort, then get up on the wall walk and take them out stealthily and set the brazier trap **(10)**. Now you can free the prisoners in the cages. You receive the 100 XP regardless of whether they make it out of the fort.

TALK TO HARKHUF

Enter the building **(11)** and talk to Harkhuf through the well cover. He tells you Sefetu wears the key around his neck. You'll have to kill him **(13)** to get the keys. Use Senu to mark Sefetu.

FIND AND GET THE KEY FROM SEFETU

Head up the ladder in Harkhuf's building to access the second floor and take the first treasure. If there is a guard right outside one of the second-floor doorways, then stealthily kill him. Be careful; there could be two soldiers on the floor above, so exit back through the first-floor doorway near the cages.

Head up to the southern wall walk, taking out soldiers along the way. Occasionally stop to look inside the fort for potential targets. Use the south wall ballista, if you can do it stealthily (kill lone soldiers). Always use the tops of towers for the best vantage point. Travel along the west wall walk to the second brazier and set the trap **(12)**.

SEFETU'S BUILDING

Enter Sefetu's building **(13)** through the east doorway on the second level. Take the treasure on the left as you enter. Sefetu is often on the lower floor next to a table with a treasure. Perform a drop assassination on him. If you don't have the ability to automatically loot, then confirm the kill to acquire the key. Take the third treasure.

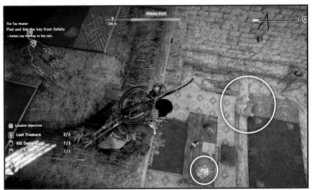

RESCUE HARKHUF

Make your way to the northwestern building **(14)** and get the last treasure on the first floor. A Level 17 captain patrols this area. Take him out now as well.

Return to Harkhuf **(11)** and use the key to free him from the floor cell.

ESCORT HARKHUF OUTSIDE NIKIOU FORT

The fort's southern area should be mostly clear of soldiers now; this is the direction Harkhuf runs after you free him. Hunt down the remaining location objectives. If you've been following this strategy, then there should be a commander remaining. He often patrols outside the fort walls. Hunt him down and kill him.

SPEAK TO HARKHUF

Talk to Harkhuf in the woods **(15)** to the fort's south to complete the quest.

INTRODUCTION
THE ESSENTIALS
MAIN QUESTS
SIDE QUESTS
ACTIVITIES
ATLAS
REFERENCE & ANALYSIS

THE OSTRICH

Prerequisite: Discover Sapi-Res Nome

SUGGESTED LEVEL: 17	REWARDS: 1,000 XP

FIND AND KILL THE TAX COLLECTOR

A woman **(1)** tells Bayek that her brother has locked himself in his house. Bayek agrees to help them out.

Ride toward the marker that appears by the shore **(2)** of Lake Mareotis. Use Senu to discover the tax collector in Camp Shemu.

CAMP SHEMU

Prerequisite: Approach the camp

SUGGESTED LEVEL: 16 or higher   **LOCATION REWARD: 400 XP**   **LOCATION OBJECTIVES: Kill one captain, loot one treasure**

Climb the south wall **(2)** of the brazier watchtower. Head to the top of the tower **(3)** and set the brazier trap. There's about ten soldiers, Levels 15 to 17, in this small camp. A soldier often stands alone on the pier **(5)**, but don't take the shot if you can't kill him with one arrow.

With the trap set, you can hang on the edge of the brazier tower's south handrail and whistle to draw enemies up the stairs. Lure them to the edge and then grab them and throw them down to their death. We lured the tax collector to his death this way.

Use the weapons on the ballista platform **(4)** to take out the others to reach the treasure in the tent **(7)**. Use the ballista nearest the main gate to take out the soldiers there **(6)**. This is a good way to eliminate the captain if you have not done so already. Once you kill the tax collector, the quest ends successfully.

TASTE OF HER STING

Prerequisite: Discover Sapi-Res Nome

SUGGESTED LEVEL: 17

REWARD: 3,000 XP

SAPI-RES RUINS INVESTIGATION

You discover yet even more signs of a gruesome killing **(1)** in the middle of Sapi-Res Nome.

Investigate the Prayer to Serqet **(2)** parchment on the ruins block; the sarcophagus **(3)**, which is inscribed with the mark of Serqet but missing a body; and the heavy cart tracks **(4)** in the mud. The final clue is at the bottom of the pool **(5)** in the middle of the ruins. Dive to the bottom to investigate the body that was ravaged by hippos. Grab the treasure while you're down there to complete the location objective.

You find the next ritual site after you explore the old temple in Ka-Khem Nome, which you do during Side Quest: The Old Library.

THE NEW KID IN TOWN

Prerequisite: Discover Sapi-Res Nome

SUGGESTED LEVEL: 18

REWARD: 1,000 XP

SPEAK TO RAMESSU

Speak to Ramessu **(1)** on the platform in front of the Temple of Horus.

SPEAK TO NEHI

Nehi **(2)** abandoned his ox cart.

FIND AND BRING NEHI'S CART BACK TO HIM

Send Senu up for recon to pinpoint the location of the missing cart **(3)**. Near the ox cart is a white lioness. Get to high ground and volley arrows at her until she's dead. You also encounter a few Level 18 bandits. Run them through with a long weapon while on a horse. When the threat is over, take the reins of the ox cart and drive it to Nehi's house **(4)**. Park the cart in the marker.

SPEAK TO NEHI

Speak to Nehi, who is patching the roof of his home. He shows you some strange writing on the walls inside. Bayek observes that some of the message is missing.

SPEAK TO RAMESSU

Return to Ramessu **(1)**. Use Senu to locate the three people around town: **(5)**, **(6)**, and **(7)**.

FIND AND SPEAK TO THE TOWN PEOPLE ABOUT THE HIEROGLYPHS

Talk to the closest homeowner **(5)**. Inspect the writing inside his home **(A)**. Bayek believes it's part of the same message.

Speak to the Nebefer **(6)** and then enter her home **(B)**. Inspect the hieroglyphs on her wall.

Speak to the farthest homeowner **(7)**, who is digging out a home across from his own **(C)**. Scale his wall to reach an open balcony door. Inspect the writing on the interior wall near the treasure chest. You decipher a prophetic message and receive the Hieroglyph Papyrus quest item.

EXPLORE THE REGION OF LETOPOLIS TO DISCOVER THE TEMPLE OF A MILLION YEARS

The clues point to the ruins **(8)** south of the Temple of Horus. Ride there now and send Senu up to mark a few bandits guarding the entrance to the buried temple.

Defeat the bandits and the lionesses to get close to the temple entrance. You must slip through a narrow gap in the recessed brick wall to gain entry.

INVESTIGATE THE BURIED TEMPLE

Light a torch and head down the stairs to a pile of large vases obstructing the pathway. There are cobras inside the large vases. Shatter the vases with arrows and then shoot the snakes.

Loot the treasure on the floor to your left. Use Animus Pulse to locate the four clues. Investigate the skeletons leaning on a column to your right. Investigate the vase of poison on the dais and the statue of Sekhmet. Lastly, inspect the prayer papyrus to Sekhmet on the table. With these clues, Bayek solves the mystery.

SPEAK TO NEHI

Exit the temple and head back to town and speak to Nehi **(4)**, who is now inside his home.

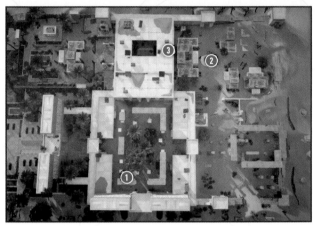

WORKER'S LAMENT

Prerequisite: Discover Sapi-Res Nome	
SUGGESTED LEVEL: 18	
REWARD: 1,000 XP	
UNLOCKS: Side Quest: The Old Library	

FIND AND CHIEF NITO

Find Chief Nito **(1)** in the Temple of Horus.

FIND AND SPEAK TO THE WORKERS

Use Senu to locate the well **(2)** on the temple's northeast side. Enter the well and speak to the worker inside.

RESCUE THE WORKERS FROM THE COLLAPSED TUNNEL

Head inside the tunnel at the bottom of the well. Break down the wooden barrier with a weapon and talk to Ipuy, the first worker you find in the tunnel.

CARRY IPUY OUT OF THE TUNNEL

Pick up Ipuy and carry him back to the well entrance and set him on the ground next to the first worker you talked to.

HELP BABA

Head back in and light a torch and then break the next barrier down. Squeeze through a narrow crack in the tunnel wall and shoot the cobras with arrows or slash them with a weapon. Enter the library vault to find Baba alive and doing well.

REPORT BACK TO NITO

Before you leave, check out the back of the library and inspect the History of the Keepers of the Old Library parchment on the middle table. This unlocks Side Quest: The Old Library. On the ceiling is a sealed entrance hole that allows access to the temple above. Shoot the wood with a couple arrows to break it and then climb out of the temple through this hole.

LOCATION OBJECTIVE: FIND PAPYRUS PUZZLE

When you leave the well through the hole in the secret library's ceiling, you come up inside the Temple of Horus near the Sea of Sand Papyrus Puzzle. Take it from the east wall behind the black, bird-faced-lion statue **(3)**. See the Papyrus chapter in Activities for more details.

Talk to Chief Nito **(1)**.

THE OLD LIBRARY

Prerequisite: Discovered during Side Quest: Workers' Lament; Lethopolis Temple

SUGGESTED LEVEL: 18

REWARD: 1,500 XP

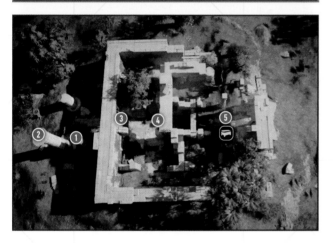

EXPLORE THE EAST BANK OF THE NILE

Be careful around the ruins; they're guarded by bandits.

Synchronize with the Viewpoint **(2)**. To do this, climb the adjacent pillar **(1)** and then leap over to the Viewpoint to reach the top.

Enter the north entrance **(3)**. Put an arrow in the head of the bandit **(4)** near the descending stairs just to clear the way and not start a fight with everyone.

Head down the stairs to the subterranean chamber, and use Animus Pulse to mark all the loot. Take the treasure and you'll discover the sword is not here.

REACH THE BANDIT CAMPS

Check your world map to find the bandit camp marker to the north. Be cautious on your approach. Stop and dismount in some tall grass and send Senu up to investigate.

FIND AND STEAL THE SWORD OF PTAH

DASOS HIDEOUT

Prerequisite: Approach the hideout

SUGGESTED LEVEL: 18

LOCATION REWARD: 400 XP

LOCATION OBJECTIVES: Kill two captains, loot one treasure

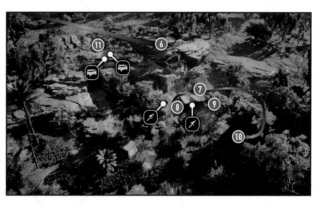

Have Senu search and mark enemies and the sword's location. This hideout is divided in two sections—the exterior camp and the cave interior hideout. The treasure you seek is inside the cave. The exterior camp is occupied by around eight Level 18 bandits with a Level 19 captain. The interior cave section is occupied by a pack of hyenas.

To reach the captain, get on the cave's rooftop **(6)**. Drop down the ledges, using the tall grass for cover, and keep moving down to the ground behind the main tent.

From behind the tent **(7)**, move left **(9)** or right **(8)** and remain in tall grass. If enemies are in groups together, then shoot vases in the distance to force them to patrol. Once they are moving about, you can divide and conquer. Travel through tall grass along the camp's edge **(10)** and get more headshots or lure victims to tall grass ambushes.

Lure the captain into the bushes and execute him. You could leave everyone else alive and then return to the rock top **(6)** and enter the hole to the cave. Shoot the hyenas with arrows before you drop in and gab the treasure and the quest item from the second chest. Once you have the Sword of Ptah, you complete the quest.

TASTE OF HER STING

Prerequisite: Complete one ritual site investigation (there are four)

SUGGESTED LEVEL: 17	REWARDS: 3,000 XP

RITUAL SITE: KA-KHEM NOME OLD TEMPLE

OLD TEMPLE INVESTIGATION

You may run across the finale to this quest while in the old temple **(1)** during Side Quest: The Old Library. Once you have cleared the bandits from the entry, head down the stairs and activate Animus Pulse to locate the clue markers.

There are only two clues to investigate: the scorpion marked sarcophagus **(2)** and the large crack in the wall **(3)**. The crack in the wall is not wide enough to squeeze through. You must find another way in.

FIND THE CAVE ENTRANCE

Send Senu up to search to the east for the cave entrance **(2)**, which is extremely close to the Hathor Stone Circle (see the Activities section for more information on Stone Circles).

EXPLORE THE CAVE

Light a torch and enter the cave through a crack in the wall. Slide under a short, low hole. Head to the tunnel intersection. Head left and slip through the crack in the wall to enter the chamber where the chanting originates.

SPEAK TO THE PROPHET OF SERQET

The room is dark and filled with collectibles. Upon closer inspection, you find three figures. Approach the marked man.

KILL THE PROPHET OF SERQET

The two goons with the marked man are Level 15 and not much of a challenge. Finish them off first and then concentrate your attacks on the prophet, who carries a very large shield and spear. Use a heavy blunt weapon or spear while dodging behind. Once you break his defense, unleash a special move if you have enough built-up adrenaline. Killing this foe and confirming the kill completes the quest. Raid the chest in the chamber for a rare item. Loot all the containers and then wash your hands of this case.

GIZA

PRECIOUS BONDS

Prerequisite: Complete all four ritual site investigations

SUGGESTED LEVEL: 18 | **REWARDS: 2,000 XP**

FREE THE PRISONER

KHUFU TEMPLE HIDEOUT

Prerequisite: Approach the hideout
SUGGESTED LEVEL: 17
LOCATION REWARD: 400 XP
LOCATION OBJECTIVES: Kill one captain, loot one treasure

Use Senu to mark the enemies and treasure. While up there, she may spot the prisoner **(1)** through a concrete rooftop, which triggers this mission to start. You'll discover bandits with a Level 29 captain inside. They are mostly grouped in the central camp area, guarding the treasure **(2)**. You should be Level 22 or 23 by now, so stealth kills should be no problem.

Climb up the east wall and head right for the arrow supply **(3)**. Keep the high-ground advantage by remaining on the rooftops and thick walls. Single out the enemy loners. The captain may patrol the pathway right below the arrows. If so, perform a drop assassination on him.

You can get right up behind the main tent, using the large amounts of tall foliage. Slide under the small flap in the back of the tent and grab the treasure **(2)**. Investigate the chamber in the southwest corner to find the prisoner **(1)**.

SPEAK TO THE PRISONER YOU JUST SAVED

Bayek frees a scavenger named Oba imprisoned by bandits. Oba is fixated on retrieving a valuable ring he claims is rightfully his. Escort Oba back to his quarters.

Exit the hideout on the south side, call your horse, and follow Oba as he finds his horse. He goes to the Eastern Cemetery Mastaba; his camp **(4)** is right beside it.

Back at the camp, Oba tells his brother that you are here to help find the ring as well as their third brother, who may be around the Sphynx.

FIND AND RESCUE RASHIDI

Ride southwest to the Sphynx and send Senu up to locate Rashidi in the Khentkawes Hideout in Eesfet Oon-m'Aa Poo.

KHENTKAWES HIDEOUT

Prerequisite: Approach the hideout
SUGGESTED LEVEL: 18 or higher
LOCATION REWARD: 600 XP
LOCATION OBJECTIVES: Kill one captain, kill one commander, loot two treasures

The Level 19 captain rides around the perimeter of the hideout on a horse. Before you infiltrate the hideout, track him down and kill him to keep him from seeing you as you climb the tops of walls.

The Level 20 commander patrols the rooftop above the imprisoned Rashidi **(6)** and areas near the prison building. Approach from

the south through the sunken wall **(5)**. Clear enemies stealthily and make your way to the arrow supply rooftop **(6)** above the prisoner. Move around the rooftop looking for loners to shoot. You will likely get a drop assassination opportunity on the commander as he walks the grounds around the building.

Use the tall walls and bushes to stealthily attack the remaining bandits and then get the treasures from the tents **(7)** and **(8)**. You can even release the captive hyena **(9)** to cause a distraction. When the hideout is clear, free Rashidi **(6)**. He is weak and you must carry him.

CARRY RASHIDI OUT OF THE BANDIT HIDEOUT

Carry him out the south hall and back out the way you entered **(5)**. Drop him on the ground when you've gone far enough.

SPEAK TO RASHIDI

You tell him that his brothers Oba and Nebti sent you to rescue him and the ring. Bayek is shocked to learn that he doesn't have the ring. He said yet another brother, Turo, punched him in the face and took the ring to Hemon Tombs to trade it.

FIND TURO

HEMON MASTABA

LOCATION OBJECTIVES: Loot two treasures

Ride north, and when you pass the pyramid, send Senu over Hemon Tombs **(10)** to assess the situation. Ride into the tomb. It's a scene of death, both bandits and hyenas. Head under the overhang **(11)** to the north to find a small clearing in a barricaded entryway. Slide under it to get inside.

Light a torch and investigate the tomb. Loot the two treasure chests in the room, and then interact with Turo's dead body. A hyena has eaten the hand that the ring must have been on.

HUNT THE HYENA THAT ATE THE RING

Send Senu up in the air to mark the hyena **(12)** to the southwest. Take off after it. While riding, select your long weapon and the bow you want to use on the hyena. After you eliminate the hyena, dismount and confirm the kill to obtain the ring. The Giza Scavengers' Ring is added to your quest items.

BRING THE RING TO THE SCAVENGERS

Return to the brothers' camp **(4)** and return the ring. You get to choose which brother receives the ring—the choice doesn't affect the outcome. Watch as they fight over the ring and then panic as it goes missing all over again.

WHAT'S YOURS IS MINE

Prerequisite: Complete all four ritual site investigations

SUGGESTED LEVEL: 19	REWARDS: 3,500 XP

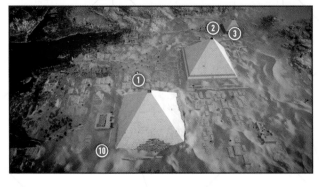

INTERACT WITH THE UNCONSCIOUS MAN

Find a man **(1)** lying unconscious in the sand to the south of the Viewpoint pyramid. Corteseos is a geographer and he's missing his notes. All he remembers is the sounds of horses galloping off.

FIND THE THIEVES WHO ATTACKED YOU

The hoofprints lead south. Head toward Menkaure's Pyramid. Send Senu to pinpoint the area of interest. Enter the small ruins at the base of Menkaure's Pyramid.

INVESTIGATE THE RUINS TO TRACK THE THIEVES

Inside the ruins **(2)** you can interact with a large rock near a small hole in a wall. Looks like someone small dug their way out. The hole is too small for you to crawl through. You must find another way in.

Explore the interior of the ruins to the southeast and speak to the small child. He seems suspect when you ask if he's alone but avoids giving you an answer.

Exit the ruins and go to the back side. There is a series of small blocks you must move away from another small access hole.

Move all the blocks to get inside. Once inside, you find a small boy sitting alone. He says that they were forced to hide the stolen items in Menkaure's pyramid.

EXPLORE MENKAURE'S PYRAMID TO RECOVER THE STOLEN ITEMS

Head to the tunnel entrance **(3)** on the north side of Menkaure's Pyramid. Light a torch and follow the tunnel. You discover an upper pathway and a lower one. Both lead to the same chamber. Take either route.

Inside the open chamber is a very large ornate box, likely a sarcophagus. Loot the chest behind it. If you entered this chamber using the lower path, then you passed another hallway just outside the entrance of this chamber. Take that pathway now. Bayek finds his stolen feather.

A small boy attacks you, saying that this is his pyramid. He tells you that Corteseos's notes were taken by bandits from the hills west of the Hermon Tombs and that they have Anta too.

> ### LOCATION OBJECTIVE
>
> The location objective for Menkaure's Pyramid is to find the Ancient Tablet. For help with this, see the Activities section of this guide.

REACH THE BANDIT HIDEOUT WHERE ANTA IS HELD CAPTIVE

Exit the pyramid and ride northwest toward the marker. If you head directly for the marker, you'll encounter an ibex and hyena hunting opportunity. A little bit farther you may be spotted by bandits. Finish them off along the way.

EXPLORE THE HIDEOUT IN SEARCH OF ANTA AND RESCUE HER

ADORER OF THOTH TOMB
LOCATION OBJECTIVES: One Ancient Tablet

Following the marker places you at the typical entry **(4)** to the tomb. Fly Senu above the mountain, where you find a large hole **(5)**. This is the suggested entrance to the tomb. Senu can also mark the enemies below the hole through the mountain. Ditch the horse and climb the mountain to this entrance.

Carefully drop down into the hole, latching on to lower handgrip points as you descend to a ledge you can stand on. Look at the Level 19 bandits in the darkness below. Many of them are gathered around a fire and an oil vase. Shoot the vase and duck back on your ledge. Many will burn to death; shoot arrows through the survivors before dropping down into the tomb.

You can either move around on the floor of the tomb or traverse higher along the narrow ledges and platforms that span the tomb. We suggest staying up high and exploring until you rid the tomb of enemies.

At the end of the tomb, you find Anta in a cage near the balance platform puzzle. Anta turns out to be a dog. Do not free her yet unless you want her running off without you.

WEIGHT AND PLATFORM PUZZLE

To solve the balance platform puzzle, simply move the single weight off the platform **(7)** closest to Anta **(8)**, walk up the ramp, and drop it on the higher moving platform **(6)**. Now take the weights from the ground and place three more weights on moving platform **(6)**. With it securely weighted down, head back up the ramp **(6)** and jump from the ramp's top (not the platform) to the now-raised platform **(7)**. Enter a room to find the Ancient Tablet and some good loot. Climb back out of the chamber and rescue Anta **(8)**.

> ### CARBON CRYSTAL, BRONZE, AND SILICA
>
> Dive into the deep pool behind the baboon statue. Follow the watery tunnel to a cave where you find a carbon crystal, some bronze, and silica.
>
>

Free Anta from her cage and she'll run for the main exit. If you left anyone alive, eliminate them on your way out so they don't harm your four-legged friend.

ESCORT ANTA BACK TO THE CHILDREN

Anta runs out of the tomb and heads south to the children **(9)**. Catch up to her to talk to the kids. They say they saw the horseman, who probably has Corteseos's notes. They say he's near Khufu's Pyramid **(10)**.

FIND AND ASSASSINATE THE BANDIT HORSEMAN

Head east past Khufu to track down the horseman. Select a long weapon and have your strongest warrior bow handy. When you spot the bandit, start in with arrows and then ride in close and take him out with a few passes of the long weapon.

BRING CORTESEOS'S NOTES BACK TO HIM

Dismount and confirm the kill to take the notes. Head back to Corteseos **(1)** to give him his notes.

A DREAM OF ASHES

Prerequisite: Unlocks during Main Quest: The Lizard's Mask

SUGGESTED LEVEL: 21	REWARDS: 2,500 XP

TALK TO THE SEER

This quest unlocks during Main Quest: The Lizard's Mask. As soon as you leave the Seer **(1)** and meet Aya outside, walk right back in and take this quest. Aya will now fight with you for a little while.

FIND THE SEER'S CLIENTS AND BRING THEM THE AMULETS

Use Senu to locate the three targets: **(2)**, **(3)**, and **(4)**. We suggest heading to the beggar first, as he is the closest.

OMORFI VILLA

Prerequisite: Approach the villa
SUGGESTED LEVEL: 20
LOCATION REWARD: 300 XP
LOCATION OBJECTIVES: Loot one treasure

You'll most likely approach this villa from the south road. Duck into the bushes to hide from the soldier patrolling the upstairs room. He could spot you from the balcony **(6)**. Put an arrow in his face and then look below; take out any other lone soldiers down there. Leap to the balcony and enter the villa.

Head to the stairs and wait to see if a patrolling solder enters the house. If so, lure him up the stairs and assassinate him from around the corner on the landing. Raid the treasure on the first floor to complete the location objective.

Defeat any soldiers around the prisoner **(2)** that could spot you. Also make sure there are no soldiers near the escape route—the south gate **(7)**. Now free the beggar.

ESCORT THE BEGGAR OUT OF THE VILLA

Walk the beggar through the east gate **(7)** and out to the street.

GIVE THE AMULET TO THE BEGGAR

Speak to the beggar to give him the amulet of protection.

RESCUE THE ADVENTURER

Head west to the ruins **(3)**, where Nomad's Bazaar is located. Drop down into the pit behind the pillars and follow the dark tunnel with a lit torch. Vault over a tree root and then climb a cave wall to reach the chamber under the Temple of Ptah. A handful of soldiers are here.

Lure the soldiers up into the tunnel to defeat them or just jump down into the ruins and have a good brawl. Loot the treasure.

Look for a tunnel exit to the north beyond the candlelit dais. Light a torch and enter that tunnel.

When you reach the edge of the path where the water begins, there's a small ledge to the left. Drop onto that ledge. Follow it around until you spot a crack large enough to fit through.

Follow the tunnel to an open cave chamber, where you find cobras and the dead adventurer. Give the amulet to the adventurer and leave the tunnel system the way you came or by continuing to head north.

RESCUE THE PHILANDERER

The philanderer **(4)** is being moved in a prison cart driven by a Roman soldier and closely watched by a team of mounted soldiers. Any soldiers who happen to be on the road when the attack happens join the fight. Fill up on arrows and use your strongest bows; also have the strongest heavy blunt or spear ready for some jousting action.

Cut off the prison cart and take out the driver with some arrows to the head (watch out because he fires arrows too); then leave quickly. Reach an area where you can fight the horseman on your own terms. Raise your shield to block the many arrows that will be flung your way. No one will regain control of the prison cart, so you can return to that when you are ready.

Use sleep darts in this situation to make things easier. When possible, carry the philanderer out of the cart. If no soldiers are nearby, then put her down and give her the amulet. If soldiers are near, carry her around a few corners to lose them and then give her the amulet.

SPEAK TO THE SEER AT THE DOCKS BY THE GREAT TEMPLE

Now ride to the docks near the Memphites Barracks and find the Seer at his boat **(8)**. Speak to him. He wishes you to take him to a sacred island **(9)** to tear aside the curtain that shrouds your nightmares.

ESCORT THE SEER TO THE SACRED ISLAND

Use the Seer's boat to reach the sacred island **(9)** to the east. Rid the island of the five crocodiles.

SPEAK TO THE SEER

Speak to the Seer near the ritual site.

FIND THE STATUE OF KHNUM

Take a boat south to the Sunken Temple of Ramses **(10)**. Use Senu to pinpoint the statue's location.

Drive the boat directly over the statue and dive in. There are two treasures below to complete the location objective and earn 450 XP. Use Animus Pulse to locate the treasures and the Statue of Khnum.

BRING THE STATUE OF KHNUM TO THE SEER

Reenter a boat and sail back to the sacred island **(9)**. Talk to the Seer to hand him the statue.

USE DAWN & DUSK BESIDE THE SEER TO MAKE THE TIME SPEED FORWARD AND INITIATE THE RITUAL

Stand at the ritual site on the small sacred island and use the Dawn & Dusk skill to change the time of day. After time passes, you discover the Seer is gone, but the quest ends successfully.

BLOOD IN THE WATER

Prerequisite: Activated from Temple of Ptah's Informant Table
SUGGESTED LEVEL: 20
REWARD: 1,000 XP

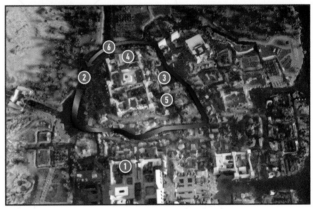

FIND THUTMOSE THE CROCODILES HUNTER

Board Thutmose's boat **(2)** and speak to him. Sit at the front of his felucca.

KILL ALL THE CROCODILES IN FRONT OF THE PALACE

Leap from the boat and head toward the front of the palace **(3)**, where the crocodiles rage. Get on the platform near the water and start killing every crocodile that comes at you. There are five crocodiles to kill. Use arrows and your most powerful weapons.

SPEAK TO THUTMOSE THE CROCODILE HUNTER AT NIGHT

Meditate the day to night and then follow the marker to the caves **(4)** below the palace. Light a torch and enter the caves on the palace's north side. Follow the marker to Thutmose, who is skinning a croc near a pool of water. He wants you to chase down to evildoers and points you in the right direction.

FIND AND ASSASSINATE THE TWO CRIMINALS

The two criminals **(5)** and **(6)** are wandering near the river by the palace and the other is on the river near the wabet. Use Senu to spot the criminals. If you have the Hunter's Instinct ability, select them to see the routes they take. Hunt them down and easily take them out with an arrow to the head or sneak up behind them and simply assassinate them. Neither of these Level 21 criminals put up much of a struggle.

You find a contract of services document on one of them. It points to the Lizard as the one paying them to cause chaos around the temple.

ODOR MOST FOUL

Prerequisite: Activated from Temple of Ptah's Informant Table

SUGGESTED LEVEL: 20	REWARDS: 1,000 XP

SPEAK TO THE PRIESTS BY THE TOMBS

You pick this job up from the temple's informant table **(1)**. Head to the tomb **(2)** northeast of the temple to find a group of priests. Speak to the priest.

FIND A WAY INSIDE THE TOMB

Use Senu to find the tomb's entrance. There's a location right around the corner from the priests **(3)** and yet a better one **(4)** around back. Go through the secret entrance to avoid detection from the bandits inside. Smash through the straw hut behind the tomb to reveal an entrance shaft.

INVESTIGATE THE STINK

Light a torch and head through the tunnel. Stop at the end of the hallway before it bends left. The three Level 21 bandits in the next room would have seen you coming in through the other entrance. Take them out stealthily. Whistle for the guards one at a time to come into your hallway. Put a hole in their neck.

Enter the room the bandits were in and climb the stairs on the room's left (east) side. Break through a wall at the top to raid a chest in a small room. Head back into the previous bandit chamber.

INVESTIGATE THE TOMB TO TRACE THE SOURCE OF THE STINK

Enter the room to the west through the broken wall. The stink is strong in this room. Activate Animus Pulse. The investigation starts with the mummies on the candlelit slab on the left.

Head down the stairs, activate Animus Pulse, and investigate from the right to the left. Mummies are on the floor in the right corner at the bottom of the stairs. They are not the cause of the smell.

At the room's other end are some offerings to chase the smell. There is also a bloodstain on the floor that leads through a barricaded wall. Smash through the wall and crawl through the crack.

The room you drop into is full of bloody mummies. Burn through the webs as you enter the adjoining room. Even more mummies. Investigate the crypt along the right wall. You see the flesh has decayed but the wrappings are still intact. Exit the tomb.

REACH THE WABET TO INSPECT THE MUMMIFICATION PROCESS

WABET

Head north to the wabet **(5)** and enter to begin the investigation.

INVESTIGATE THE WABET'S MUMMIFICATION PROCESS

Find the embalmer **(6)** in the northeast corner of the main room. He tells you that he uses natron, not salt, and says you should see the expert out back. On your way out to see the expert, you find the Burning Bush Papyrus Puzzle on a table in a small room in the back.

SPEAK TO THE WORKER IN THE YARD ABOUT NATRON

The natron expert tells you there's salt in the natron and points you to the warehouse just north of the Great Temple.

REACH THE WAREHOUSE WHERE THE TAINTED NATRON IS KEPT

NATRON WAREHOUSE

Head southwest to the warehouse **(9)**. Enter the facility to catch a masked man inside.

FIND THE CAVE WHERE THE BANDITS ARE MIXING NATRON

TEMPLE CAVE ENTRANCE

Send Senu up to find the northwest cave entrance **(10)** underneath the Temple of Ptah. Run through the temple neighbor's backyard and into the hidden tunnel entrance. Light a torch and follow the tunnel to a chamber with four Level 20 bandits. Lure the closest guard to the tunnel entrance to you and assassinate him from around the corner.

Push into the room and hide behind an object. Throw a torch to get the distant guards' attention. When they start investigating, put arrows in their heads to complete the quest. Take a Legendary weapon from one of the bandits.

CHILDREN OF THE STREETS

Prerequisite: Discover Memphis

SUGGESTED LEVEL: 23

REWARD: 2,500 XP

CATCH THE THIEF

While in South Memphis **(1)**, you come across a shopkeeper yelling for your help stopping a thief. Chase the boy down the alley, through the streets, and up some stairs.

At the top of the stairs, he drops into a hole in a rooftop **(2)**. Expect a fight with three bandits in the building below. Shoot arrows down into the hole to take out as many as you can and then jump down and fight the remaining bandit(s).

Talk to the street urchin after rescuing him from bandits.

REACH THE MEMPHIS SHIPYARD

Head to the Memphis shipyard **(3)**.

INVESTIGATE THE SHIPYARD IN SEARCH OF KAWIT

MEMPHIS SHIPYARD

Enter the large hole in the ship's east side and investigate the ropes **(4)**. You learn there are traces of oil. Investigate the doll **(5)** on the broken cage on the boat's east side. Inspect the broken, burned ship mast **(6)**. It's quite colorful.

Speak to the oil salesman **(7)**. He refuses to help without you paying him something. To make him talk, start destroying his vases of oil **(8)**. Now talk to the oil salesman and he'll spill the beans.

FIND KAWIT AND THE CHILDREN BY THE KIDNAPPER'S SHIP

Head south along the shoreline and send Senu up to pinpoint Kawit's location at Apagogeas Hideout **(9)**.

APAGOGEAS HIDEOUT

Prerequisite: Approach the hideout
SUGGESTED LEVEL: 23
LOCATION REWARD: 600 XP
LOCATION REWARDS: Kill one captain, loot one treasure

Approach the small island camp from the water **(9)** west of the camp. The Level 24 captain **(10)** and his crew—four Level 23 bandits—occupy the hideout. The captain patrols back and forth across the small island, but you may catch him relieving himself in the tall grass; easily reach this by following the path of tall grass along the shoreline. Come up through the grass and assassinate him.

Find a captive child **(11)** hiding behind some bags on the ship. He tells you Kawit was taken to a house in the city near the temple of Hathor and that a rich lady named Gaia owns it. Grab the treasure from the tent to complete the location objective.

FIND AND RESCUE KAWIT IN GAIA'S VILLA

MEMPHIS VILLA

Head back to town and send Senu up to locate Kawit at Gaia's house **(12)**. Mark the Level 21 to 23 bandits as well. Approach the villa from the neighboring rooftop **(12)** and drop down onto the vine-covered pergola that covers a stairwell to the prison. Walk to the edge and perform a drop assassination on the prison guard **(13)** standing in the stairwell.

FIND THE KEY TO OPEN KAWIT'S CELL DOOR

Enter the basement and speak to Kawit **(14)**. She tells you that one of the bandits has a key to the cell. Send Senu to locate the key holder **(15)**.

Crouch-walk up the stairwell and stop at the end to stay hidden from the group of bandits in the courtyard area. If the key holder does not move from the group, throw a torch near them to break up the party. The key holder is forced to patrol in your direction. When he crosses the top of the stairs **(16)**, stealthily assassinate him and take Gaia's villa cell key.

RESCUE KAWIT

Use the key to free Kawit and Matia. This unlocks Side Quest; Mortem Romanum.

TAIMHOTEP'S SONG

Prerequisite: Complete Main Quest: The Lizard's Mask after completing objective "Speak to Pasherenptah about Taimhotep"
SUGGESTED LEVEL: 22
REWARD: 2,000 XP

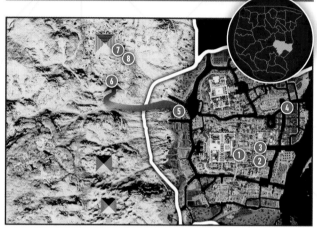

SPEAK TO TAIMHOTEP

This quest unlocks after you kill the soul eater during Main Quest: The Lizard's Mask. Afterward, you can find Taimhotep weeping on a bench in her temple garden **(1)**. Speak to her.

FIND THE SHOP AND GET A FERTILITY TALISMAN

Send Senu up to find the magic goods shop **(2)**. It's in an underground tomb. Light a torch, enter, and explore.

EXPLORE THE SHOP TO FIND A FERTILITY TALISMAN

Meet the curious shop owner inside. She leaves the shop while you investigate. Use Animus Pulse to mark the clues in the room. Inspect an inventory sheet where the talisman in blue faience is listed.

Use Animus Pulse again. A mark pops up under a sheet hanging against a wall. Push through the sheet to find a moveable shelf. Push it forward. This reveals a small

secret room. Collect the loot from the floor and inspect the final clue on the table in the back. It's the fertility talisman.

HUNT BIRDS AND BRING THEIR TROPHIES BACK TO TAIMHOTEP

YOU NEED TWO FLAMINGO TONGUES AND TWO HERON FEATHERS

Three thugs enter and attack as you start to exit the magic shop. Just be ready for them with a bow in hand and shoot one after the other in the head.

If you have sold all your animal parts and need to find the flamingo tongues and heron feathers, then head to the boat slip around the Memphites Barracks **(3)**. Shoot a couple and collect their tongues.

Fast Travel to the Viewpoint **(4)** to the northeast. Remain on the pillar and begin hunting heron; they like to land in the water below. Shoot a couple and grab their feathers.

You can now find Taimhotep at a stable **(5)**.

ESCORT TAIMHOTEP TO THE PYRAMID OF DJOSER

SAQQARA NOME

Mount the camel at the stable and follow Taimhotep and her maid. You shouldn't run into any trouble until you must pass through Per Our Hideout **(6)**. This is a bandit-occupied hideout just south of the Djoser pyramid in Saqqara Nome.

PER OUR HIDEOUT

Prerequisite: Approach the hideout
SUGGESTED LEVEL: 23
LOCATION REWARD: 300 XP
LOCATION OBJECTIVE: Loot one treasure

Taimhotep stops just before entering the gates **(6)** of Per Our Hideout. Ride through the front gate; not much of a battle occurs since all the bandits are on foot. You move so quickly away from them that not much of a chase occurs, even though her maid does not take the most direct exit route.

Taimhotep and her maid dismount near the base of the pyramid and climb a dune to reach the top of a wall walk, where the ritual settings are in place. When Taimhotep is at the ritual site, guard her during the moon-lit ceremony.

THE BAKER'S DILEMMA

Prerequisite: Discover Memphis
SUGGESTED LEVEL: 23
REWARD: 1,000 XP

FIND AND RESCUE THE BAKER'S TASTER

Talk to the cursing baker **(1)** in northeast Memphis.

Send Senu up to track down the prison cart that is on a short route around a city block; this includes going very close to the Memphites Barracks **(2)**. The prison cart is driven by an archer and is followed closely by a couple soldiers. No matter what part of town you choose to ambush the prison cart, additional soldiers in the area respond. However, we still suggest ambushing it as far away from the barracks as possible to minimize reinforcements.

Once you deal with the threat, get into the back of the cage and pick up the taster. Put him on a horse and take him to the baker **(1)**. Drop him in the marked location at the bakery. He tells you that he uncovered a plot to poison the lady Taimhotep. He thinks the cakes will be at the garrison.

FIND AND DESTROY THE JARS OF POISONED CAKES

MEMPHITES BARRACKS

Prerequisite: Approach the camp

SUGGESTED LEVEL: 23 **LOCATION REWARD: 600 XP** **LOCATION OBJECTIVES: Kill one captain, kill one commander, loot two treasures**

Send Senu up over Memphites Barracks to locate the poison cakes and to mark enemies, the captain, and the brazier. Reach the rooftop of the house **(2)** to the north. You can leap from the house's rooftop to two Y-branched trees, and then latch on to the top of the barrack's wall walk. From there, stealthily shoot any soldiers in sight and any near the brazier **(3)**.

Set the brazier **(3)** trap. This helps you avoid the Phylake in Memphis if the alarm is set. Pivot west from the brazier and enter the second level of the main barracks building. Walk to the edge inside and look down to your right. You can spot the commander **(4)** in the room with the treasure.

Sometimes the commander is next to the treasure and sometimes he's on the room's other side **(5)**. Either way, get into a position above him, quickly shoot his guard in the head, and then drop assassinate him before he spots you. Duck into the hiding booth in his room to avoid detection from any other guards who may have heard commotion.

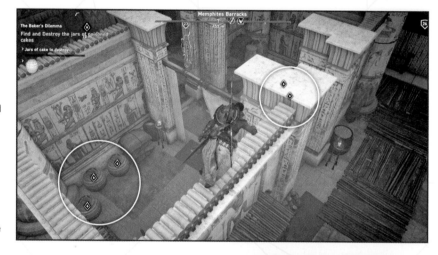

Sneak around the barracks using the tops of walls, the haystack, or the hiding booth. Eliminate anyone within earshot of you smashing the six cake vases, which are indicated with objective markers. They are in the rooms **(6)** across the hall from the commander's. Destroy them with arrows or a blunt weapon.

Return to the wall walk and head to the barracks' east side to reach the last two vases of poisoned cakes. They're under the overhang of a small building, where you also find the second treasure and the captain. Stand on the wall walk **(7)** and shoot the remaining vases **(8)** with arrows. To complete the location objective, begin your assault on the captain, loot the treasure inside, and escape.

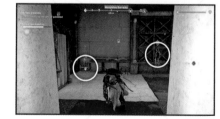

MORTEM ROMANUM

Prerequisite: Complete Side Quest: Children of the Streets

SUGGESTED LEVEL: 30	REWARDS: 1,500 XP

FIND AND ASSASSINATE GAIA

You find a dead body in the house where the children from Side Quest: Children in the Streets stay. Kawit rushes in and says that the dead man was the one they called "Father." She says Gaia is responsible for his death. She sails down the Nile today.

Send Senu north along the coast toward the marker in the Nile. You'll spot Gaia's ship near the Viewpoint **(2)**. If it's active, travel to that portal to save time reaching the ship **(3)**.

You may catch the ship as it travels south and makes a quick stop near the corrupted cache (loot treasure location) **(4)**. Dive into the water near the ship, come up under it, and latch on to the side. Pull up to the top edge and hang from the deck to remain stealthy. Begin whistling to lure the bandits so you can grab them and throw them overboard.

If you are spotted or are fighting on deck and things get too rough, then jump into the water and swim under the boat to return to stealth. Approach Gaia (from stealth or not) and assassinate her. Confirm the kill to complete the quest.

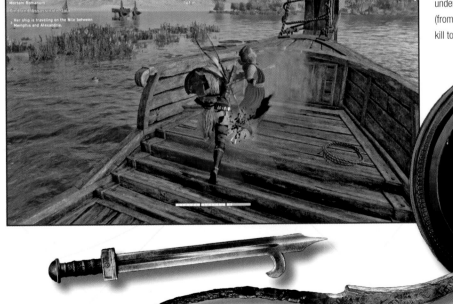

INTRODUCTION

THE ESSENTIALS

MAIN QUESTS

SIDE QUESTS

ACTIVITIES

ATLAS

REFERENCE & ANALYSIS

FIRST BLOOD

Prerequisite: Discover Saqqara Nome

SUGGESTED LEVEL: 18

REWARD: 1,500 XP

INVESTIGATE THE TOMB WHERE BAYEK KILLED THE HERON

GETTING INTO THE INVESTIGATION CHAMBER

The pyramid in which the Heron died is inaccessible. It's through the high west entrance **(2)**. Before you enter, you must unblock an obstruction. To do this, enter the pyramid through the lower north entrance **(1)**. Light a torch and walk cautiously; there are cobras on the ground through the first doorway in the tunnel. Defeat them.

Climb up the back wall in the cobra room. Enter a high tunnel and continue to the dead-end shaft. Begin climbing the wood framing on the wall. Pull up into the next room and break the wall.

This reveals a barred window with a view into the tunnel behind the blocked shelf in the west entrance. Look inside the room through the bars

to spot the large vase blocking the shelf. Break the vase with arrows and then exit the pyramid.

THE WEST ENTRANCE

Push the unblocked shelf in the west tunnel, walk around to the back side of it, and enter the chamber.

Interact with the cross near the tablet. Raid the treasure on the opposite wall to complete the location objective.

Investigate the arrow below the breakable wall. This is the arrow Bayek used to scratch the heron tattoo off his arm. Break through the wall and enter the next chamber.

There are three clues to investigate in this chamber: the mummified heron, the tomb fit for a pharaoh, and the mask in the corner. Vases block the mask. Be prepared for a cobra in one of the vases. Shoot it and then investigate the mask.

Bayek pieces together what happened from the clues.

SECRETS OF THE FIRST PYRAMIDS ULC

Prerequisite: Discover Saqqara Nome

SUGGESTED LEVEL: 23

REWARD: 4,000 XP

Exclusive for Deluxe and Gold editions of Assassin's Creed Origins.

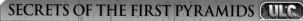

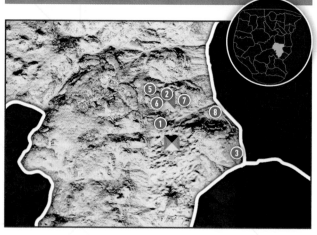

FIND MERKES THE SCHOLAR

When you explore the area around the Bent Pyramid in Saqqara, you happen upon a man **(1)** being chased by bandits on camelback.

FIND MERKES THE SCHOLAR

Give chase and shoot the pursuers with arrows with a strong warrior bow.

SPEAK TO MERKES

Bayek meets a scholar named Merkes and agrees to help him.

Merkes has one of the three artifacts he needs for his research. The other two are in the Tomb of Sneferu **(2)** and in Hugros Hideout **(3)**. Send Senu up to pinpoint these locations.

TOMB OF SNEFERU

Climb the northernmost pyramid to enter through the open tunnel on the north side. Light a torch and follow the tunnel. At the bottom of

the first sloping tunnel is a very small shaft that you must crouch to walk through.

This opens into a room with a burnable lamp. To the right of the lamp is a "pass-through crack."

Slide down the slope in the next tunnel and cross the bridge over the pool of water. At the end of the tunnel is a deep shaft. Jump to the opposite wall and climb down to the floor. Slide under the wall through the open slot in the blocks at the bottom of this shaft. This places you in the chamber with a weighted platform challenge.

THE FIRST BALANCE PLATFORM CHAMBER

The first balance platform chamber has a simple solution. As you enter the chamber, pick up the weight **(A)** to the right and walk onto the

first moving platform **(B)** near the weight you picked up. This drops the platform to the ground. Now push the large shelf **(C)** along the rails onto the same platform. This provides enough counterweight for you to jump from the next shelf **(D)** on the floor to the second platform **(E)**. Now it won't lower from your own weight and you can enter the next chamber **(F)** above the raised platform.

THE SECOND BALANCE PLATFORM CHAMBER

Smash the vase in the corner that's keeping you from entering the second balance platform chamber. In the first chamber, you see two counterbalancing platforms—one on the left **(G)** with a vase on it and one on the right **(H)** with five weights on it. There's a high room **(I)** accessed through the upper platform in the back of the room. The puzzle in the chamber to your right leads to the artifact you need.

Break the vase **(G)** with an arrow. Climb atop the large, wood-framed vase in the left corner to jump to the platform **(G)** that held the

vase. Continue to jump from the platform to the high ledge in the back of the room. There is a treasure in the right corner. Do not confuse this chamber with the next, because it's very similar.

THE THIRD BALANCE PLATFORM CHAMBER

Enter the final balance platform chamber. On the right is a balance platform **(J)** with two weights on it. In front of that is a wood scaffold **(K)** used as a jumping platform to access the second balance platform **(L)** in the room. This platform is raised and when you jump on it now, it lowers and does not allow you to reach the room above **(M)**.

Simply take two weights off the balance platform **(H)** in the previous chamber and place them on platform **(J)** with the other weights. Now it is heavy enough to stay down as you jump from the corner scaffold **(K)** to the balance platform **(L)**; then jump to reach the high ledge that leads to the final chamber **(M)**.

ARTIFACT AND ANCIENT TABLET CHAMBER

As you enter, there are four chests on the room's left side. The fourth one **(N)** is the artifact you need. Make sure you interact with the ancient tablet in the back of the chamber to complete the location objective and earn an Ability Point.

EXITING THE TOMB

In the ancient tablet room, use the slide-under open block near the left wall for a quick way out of the tomb. You'll slide down a ramp, swim underwater through a long tunnel,

and climb out of a tall shaft to reach the outside on the pyramid's west side.

HUGROS HIDEOUT

Prerequisite: Approach the hideout
SUGGESTED LEVEL: 23
LOCATION REWARD: 400 XP
LOCATION OBJECTIVES: Kill one captain, loot one treasure

The Hugros Hideout **(3)** is inside a very large cave. It's best to approach from the mountaintop above the cave opening. Once inside, use Senu to mark enemies through the rock to make it easier to find them. Stand above the entrance and shoot the patrolling bandit near the water below; then drop to the lower ledge **(4)**.

Shoot the bandit on the ledges to the left, deeper in the cave. He stands near an arrow supply.

Now get to his ledge and move across the short bridge back to the right side. Along this bridge you can pivot to your left and shoot a bandit standing on the next ledge. After the bridge, hide in the grass to the right of the next cave opening; a couple bandits are gathered deeper in the cave.

Get their attention by shooting a vase near them. If two bandits investigate your location, assassinate one and either take the other out with a weapon or dive into the water below to avoid detection.

If you dive into the water, you find a nook with loot and discover a lot of tall grass that allows you to move around undetected. You can head back to shore through the tall grass

and reach the treasure chests near the tents, one of which contains the artifact.

SPEAK TO MERKES

Finish off the captain in the cave to complete the location objective and then return to Merkes **(5)**, who is now at the northwest edge of the Sneferu's pyramid. There's one part missing and it's at the top of Sneferu's pyramid.

REACH THE TOP OF THE TOMB OF SNEFERU

Climb the west side of Sneferu's pyramid. At the top, you spot the third artifact in the capstone **(6)**. Bayek places the three artifacts in the empty slots to complete the diagram. It points you to a vault in the ruins to the east.

SPEAK TO MERKES ABOUT THE DIAGRAM

Merkes **(7)** has moved to the pyramid's east side, so while on top, shimmy around to the east side and slide down the pyramid. Talk to Merkes.

ESCORT MERKES TO THE TEMPLE RUINS

Merkes mounts the nearby camel. Take the one next to him and escort him east to the ruins **(8)**. You dismount and walk into the ruins to the vault entrance **(9)** covered in sand.

Bayek uncovers the vault entrance. Shoot the wooden barricade from the entrance.

ESCORT MERKES INTO THE VAULT

Drop into the vault, light a torch, and follow the tunnel until you cross some cobras. Shoot the cobras and continue down a ladder into the final chamber, where you discover a treasure with a rare weapon inside and a model pyramid in the middle of the room.

SPEAK TO MERKES

Talk to Merkes to complete the quest.

RITES OF ANUBIS

Prerequisite: Discover Saqqara Nome

SUGGESTED LEVEL: 23

REWARD: 1,500 XP

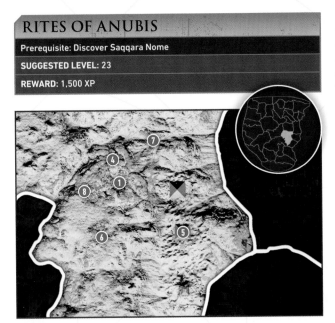

SPEAK TO NEFERTARI

NITRIA

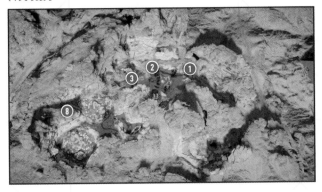

FOLLOW NEFERTARI

Follow Nefertari as she catches you up on the natron mine. Her first stop is at a wounded worker **(2)**; she administers natron to disinfect the wound.

The next stop is at the top of the hill **(3)**. Nefertari asks you to light the three torches at the Anubis shrines. There's one to the south **(6)**, one atop the natural well **(4)**, and one inside the Bent Pyramid **(5)**.

FIND AND IGNITE THE THREE CEREMONIAL TORCHES

Send Senu up in the air to locate the three torches. Head to the north one first **(4)**. Head across the mine and climb the cliff to reach the natural well.

INVESTIGATE THE WELL FOR THE MISSING TORCH HEAD

NATURAL WELL

Activate Animus Pulse when standing at the top of the well. Interact with the fallen torch and the broken fence with traces of blood. Dive into the well below and pull up to the ledge to interact with the pool of blood. Dive into the water and interact with the floating body. Lastly, dive underwater and find the torch head.

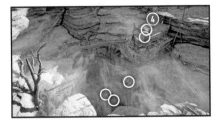

INVESTIGATE THE WELL FOR THE MISSING TORCH HEAD

NATURAL WELL

Activate Animus Pulse when standing at the top of the well. Interact with the fallen torch and the broken fence with traces of blood. Dive into the well below and pull up to the ledge to interact with the pool of blood. Dive into the water and interact with the floating body. Lastly, dive underwater and find the torch head.

REPAIR THE BROKEN WELL

Place the ceremonial lamp piece on the lamp (Bayek stands it up and finds a charm under it). Light the ceremonial torch with your own torch. Ride to the Bent Pyramid **(5)**. Following the road, you'll pass the stranded natron caravan **(7)**. Be careful of the bandit ambush that occurs if you loot the treasure. It's worth it.

THE BENT PYRAMID OF SNEFERU

Enter the Bent Pyramid of Sneferu **(5)**. For instructions on getting into the chamber, see Side Quest: First Blood. This is also where the torch is located. Once inside, light the torch and then head for the final torch at the hyena lair.

SAQQARA HYENA LAIR

On your way to the hyena lair **(6)**, you will likely encounter some bandits on horseback. Defeat them before you get to the hyena lair so you don't have double the enemies to deal with.

Defeat the Level 23 hyenas and the Level 25 leader to complete the location objective. Use Animus Pulse to locate some strange clues. Check out the hanging pig carcass and the charms in the cave containing the torch.

Light the torch in the cave and collect the loot (treasure is behind the pig carcass and the hyena parts).

SPEAK TO NEFERTARI

NITRIA

Speak to Nefertari **(8)**, who is at the end of a long, high platform overlooking Nitria. This unlocks Side Quest: When Night Falls.

Prerequisite: Complete Side Quest: Rites of Anubis

SUGGESTED LEVEL: 23 | **REWARDS: 2,000 XP, Rare Mount**

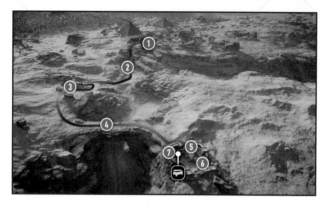

SPEAK TO SUPHIA AT NIGHT ABOUT THE REBELS' NEEDS

NITRIA

Talk to Suphia **(1)** at night.

Mount your horse and follow Nefertari and her rebel contact as they ride north down the trail out of Nitria. Select a warrior bow, a fast light bow, and a long weapon such as a spear or heavy blunt. You could run into random traveling bandit trouble where your route meets the main road **(2)**.

Trouble is certain as you pass a bandit outpost along the curvy road incline **(3)**. Have the warrior bow ready to splatter some bandits. You'll be in the clear once you get beyond the rock bridge **(4)**. Enter Ekdikesis Outpost and meet your posse in the left corner **(5)**.

CARRY THE WOUNDED REBELS TO THE BACK OF THE FORT

EKDIKESIS OUTPOST

Prerequisite: Approach the Outpost
LOCATION REWARD: 300 XP
LOCATION OBJECTIVES: Loot one treasure

As you enter the gate, find the treasure behind a supply stack in the corner to the right.

Now pick up the three wounded bodies **(5)** and

place them on the blankets **(6)** in the back of the fort. Meditate to nighttime (if it's not already) before you drop the third wounded rebel on his blanket. Suphia doublecrosses you and lights the brazier, calling the regime! A battle with Roman soldiers occurs instantly.

DEFEND THE REBELS

A small force of about five soldiers and archers attacks. The main threat is the Level 23 leader named Uset. He's heavily armored and has a full body shield. Run from him to take out the problematic fire archers first and then try to sweep up the other soldiers before taking on Uset. Use shield break moves on him and dodge often to get behind him to land sword or spear strikes. You can also escape the battle and run to the top of the wall, then come back down over Uset for a leap attack.

CONFRONT SUPHIA

After clearing the regime from the fort, climb the ladder to the brazier tower and deal with Suphia.

A REBEL ALLIANCE

Prerequisite: Discover Saqqara Nome

SUGGESTED LEVEL: 24 | **REWARDS: 1,500 XP**

DISCOVER THEODOROS'S PRISON CART

SAQQARA NOME

When traveling along the main road west of Nitria, you encounter a small troop of soldiers taking a break from transporting the prisoner, Theodoros **(1)**. Break's over when you approach; they get up and mount their horses. Stage your attack here or lure them southwest down the road to a band of Theodoros's men **(2)** waiting to ambush the soldiers and free him themselves.

Use a warrior bow and a light bow with good speed to finish off the soldiers guarding the prisoner. When they are all dead, enter the back of the prison cart. Carry Theodoros out and speak to him.

ESCORT THEODOROS THE REBEL TO BAKCHIAS

BAKCHIAS

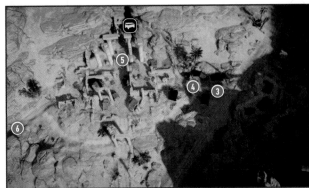

Theodoros mounts a horse and continues telling you his life story as you escort him down the road and into the small camp of Bakchias **(3)**. Dismount and follow him as he heads deeper into the camp.

Not too far into the camp, a battle breaks out **(4)** between Roman soldiers and the rebels. Help them defeat the Level 24 enemies. Concentrate your efforts on the large brute with the full-length shield first. Use shield break moves and dodge to get to his fleshy backside. Unleash an adrenaline special attack on him to finish him off. Then help the rebels kill the weaker soldiers.

Follow Theodoros to the northern headquarters section **(5)** of Bakchias.

Before you head off on the mission, head farther north to the back of the headquarters area. Find the hole on the right that leads down to a tunnel. Loot the containers in the first room, kill the cobras in the hallway, and climb the ladder to a small ledge where the treasure is located.

FIND THE SCRIBE IN KARANIS AND BRING HIM TO THEODOROS

KARANIS

Ride west out of Bakchias **(6)**, heading for the city of Karanis **(7)**. Synchronize with the Viewpoint **(7)** on top of the Sarapeion of Karanis.

Get to Derratos's scribe while he rests around nighttime. From the Viewpoint **(7)**, slide down the rope **(8)** at the edge of the Sarapeion rooftop to the rooftop **(9)** below. Get on the wall walk **(10)** above the scribe's pergola.

Put the two Level 24 soldiers **(11)** to sleep with darts. If you don't have them, shoot one after the other in the head very quickly with arrows.

CARRY DERRATOS'S SCRIBE TO BAKCHIAS

Pick up the sleeping scribe, put him on a horse, and ride back to Bakchias **(5)**. Take the scribe off the horse and place him in the marker at Theodoros's feet.

This unlocks the Level 25 Side Quest: Rebel Strike.

FAIYUM

AMBUSH AT SEA

ULC

Prerequisite: Complete Main Quest: Pompeius Magnus

SUGGESTED LEVEL: 28   **REWARDS:** 3,000 XP   **UNLOCKS:** Exclusive for Deluxe and Gold editions of Assassin's Creed Origins.   **DETAILS:** A flamboyant storyteller on the streets of Faiyum entertains Bayek with a wild account of Aya and Phoxida's first naval mission against the Gabiniani.

SPEAK TO THE STORYTELLER

LEGEND

1   Storyteller (Quest Start)

Locate and speak to the storyteller **(1)** on the eastern coast of Faiyum Oasis. Without knowing you are the main character's husband in the story, he begins to tell you about the incredible sea battle.

SINK THE GABINIANI FLEET

Travel the 700+ meters to the Gabiniani fleet. As you near, you come up against four battleships. Avoid driving right down the center or you can get surrounded. Instead, steer to the left side of the leftmost ship or the right side of the rightmost. Shoot for the weak spots and take advantage of any ramming opportunities that arise.

One more ship of equal size appears after you destroy the first four. Steer beside it and destroy it as you did the previous ships.

SAIL EAST TO THE MAIN GABINIANI FLEET

Now travel east around 1,000 meters to confront the main Gabiniani naval force. There are three ships: two the size of what you've faced already and one massive warship, the pride of their fleet. Brace for impact from fireballs as you approach.

Steer around the large ship and ram one of the smaller ones. You need to attack the large one when the opportunity arises, but do this only after you sink the little ones.

There are three areas of weakness on each side of the large warship. When you can, ram the sides of the ship to do the greatest amount of damage and to recharge your weapons more quickly. Use firebombs when at close range and between arrow attacks. Continue to circle the ship and avoid getting too far in

front of it so you can avoid being rammed by the warship.

After defeating the warship, you are returned to Bayek and the storyteller finishes his tale. You receive a letter from Aya. In it she conveys the news of an alliance being made with Pompey, but those they've tracked so far were not their son's killers. There are two more they must now chase down: the Scorpion and the Jackal. These two are with Pompey's royal guard. Aya will join you in Herakleion.

MURDER IN THE TEMPLE

Prerequisite: Discover Faiyum

SUGGESTED LEVEL: 24   **Reward:** 1,000 XP

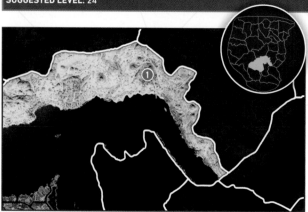

The local phylakitai **(1)** at the Sarapeion asks Bayek to help his murder investigation.

INVESTIGATE THE TEMPLE

KARANIS

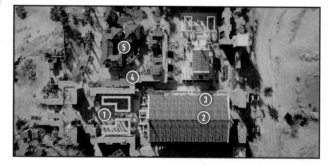

Enter the Sarapeion of Karanis **(2)** and begin the murder investigation. Inspect the overturned and bloody chair, then the green paint on the statue's left foot. Climb up the statue and jump from the left arm to the right. Inspect the Wadjet mask on its right shoulder.

Follow the painted green wood platform from the right arm to the second-level room. Inspect the Killer's Letter on the bloody lounge chair.

In the next section of the second-floor room, find the papyrus puzzle **(3)** for the temple on a table behind the screen.

SPEAK TO THE PHYLAKITAI

Return to the first floor and talk to the phylakitai about what the letter said.

KILL THE BANDITS HOLDING THE HIGH PRIEST

Follow the phylakitai as he runs out of the temple, turns left, and heads up a ladder on a tall city wall **(4)**. Killers are harassing the priest in the nearby courtyard **(5)**.

Three bandits are about to kill the high priest. Take one out with an arrow to the head before they start scrambling. Either remain on the wall flinging arrows or leap down there and get your hands dirty. Just finish them off. There are two archers and one with a full-body shield. Save the priest.

Afterward, both the high priest and the phylakitai thank you. Stick around in the courtyard after completing the quest; a lady runs up to you, asking for your help. This unlocks Side Quest: Feeding Faiyum.

FEEDING FAIYUM

Prerequisite: Complete Side Quest: Murder in the Temple
SUGGESTED LEVEL: 24
REWARD: 2,500 XP

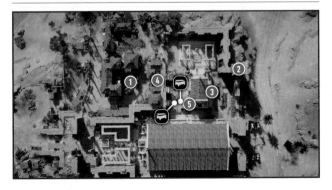

SPEAK TO THE STONEMASON'S WIFE

Speak to the stonemason's wife **(1)**.

SPEAK TO THE STONEMASON

Speak to the stonemason **(2)** on the northwest fortifying wall.

INVESTIGATE BENEATH THE KARANIS TEMPLE

Have Senu search the area around the temple. Mark the soldiers around and under the temple. You can also find two different entrances to the tunnel below the temple. We suggest using the north one **(3)** closest to the stonemason's position. The one farther south **(4)** makes a good exit.

Jump down to the tall scaffold with the jutting poles. You can survive the next jump to the tunnel entrance by performing a drop assassination on the soldier below.

UNDERGROUND STASH

Enter the tunnel cautiously and eliminate the three soldiers inside.

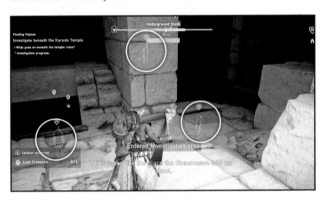

Break down the stick doorway that seals the small room **(5)** with two treasures inside. The underground stash! This completes a location objective.

Enter the room behind the hanging canvas. Use Animus Pulse to identify the clues in the room. Inspect the message from the butcher on the floor near the fire can.

FIND AND GET THE PAYMENT NEAR THE BATHING SOBEK STATUE

SUNKEN TEMPLE OF PNEPHEROS

Exit the tunnel and head southwest out of town. Ride toward the marker off the coast near the Sunken Temple of Pnepheros **(6)**. Send Senu up over the statue in the water. Have her mark the treasures below. Notice the crocodiles in the water and the soldiers on the boats.

Sail a boat or just swim over the objective marker and then dive underwater. The crocodiles do not bother you; they're too busy harassing the soldiers who are also looking for the stash.

Head down into the chamber below the feet of the sunken statue. Loot the chest at the bottom of the stairs. Bayek mentions the engraving on the chest depicting Soknopaiou, the village west of here. Continue into the underwater chamber and open the glowing chest. Loot the treasure bags around it. Bayek mentions the coins in the bags possibly came from the storehouse.

Collect the treasure near the pillar before the stairs that lead beneath the statue and nab the treasure above the chamber behind the statue to complete the location objective. Swim to shore and ride west to Soknopaiou Nesos **(7)**.

FIND THE STOREHOUSE IN SOKNOPAIOU NESOS

SOKNOPAIOU NESOS

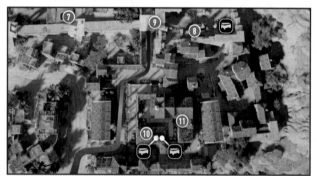

Send Senu to locate the storehouse **(7)** and the guards around it. There are two entrances into the tunnels under the storehouse. Continue flying Senu around areas we've marked on our map so you can find the east entrance **(8)** and treasures.

We like using the east entrance. Ride through the main gate **(9)**, climb the partial wall, and drop-assassinate the soldier near the stairs when the second soldier walks away.

INVESTIGATE THE STOREHOUSE

THE STOREHOUSE

The storeroom is at the end of the tunnel. There are three Level 24 to 25 soldiers inside. You can hit them with sleep darts, start with arrows, or just go in there and slaughter them with a heavy blunt.

There are three clues inside the storehouse—ledger entries and grain on the floor. Inspect the urgent message for the butcher to get the butcher's location. It's on the table under the wall torch where one of the guards was sitting.

CONFRONT THE BUTCHER IN HIS UPSTAIRS OFFICE

VAULT OF SPLENDORS

Head out of the storehouse through the cavelike tunnel to the east. Climb the ladder slowly as you come up inside a small house **(10)** with a couple very large brutes inside. This is the Vault of Splendors. There are two treasures to loot after you kill the guards. One brute has his back to you as you come out of the hole. Assassinate him and then throw a sleep dart at the second brute at the door in case he turns around. Assassinate him and then loot the two chests in the room.

Exit this house and look left for the ladders on the side of the neighboring home **(11)**. This is the butcher's building (it also has a Viewpoint on the rooftop). Before you climb up to his office, select weapons you would choose if you were suddenly surrounded by three assailants in a small room. Climb the ladders. When you approach the open door, a cinematic introduces you to the butcher and his two bodyguards.

ASSASSINATE THE BUTCHER IN HIS UPSTAIRS OFFICE

You go up against the butcher's two "bodyguards." They are weak, Level 23 goons with no armor and no moxie. Finish them off quickly and use your adrenaline special attack on the butcher. Confirm the butcher's kill to complete the quest.

CURSE OF THE WADJET

Prerequisite: Discover Faiyum

SUGGESTED LEVEL: 25	REWARDS: 3,750 XP

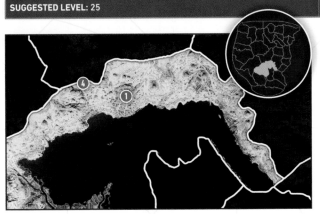

INVESTIGATE THE CURSE OF WADJET IN THE GREEK

SOKNOPAIOU NESOS

Speak to the stuttering man **(1)** in Soknopaiou Nesos.

Head north to the crime scene **(2)**. Inspect the bloody, burned body on the ground. Shoot the vase and kill the cobra inside. Speak to the Greek guy in green who is bent over cleaning up the mess.

FIND THE CARETAKER'S SHRINE

WADJET'S BURROW

Location Objective: Loot one treasure
REWARD: 300 XP

Send Senu west to find the entrance **(3)** into the Wadjet's Burrow. Enter the cave entrance. Throw torches into the main room to ignite all the oil vases inside and to burn most of the cobras

hiding inside large vases. Scan the floor with a bow to find living cobras. Kill them. Collect all the loot and find the treasure against the back-right wall to complete the location objective.

EXPLORE THE CARETAKER'S SHRINE

Read the Caretaker's Letter on the candlelit table in the back of the cave.

ASSASSINATE THE WADJET-WORSHIPPING CARETAKER

The racist guy and two very competent bandit fighters, who are well armored and skilled with their weapons, are waiting to ambush you outside the cave **(3)**. Slowly move around the last bend in the tunnel and take out the racist with an arrow to the head; then quickly weaken the two bodyguards with arrows before they rush you.

If the battle starts in the narrow tunnel, run outside and deal with them in the open. Fight around the vase outside, so when they get smashed, the cobra inside could preoccupy one of the bandits long enough for you to kill the other. Dodge often to get beside or behind the target; their large shields prevent most straight-on attacks. Try a very powerful, quick sword. Use your adrenaline special to finish off one of them. Confirm the main target's death.

FIND AND RESCUE THE HOSTAGE IN PANNOUKI

PANNOUKI HIDEOUT

Prerequisite: Approach the Outpost
SUGGESTED LEVEL: 26
LOCATION REWARD: 300 XP
LOCATION OBJECTIVES: Kill one captain, loot one treasure

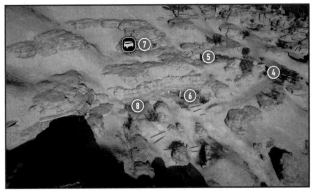

Head northwest to the Pannouki Hideout and avoid the two guards **(4)** east of the hideout. Send Senu to locate the hostage. Find the guard platform **(5)** with arrows higher up the mountain and above the main entrance **(6)**. Use the ladder in the hole to access the first landing. Mark the two bandits in the room below using a bow. If you have sleep darts, crouch and hit them in the legs to put them to sleep. Drop down and execute them. This often forces the Level 27 captain to patrol. Hide behind the hallway corner and stealthily execute him when he shows up. Alternatively, throw torches down the hole and the entire place will go up in flames, but the hostage will be safe.

Slide under the hole in the wall and take the treasure to complete the location objective. Pick up the hostage near the treasure and carry him out the main entrance **(6)**. Head west to avoid any enemies you may have left alive. If that exit is still heavily guarded, stick to the right walls, heading west from the hostage's pickup location. You'll enter a front room with barricaded windows. One window has a V-shaped opening **(8)** that you can slip through while holding the hostage. Once clear of the hideout, put him down and talk to him.

SPEAK WITH THE HOSTAGE

Speak to the freed hostage. He thanks you without a stutter. This completes the quest.

REBEL STRIKE

Prerequisite: Complete Side Quest: A Rebel Alliance

SUGGESTED LEVEL: 25	REWARDS: 1,000 XP

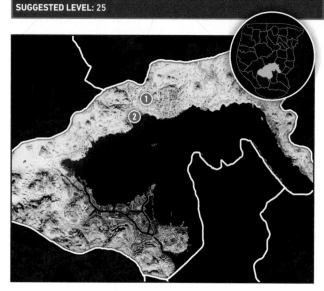

RAID THE CAMP WITH THEODOROS AND HIS MEN

Find Theodoros's rebel troops **(1)** camping in the hills north of the Beached Trireme Camp **(2)**. Talk with them and then wait for Theodoros to arrive. Follow his men to the horses nearby and ride south to the camp.

BEACHED TRIREME CAMP

Prerequisite: Approach the camp
SUGGESTED LEVEL: 25
LOCATION REWARD: 600 XP
LOCATION OBJECTIVES: Kill one captain, loot one treasure

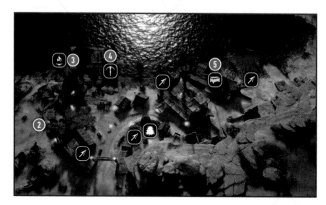

The camp is full of soldiers of every type. There's also a Level 27 captain and Derratos, a Level 25 soldier armed with a heavy blunt mace.

Theodoros's men enter through the east beach entrance **(2)**. Follow them in and assist with any enemies near the gate. Get to the top of the brazier tower **(3)** and set the trap. When you leave the tower, use the ballista **(4)** on any enemies in sight.

Afterward, it's all about moving around cautiously and picking your targets. Help the rebels eliminate everyone in the camp and on the docked ships, including the captain and Derratos. Yellow markers appear above the few remaining enemies to help you find them.

CONFIRM DERRATOS'S KILL

When the battle is won, look for Derratos's corpse and confirm the kill. Speak to Theodoros again. Get the treasure from the westernmost ship **(5)** to complete the location objective.

THE BRIDE

Prerequisite: Approach the bride on the cliff's edge
SUGGESTED LEVEL: 26
REWARD: 2,250 XP

SPEAK TO THE GIRL

SOKNOPAIOU NESOS

A young woman **(1)** stands inert on a high cliff in Soknopaiou Nesos. Climb up the cliff and talk to her.

STAY WITH THE GIRL

Remain talking to the girl. Eventually you decide to bring her a feather.

GET A HERON FEATHER

If you don't
have any heron
feathers in your
inventory, head
down to the
beach **(2)** to the
southwest to find
a flock of heron
by the water.

Approach slowly and stick an arrow in one. Grab the feather.

GIVE THE GIRL THE HERON FEATHER

Return to the girl on the cliff **(1)** to give her the feather.

FOLLOW TUAA

Follow Tuaa down the cliff. She continues to chat as you head back toward town.

DEFEND TUAA FROM THE LEOPARDS

Before you can round
the last turn into town, a
pack of Level 15 to 26
leopards attacks **(3)**. Use
a powerful and quick
sword to slice and dice
them up before they can
harm your friend.

ESCORT TUAA TO THE DOCKS

Call you mount. Tuaa will ride with you. Head to the pier **(4)**. Walk her into the marker on the pier to complete the quest.

SOBEK'S GOLD

Prerequisite: Discover Faiyum
SUGGESTED LEVEL: 27
REWARD: 2,250 XP

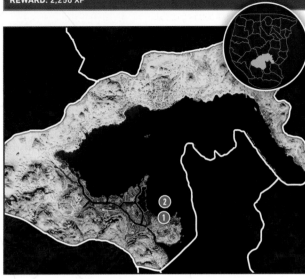

FIND AND GET THE GOLD SOBEKS

EUHEMERIA

A young priest **(1)** is accused of stealing gold icons. Bayek sets out to prove the boy's innocence.

Grab a boat from the
shore and sail out
toward the Okteres
Blockade **(2)**. This is
a group of four large
battleships parked off
the coast of Euhemeria.
Send Senu up to locate

the two gold Sobeks. There's one on the bow of a ship in the blockade, and the other is deep underwater in the sunken trireme wreckage.

SUNKEN TRIREME

Prerequisite: Approach the sunken ship
LOCATION REWARD: 450 XP
LOCATION OBJECTIVES: Loot two treasures

Dive underwater and get the Gold Sobek Statue **(2)** from the sunken trireme before tackling the blockade. Dive in just east of the third ship in the blockade, and use Animus Pulse to locate the two treasures in the wreckage and the statue between the two chests.

Prerequisite: Approach the blockade

SUGGESTED LEVEL: 28   LOCATION REWARD: 900 XP   LOCATION OBJECTIVES: Kill one captain and one commander, loot two treasures

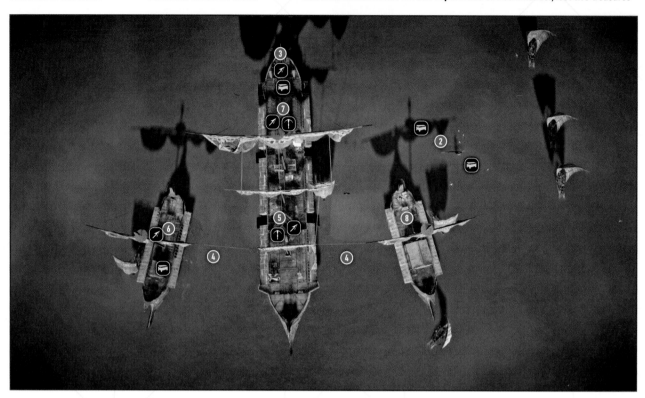

All three ships in the blockade are connected via high mast ropes **(4)**. This makes traveling from one ship to the next a snap. And being that high keeps you out of sight.

You can use the ballista on the south platform to shoot enemies on the west ship **(6)** and use the north ballista **(7)** to shoot enemies on the east ship's stern **(8)**; there's not enough pivot to cover the entire east ship.

You can dive into the water to avoid detection. There's always the hang-on-the-edge trick to throw unsuspecting soldiers overboard, which is a good way to start the attack.

Defeat everyone on the three ships and collect the two treasures to complete the location objective. Grab the Gold Sobek Statue **(3)** from the stern of the center ship to complete the objective.

GIVE THE GOLD SOBEKS TO THE SOBEK PRIEST

Have a warrior bow ready when you return to the elder priest **(1)**. A battle begins with the elder and two of his large brute bodyguards.

SAVE THE YOUNG PRIEST

Shoot the elder priest dead before his goons can get to you. Destroy the two Level 27 brutes. After all aggressors are dead, approach the poor priest boy.

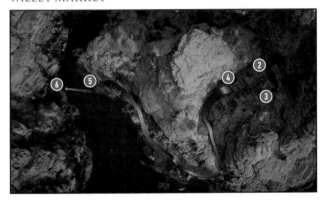

across the river. She's being held captive by three very capable Level 27 to 29 bandits.

RESCUE THE GIRL'S MOTHER

You can take the boat across the river and just start fighting or you can jump in the water, get close enough to get a one-hit-kill headshot, and then finish off the last two in a swordfight. Or you can swim underwater up to the shore, enter the tall grass to stay stealthy, and lure the bandits to their death. Use sleep darts to keep things under control. The bandit with the shield is a very capable fighter, so make him the stealth kill target.

After you deal with the threat, free the girl's mother. She gives you a Siwan Legendary sickle sword.

FIND AND INVESTIGATE THE SIWAN STALL IN VALLEY MARKET

EUHEMERIA

A man **(1)** wanders the northern streets of Euhemeria and tells you to check out the Valley Market.

VALLEY MARKET

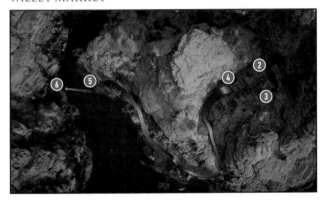

Follow the objective marker south to the narrow valley to discover the Valley Market **(2)**.

LOCATION OBJECTIVE: PAPYRUS PUZZLE

Find the Blasphemer Papyrus Puzzle on a table at a market booth **(3)** in the row of shops on the upper west ledge. For information on solving the puzzle, see the Activities section.

Approach the sales booth **(4)** and inspect the fake treasure on the table of the Siwan treasure shop. Talk to the little girl at the booth.

THE ESSENTIALS

MAIN QUESTS

SIDE QUESTS

ACTIVITIES

ATLAS

REFERENCE & ANALYSIS

SPEAK TO THE HEALER IN EUHEMERIA SLUMS

EUHEMERIA SLUMS

Talk to the young woman healer **(1)** in the Euhemeria slums.

INVESTIGATE THE STRANGE SICKNESS IN EUHEMERIA HARBOR

Follow the healer west down the road to the shell of a building. Activate Animus Pulse to locate the clues. Interact with the filthy bowls on the ground and the dead body on the gurney.

Enter the storage room behind the wall and investigate the seasoning urns and the rancid food in large vases.

food comes from and she tells you a merchant makes it for the poor. He's in the south section of town. She shows you the way.

FOLLOW THE HEALER TO THE MERCHANT'S HOME

Follow the fast healer as she runs west and then crosses the wooden bridge into town. Continue to follow her east to the estate **(2)**.

INVESTIGATE THE FOOD MERCHANT'S HOME

Pass through the merchant's home to the backyard, hop the fence, and select a powerful warrior bow. Enter the small building in the back **(5)** and you'll meet the merchant responsible for the rancid food that's making people sick. He has two soldiers with him.

ASSASSINATE THE FOOD MERCHANT

Draw your warrior bow and shoot the Level 28 soldiers directly in the face as soon as the cinematic ends. One shot apiece should do them in. The merchant is the lesser of the three evils, so save him for last. Confirm the merchant's death to complete the quest.

FIRES OF DIONYSIAS

Prerequisite: Meet Hotephres during Main Quest: The Crocodile's Scales

SUGGESTED LEVEL: 37

REWARDS: 4,500 XP, Rare Shield

SPEAK TO THE FARMERS OF DIONYSIAS

Talk to the young, tough woman named Zahra **(1)** in the ashes of her farm in Faiyum. She wants your help.

FOLLOW ZAHRA

Mount the nearby horse and follow Zahra west out of her farm and into Dionysias. You stop at a farm villa **(2)** where bandits have invaded and are holding the landowner in captivity.

FIND AND RESCUE THE GREEK LANDOWNER

Zahra insists on fighting by your side. Send Senu up to locate the landowner on the villa's second floor. You'll also find several Level 37 bandits scattered throughout the property.

Use the warrior bow on the bandit at the front gate; then climb the yard wall so that you enter the grounds behind the remaining bandit in the front yard. Assassinate him.

Enter the front door, sneak upstairs slowly, and assassinate the bandit with the landowner. If you have the chain assassinate ability, use it on the next bandit on the exterior balcony.

TAKE THE GREEK LANDOWNER OUT OF THE VILLA

Pick up the landowner and carry him downstairs and out the front door. Exit the yard and set him down to talk to him.

SPEAK TO THE GREEK LANDOWNER

When you ask if he knows where the bandit nest is located, he tells you that servants tracked riders coming south form the White Desert.

FIND AND ASSASSINATE THE BANDIT LEADER

WHITE DESERT

Mount horses and ride south over the mountains, heading for the White Desert Sobek Ruins **(4)**. Expect to meet bandits on horseback on the mountain road **(3)**. Use a heavy blunt or your favorite long weapon to take them out while remaining on your mount.

WHITE DESERT SOBEK RUINS

Prerequisite: Approach the Ruins

SUGGESTED LEVEL: 38

LOCATION REWARD: 450 XP

LOCATION OBJECTIVES: Loot three treasures

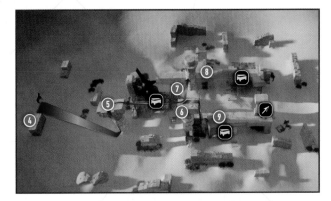

Send Senu up to locate the bandit leader when you near the White Desert Sobek Ruins. Mark the three treasures and the Level 38 to 39 bandits. A good approach is from the east **(4)**.

Climb up the northeastern pillar **(5)** and cross the rope connected to the next pillar **(6)**. From here you can wait for patrols to line up underneath you, where assassinations

will be stealthy. Cross the rope heading south to drop-assassinate the bandit patrolling **(7)** below, or put arrows in the heads of the bandits on the ledge **(8)**.

Eventually the leader **(9)** sits at his desk with the treasure. Drop down the north side of the ruin walls to assassinate him from behind. When you confirm the kill, you receive a letter: the Blessing of Ra. It's a letter from Son of Ra, so this wasn't the guy you're looking for. Before you leave, collect the treasures.

FIND AND ASSASSINATE THE BANDIT LORD, SON OF RA

DIONYSIAS CARAVANSERAI

Prerequisite: Approach the fort
SUGGESTED LEVEL: 38   **LOCATION REWARD: 900 XP**   **LOCATION OBJECTIVES: Kill one captain and one commander, loot two treasures**

Travel northwest to Dionysias Caravanserai **(10)** back in Faiyum. Send Senu over the medium military stronghold to mark the Son of Ra (who is in a cage). Mark all the bandits and treasures too. Be aware, if you have not killed him already, Phylake, Ra's Mercy, is in the area. Make setting the brazier trap priority.

Climb up the northwest tower **(10)** and pull the solider out of the window (if he's there). Access the rooftop to set the brazier trap. Head northeast through the next tower and grab some arrows. Continue across the top of the commander's office **(11)** and leap into the haystack on the wall walk.

If the commander is not in his office, wait until he sits down at his desk or take him out another way. If he is sitting at his desk, assassinate him from behind. However, this could cause attention if it comes to combat. Use the hiding booth in his office to hide from investigating bandits.

From this wall walk, use the fire from the commander's doorway to light arrows. Shoot the oil vases around the prisons **(12)** to light up the entire area and defeat the caged Son of Ra without laying a finger on him. You also burn the lions in the cages next to him.

Continue through the fort, taking full advantage of the many hiding booths, high towers, suspended ropes, and ballista **(13)** to take out the remaining occupants. The captain **(14)** hangs out in the shipping area at the fort's north end.

CONFIRM THE KILL

After defeating the Son of Ra, confirm the kill to enter the kill room, where you help him pass into the next realm.

SPEAK TO ZAHRA

Head to the small village street north of the fort to find Zahra **(15)**. She is delighted you helped her stop the farm burnings.

DEMONS IN THE DESERT

Prerequisite: Meet Hotephres during Main Quest: The Crocodile's Scales

SUGGESTED LEVEL: 39

REWARDS: 2,500 XP

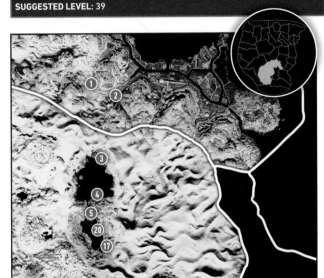

SPEAK TO THE MADMAN

Speak to the madman **(1)** wandering the streets around Dionysias Caravanserai.

FIND AND SPEAK TO THE BOY

Ride southeast to the broken tower **(2)**. Send Senu up to locate the boy in the tower, which is surrounded by a pack of Level 39 hyenas. Ride in with a long weapon and start playing hyena polo. Defeat them all and then talk to the boy.

He tells you that their village was attacked by bandits and that he's going back.

FOLLOW RAHOTEP THE SURVIVOR

Follow Rahotep to his camel to the south. Follow him through the sandstorm into the region of White Desert Oasis. Select your warrior bow and be ready to attack another pack of hyenas at the lake **(3)**.

Kill the hyenas, and Rahotep continues his journey across the lake to the south shore **(4)**. When you reach shore and speak to Rahotep, you convince him to stay back so he won't get hurt.

FIND AND RESCUE THE FARMERS OF DIONYSIAS

DESERT WATERFALLS HIDEOUT

Prerequisite: Approach the hideout

SUGGESTED LEVEL: 39 or more   **LOCATION REWARD: 900 XP**   **LOCATION OBJECTIVES: Kill one captain and one commander, loot two treasures**

INTRODUCTION

THE ESSENTIALS

MAIN QUESTS

SIDE QUESTS

ACTIVITIES

ATLAS

REFERENCE & ANALYSIS

From the shore **(4)**, head toward the first guard tower using the tall grass **(5)** for cover. Shoot the bandit out of the tower **(6)**. Quickly put arrows in the two bandits guarding the gate **(7)**.

Enter the hideout through the gate **(7)** and take a distant shot at the bandit **(8)** near the bridge at the shallow stream. Get into the tall shrubbery around the large round hut **(9)** and pick off nearby bandits with arrows.

If you mess up and a few begin coming for you, then throw sleep darts at them and finish them off with a warrior bow or a stealth assassination as they sleep. This is a great way to take out any high-level enemy, such as the captain in the area.

When the entry area is clear, run into the cave between the two waterfalls and grab the treasure. Enter the captain's tent **(11)** and steal the other treasure.

Head to the hideout's southwest corner **(12)** and eliminate the bandits camping out around the tower.

The commander patrols the pathway in front of the prisoners **(14)**. Now that it's only you and the commander in the area, take some shots at him. Even if he puts up a fight, he has no backup. Eliminate him. You could release the crocodile from the cage **(15)** using a fire arrow and let him distract the commander while you attack him from behind.

ESCORT THE FARMERS OUT OF THE HIDEOUT

Release the farmers from the cell **(14)** and follow them out the southeast exit **(16)**. They'll assist you in eliminating any remaining bandits you encounter on the way.

You and the farmers meet up with Rahotep on the east road. He discovers his father is not among the crowd. One of the farmers told him that the demons took him to the crocodile pit. Rahotep rallies the group together to free his father. Resupply your arrows from the camp in preparation for the next battle.

RESCUE RAHOTEP'S FATHER FROM LARDER STATION

LARDER STATION HIDEOUT
Prerequisite: Approach the hideout
SUGGESTED LEVEL: 39
LOCATION REWARD: 600 XP
LOCATION OBJECTIVES: Kill one captain, loot one treasure

Ride east down the road to Larder Station Hideout **(17)**. Use your warrior bow and sleeping darts to take out the captain and then help the others defeat the remaining bandits.

CARRY RAHOTEP'S FATHER TO THE DOCKS OUTSIDE THE CAMP

Find the treasure in the farthest hut **(18)**. Pick up Rahotep's father from the pier **(19)**. Carry him out of the camp and place him on the dock **(20)**.

FAIYUM OASIS

THE CHAMPION

Prerequisite: Discover Faiyum Oasis

SUGGESTED LEVEL: 28

REWARDS: 2,250 XP, Rare Shield

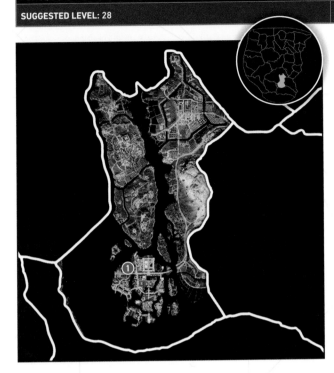

HELP THE OLD FIGHTER

KROKODILOPOLIS

Head to the bulkhead northeast from the arena to find some brawny fellows fistfighting in the middle of an excited crowd. Talk to the old one, and watch him get his butt beat by the younger gladiator.

Interact with the winner of the bout and a challenge begins: a fistfight between you and the young gladiator. You have all the moves you are accustomed to but no weapons. You can block, hit light or hit hard, target the opponent, and dodge. Annihilate him. Interact with the old fighter who's lying on the ground.

FOLLOW THE OLD FIGHTER

Follow the old man as he heads south in front of the arena. He asks you to take his place in some of his fights, cheerfully assuming the role of the fight teacher, much to Bayek's bemusement.

The old man leads you to another street fight location **(2)** in someone's backyard near the water.

SPEAK TO THE OLD FIGHTER

When you are ready to start the fight, speak to the old man and he'll give you some fighting tips.

DEFEAT THE CHALLENGER

This fight is much like the last. This guy rushes you at the start, so begin with a blocking move and then just unleash on him continually, alternating between hard and light attacks. He runs away before you can finish him off.

SPEAK TO THE OLD FIGHTER

Speak to the old fighter. He is impressed and finally asks your name. He tells you the next fight is at the lighthouse at night.

MEET THE OLD FIGHTER ATOP THE LIGHTHOUSE

Go to the top of the lighthouse **(3)** during the day and then meditate the time to night.

FOLLOW THE OLD FIGHTER

The old fighter never shows up once you reach the top of the lighthouse. You hear him calling to you from the ground. Jump from the extended post to dive into the haystack below. When you ask him why he sent you up there, he says that it was good exercise.

RACE THE OLD FIGHTER

A short distance from the lighthouse, Hilarus **(4)** challenges you to a race on foot. The race stops just as you cross the second bridge **(5)**. To blow him away, call your mount and have him race you while you ride.

FOLLOW THE OLD FIGHTER

Follow Hilarus another block west to the brothel **(6)**.

SPEAK TO THE OLD FIGHTER

Speak to the old fighter inside the brothel when you are ready to begin the final fight.

DEFEAT THE BROTHEL CHALLENGER

The guy you fight inside the brothel is a joke. You must be getting suspicious now. When you beat the Level 28 fighter to a pulp, more fighters jump out of the crowd and Hilarus joins in on the brawl.

FIGHT ALONGSIDE HILARUS, THE CAMEL OF HERMES

Hilarus is very capable of handling his opponent. Target-select your new opponent and beat the daylights out of him. Release an adrenaline special on him to end the fight then and there. When the quest is over the old man is released from your services as fight trainer.

THE MAN BEAST
Prerequisite: Discover Faiyum Oasis
SUGGESTED LEVEL: 28
REWARD: 3,000 XP

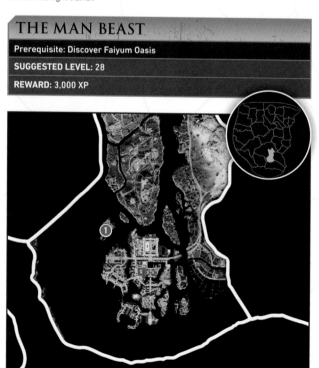

TALK TO THE FISHERMAN

KROKODILOPOLIS

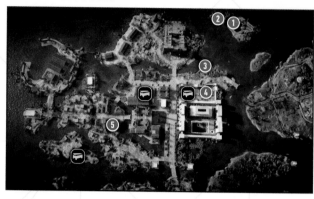

Talk to the fisherman **(1)** on the small northwest island in Krokodilopolis.

INVESTIGATE THE AREA AROUND THE MAN BEAST

Follow the nearby objective marker to the investigation area **(2)** on the same island. Use Animus Pulse to locate the three clues: baskets of fish bait meat (possibly human); broken vases on the shore; and rotting, waterlogged, bloody flesh in the water next to the vases.

FIND THE SOURCE OF THE BODY PARTS

Head to the end of the pier and talk to the little boy. Take a boat and follow the trail of blood floating on the water's surface. Send Senu up to locate the cave entrance **(3)** across the river to the southeast. Exit the boat and enter the watery cave.

EXPLORE THE CAVE

Once in the cave, dive deep underwater and swim through the many floating body parts in the tunnel below to reach a dry, subterranean chamber. Beware of the crocodile when you surface. Wipe it out and then use Animus Pulse to locate clues. You find half-eaten bodies near the crocodile you just killed, and on the other side of the short wall is a seating area.

Head to the right nook to free the prisoner. He tells you that the embalmer is throwing people to the crocodiles while spectators watch. The prisoner says he was kidnapped from the market.

FIND AND ASSASSINATE THE EMBALMER

Follow the bright light in a nearby corner to find a ladder that leads to an exit above. This opens into the embalmer's work area **(4)**.

Use Senu to locate the embalmer **(5)** in Greek Square. Get to the rooftops just before reaching your target. Take out the embalmer and then his large brute bodyguard to complete

the quest. If you have the chain assassination ability, use it.

SOBEK'S TEARS

Prerequisite: Discover Faiyum Oasis

SUGGESTED LEVEL: 29

REWARD: 3,000 XP

SPEAK TO THE GUARDIAN

KROKODILOPOLIS

Talk to the guardian **(1)** on the Temple of Sobek steps.

INVESTIGATE THE SACRED POOL IN THE TEMPLE OF SOBEK

Head north from the steps into the temple and approach the pool **(2)** where the albino crocodile Petsuchos is located. Use Animus Pulse to locate the clues around the pool area. Do not attack Petsuchos.

Investigate the blood on the staircase, the foul-smelling liquid next to the blood on the stairs, and the carcass. The last clue can be seen in a drain through an impassible grate. You must find another way around.

Follow the blood from the stairs out of the pool and into a nearby well **(3)**. Jump into the well and follow the tunnel to the last clue. The final clue is a discarded priest robe covered in blood. Follow the blood trail outside the tunnel.

FIND THE INJURED PERSON

Use Senu to find the injured person (4) on the east shoreline. Have your warrior bow ready to take out the crocodile near the body. Interact with the body to read the Ptolemy soldier's note. You're now looking for Melina the Hibiscus at the southern docks.

ASSASSINATE MELINA THE HIBISCUS

NEORION NAVAL ARSENAL

Prerequisite: Approach the blockade

SUGGESTED LEVEL: 30   **LOCATION REWARD: 900 XP**   **LOCATION OBJECTIVES: Kill one captain and one commander, loot two treasures**

Take a boat near the dead body and paddle it to the Neorion Naval Arsenal (5). Send Senu up to locate Melina the Hibiscus. Your target is usually on the base's west end, but she moves around. You can usually take her out by performing a drop assassination from a rooftop. You get the Letter from Sehetep from her, which points to Sehetep as the one paying her to poison Petsuchos.

Start by docking your boat on the base's southeast side (5) to remain hidden from the two brute guards at the mouth of the docking bay. Scale the wall and enter the first guardhouse,

where you can collect the treasure from the chest on the left wall. There's a hiding booth next to the chest in case a soldier's patrol takes him up the stairs and into this room while you are there.

Continue out of the house, following the wall walk to the gate guardhouse (6). There's a soldier on the balcony outside the fort. Kill him from behind or leave him alive and get to the rooftop of the same guardhouse.

Walk across the rope stretching from this guardhouse to the rooftop of the (Level 31) commander's quarters (7). The commander is often sitting at the desk with the second treasure and with his back to the balcony doorway. Enter in a crouch and assassinate him. Take the treasure and leave. Get back on rooftop.

Return to the commander's rooftop and use the beam on the west end to jump to the boathouse rooftop (8). From here, jump off the beam sticking out on the northeast end

and get to the brazier (9) to set a trap. If you don't need to worry about the alarm, then track down the captain that patrols the west end (10). Drop-assassinate him using the rope suspended from the boathouse to the west guardhouse. Use the haystacks to lure him to you if a rooftop drop is not an option. Melina also starts her patrol from the west end. If you have not taken her out already, use arrows or a drop assassination.

SPEAK TO THE GUARDIAN

Use the Viewpoint at the temple to get back to the guardian (1). Speak to him.

THE JAWS OF SOBEK

Prerequisite: Discover Faiyum Oasis

| SUGGESTED LEVEL: 28 | REWARDS: 3,750 XP | UNLOCKS: Side Quest: Bad Faith |

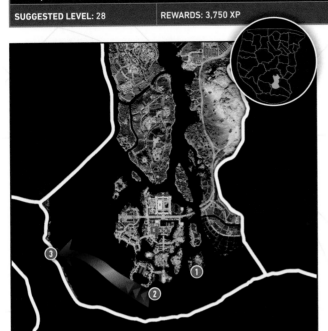

INVESTIGATE THE TANNERY'S STOREROOM

KROKODILOPOLIS

You find a pool of blood beneath the tannery's **(1)** door in Krokodilopolis. You can't break the door down, so climb to the rooftop and drop in through the skylight. Use Animus Pulse to locate the clues in the tannery.

Investigate the gold in the crate near the sealed and bloody doorway, the hanging crocodiles, the baby croc mummies, and the crocodile mummies on the floor that are stuffed with gold and valuables.

REACH THE DOCK NEAR THE TANNERY

Climb back out of the hole in the ceiling and talk to the man outside to the north. You notice that soldiers are harassing him. Shoot the soldiers in the back of the head with arrows before you get close.

RESCUE AND SPEAK TO THE MAN

Free the prisoner and talk to him. The priest tells you that the cult has a trireme that follows trade routes south of the city.

FIND AND GET THE MANIFEST FROM THE CULT'S TRIREME

Send Senu up to locate the ship. Currently it's around the Neorion Naval Arsenal in the south, but it sails along a route from the naval base to the northwest, heading for the Trireme Stranding Camp **(3)** on Uab Nome's coast. By the time you steal a sailboat from the shore and catch up to the trireme, it'll be passing the base.

Sail up to the back of the cult's ship, get onto the aft, and crawl up. There are five soldiers onboard. Stand up high above them on the aft and use sleep darts on those you can see; then leap down and kill the others, coming back to assassinate the sleeping. Or hang off the deck's edge and lure and pull enemies into the water.

Follow the marker on the ship to the table and interact with the instructions. It says the cargo is being delivered to the Trireme Stranding Camp **(3)**.

GET EVIDENCE TO EXPOSE THE CORRUPTION

If the ship is still moving after you rid it of its crew, then you can ride it close to the stranding camp; otherwise, get off, get a sailboat, and get to the camp.

153

TRIREME STRANDING CAMP

Prerequisite: Approach the blockade

SUGGESTED LEVEL: 30   **LOCATION REWARD: 600 XP**   **LOCATION OBJECTIVES: Kill one captain, loot one treasure**

Exit your boat and use the tall grass along the shore to get past the gate (3). Lure the archer (4) standing near the gate to the grass and assassinate

him. Or if his back is to you, sneak up behind him and kill him.

Use the grass along the back of the camp, next to the canyon wall, to get deep into the camp without being spotted. Ignore the guards with their backs

to you at the canyon gate (5). Keep moving for the next patch of tall grass behind the tents.

If there are multiple guards under the pergola (6) behind the captain's tent (7)—where most of the soldiers in this camp hang out—then meditate to see if they all leave or if only one remains. Lure him behind the tents in the tall grass and assassinate him.

Now using the captain's tent to hide attacks, begin luring guards from in front of the tent to your kill zone. You can move to the grass on both sides of the tent for cover and to get away from multiple searching guards.

The captain (8) often sits at the desk in his tent. If you have gotten rid of the two brute bodyguards from the front of the tent, then you can sneak in and assassinate the captain from behind. Interact with the shipment correspondence (evidence) on the captain's desk. Interact with the crocodile mummies on the floor in the back of the tent. Take the treasure and find this evidence to complete the location objective and the quest.

BAD FAITH

Prerequisite: Complete Side Quest: The Jaws of Sobek

SUGGESTED LEVEL: 29	REWARDS: 1,500 XP, Legendary Scepter

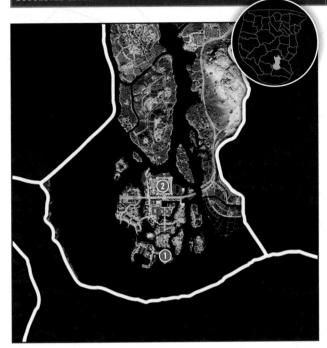

SPEAK TO PADIASET, PRIEST OF SOBEK

SOUTH SOBEK TEMPLE, KROKODILOPOLIS

Talk to Padiaset **(1)**, who kneels in the Sobek Temple courtyard near a dead Roman soldier. Use the Viewpoint on the North Sobek Temple **(2)** to get there quickly.

FIND AND ASSASSINATE SEHETEP

NORTH SOBEK TEMPLE, KROKODILOPOLIS

LOCATION OBJECTIVES: Find one papyrus puzzle

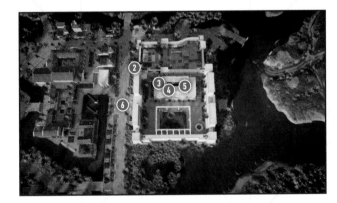

Use Senu to locate Sehetep inside the temple. If you arrived on the Viewpoint, then simply drop down to the wall walk, hop over to the temple rooftop, and enter the temple through the second-story windows **(3)**. When you drop to the floor inside, find the Sobek's Rage papyrus puzzle on a table in the corner. For details on the treasure it leads to, see the Activities section.

With Sehetep marked, drop through the hole in the floor to reach the top of a column **(5)** in the temple's first level.

From the top of the column, drop-assassinate Sehetep. Make sure you are targeting him and not his bodyguard. Deal with the bodyguard after the assassination. That way Sehetep does not run off and find another soldier to protect him.

SPEAK TO PADIASET, PRIEST OF SOBEK

Exit the temple through the south entrance and find Padiaset **(6)** on the sidewalk waiting for the good news.

SHADYA'S REST

Prerequisite: Complete Side Quest: The Jaws of Sobek

| SUGGESTED LEVEL: 30 | REWARDS: 1,500 XP | UNLOCKS: Side Quest: Fighting for Faiyum |

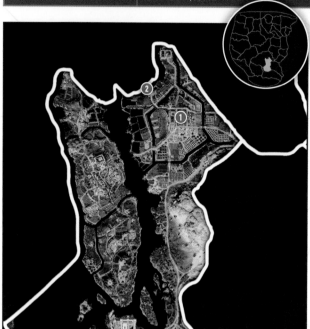

SPEAK TO HOTEPHRES AT PHILADELPHIA FARM

PHILADELPHIA FARM, FAIYUM OASIS

You can find Hotephres **(1)** with one of his servant girls on the second-floor balcony of their Philadelphia Farm estate.

Interact with Hotephres to follow him to find Khenut.

FOLLOW HOTEPHRES

Hotephres sprints out of his house and to a couple horses outside. Follow him to Khenut **(2)** at Shadya's Shrine by the lake.

BRING A HERON FEATHER TO SHADYA'S SHRINE

Khenut is in serious mourning, and Bayek thinks he knows a way to help. He needs a heron feather. A marker appears to the southwest. Run there but slow down before you reach the destination **(3)** so you don't scare all the heron off. Sneak up to the flock and put an arrow through only one of them. Take the feather and head back to Khenut at the shrine **(2)**.

When you return to the shine, a brute Ptolemy captain is seen harassing a farmer. Khenut goes off on the captain, taunting him. He leaves without escalation.

ASSASSINATE THE PTOLEMY CAPTAIN OF PHILADELPHIA

Bayek is not going to stand around and let that kind of thing happen without someone feeling some pain. The captain has not gotten far. Send Senu up to locate him **(4)** just 90 meters away to the east. He travels with two Level 29 soldiers. He's a Level 31 brute and they're walking to a small group of Level 29 soldiers. There will be a big brawl if you don't try to take some down stealthily.

Use the abundance of tall grass for cover as you put arrows in heads and move to avoid detection. Lure others to their doom, but mostly, kill that captain. You receive the Fort Insignia quest item when you confirm the kill. You don't recognize it but hope that your friends might.

SPEAK TO HOTEPHRES ABOUT THE FORT INSIGNIA

Return to the shrine **(2)** and ask about the insignia. This unlocks Side Quest: Fighting for Faiyum.

FIGHTING FOR FAIYUM

Prerequisite: Complete Side Quest: Shadya's Rest

SUGGESTED LEVEL: 30

REWARDS: 4,500 XP

INTRODUCTION

THE ESSENTIALS

MAIN QUESTS

SIDE QUESTS

ACTIVITIES

ATLAS

REFERENCE & ANALYSIS

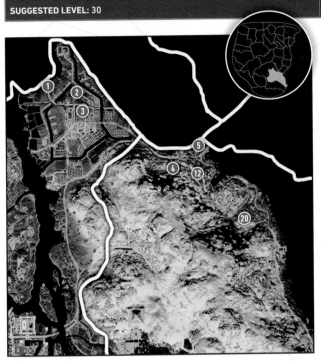

SPEAK TO HOTEPHRES AT PHILADELPHIA FARM

PHILADELPHIA FARM, FAIYUM OASIS

Speak to Hotephres and Khenut **(1)** at Shadya's shrine.

SPEAK TO THE FARMER

Head east into the fields to find the farmer **(2)**. He won't talk seriously about retaliation until his work is finished.

BURN THE PYRES FOR THE FARMER

Help the farmer finish his job. Light a torch and light the three, objective-marked straw pyres on fire. Alternatively, you could light arrows on the

pyres the farmer lights and then shoot flaming arrows at the targets. Or throw firebombs at them.

SPEAK TO THE FARMER

The farmer tells you that he and other farmers do not respect Hotephres, but when the farmer learns that you defeated the captain, he is

willing to stand behind you in an uprising. He agrees to spread the word.

SPEAK TO HOTEPHRES AT THE PHILADELPHIA FARM

Hotephres is now on his farm estate balcony **(3)**. When you share the farmer's news, the conversation is interrupted by soldiers on the grounds searching for you.

DEFEND THE PEOPLE OF PHILADELPHIA

Hotephres is fired up and takes off running through the house to get down to the courtyard to fight the three Level 28 and 29 soldiers. Select a warrior bow and leap from the balcony, down to the top of the statue. Drop-assassinate one of the three soldiers below. Shoot the remaining soldiers in the face.

You will likely kill all three of them before Hotephres makes it through his estate to reach the battle. A conversation between you, Hotephres, and Khenut occurs as soon as the battle is won.

FOLLOW KHENUT

Follow Khenut as she mounts a horse outside the courtyard. Mount the other horse and follow her into Haueris Nome, where you meet a group of rebels **(4)**.

The rebels' leader has been captured and is held at the nearby dam **(5)**.

CLEON'S DAM

Prerequisite: Approach the blockade

SUGGESTED LEVEL: 31

LOCATION REWARD: 600 XP

LOCATION OBJECTIVES: Kill one captain, loot one treasure

Send Senu up over the nearby dam to find the rebel leader and to mark the Level 30 to 31 soldiers. Defeat as many of the soldiers as you can because

once you free the Faiyum rebel leader, he's going to choose a dangerous route to freedom and will want to fight. For this reason, we suggest setting the brazier trap before you free him.

A good approach is avoiding the gate guards and diving into the water on the dam's southeast side **(5)**. Reach the middle watchtower's rooftop and set the brazier trap **(6)**. Jump back into the water and swim northeast toward the dam's other end. Scale the wall and hang on to the top edge **(7)**, looking for patrolling soldiers. Lure any in the area to the edge and throw them over.

Sneak up behind the guard **(8)** at the northeast dam entrance and assassinate him. If another guard is across the road, do the same to him.

There's a hiding booth next to the northwest tower that you can use to lure nearby soldiers to their silent death.

Get into the water **(9)** on the dam's northwest side and then scale the northwest side of the captain's tower (he usually stands guard at the top of the tower). Pull up slowly into the guard tower, assassinate the captain **(10)**, and take the treasure to complete the location objective.

From the captain's tower, look down to the captive rebel **(11)** and see how many soldiers are guarding him. If more than one, you can put arrows in them. If only one, you can glide down the connecting rope and assassinate him. Free the prisoner **(11)**.

ESCORT THE LEADER OF THE FAIYUM REBELS

The rebel leader heads straight across the bridge toward the captain's tower **(10)** and gets onto the dam road heading for the south entrance and guard booth. Defeat the remaining soldiers with

the leader's help. Beware that there may be a Phylake in the area, and this crazy guy you just freed may lead him right to you. See the Activities section for tips on finding and defeating all of them in "Phylake's Prey."

The leader takes you to a spot in the hills **(12)** not far from the dam.

FORT BOUBASTOS

Prerequisite: Approach the blockade

SUGGESTED LEVEL: 31　　　**LOCATION REWARD: 1,500 XP**　　　**LOCATION OBJECTIVES: Kill two captains and one commander, loot four treasures**

Head southeast to Fort Boubastos. You approach the northwest section of the base. Take advantage of this location to easily take out the

captains. Simply step through the V-opening in the wooden fence **(13)** and enter the tall grass on the other side. The captain often patrols here and stops with his back to you in this exact spot. Assassinate him from the tall grass.

Walk south with the canyon wall on your right, sticking to the tall grass and the canyon wall as it opens to a small area with a guard tower. Continue around the tower, slipping by soldiers, and sneak into the tunnel entrance **(14)** behind the tunnel guard.

An alternate route is to dive into the hole **(15)** and swim through a long subterranean tunnel to come up in the prison **(16)**. There's usually a guard there. Sneak up beside him and assassinate him. Both the tunnel entrance **(14)** and the water tunnel entrance **(15)** lead to the prison **(16)**. Release the prisoners to cause more distractions.

Once you come out of the prison, the rebels and farmers enter the base and start attacking soldiers. All chaos breaks loose. Use the chaos to your advantage and just run to the brazier **(17)** and set the trap so you and the rebels don't have to face reinforcements.

KILL THE COMMANDER

Head for the central building **(18)** with the commander and the insanely huge brute captain. Climb the wall to the rooftop. Use the hole in the ceiling to drop down on the captain. That's the easy part. Now defeat the captain. Use sleep darts and multiple assassinations from behind to take the beast down. Confirm the kill, take the two treasures from the little ground-floor room, get the one from the upstairs room, and then trot across the fort to get the treasure in the chambers near the main gates.

SPEAK TO HOTEPHRES AND KHENUT OUTSIDE FORT BOUBASTOS

Head out the gates **(19)** to the southeast and go to the top of the hill. Hotephres and Khenut **(20)** await you there. They thank you.

Shadya liked you immediately, you know. You always have a home here, if you need it.

RECON WORK

Prerequisite: Discover Herakleion Nome

SUGGESTED LEVEL: 31

REWARD: 1,500 XP

INTERACT WITH THE INFORMANT TABLE

Head to the Herakleion in Herakleion Nome and interact with the informant table **(1)** at the bulkhead. Accept the only available job, "Recon Work."

FIND THE MILITARY CAMP

MITHIDRATES ROMAN CAMP

Prerequisite: Approach the camp

SUGGESTED LEVEL: 31   **LOCATION REWARD: 600 XP**   **LOCATION OBJECTIVES: Kill one captain, loot one treasure**

Take a boat northeast to the northeasternmost island in Herakleion Nome to find the Mithidrates Roman Camp **(2)**. Fly Senu over to mark all the soldiers and the treasure. The ship that is docked at the camp holds the treasure.

Climb the southwest watchtower **(2)** and grab some arrows (set them on fire). Shoot one of the three soldiers—one being the captain—sitting under the nearby tent **(3)**.

As soon as you fire, hang off the back of the watchtower so if they climb up, they won't see you. Then attack again and perform a drop assassination on the remaining one.

Now you can move more freely around the camp using the tall grass and building interiors for cover. You could enter the closest building **(4)** to your watchtower, shoot three soldiers across the yard **(5)** and **(6)**, and duck behind the doorway if an arrow doesn't kill one of them.

Don't free the prisoners yet; wait until you've eliminated all the soldiers in the camp. Use the tall grass **(7)** near the building just beyond the prisoners for cover as you shoot the soldiers on the ship **(8)**.

INVESTIGATE THE MILITARY CAMP

This objective simply means "free the prisoners" **(6)**.

SPEAK TO THE PRISONERS

Once free, talk to the guy with the marker over his head. Complete the location objective by looting the treasure on the ship **(8)**.

INTRODUCTION
THE ESSENTIALS
MAIN QUESTS
SIDE QUESTS
ACTIVITIES
ATLAS
REFERENCE & ANALYSIS

LOOSE CARGO

Prerequisite: Discover Herakleion Nome

SUGGESTED LEVEL: 31

REWARD: 1,500 XP

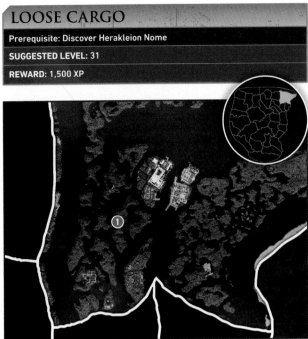

RESCUE THE ROMAN HUNTER

There's lions, fowl, and crocodiles infesting the land and sea around the Zoiontegoi shipwreck. Use a long weapon to defeat the Level 32 lions and crocodiles that devoured soldiers around the camp. A Roman hunter is locked in a cage **(1)**. Free him afterward. Find the treasure on the shipwreck to complete the location objective.

SPEAK WITH THE ROMAN HUNTER

The Roman said they had spent weeks capturing animals for the gladiators to slaughter. This completes the quest.

Prerequisite: Discover Herakleion Nome

SUGGESTED LEVEL: 31	REWARDS: 1,800 XP

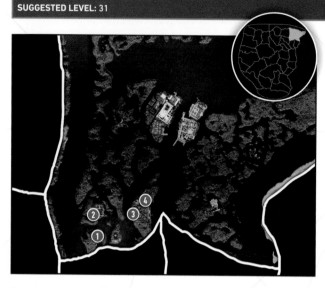

REACH THE SOURCE OF THE WHISTLE

HUNTRESS CAVE

You find an old friend named Tahira **(1)** at the Huntress Cave on the southwesternmost island in Herakleion. She takes off running. Before you follow her, duck into the cave and get the treasure to complete the location objective.

FOLLOW TAHIRA

Follow Tahira north to the Shrine of Sobek ruins **(2)**.

CLIMB THE RUINS

Climb up on the nearest pillar and make your way to the marker.

MEET TAHIRA IN THE HUNTER'S VILLAGE

Head east to Natho **(3)**. The next objective activates when both you and Tahira step foot on the island.

FIND AND RESCUE SOBEK'S CHILD

CARCER ROMAN COMPOUND

Prerequisite: Approach the compound
SUGGESTED LEVEL: 31
LOCATION REWARD: 600 XP
UNLOCKS: Side Quest: Predator to Prey
LOCATION OBJECTIVES: Kill one captain, loot one treasure

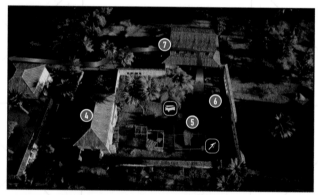

Head north toward the marker and send Senu up over Carcer Roman Compound to locate the crocodile **(5)** in the cage. Mark all the soldiers in the compound. You face about seven Level 31 to 32 soldiers and the Level 33 captain.

If there's a guard on the west side of the west house **(4)**, assassinate him and then climb onto the rooftop. Crouch down and get into a position

where you can get a clear arrow shot at the front door of the crocodile cage **(5)**.

Shoot a few arrows until the cage door breaks open. Sobek's child (the enormous white crocodile) will help you eliminate the soldiers. Releasing the lions from their cages might help too. Shoot the oil vase **(6)** near the campfire to burn up some soldiers. Jump down into the courtyard and help the crocodile finish off the soldiers.

Take the treasure from beside the tree with the hippo carcasses after destroying the enemy.

ESCORT SOBEK'S CHILD

Now the huge crocodile travels to the shrine. Mark the shrine **(2)** on your map to help you with directions. Exit through the barn and veer left to exit through the west doorway **(7)**. Head to the shrine by swimming through the Nile or using a boat. You may run into some hyenas when you reach the first island. Slaughter them and continue to the shrine.

You'll also encounter a few Roman hunters on the island. Help Sobek's child eliminate them.

Tahira thanks you when you finally get Sobek's child back home, and the large white crocodile joins its partner at their home in the shrine.

PREDATOR TO PREY

Prerequisite: Discover Herakleion Nome; Complete Reunion

SUGGESTED LEVEL: 31

REWARDS: 2,250 XP, Rare Hunter Bow

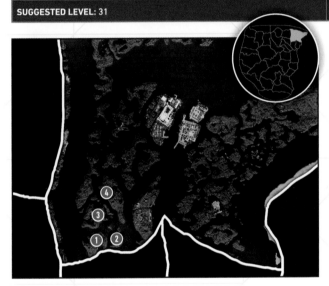

SPEAK TO TAHIRA

HUNTRESS CAVE

Tahira invited you to her home at the Huntress Cave at the end of her previous side quest, Reunion. Head back to the cave to find her at her camp again **(1)**. Talk to her.

FOLLOW TAHIRA

DESHER BLUFF

Follow Tahira as she runs east to the next island. Send Senu up to locate the hunters around Desher Bluff **(2)**. Tahira leads you to the treasure on the shore near the dead body. Grab the treasure to complete the location objective.

KILL THE ROMANS HUNTING FLAMINGOS

You can eliminate all the soldiers stealthily by taking advantage of the tall foliage around the bluff.

FOLLOW TAHIRA

Follow Tahira as she runs toward the next island **(3)**. If there's a boat available near the shore when you are about to cross the Nile, then use it (watch how fast Tahira treads through water when you sail next to her).

KILL THE ROMANS HUNTING CROCODILES

Now you head back to the Sobek Shrine **(3)**. Use Senu to mark all the soldiers around the ruins. There's around five Level 31 soldiers.

Reach the top of the pillars to launch an arrow attack or use the tall grass to perform stealth assassinations.

If you want to claim the treasure from this location, then dive into the water below the Viewpoint statue and swim into the subterranean chamber. The treasure is in a second chamber to the left, through a passage almost completely blocked by large vases.

FOLLOW TAHIRA

After defeating the crocodile hunters, follow Tahira north to the hippo lair **(4)**. There are only about four hunters on this island and can be difficult to find. Use Senu to track them down. Once you have killed one of them, they become marked, making it easier to find them. The hunters often kill the alpha hippo, completing the location objective for you.

UAB NOME

SEVEN FARMERS

Prerequisite: Discover Uab Nome

SUGGESTED LEVEL: 30	REWARDS: 3,750 XP, Rare Predator Bow

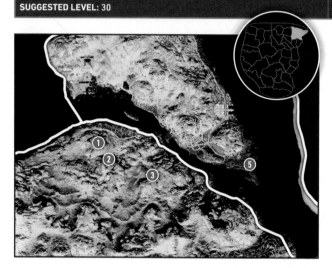

SPEAK TO RAI

UAB NOME

A small group of farmers is planning their last stand against bandits. Their leader, a woman called Rai **(1)**, asks for Bayek's help.

FOLLOW RAI

Follow Rai as she heads southeast toward the Horus Stone Circle **(2)**. Along the way, be prepared to battle a pack of Level 28 hyenas.

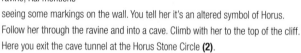

When you reach a deep ravine, Rai mentions seeing some markings on the wall. You tell her it's an altered symbol of Horus. Follow her through the ravine and into a cave. Climb with her to the top of the cliff. Here you exit the cave tunnel at the Horus Stone Circle **(2)**.

She continues to the cliff's edge just beyond the stone circle. Approach her to talk to her. Before you leave, you can complete the Horus Stone Circle challenge (see the Activities section for help) and synchronize with the nearby Viewpoint. Dive into the water below for a shortcut off the cliff.

Return to Rai's brothers **(1)**. You tell them that she is staying on the cliff and will signal when the bandits approach. Bayek suggests setting traps with oil vases in areas where the enemy will pass.

SPEAK TO THE LOOKOUT WHEN YOU ARE READY

The battle is not any more severe than other battles in the past. Set up oil pots to shoot with fire arrows, then put them in the two narrow passages below the guard tower. Speak to the lookout in the watchtower when you are ready to start the fight.

KILL THE BANDITS

If it was daytime, then time changes to night and the battle begins. You start in the watchtower. Set your arrows on fire with the small lamp there. Start shooting oil vases or the bandits.

There are six Level 29 bandits below; all are marked. You can take most, if not all, of them out from the tower. Kill all six bandits to complete the objective. One of the brothers tells you that the bandits are only coming for their father's bow. Bayek offers to hunt down their leader. Rai says they could be camping in the foothills to the southeast. She gives you her father's bow, knowing it will be safer with you. You earn the Broken Bow.

FIND AND GET INFORMATION ON THE BANDIT LEADER

Follow the marker southwest. When you get close and are prompted, send Senu up to locate the target (3) through the cliff rock inside Senehem Depths.

SENEHEM DEPTHS

Prerequisite: Approach the cave
SUGGESTED LEVEL: 30
LOCATION REWARD: 450 XP
LOCATION OBJECTIVES: Loot one treasure

Instead of entering the Senehem Depths through the front door (4), climb to the cliff's top and drop in through the hole (3) southwest of the main entrance. This way you can deal with the bandits guarding the entrance from behind them when you leave. You drop into a locus nesting area. Ignore them and drop to the floor; head to the right to the marker.

You find the Bandit Letter on a table on the cave's right side.

Steal the treasure at the bottom of the wall of hives (also next to a skeleton) to complete the location objective.

FIND AN ANCIENT TOMB

Exit the cave through the front entrance. Call a mount and trot out of there, or finish off the front entrance guards and not worry about escaping.

Follow the marker northeast. Cross the Nile (you'll have to swim or find a boat) and travel through Etesias' Olive Grove, which is occupied by Roman soldiers. Call Senu to find the entrance to the Tomb of Smenkhkare (5).

TOMB OF SMENKHKARE

Prerequisite: Approach the tomb
SUGGESTED LEVEL: 30
LOCATION REWARD: One Ability Point
LOCATION OBJECTIVES: Find the Ancient Tablet

There is a lion around the tomb's entrance **(5)**. Be prepared to defeat it before you head down the stairs into the tomb. At the bottom of the stairs, inspect the wall to find the markings are like those on Rai's bow.

ASSASSINATE THE BANDIT LEADER

Smash through the cracked wall at the bottom of the stairs and enter the tomb. Light a torch. Take the first hallway on the right to reach a dead-end treasure room with two chests. Raid the chests and return to the previous hallway. Turn right to continue deeper into the tomb.

WEIGHTED PLATFORM CHAMBER PUZZLE

In the next chamber, dive into the water at the bottom of the pit. Do some exploring underwater for some treasure. You come up into a very large chamber with counterweight balance platforms.

Use the series of two solid platforms and two balance platforms arranged all in a row to reach the upper walkway. On the walkway is a small table and a large crack in the

wall (through the crack is a small room containing a single Silica).

Follow the upper walkway to the next set of balance platforms. Now you must run and jump from the first balance platform to a solid one. From here, continue running without stopping. Jump from the solid platform and grab on to the hanging wench. Swing around the corner to the next balance platform. Quickly run and jump from the platform before it falls under your weight. Reach the final ledge.

Now you reach a large ledge with an opening marked with lit torches. Inside the next room, mark a handful of enemies (Level 29 to 31). The bandit leader is marked with an objective marker. Use the torch near the entry to light your arrows and shoot those that you can get with a clear shot.

Move around the edges of the large chamber, taking out bandits until you can get to the leader. There are plenty of walls, columns, and even a large sarcophagus to hide behind as you sneak up on the leader. Eliminate him and confirm the kill to complete the quest. He's also in the same room with the Ancient Tablet. It's at the back side of the large central sarcophagus.

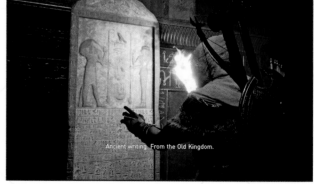

ATEF-PEHU NOME

THE MATRIARCH

Prerequisite: Discover Atef-Pehu Nome

SUGGESTED LEVEL: 31	REWARDS: 3,750 XP

TALK TO MERITMAAT

While in Kerke in Atef-Pehu Nome, speak to the village leader Meritmaat **(1)**.

FIND AND RESCUE THE HOSTAGE

KERKE WHARF

Prerequisite: Approach the Wharf
SUGGESTED LEVEL: 31
LOCATION REWARD: 600 XP
LOCATION OBJECTIVES: Kill one captain, loot one treasure

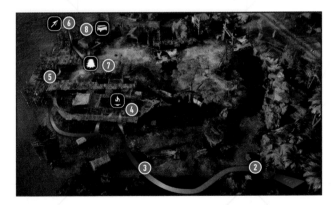

Head northwest to the Kerke Wharf **(2)**. Send Senu up to locate the hostage in one of the tents.

Enter through the tall grass near a passable barricade **(2)** in the water on the camp's north side. Travel as close as possible to the dry-docked ship with the brazier on deck **(4)**. A bandit patrols the deck but often walks away while a foot soldier approaches the grass near you **(3)**. Assassinate the soldier in the grass; then climb up the dry-docked ship to set the brazier trap **(4)**. Assassinate the bandit if he's near it.

Drop back down to the ground on the ship's north side and enter the Nile. Crouch-walk under the docks. A soldier may be sitting **(5)** in the shallow water to the left as you pass under the docks. Assassinate him.

A ship may also dock at the pier while you are there. A good place to be if this happens is in the guard tower **(6)** or underwater. Wait for the ship to sail away or silently take the crew out. Use the haystack **(7)** to eliminate a couple enemies in the yard. If the bandit was not on the dry-docked boat, then he could be sitting around the fire. Lure enemies to the haystack and kill them. Assassinate the captain as he sits in his tent **(8)**.

Find the hostage **(8)** next to the treasure in the tent. Grab the loot and then pick up the hostage. You can carry her out of the camp the way you entered or head out through the shallow water on the south side (making sure no more soldiers are in that area).

SPEAK TO THE RESCUED HOSTAGE

Drop the hostage outside the restricted zone and talk to her. She tells you the commander was going to send her off on the next opium shipment and that he's currently on a ship somewhere.

SPEAK TO MERITMAAT IN KERKE

Return to town. Follow the marker to Meritmaat's second-floor exterior balcony **(9)**, where she is waiting to see if she can call you a hero. You tell her the commander was not at the camp, but you can follow the opium shipments that should lead to him.

FIND AND GET INFORMATION ON THE COMMANDER

Travel northeast along the shoreline road. Watch the marker out in the Nile. When you get somewhat close, head to the shoreline and procure a boat. Sail toward the marker, and send Senu to locate the opium ship **(10)**.

Board the ship and put the biggest threat to sleep (the brute). Assassinate his comrade and then the sleeping brute. Kill the remaining soldier onboard and then locate the manifest on the table in the cabin. You learn the ship unloads in Memphis.

TRAVEL TO MEMPHIS

You've been to Memphis already. Use a Viewpoint to travel close to the commander's location **(11)**.

ASSASSINATE THE COMMANDER

MEMPHIS CHANNEL

Follow the marker to find the commander and a bunch of his soldiers at a dock where the opium shipments are delivered. The commander often patrols the sidewalk next to the boat. You can easily wait for him at the top of the nearby bridge and perform a drop assassination on him. Afterward, dive into the water to escape detection.

If you silently assassinated the commander, then you acquired a letter from him after killing him. If you fought with him, then you have to confirm the kill to receive the letter. In the Strange Confessions letter, you learn that he came to view Meritmaat's daughter as his own and that she's very much alive; he could not bring himself to kill her.

SPEAK TO MERITMAAT'S DAUGHTER IN MEMPHIS

Follow the marker to locate Meritmaat's daughter **(13)** walking near Nomad's Bazaar. Speak to her.

GREEN MOUNTAINS

ONE BAD APPLE

Prerequisite: Complete Main Quest: The Final Weighing

SUGGESTED LEVEL: 35	REWARDS: 3,000 XP, Legendary Spear

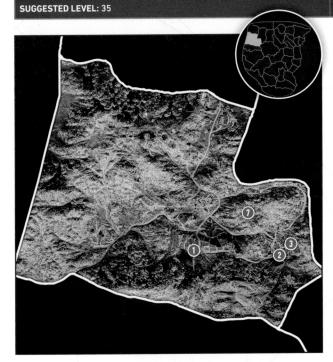

You find Crios standing on a table.

You receive this quest when you help Praxilla **(1)** in Green Mountains during Main Quest: The Final Weighing.

SPEAK TO PRAXILLA AT THE CLINIC

BALAGRAE, GREEN MOUNTAIN

Praxilla sits outside her clinic **(2)** in Balagrae. She wants you to speak to her friend Crios.

FIND PRAXILLA'S FRIEND CRIOS AT THE ASKLEPIEION

Use Senu to locate Crios at the Temple of Asklepieion **(3)**. Continue to scan for enemies all around the temple, focusing mainly on those soldiers around the right-front side. Climb the side of the temple and crawl into the high open window **(3)** on the north side.

CARRY CRIOS TO PRAXILLA'S CLINIC

Pick up Crios and head down the stairs to the first floor. Exit through the east door **(4)**. Head toward the clinic. Use the tall shrubs to move stealthily.

Jump onto the southwest corner yard wall **(5)**. Leap to the pole sticking out of the nearby rooftop. Run across the rooftops using the suspension ropes to reach the next house. Drop into the clinic courtyard and put Crios on the marked blanket **(6)**.

FIND THE SHRINE OF WHISPERS

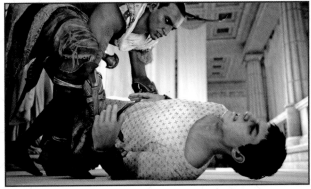

Travel northwest into the mountains toward the marker, and send Senu to locate the entrance to the Shrine of Whispers **(7)**.

Climb the mountain and get right above the entrance to the shrine to avoid the five soldiers at the entrance. From above, or by dropping down into the corner, throw sleep darts at each of the guards and then assassinate them. If you need arrows, you can find them at camp in front of the shrine entrance. Enter the shrine cautiously; there are few soldiers inside.

ASSASSINATE THE PRIESTESS MELITTA

There are two soldiers guarding Praxilla. Melitta has an objective marker. Work your way around the room and throw sleep darts at the two soldiers and then execute them. Melitta

runs away but you can throw a sleep dart at her or use arrows. Assassinate her.

RESCUE PRAXILLA AND ESCORT HER OUT OF THE SHRINE

Untie Praxilla and escort her from the shrine. If you killed all the guards at the entrance, then just walk outside the restricted zone to complete the quest.

PLAYING WITH FIRE

Prerequisite: Complete Main Quest: The Final Weighing

SUGGESTED LEVEL: 33

REWARD: 2,250 XP

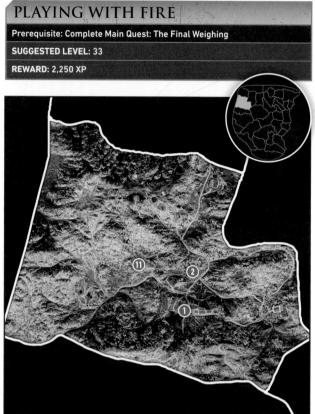

You receive the quest when you help Praxilla **(1)** in Green Mountains during Main Quest: The Final Weighing.

FIND AND RESCUE KADE FROM THE KYRENAIKA CITADEL

Travel to the Roman Kyrenaika Citadel and send Senu up to locate Kade in a prison cell **(2)**.

Kade gets revved up and ready to kill Romans. For an easier quest, get him out of the restricted zone without him seeing any Romans. If it goes badly, he will follow a trail of Roman soldiers right into the heart of the citadel and you'll be in an unbalanced war. Therefore, a good strategy is to clear all the soldiers from the small camp on the citadel's south side.

Enter through the hole in the barricade **(2)** in the tall grass. Slip into the back flap of the tent to assassinate the guard who often stands in front of the tent **(3)**. There are multiple arrow supplies here. Return when you need to resupply.

Make sure the nearest tower **(4)** is clear, then clear all the soldiers from around the east entrance **(5)**. If occupied, clear the soldier in the central guard tower **(7)**. Head west on the lower level and use the tall grass **(6)** near the shelters. Lure anyone patrolling nearby to a grassy kill zone.

Move to the west entrance **(8)** and kill any guards in the watchtowers. Work your way up to the prisons. You can head through the building **(9)** and use the hiding booth on the second level near the exit to lure guards outside to their demise.

HELP KADE SAVE THE OTHER PRISONERS

Before you free Kade **(10)**, open the cells— **(A)**, **(B)**, and **(C)**—and free the prisoners. This way, Kade won't have time to go find trouble while you are busy freeing the prisoners, which is the next objective. The citadel is a heavily trafficked fort with patrols coming and going all the time, so the east gate road is going to be busy. Before you free Kade, check the east entrance one more time to ensure no soldiers are in sight.

ESCORT KADE OUT OF THE PRISON AREA

Free Kade and run west into the hills and as far away from the heavily trafficked road to the southeast as possible. Stay a good distance ahead of Kade so he won't be tempted to look for trouble.

SPEAK TO KADE

You tell him his mother, Nanet, is safe and that Praxilla took her to Balagrae. He tells you that a Roman engineer at the aqueduct invented a special ballista that could help the cause.

SPEAK TO VITRUVIUS THE ENGINEER AT THE AQUEDUCT

Travel northwest through the mountains to reach the aqueduct. If you've been there before, then use the Viewpoint to Fast Travel. If you have not already started Side Quest: The Good Roman, then when you approach Vitruvius **(11)**, the intro cinematic for that quest begins.

HELP VITRUVIUS WITH HIS PROBLEM

If you have not completed The Good Roman, then do it now so you can reach the next objective in this quest. For help, page down to the next side quest. After completing The Good Roman, you must speak to Vitruvius again. He starts telling you his life story.

FOLLOW VITRUVIUS

Follow Vitruvius as he travels to the other side of the aqueduct. He tells you that General Agrippa must have his notes on the special ballista. He says he cannot be part of a Roman sabotage but if you get the notes, he'll destroy them.

FIND AND STEAL THE FORMULA FROM GENERAL AGRIPPA

KYRENAIKA ROMAN CITADEL

Prerequisite: Enter the Citadel

SUGGESETD LEVEL: 35   **LOCATION REWARD: 900 XP**   **LOCATION OBJECTIVES: Kill two captains and one commander, loot four treasures**

Travel back to Kyrenaika Roman Citadel **(12)** to kill the general and get the notes. This time you must go inside. You might as well kill everyone there to complete the location objective. Use the watery tunnel entrance **(12)** to get inside. You exit into the southernmost

fort prison **(13)**. Climb to the top floor and access the wall walks. Begin clearing soldiers from the walks and then get to the top of the guardhouse **(14)** to assess the situation.

Assassinate soldiers as they patrol alone. Return to your perch to watch for the next soldier to leave. To stir things up, kill a lower-level guard with a single arrow and then quickly hide behind the roof peak. This creates more opportunity to single out soldiers for

assassinations. The hiding booth outside the south wall is a great backup kill zone.

Keep an eye on the nearby guard tower **(17)**. If it gets occupied, then shoot the soldiers from your perch **(14)** before they blow your cover.

Using the rooftops, arrow supplies, ballista, and hiding booth in this corner of the fort allows you to cleanly eliminate most everyone in the courtyard **(16)**. This includes General Agrippa. Make a special trip up the middle wall walk to set the brazier trap **(15)** and then return to your comfortable kill zone until the numbers have thinned and you can move around more freely.

General Agrippa—who wears an alpha lion's pelt—is a tough cookie to put down. A clean assassination is unlikely. It'll most likely end up in a fight. It's best to clear all the soldiers from the area and leave him for last so you don't have to deal with his reinforcements. Confirm his kill to receive Vitruvius' Formula.

DESTROY THE GREEK FIRE STOCKPILES

Three objective markers appear, indicating the location of the Greek Fire stockpiles: **(18)**, **(19)**, **(20)**. These take you into the fort's east side, where you must eliminate even more soldiers, allowing you to move without constantly looking over your shoulder.

CARPE DIEM

When you enter the building **(21)** where the captain sits at a desk, you can find the Report from Brutus Severus on his desk. This initiates the Carpe Diem side quest. One of the four treasures is also located on his desk.

Use fireballs or torches to destroy the vases of Greek Fire. Return to the aqueduct when the job is done.

RETURN TO VITRUVIUS AT THE AQUEDUCT

Return to Vitruvius **(11)** at the aqueduct camp. Find him around his tent and speak to him to complete the quest.

THE GOOD ROMAN

Prerequisite: Discover Green Mountains

SUGGESTED LEVEL: 33

REWARD: 3,750 XP

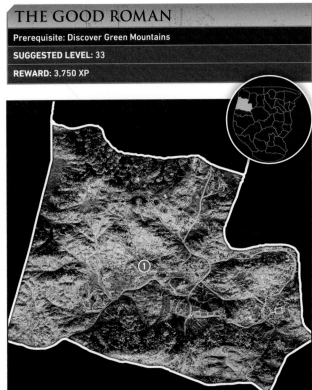

FIND DEDI AT THE CONSTRUCTION SITE

AQUAEDUCTUS KYRENAIKE, GREEN MOUNTAIN

SPEAK WITH VITRUVIUS

While syncing with the Viewpoint atop the aqueduct, you can spot a workers' camp below **(1)**. Investigate the commotion in the camp. Speak to Vitruvius, the Roman surveyor standing up for the rights of the Siwan workers. Vitruvius's dioptra has been stolen and work has stopped. Bayek must find the tool.

FIND DEDI AT THE CONSTRUCTION SITE

Climb to the aqueduct's top and follow the marker to locate Dedi **(2)**. He thinks you are there to flog him and runs from you. Catch him and he'll tell you that he left the dioptra in the cave; when he came back from lunch, it was gone.

FIND AND COLLECT THE DIOPTRA PIECES

NECROPOLIS HIDEOUT

Prerequisite: Approach the hideout

SUGGESTED LEVEL: 34

LOCATION REWARD: 900 XP

LOCATION OBJECTIVES: Kill one captain and one commander, loot two treasures

There are three pieces of the dioptra to find in and around the cave **(3)**. Run along the aqueduct's top and enter the cave tunnel. Send Senu up over the mountaintop to locate the three pieces of the dioptra, two of which are in an exterior ruins outpost. Climb the waterfall inside the cave to continue to the next cavern, which is very dark.

FIRST DIOPTRA PIECE

Jump into the pool of water in the dark cave and climb the north cave wall. You find a well-lit wooden walkway above and a bandit to your left. Kill this guy and fill up on arrows. You can go three directions from here; just remember that you will be returning to this cave later. You can head outside through the sunlit exit behind the bandit you killed (this is the exit you need to use later) or you can head deeper into the cave system through one of the two tunnels on the opposite side.

Travel through the higher cave tunnel on the right where the objective marker appears. A bandit patrols this tunnel.

Kill the bandit in the tunnel. He was guarding the Dioptra Piece. Pick it up from the table on the right. Break the large vase on the floor next to the

Dioptra Piece to reveal a small slide under hole. Find the first treasure inside the hidden room. Exit the room through the same small slide under hole.

SECOND DIOPTRA PIECE

Continue through the unexplored direction of the tunnel. You reach a large, well-lit cave occupied by three bandits. Assassinate the closest one and then put arrows in the other two. During the battle, the captain may come running out of a nearby tunnel. Assassinate him as well. Instead of heading outside from this cave, turn back and retrace your steps to the last cavern where you came up through the large hole in the floor (the one where we mentioned you will be returning to).

Exit the cave into that sunlit area where you find a guy hanging from a tree. Climb the stairs behind and to the right of the hanging man; then climb a ladder to a ledge where the tunnels continue through the mouth of a cave (that looks like it has teeth).

You find a fire in the middle of the next clearing, a haystack you can hide in, and a dark cave continuing along the ground level. Enter the cave and head down the southwest tunnel. There you find the commander. Kill him and any of his guards.

Free the rebels in captivity in this cave. Head to the platform atop the northwest cages. Read a letter near a guy hanging on the wall. You receive Side Quest: Taking Liberty.

On this ledge's south end is the second Dioptra Piece. Pick it up.

THIRD DIOPTRA PIECE

Freeing the captives gets the bandits outside the cave in an uproar, and they flood into the cave looking for you. One of the bandits is tagged with an objective marker. Kill this one to acquire the final Dioptra Piece. If he does not rush into the cave, then you'll find him outside in the ruins near the last treasure.

The final treasure to complete the location objective is outside. If you follow the tunnel where the bandits were coming from, then you reach an exterior mountain ledge. Send Senu up and you'll find a camp with an insane number of high-level soldiers. The treasure is located here. If you didn't get the last Dioptra Piece, then the bandit holding it will be here too. Have Senu mark the target; then just rush in, steal it, grab the treasure, and get out quickly, if you don't want to battle everyone.

BRING THE DIOPTRA TO VITRUVIUS AT THE AQUEDUCT

Use the aqueduct Viewpoint to travel back to the workers' camp **(1)**. Dive into the haystack below and talk to Vitruvius.

TAKING LIBERTY

Prerequisite: Discover Green Mountains

SUGGESTED LEVEL: 33

REWARD: 2,250 XP

FIND THE LETTER FROM HAPTI

NECROPOLIS HIDEOUT

During Side Quest: The Good Roman, Bayek finds a letter in the Necropolis hideout. We suggested taking that mission then. If you did not, return to the cave where the prisoner cages are located and read the letter above the row of cages.

FIND THE WORKER HAPTI AT THE QUARRY

Travel toward the marker in the southwest **(2)**. Ride past the Roman camp of Surus and then launch Senu to find Hapti in the Roman quarry camp.

Prerequisite: Approach the camp

SUGGESTED LEVEL: 33   LOCATION REWARD: 600 XP   LOCATION OBJECTIVES: Kill one captain, loot one treasure

You can start this objective by avoiding all combat, but eventually you'll have to attack the soldiers in the camp. Head up the south

wall of the mountain **(2)**. Sneak north into the cave **(3)**, where you find Hapti. Unfortunately, he is dead and has been left on the cave floor to rot.

FIND AND RETRIEVE HAPTI'S WEDDING BRACELET

Send Senu over the camp and locate the soldier with the wedding ring. Eliminate everyone in the camp so you can get to the ring and complete the location objective. Use the many guard towers in the camp to replenish and shoot flaming arrows at the soldiers. Consider making the brazier tower your first visit. Set the trap so you aren't battling reinforcements.

Do not free the captives inside the lower caves near the pool; it's a trick—they're enemy soldiers. Chase down the soldier with the ring, kill him, and take the ring. Before you leave the camp, take the treasure from the tent and make sure to kill the captain.

BRING THE BRACELET TO HAPTI'S WIFE

Travel southeast to find Hapti's wife **(4)** at the honey farm. You deliver the bad news and she accepts it the best she can. This completes the quest.

HALO OF THE HUNTRESS

Prerequisite: Discover Green Mountains

SUGGESTED LEVEL: 34	REWARDS: 2,250 XP

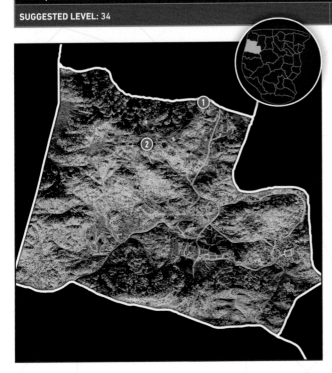

SPEAK TO THE ORACLE

ORACLE OF APOLLO

Find this side quest on the northern border of the Green Mountains inside the Oracle of Apollo. To the right, as you enter, is the Wet Work Papyrus Puzzle (see the Activities section for details). In the cave to the left, lying on the ground, is the oracle **(1)**. Speak to her.

FIND AND RETRIEVE THE HALO OF THE HUNTRESS

COLLIS ROMAN HUNTING CAMP

Prerequisite: Approach the camp
SUGGESTED LEVEL: 34
LOCATION REWARD: 600 XP
LOCATION OBJECTIVES: Kill one captain, loot one treasure

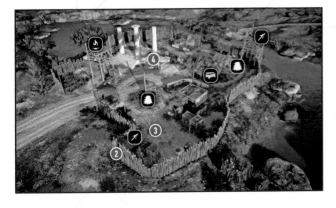

Travel southwest to the Lake of Tears, where you can synchronize with a Viewpoint and find the Collis Roman Hunting Camp. Have Senu locate the halo, which is in the underground temple.

There's some tall grass next to a V-shaped gap **(2)** in the wooden spike fence just right of the entryway. The captain **(3)** often sits near a fire just through this opening. You can throw

a sleep dart at him and anyone around him and then push through the gap and assassinate them while they sleep.

Move around the tall grass to find opportunities to defeat the remaining soldiers. There's not many, but this camp is frequented by many mounted soldiers. You can avoid them by quickly entering the subterranean temple **(4)**. If you get in a serious

battle with many soldiers and need to escape, simply jump into the water surrounding the camp and dive under to lose them.

Head down the stairs into the temple and break the cracked wall on the right to enter the hidden room. The halo is in the middle of the chamber on the floor near the statue. Take it to complete the quest.

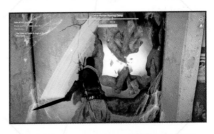

UNSEEING EYES

Prerequisite: Discover Green Mountains

SUGGESTED LEVEL: 35

REWARDS: 3,000 XP

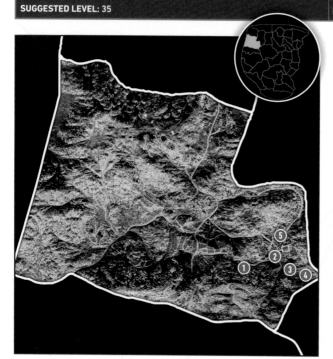

SPEAK TO THE BLIND MAN

BALAGRAE

Find the old blind man **(1)** lying on the side of the road southeast of Balagrae. Speak to him.

CARRY THE BLIND MAN TO THE CLINIC IN BALAGRAE

Pick the blind man up and place him on your mount. Follow the marker to the Praxilla's clinic **(2)**. Drop him on the marker on the blanket next to the healer Theramenes.

SPEAK TO THE HEALER THERAMENES

Theramenes says he can help but first he needs some ingredients and gives you a list.

COLLECT THE INGREDIENTS FOR THE MEDICINE

You need to collect two ibex horns and three snake venom. A marker appears on the map to the southeast. Head there now and send Senu up to scan the ground in that area **(3)** for cobras. You can find more than you need. Kill a few and collect the remains.

Just a little farther east are many ibex **(4)**. Hunt three and collect the remains.

BRING THE INGREDIENTS TO THERAMENES IN THE CLINIC

Return to Theramenes **(2)** at the clinic and hand over the supplies. Now he says he needs Silphium from the depot.

FIND AND STEAL SILPHIUM EXTRACT FROM THE DEPOT

DEPOT

Head north to the depot **(5)**, which is directly across the street from Balagrae Roman Barracks. You don't want to cause a big ruckus or you'll have reinforcements coming over from the barracks. Send Senu up to locate the extract **(8)** and to mark the soldiers around the barn.

Approach the barn from the big boulders **(5)** in the back corner. Enter the tall grass and drop to the ground in more tall grass. There are usually two guards behind the barn.

You may catch one relieving himself **(6)** and the other **(7)** at the doorway. From the tall grass, assassinate the urinating guard and perform a chain assassination on the guard at the door.

Come back around the corner of the barn and throw a sleep dart at the guard **(8)** in the large entrance. Enter the barn and take the Silphium extract from the ground on the barn's bottom level.

BRING THE EXTRACT TO THERAMENES

Back out of the barn the way you entered. You could cut through the Asklepieion's yard, jumping the fence for a more direct route back to the clinic **(2)**. Give the extract to the healer to complete the quest.

CARPE DIEM

Prerequisite: Discover Green Mountains

SUGGESTED LEVEL: 35 | **REWARDS: 2,250 XP**

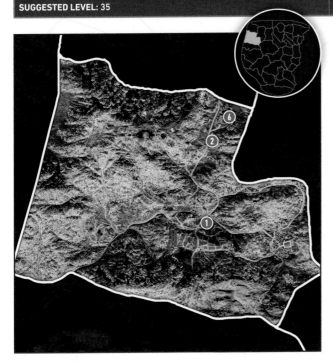

Follow the marker north along the main road from the citadel. When you get close, head off road to avoid detection, going east into the wilderness. Use Senu to locate the captive freedom fighter.

There's around six soldiers at this outpost, but this is a heavily trafficked road and an obvious fight or dead body could get passerby's attention.

Sneak down to the large boulder **(3)** behind the outpost and throw a sleep dart at the guard **(4)** in the field to the south. Sneak over to him and assassinate him in his sleep. Sneak to the tall grass in front of the boulders you were behind. Along the way, throw sleep darts at anyone on the outpost platform.

Continue throwing darts until you are out, if necessary. Once everyone is asleep, walk up to them in the order they went to sleep and assassinate them. If you see patrols coming down the road, then get to the tower **(5)**, collect arrows,

and wait for them to pass. Put arrows in them as they patrol.

Now release the freedom fighter **(6)** at the front of the outpost platform.

FIND AND RESCUE THE FREEDOM FIGHTER APATE

This quest is often discovered while on Side Quest: Playing with Fire in the Kyrenaika Roman Citadel. You can find the Report from Brutus Severus on the captain's desk. This initiates the Carpe Diem side quest. Page over to Playing with Fire if you need to see a map of the fort with this building pinpointed.

ESCORT APATE TO SAFETY

With Apate following you, head east up the mountain to get away from the busy road.

SPEAK TO APATE

She tells you that if you attack the fort, then she and her freedom fighters will help you.

ROADSIDE OUTPOST

INTRODUCTION

THE ESSENTIALS

MAIN QUESTS

SIDE QUESTS

ACTIVITIES

ATLAS

REFERENCE & ANALYSIS

FIND AND ASSASSINATE BRUTUS SEVERUS

PRASINOS OUTPOST

Prerequisite: Approach the outpost

SUGGESTED LEVEL: 37   **LOCATION REWARD: 900 XP**   **LOCATION OBJECTIVES: Kill one captain and one commander, loot two treasures**

During the day, Severus is in the Prasinos Outpost and at night he leaves the camp with only his most trusted men. We suggest getting him while he's in the camp (they have ballistae and the freedom fighters will help).

Head north to Prasinos Outpost. Use Senu to locate Severus during the daytime. March up to the front gate and eliminate or avoid anyone leaving or entering the base.

Climb the south fence **(6)** between the gate entrances, and grab arrows from the nearby supply. Sneak west and climb to the watchtower's top. Pass by the ballista **(9)** and continue to the end of the next watchtower **(7)**. Put an arrow in the guard in the corner watchtower **(8)** to cover your flanks.

Now man the nearby ballista **(9)**. From this high perch, strategically shoot all the lone soldiers in sight, not allowing anyone to escape your kill zone. This is such a high perch it's just beyond many of your targets' range of sight. If they get close enough to see you, they will try to flank you. You have 20 bolts; make them count. Make the commander **(10)** on the central bridge platform your first target.

You can also kill your main target as he patrols around this bridge platform area. Concentrate your fire on Severus first and then his bodyguard.

When you have shot everyone you can, begin hunting soldiers with your bow. Remain on the high platforms and pick off soldiers below. Loot the treasures and then confirm Severus's death. You then receive Orders to Brutus Severus and the quest completes.

SHADOWS OF APOLLO

Prerequisite: Discover Green Mountains

SUGGESTED LEVEL: 38

REWARDS: 3,000 XP

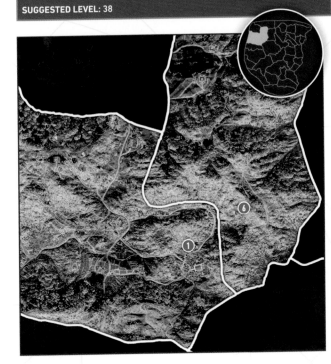

FREE THE PRISONER

BALAGRAE ROMAN BARRACKS

Prerequisite: Approach the barracks

SUGGESTED LEVEL: 37

LOCATION REWARD: 600 XP

LOCATION OBJECTIVES: Kill one captain, loot one treasure

The prisoner who initiates this quest is in a cell in the basement of Balagrae Roman Barracks **(1)**. Approach this site, using the mountain

behind it for cover. Work your way down to a low rock ledge **(2)** with tall grass on it. From here you can hide and hit many of the soldiers inside the base.

When you've taken down all you can from there, drop to the haystack below and restock your arrows from the supply next to the hiding booth. Climb to the top of the building **(3)** and see how many more soldiers you can kill with one hit. It's best to clear the site before you bring the prisoner out.

When everyone is dead, head into the building and creep upstairs to see if you can catch the captain while he's sitting. If not, use the hiding booth on the first floor to assassinate him during his patrol route.

The cellar stairway is near the back door (the mountain side of the base). Head down and take the treasure from the corner and then free the prisoner.

ESCORT THE PRISONER OUT OF BALAGRAE BARRACKS

Once freed, the prisoner must exit the barracks through the front gates **(4)**. If you've killed everyone except those in the small camp **(5)** in front

of the barracks, then you could climb the southeast corner wall (while he's following you) and head south. This forces the prisoner to exit the barracks through the front gate, taking the most direct route to you while avoiding the small enemy camp **(5)** out front.

SPEAK TO THE PRISONER

The prisoner will talk once out of the restricted zone.

FIND AND RETRIEVE THE SPY LIST

HYDRAX ROMAN CAMP

Prerequisite: Approach the camp
SUGGESTED LEVEL: 37
LOCATION REWARD: 600 XP
LOCATION OBJECTIVES: Kill one captain, loot one treasure

Travel northeast to the Hydrax Roman Camp **(6)** in Marmarica. When you get close, send Senu up to locate the spy list on the Centurion. Scale the mountain and the side of the fort walls **(6)** to reach the brazier **(8)**. Sometimes the captain patrols both the brazier platform and the stair landing **(7)** on the opposite side of the central guard tower. You may be able to get an arrow in his head before you climb the walls.

There are usually a few soldiers inside the building **(9)**. Use the rooftop as a vantage point to shoot arrows at the soldiers down in the camp; then hide behind the peak of the roof so they don't see you. Continue to watch for those soldiers in the room below you. Pick them off as they leave on patrol or run in and slaughter them.

The Centurion is marked. Kill him and confirm the kill to obtain the Apollodorus' Agent in Kyrenaika quest item to complete the quest. The treasure for this location is inside the building **(9)**.

KYRENAIKA

THE FLEA OF CYRENE

Prerequisite: Discover Kyrenaika

SUGGESTED LEVEL: 34

REWARD: 2,250 XP

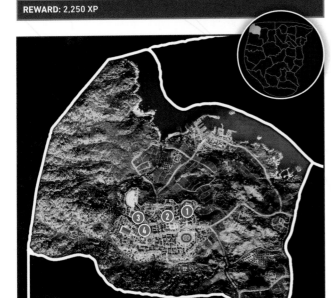

LEAP FROM THE TEMPLE OF ZEUS

Dive from the Viewpoint atop the Temple of Zeus. Afterward, find the boy in the street and speak to him.

SPEAK TO ESIO

Talk to the little boy Esio **(1)**, who you impressed with your jump into the pool. He wants to see you do it again from another spot.

FOLLOW ESIO

Follow Esio to the street in front of the Roman baths **(2)**.

LEAP FROM THE TOP OF THE ROMAN BATHS

Climb to the top of the Roman baths. Jump from the flagpole into the hay from the crashed cart in the street below.

FOLLOW ESIO

Now follow him through the crowded streets to the Apollonion of Cyrene. Even more kids are trailing behind you now.

LEAP FROM THE TEMPLE OF APOLLO

Now climb to the rooftop of the Temple of Apollo **(3)**. Leap from the statue at the peak of the roof down into the pool of water below.

FOLLOW ESIO

Follow Esio to the Akropolis tower **(4)**. The kids stop near a small waterfall pool below a cliff, where the Akropolis tower can be seen…way above.

LEAP FROM THE AKROPOLIS TOWER

Climb up the waterfall rocks and then scale the walls of the Roman Akropolis.

Walk to the end of the flagpole jutting from the corner of the guardhouse's rooftop. Leap into the small waterfall pool below.

SPEAK TO ESIO

Get through the crowd of your young admirers and speak to Esio. He congratulates you and officially names you the Flea of Cyrene.

THE LURE OF GLORY

Prerequisite: Discover Kyrenaika

SUGGESTED LEVEL: 35

REWARD: 1,500 XP

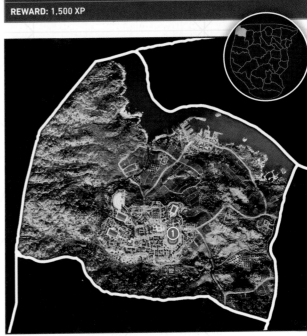

MEET THE OWNER OF THE CYRENE ARENA

Talk to the owner **(1)** standing at the front door to begin and end this quest. He welcomes you to bleed for gain and glory in Cyrene.

THE MOUSETRAP

Prerequisite: Discover Kyrenaika

SUGGESTED LEVEL: 35	REWARDS: 3,000 XP, 1,000 Drachmas	UNLOCKS: Side Quest: Cat and Mouse

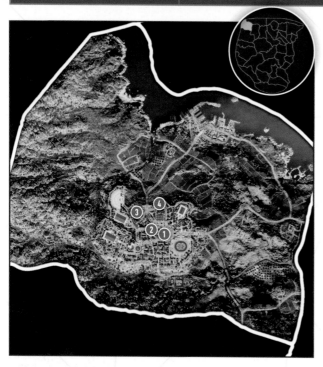

SPEAK TO THE MOUSE

Speak to Mouse **(1)** in the town square. He says he has trinkets, bows, blades, and scepters for sale at his shop and wants you to follow him there.

FOLLOW THE MOUSE

Follow the Mouse west to his shop **(2)** a short run from the square.

KILL THE ROMAN SOLDIERS

As you reach his shop, three Roman soldiers ambush you. Whip out the sword and slaughter them, or put them all to sleep and avoid the struggle. Assassinate them in their sleep-dart-induced slumber.

SPEAK TO THE MOUSE

Speak to the Mouse under his shop tent. He thinks the Romans stole his chest of trinkets and asks you to retrieve it for him.

FIND AND RETRIEVE THE MOUSE'S STASH FROM THE ROMAN BARRACKS

CYRENE BARRACKS

Prerequisite: Approach the barracks

SUGGESTED LEVEL: 35 | LOCATION REWARD: 900 XP | LOCATION OBJECTIVES: Kill one captain and one commander, loot two treasures

Head northwest to the street on the west side of the Cyrene Barracks. Walk onto the rooftop **(3)** of its westernmost building and look around.

Down in the fort to the left (north), two guards **(4)** are usually on break together. The captain often patrols around here too. Or you can find him in the lower courtyard to the northeast **(5)**, but he won't settle there for long. He also frequents the interior of the building you're standing on **(3)**.

Before you set the brazier trap on the next rooftop **(7)**, make sure none of the previously mentioned enemies see you. The same goes for the soldier **(6)** standing guard to the south. Use arrows or a combination of sleep darts, arrows, or wrist blade assassinations. Once you clear the west area, you can safely venture east into the barracks.

Clear the south courtyard **(8)**; there's usually a couple soldiers here. And watch the wall walk. Put arrows in the soldiers who patrol the outer walls.

The commander **(9)** is very comfortable at his desk on the central building's second floor. If you've cleared the soldiers almost everywhere in the lower courtyard, you could enter through most any doorway and climb the stairs to sneak up behind him and assassinate him, or you could travel by rooftops, drop down to his north balcony, and come up behind him through the second-floor entry.

BRING THE STASH TO THE MOUSE

Before you grab Mouse's stash **(10)** from the cellar of this building—which is in the same room with one of the two treasures—we suggest killing the large brute guard at the main barracks exit **(11)**. You have to carry the chest out and you cannot climb ladders with it in your hands. One option is to go out the main gate. Grab the final treasure in the southeast building before you leave. Once through, the trader's building **(12)** is just 100 meters to the northeast.

Enter the trader's building and climb the stairs to the second level, where you find Mouse at his desk. Drop the chest on the floor on the marker near the doorway to his balcony.

SPEAK TO THE MOUSE

Speak to the Mouse to complete the quest and collect your rewards.

Then money, I will shower you with riches to make
Croesus jealous

FOUNDING FATHER

Prerequisite: Discover Kyrenaika

SUGGESTED LEVEL: 35

REWARDS: 3,000 XP

SPEAK TO THE PRIEST IAKCHOS

Near the Tomb of Battos **(1)**, talk to the Priest Iakchos controlling a crowd of protesters.

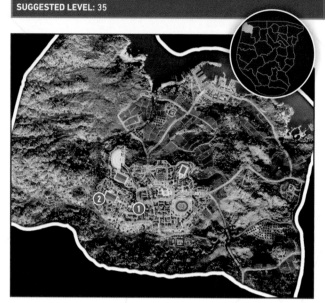

CYRENE BARRACKS

INVESTIGATE WHY THE TOMB OF BATTOS IS CLOSED

Climb up any of the tomb's pillars. Jump through the hole in the roof to land in a shallow pool of water inside. Take the Underground Currents Papyrus Puzzle from a table against the wall and then head down the stairs into the crypt.

Inspect the two display cases on either side of the Battos statue on the back wall. There are two objects missing from the shrine: a bow and a medallion.

FIND AND COLLECT BATTOS' STOLEN RELICS

Return upstairs, climb a wall, then crawl out of the hole in the ceiling. Send Senu up to locate the two missing items. They are inside the south section of the Roman Akropolis fort **(2)** to the west.

Have Senu mark all the enemies on the south section of this massive fort.

Climb up the front, south corner wall walk **(3)**, if there are no guards patrolling up there. It's usually clear. Climb to the top of the higher wall walk. Peek over to make sure no one is patrolling nearby; if so, sneak up and assassinate them from behind.

Sneak up behind the solider looking out the south window in the first guardhouse **(4)**. Take arrows from inside if necessary.

Shoot the soldiers on the wall walk to the west: **(5)**, **(8)**, and **(9)**. Use arrows or sleep darts and then assassinate them in their sleep.

On the south wall walk, reach a vantage point **(6)** where you can shoot an arrow through an open window and into the head of a soldier **(7)** sitting in a building.

Climb up the guardhouse **(10)** and set the brazier trap. If there is a guard inside this house, drop down through the ladder hole and kill him.

Head to the walk's east edge (in front of the hiding booth) and through the opening **(11)** in the railing. Shoot any soldiers in the courtyard below **(12)**. Eliminate everyone you can from the courtyard now. Use the hiding booth if you trigger a search patrol.

Crawl over the rooftop **(13)**, drop down and enter the building through the second-floor balcony. Take the Rare warrior bow from the table. Equip it if it's better than what you have.

Exit the building and cross the courtyard heading north to the treasure building **(14)**. If you have not cleared the location objective yet, get the treasure if you haven't already.

Climb the exterior stairs **(15)** slowly and while crouched. The marked Level 35 elite soldier with the medallion is on the north terrace **(16)**. He patrols this area, where there's also a large haystack. From around the stair wall, throw sleep darts at the thief and then execute him in his sleep. Take the Medallion of the Battos.

BRING THE RELICS TO THE PRIEST NEAR THE BATTOS TOMB

Since you have cleared the route, retrace the steps that led you to this medallion to escape the fort. Or take your chances and run through the main south gate, mount a horse, and outrun pursuers.

When out of conflict, speak to the priest **(1)** at the tomb to complete the quest.

PAX ROMANA

Prerequisite: Complete Main Quest: The Final Weighing and Side Quest: The Good Roman

SUGGESTED LEVEL: 35 | REWARDS: 5,250 XP, Rare Hunter Bow

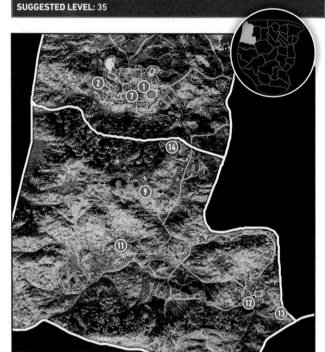

FIND THE DEED TO LEANDER'S VILLA

Talk to Diocles in town square **(1)**. He asks you to get the deed to Leander's villa, as it should be returned to the people.

Travel west to the Roman Akropolis **(2)**. Climb the northwest wall **(3)** in the corner closest to the building **(4)** with the cellar access. Defeat any nearby soldiers on the wall walk who could alert others or light a brazier. Jump down into the courtyard and defeat just enough soldiers necessary to run into the northwest building's first-floor entryway **(4)**. Once inside, follow the

marker into the room on the left and drop down into the cellar hole.

Grab the Deed to Leander's Villa from the table on the right inside the cellar cave.

BRING THE DEED TO DIOCLES

Head to the building's top floor **(4)** and exit onto the balcony **(5)**. Run across the rooftops and jump from the flagpole to the wall walk.

Head back the way you came (toward the objective marker) and veer left as you pass through the first guardhouse. Leap from the flagpole at the corner of the wall walk **(6)** into a haystack below. Now run or ride to Diocles **(7)** at his home to give him the deed.

Take Diocles's carbon crystal from his balcony table before you leave.

FIND VITRUVIUS

Travel southeast to Green Mountain, where you find Vitruvius on the side of the road with some workers **(8)**. Talk to him.

FIND AND RETRIEVE VITRUVIUS'S MANUSCRIPT

DESPERATE GULLY HIDEOUT

Prerequisite: Approach the hideout

Suggested Level: 35　　　　　　　　　**Location Reward: 600 XP**　　　　　　　　　**Location Objectives: Kill one captain, loot one treasure**

Send Senu up to the north to locate the manuscript inside the Desperate Gully Hideout **(9)**. Most of the bandits are in the hideout hole, which makes it easy for you to circle around the hideout using the cliff edges and tall grass for cover. Take out the one bandit that patrols the walkway to the top of the hideout; then shoot the fish in the barrel. Use arrows or a sleep dart and arrow combo. This is not a difficult area to clean out.

The bandit with the manuscript is equipped with a shield and large sword. Defeat him to grab the De Architectura manuscript. Kill the captain and collect the treasure **(10)** to complete the location objective.

RETURN DE ARCHITECTURE TO VITRUVIUS

Ride southwest to the aqueduct to return the manuscript to Vitruvius **(11)**.

SPEAK TO PRAXILLA AT HER CLINIC

Travel southeast to Balagrae to speak to Praxilla **(12)** at her clinic.

FIND CRIOS

Travel southeast out of Balagrae toward the marker and then send Senu up to locate Crios **(13)** when you get close. You'll find Crios stranded on a large boulder with a circling, hungry lion.

RESCUE CRIOS

Jump onto the boulder and locate the lion circling below. Shoot it with arrows or slay it with a weapon. Or, if you have the ability, tame it.

SPEAK TO CRIOS

Talk to Crios once the lion is gone.

MEET WITH YOUR FRIENDS AT THE ORACLE OF APOLLO

Cyrene's Triumvirate! Heralds of a new peace for this outpost of Rome

Use the Viewpoint at the Oracle of Apollo **(14)** to Fast Travel to your gathering of close friends. Approach them as they stand waiting for you at the overlook.

INTRODUCTION

THE ESSENTIALS

MAIN QUESTS

SIDE QUESTS

ACTIVITIES

ATLAS

REFERENCE & ANALYSIS

CAT AND MOUSE

Prerequisite: Complete Side Quest: The Mousetrap

SUGGESTED LEVEL: 36   **REWARDS:** 3,000 XP

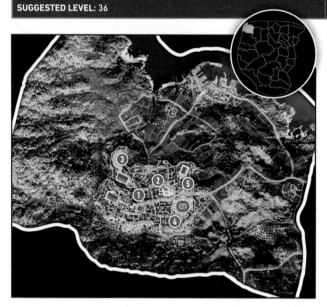

RESCUE THE MOUSE

Track down the Mouse **(1)**, who is held captive in a jail cart traveling the road near the Apollonion of Cyrene. The driver is alone with no support. Simply follow the cart and hit the driver with a warrior arrow or put the horses to sleep with sleep darts to buy you more time to assassinate the driver.

CARRY THE MOUSE TO SAFETY

Open the cage and pick up the Mouse. Carry him away from the cart until the "Speak to the Mouse" objective becomes active. Then drop him.

FIND THE MURDER SITE AT THE BATHS

Head northeast to the Baths **(2)** and find the open window up on the building's southwest side. There are many soldiers patrolling inside; having direct entry into the investigation room makes things easier.

INVESTIGATE THE MURDER SITE

Inspect the bloodstains on the floor near the locked door to reach the next objective.

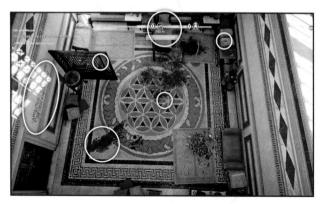

INVESTIGATE THE REST OF THE BATHS

Climb the wall behind the bed with the beads clue on it; then stand on the top and look down at the few guards below. One is guarding the room you need to get into (the one that the bloodstains lead to).

Throw sleep darts at one or both of the guards and then drop-assassinate the other. Run into the room quickly, and investigate Paulus Aurelius's body in the back before more guards track you down. You acquire the On the Usurer Paulus Aurelius note, which names the actor Metrobius as the next victim.

FIND METROBIUS AT THE THEATER OF APOLLO

Get back to the investigation room by climbing the walls. Exit the Baths through the same open window used to enter.

Mount up and ride to the amphitheater **(3)** in northwest Cyrene. On the ground before the stage is another dead body, but you need to destroy the lion before you can investigate.

EXAMINE METROBIUS'S CORPSE

Interact with Metrobius's corpse to obtain the On the Pickled Ham Metrobius note. The note mentions the next scene takes place at the brothel, the Wolf's Den.

FIND THE WHORER AT THE WOLF'S DEN

Mount up and ride southeast to the Wolf's Den **(4)**. Have the warrior bow ready before you approach the body.

EXAMINE THE WHORER'S CORPSE

You find yet another note on the dead victim: On my father the Whorer Akakios. It reads, "Father you die. You will be quiet now mother?"

KILL VESTA THE MURDERER

As soon as you are done examining the father, draw your warrior bow and look west to the open doorway. The murderer is coming at you from inside the building. Fill him with holes. Confirm the kill to receive the On Vesta's Son Oidipous note.

SPEAK TO THE MOUSE

Travel north to find the Mouse **(5)** hiding in some bushes south of the Temple of Zeus. You let him know that he is in the free and clear, the killer has been killed, but you have his letters as proof.

ABSOLUTE POWER

Prerequisite: Discover Kyrenaika

SUGGESTED LEVEL: 36

REWARDS: 4,500 XP

INTRODUCTION

THE ESSENTIALS

MAIN QUESTS

SIDE QUESTS

ACTIVITIES

ATLAS

REFERENCE & ANALYSIS

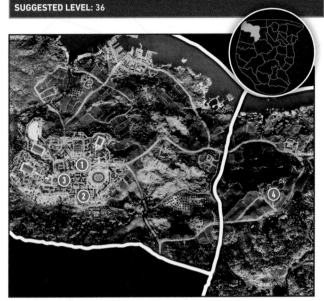

FIND THE MAGISTRATE SIMONIDES

CYRENE

Visit and speak with Diocles **(1)** in Cyrene's town square to begin this quest.

FIND THE MAGISTRATE SIMONIDES

Send Senu up to locate Simonides **(2)**. He's to the south in the craftsmen district. You can find him on the ground in a small alley near the south wall walk. Speak to him. Pick him up and carry him.

BRING SIMONIDES TO DIOCLES'S HOUSE

Either carry Simonides and run or put him on a horse and deliver him to Diocles's house **(3)** to the northwest.

FIND AND RETRIEVE LEANDER'S LEDGER

LEANDER'S VILLA

Leander's farm **(4)** is 1,240 meters to the east in Marmarica. Ride there now. When close, send Senu up to pinpoint the ledger. The villa is heavily guarded by soldiers. Make a dash for the marker with the most direct route possible, taking out only the guards who try to stop you. Use chain attacks when faced with more than one enemy at a time.

Get to the villa's second floor and loot the two treasures in the same room as the ledger to complete the location objective.

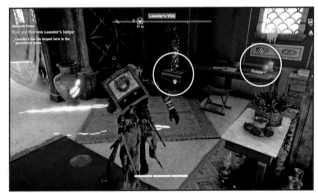

WARN DIOCLES

CYRENE

Race west (or use a Viewpoint for Fast Travel) back to Cyrene to find Diocles in the Apollonion of Cyrene **(5)**.

Defeat the two soldiers at the top of the steps.

DEFEND DIOCLES

Rush inside and stop the soldiers from killing Diocles. They come in through the back entrance. Diocles assists in his own defense. After killing the four soldiers, Diocles thanks you.

ARE YOU NOT ENTERTAINED?

Prerequisite: Discover Kyrenaika

SUGGESTED LEVEL: 37	REWARDS: 3,000 XP, Rare Regular Sword

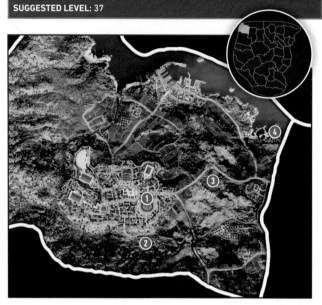

SPEAK TO THE LANISTA

Read the sign **(1)** on the wall at the stairs of the gladiator arena, or just go to the gladiator school **(2)** to begin this quest.

The lanista says his champion fighter, the Thracian Bear, has escaped and there's a bounty on his head.

FOLLOW THE LANISTA

Follow the lanista into the next area to the west, where he will pit you against three of his gladiators.

DEFEAT THE GLADIATORS

The Level 35 gladiators are pushovers compared to the gladiators you fought in the arena or any of the Roman soldiers you've crossed. Slaughter them to prove your worth. Use a long heavy blunt or heavy blade to strike multiple opponents at once.

SPEAK TO THE LANISTA

Talk to the lanista, who just witnessed you slaughter his best remaining gladiators.

REACH THE FARM MASSACRE

Travel northeast to the Silphion Farm **(3)**, where two lions roam the grounds. Kill them so you can investigate the brutal scene at the farm.

INVESTIGATE THE MASSACRE AT THE FARM

Inspect the mutilated bodies on the ground just outside the barn. Use Animus Pulse to find more clues, like the body facedown with arrows in its back inside the barn.

Inspect the two bodies bound and secured to the wall, one with a spear in the back. Shoot arrows into the well cover inside the barn to reach the clue that pings underneath the ground. Jump into the well.

Down below, you find a letter on a table: My Friends and Saviors.

FIND POLYMESTOR AT THE FINISHING VILLAGE

Travel northeast to the fishing village **(4)** and find the gladiator on the beach. He tells you he threw the lanista's sword in the sea.

FIND AND RETRIEVE THE LANISTA'S SWORD

Send Senu up to locate the sword in the water just off the pier to the east. Jump off the pier and dive down to the marked sword. Interact with it to pick it up.

RETURN TO POLYMESTOR

Get out of the water and send Senu up to mark the soldiers who have now approached Polymestor onshore where you left him.

Six soldiers surround him. Before you run up to the group, take a few of them out with arrows from a distance. Then run in and attack. Fight by the gladiator's side to eliminate the threat.

After the battle is won, the Bear thanks you and lets you keep the Rare regular word: Sword of the Free. You do not need to return it to that shady lanista.

THE SMUGGLERS OF CYRENE

Prerequisite: Complete Side Quest: Cat and Mouse

SUGGESTED LEVEL: 37

REWARDS: 4,000 XP, Rare Heavy Blade

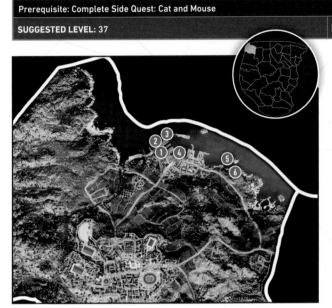

SPEAK TO THE MOUSE

Talk to the Mouse, Smithnos **(1)**, near the north coast of Cyrene. He is standing under a large shelter.

FOLLOW THE MOUSE

Follow the Mouse as he heads north to the docks **(2)**. He tells you to steal the dock manifest so you can get the Black Crow's scheduled route into the harbor.

FIND AND RETRIEVE THE BLACK CROW'S MANIFEST

APOLLONIA

Send Senu up and to the northeast over the pier to locate the soldier carrying the manifest. While scanning, mark the soldiers around the pier. You face Level 37 to 38 enemies here.

There's very few guards who stand between where you last talked to the Mouse on the docks and the shelter where the manifest carrier **(3)** is located. Just run in and catch the patrols off guard. Eliminate them quickly so as not to start a big battle with guards farther beyond the manifest location.

Shoot an arrow into the manifest holder's head, and take out the next nearest soldier so he won't see you looting the dead soldier for the schedule.

Confirm the kill to acquire the Apollonia Dock Manifest.

SPEAK TO THE MOUSE

Now run to the Mouse to the southeast. He is standing on the end of a small dock **(4)**.

FIND AND COLLECT THE SMUGGLER'S LOOT

Four markers appear onscreen, all about 300 to 370 meters away to the east. The booty was dropped near the Thibron Expedition Shipwreck **(5)**. Take the boat from the dock and sail toward the shipwreck and the markers. Shoot any nearby enemies on other smaller boats in the area.

Send Senu up to pinpoint the submerged booty. Then go swimming and retrieve the four objects from the shipwreck area. Collect the two treasures while you're down there to complete the Thibron Expedition Shipwreck location objective.

BRING THE LOOT TO THE MOUSE AT THE RUINS

Now take a boat to the shore and find the Mouse **(6)** at the Sunken Shrine of Aristoteles. When you arrive, you find soldiers attacking him.

DEFEND THE MOUSE

The Mouse's health bar appears onscreen. If you do not defend him and his health drains completely, then you fail and must retry the objective again. Fend off the five enemies to save Smithnos, who is bound and kneeling in the middle of the ruins. Use chain attacks to make quick work of them. Approach the Mouse to free him and to complete the quest.

DEAD IN THE WATER

Prerequisite: Discover Kyrenaika

SUGGESTED LEVEL: 38 | **REWARDS: 3,000 XP**

FIND AND RESCUE AGATHA'S SON

Talk to the old woman **(1)** in Apollonia. She says her son, Titus, has been imprisoned at the barracks for trying to leave the army. You tell her you'll look into it. You're a block from the barracks. Send Senu up to locate Titus in the Apollonia Barracks **(2)**.

APOLLONIA ROMAN BARRACKS

Prerequisite: Approach the barracks

SUGGESTED LEVEL: 38 | **LOCATION REWARD: 600 XP** | **LOCATION OBJECTIVES: Kill one captain, loot one treasure**

Senu locates the prisoner in the barracks' southeast corner. There's not many soldiers in this base but it's best to eliminate those on the southern half who will see you marching out the front gate with the prisoner. So, climb the southeastern wall **(2)** and kill any guards on the wall walk. Sometimes you find one in the southeast guard tower **(3)**. Set the brazier trap **(4)** just in case. Move around the wall walk looking for opportunities to perform a drop attack or bow attacks.

Enter the captain's building **(5)** from the east interior hallway entrance so you can sneak up behind him while he sits at his desk. Assassinate him and take the treasure from the same room to complete the location objective.

Once the area is clear, head back to the southeast corner and free Titus from the cell on the building's first floor **(6)**. Open the cell and free him.

LEGEND
- Ballista
- Hiding Booth

ESCORT TITUS OUT OF APOLLONIA BARRACKS

Have Titus follow you west to the main southern gate **(7)** that opens to the street. March out the main entrance and get to a secluded area quickly. Titus wants to fight Romans, and if he sees one, he will attack. If he does, finish the job quickly for him so it doesn't attract more Romans in the area and turn into a huge ruckus.

SPEAK WITH TITUS

Speak to Titus once you're out of conflict.

FIND AND ASSASSINATE THE NAVARCH

Take a boat from the barrack's pier and sail east toward the marker. When you get near the marker, send Senu up to pinpoint the navarch's ship **(8)**. Have Senu mark the five Level 34 to 35 soldiers aboard. Sail to the ship and board it. Try stealthily pulling a couple overboard from the deck's edge and maybe climbing the ropes above the ship to perform drop assassinations. After you kill the navarch (marked), the quest ends successfully.

MY BROTHER FOR A HORSE

Prerequisite: Discover Kyrenaika

SUGGESTED LEVEL: 38	REWARDS: 4,000 XP, Rare Mount

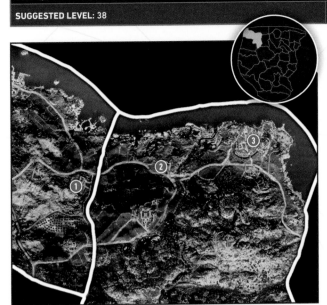

FIND AND RETRIEVE THE REQUISITION LIST

The horse master Darius **(1)** is at the stables near the eastern boarder of Kyrenaika. Speak to him.

Travel east into Marmarica to the Archile Pandocheion. When you get close to this village, send Senu up to investigate. She can locate the list **(2)** in the main house near the main road. There's also a few bandits guarding the list. When you near the building, one of the bandits picks up the list and takes it with him toward the main road.

Enter through the back door of this house and follow them out to the road; this gives you the advantage of stealth. Sneak up behind the  marked soldier and assassinate him. You can put all three bandits to sleep and then assassinate them. Confirm the kill of the list-holder if you don't have the loot on kill ability. You'll receive the Supplies Secured list.

FIND AND STEAL THE STALLION FROM CHERSONESOS ROMAN FORT

Travel northeast to the Chersonesos Roman Fort **(3)**. Have Senu scan the fort to locate Praefectus Equites. He rides his horse Hermes on his daily route around the fort. Perfect! You don't need to raid the fort right now (save it for a side activity). Simply tag the target and wait for him to exit the fort and ride on the road west of the fort, well enough away that only his bodyguard will see you kill him.

Select your warrior bow and follow Praefectus. Shoot the target first and then deal with the second mounted soldier last. With them both dead, hop on Hermes.

BRING HERMES BACK TO HIS MASTER AT THE HORSE FARM

Now ride Hermes back to the horse farm **(1)** and return him to Darius. Enjoy the ride. He's quick and agile. Don't worry, you'll earn one much like  him at the end of the quest.

INTRODUCTION

THE ESSENTIALS

MAIN QUESTS

SIDE QUESTS

ACTIVITIES

ATLAS

REFERENCE & ANALYSIS

MARMARICA

HIS SECRET SERVICE

Prerequisite: Available once Bayek leaves Siwa

SUGGESTED LEVEL: 38	REWARDS: 3,000 XP	DETAILS: Several spies have been captured, imprisoned, and tortured. Bayek must find out if any of the network remain, or the future of Egypt could be in serious danger.

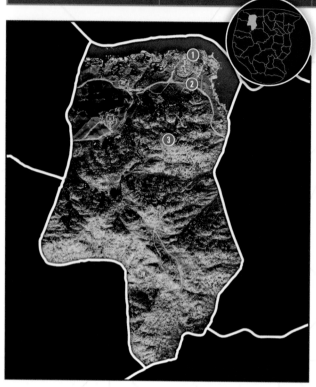

Chersonesos Roman Fort **(1)** is a big Roman stronghold, but you can ignore it as you perform this quest. Move around to the fort's northeast side and climb up the rock to find a few prisoners. You can release all of them, but you only need to unlock the northern small cage. This begins the quest.

CARRY THE PRISONER OUT OF CHERSONESOS ROMAN FORT

Pick up the prisoner and exit out the northeast side. Stick to the fort's fence line as you move toward the main road. As you descend the rocky levels, look for the shortest drops to limit damage.

SPEAK TO THE PRISONER

Set the prisoner down once you near the road **(2)**. He tells you of a spy list that's in the hands of a Roman Centurion who patrols the towers on Marmarica's eastern border.

BEMULOS ROMAN TOWER

Prerequisite: Approach the tower
Suggested Level: 38
Location Reward: 600 XP
Location Objectives: Kill one captain, loot one treasure

FIND AND RETRIEVE THE SPY LIST

Follow the road up the mountain to the south. Your destination is Bemulos Roman Tower, perched atop the high peak of northeastern Marmarica **(3)**. Watch out for high-level enemies that may attack as you push farther into their territory.

Approach the rear of the tower, and have Senu scout the area to find your target. He is near the tower, possibly resting at the campfire or inside the building. A couple soldiers always accompany him. Quietly take down the Roman soldiers who guard the tower first and hide them outside the tower walls, if possible.

Once you have eliminated everyone else, including the Level 39 captain, pick off the Centurion's guards and then kill your target to retrieve the spy list (Apollodorus' Agents in Kyrenaika).

Before you leave the tower, collect the treasure from inside the structure.

ISOLATED DESERT

PLIGHT OF THE REBELS

Prerequisite: Available once Bayek leaves Siwa

SUGGESTED LEVEL: 40	REWARDS: 7,500 XP	DETAILS: Bayek is asked to find two children who wandered away from their camp while on a treasure hunting adventure. He must first rescue the two rebels out searching for the children.

FIND AND RESCUE THE REBEL PRISONERS

Exit Rematch Ra and ride north toward Camp Hetoimazo **(2)**. About halfway there, a group of rebels may ride to the camp, giving you a hand in the fight. Continue north, dismounting just before the camp.

TALK TO NAWA

Nawa **(1)** teaches class in Rematch Ra. Talk to her to learn of two missing children, who have wandered off in pursuit of Alexander the Great's treasure. On top of that, Pharaoh's soldiers have captured Sebni and a great warrior of the village as they searched for the kids. They are held captive at Camp Hetoimazo, to the north. That is your first objective, since they may have knowledge of the children's whereabouts.

BEWARE OF THE PHYLAKE—THE GALATIAN

While exploring the desert, remain vigilant of the Phylake that patrols the territory (assuming you haven't already killed the bounty hunter). He rides the main roads that you will follow throughout much of this quest. If an enemy manages to light the brazier at one of the camps, the Phylake will respond if nearby.

CAMP HETOIMAZO

Prerequisite: Approach the camp

SUGGESTED LEVEL: 39	LOCATION REWARD: 600 XP	LOCATION OBJECTIVES: Kill one captain, loot one treasure

Sneak into the tall grass on the camp's south side to find the cages **(3)** that hold the two rebel prisoners. Before releasing them, set a trap at the brazier to eliminate the arrival of reinforcements. Set the prisoners free, and they move into the camp; no matter what you do, you must defeat the enemies.

Seek out the Level 39 captain first; put an arrow or two into the predator's head before joining the battle. Once you clear out the camp, enter the eastern tent and collect the treasure.

FOLLOW THE REBEL PRISONERS AND SPEAK TO SEBNI ABOUT THE REBEL CHILDREN

Once you are done at the camp, join the two rebels to the southeast. Speak to Sebni to discover that the children could have gone to the ancient temple of Alexander the Great to the northwest or to the nearby rebel village of Theos Elpis Rift.

FOLLOW THE REBEL TO ALEXANDER'S TEMPLE

As the two rebels split up, follow the warrior northwest to Alexander's Temple **(4)**. Continue searching for the missing rebel children. Along the way, you learn more about the inquisitive kids they seek. Four high-level soldiers greet you and the rebel at the temple. Fend them off from horseback or hop off and take them down.

INVESTIGATE ALEXANDER'S TEMPLE TO LOCATE THE CHILDREN

Follow the rebel through the opening in the temple to reach an investigation area among the ruins.

ALEXANDER'S TEMPLE
Prerequisite: Approach the camp
SUGGESTED LEVEL: 39
LOCATION REWARD: 450 XP
LOCATION OBJECTIVES: Loot two treasures

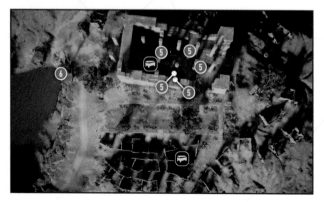

Use Animus Pulse to find the clues **(5)** and interact with them. Cobras appear throughout the temple grounds, so proceed cautiously. You see footprints next to the downed pillar, and children's sandals lie near the eastern wall. Climb the wall next to the sandals to find a torn piece of cloth; investigate the ostraca next to the bench. Descend the steps. You hear a child crying out for help. The obstacle does not budge, so you must look for another way in.

SKIP THE INVESTIGATION
It is possible to skip to the next step without performing the investigation.

FIND A WAY INSIDE THE TEMPLE

Dive into the lake in front of the temple and enter the hidden tunnel **(6)** in the northwestern corner. Follow the path to find the child, trapped with a group of cobras. Slay the snakes.

ESCORT HETANU OUT OF THE TEMPLE

Speak to Hetanu and then collect the treasure that sits on the pedestal. Destroy the pots that block the moveable obstacle and then slide it into the corner. Return to Khamet with the child. Speak with him to find out Istellah was headed to Theos Elpis Rift **(7)**.

DEFEND THE REBEL CAMP FROM THE PHARAOH'S SOLDIERS

Head southwest and enter the chasm to find the rebel camp. Pharaoh's soldiers have invaded the village, so take up arms and start killing the foes.

SPEAK TO SEBNI THE REBEL

Once the village is safe again, Sebni informs Bayek that the rival leader, Medon, has taken Istellah—possibly to Pissa Oros. Pissa Oros Citadel is a big fort in southwestern Isolated Desert. This provides two objectives for you: rescue Istellah from the fort and assassinate Medon.

FIND AND ASSASSINATE THE LEADER OF THE REBELS' ENEMIES

Head southwest along the main thoroughfare until Camp Khoikos **(8)** is within range of Senu. Send her up and find the leader Medon.

CAMP KHOIKOS
Prerequisite: Approach the camp
SUGGESTED LEVEL: 40
LOCATION REWARD: 600 XP
LOCATION OBJECTIVES: Kill one captain, loot one treasures

Medon is either inside or exiting the camp on his way toward the citadel. Bodyguards surround the leader, so take them away from the camp to limit the number of enemies—though it is possible that rebels have already started a fight in the camp.

If the battle is within the camp, make your first stop the brazier and set a trap. Move outside the area and pick off as many of the enemies as you can with your bow before entering the fray.

Try to lure the two targets away from the big group, one at a time, for a fairer fight. Medon is a Level 40 super-soldier with spears and a small shield, while the camp's captain is a Level 39 predator. Once you secure the area, collect the treasure from the biggest tent on the north side.

FIND AND RESCUE ISTELLAH THE REBEL CHILD

With Medon out of the way, it is time to rescue Istellah from the citadel. Stop short of Pissa Oros Citadel **(9)** and have Senu scout out the fort. Mark every enemy possible and note the hidden entrance on the south side, as well as Istellah's location **(10)** deep inside the stronghold. Be cautious entering through the hidden entrance, as soldiers often patrol near the opening inside the base. Check out the area with Senu before exiting.

PISSA OROS CITADEL

Prerequisite: Approach the citadel

SUGGESTED LEVEL: 40   LOCATION REWARD: 1,500 XP   LOCATION OBJECTIVES: Kill one commander and two captains, loot four treasure

You must infiltrate the fort, find the child hidden on the back of a hay wagon, and safely ride out of the enemy base. It is possible to sneak straight to Istellah **(10)**, mount the cart, and speed out. You may need to pick off soldiers with your bow if too many get in the way, but this is the quick and dirty way to complete the quest.

With four treasures, two captains, and a commander required to complete the location, it is well worth the time to sneak into the fort and stealthily head through the stronghold—picking off most, if not all, of the Pharaoh's soldiers. There are plenty of arrow stands along the way for you to restock. Be sure to hide bodies and stay hidden or risk a soldier lighting the brazier.

Attacking at nighttime reduces activity in the fort, with a captain and the commander possibly asleep. One captain spends his time in the courtyard near the east corner, while the other spends much of his time in the southern portion. The commander is in or near the well-fortified, lower room in the center of the northwest side.

Once you have eliminated most of the soldiers and found Istellah, mount the cart and take an immediate left—following the road through the archway. You can take out any stragglers along the way, but it is not necessary. Just be sure to stay on the path.

COLLECT THE LOOT

If you have not completed Pissa Oros Citadel, then collect the loot before you leave. Find two treasures in the northern room that the commander stayed in. The other two treasures are not far away on the third level. If you failed to kill both captains and/or the commander, take care of them too.

BRING THE CART TO AKROS PEAK

Follow the road out of the fort and continue to the right, alongside the fort. Follow the path straight and right at the intersections (refer to the in-game map if you lose your bearings). This leads straight to a rebel camp **(11)** at the southwest Viewpoint and completes the quest.

ACTIVITIES

There are numerous activities available to keep you busy beyond the main story line and side missions. The following activities are covered in this chapter:

- Gladiator Arena
- Hippodrome Chariot Races
- Hunting Grounds (Animal Lairs)
- Papyrus Puzzles
- Stone Circles
- Tombs
- War Elephants
- Reda's Daily Quests
- Phylakes
- World Events
- Military Strongholds

GLADIATOR ARENAS

TOTAL: 7 Bosses
OBJECTIVE: Win the fight
REWARD: XP for each kill
REWARD FOR NONBOSS EVENT: 150 XP
REWARD FOR BOSS EVENT: 500 XP or 750 XP (Elite Boss) and a piece of Legendary gear (see each boss entry)

When Bayek reaches Krokodilopolis in southern Faiyum Oasis, you can unlock the local gladiator arena by completing specific side quests. With access to the first of two arenas, you can go toe to toe with challenging bosses, but first you must complete three events.

THE EVENTS

Unlock each boss by completing three events: I, II, and III. You can select these in any order, but you must defeat all three to unlock the corresponding boss.

Each event is split into three waves with three to five soldiers per wave. Wipe out a wave to bring out the next group until you've defeated all three waves.

Once the boss is unlocked, Bayek must take down each challenge in order to unlock the next boss event. Each time you defeat a boss, you are given the opportunity to show mercy or kill your opponent. This means you can make Bayek deliver the final blow or not. There are only two bosses at the Krokodilopolis gladiator arena, but once you unlock the second arena in Cyrene, five more bosses become available.

Defeat all the bosses at an arena to unlock Elite events, which are identical to the standard events, but enemies are higher level.

HOW TO COMPETE

The rules in the gladiator arenas are simple: fight to the death. For each event, Bayek is given a specific weapon and, if possible, a shield. The same equipment is

typically used throughout the three events and boss combination. However, on a few occasions, a bow must be used to defeat some challenges.

- Shield mode is advised for most of the fights so that you remain on guard with the ability to deflect as many attacks as possible.

- Depending on the attack, evading to the side often results in an attack of your own from the side or behind the enemy.

- Learn a rival's combo attacks so that you know when to attack. Evade each strike and start your own combo as the enemy ends his maneuver.

- Each type of weapon handles drastically different from the others, so spend some time with them all. The regular sword provides quick strikes and combos. The heavy blunt is slower to hit with but can cause serious damage. The long spear and heavy blade allow for attacks from farther away but leave you vulnerable after a miss.

- In many of the events, traps create additional hazards on the battlefield. Ground spikes, spiked pillars, pits, and fire pose risks for all fighters. Always be aware of your surroundings, steering clear whenever possible. Spikes and fire damage Bayek, while falling in a pit is instant death. By placing a trap between you and an opponent, you can catch your breath and regenerate health, though enemies with long-range weapons can still attack. Keep your guard up and be ready to dodge if necessary.

Use traps around the arena to catch your breath when health gets low. Keep your enemies in view as you move to the opposite side of an object, but beware that anyone carrying a bow can still hit you. Use your shield to block incoming projectiles.

Hyenas, lions, and cobras also appear during a few of the events. Caged animals can be released by busting down a gate, but beware, as they will attack the nearest target. Use this as a distraction when health is low. Cobras may hide inside the bigger urns. Quickly dodge backward when busting them open.

Two events equip Bayek with a warrior bow, which fires multiple arrows with each shot. An ammo rack allows you to restock when arrows run out. In Seleucid, fire braziers allow you to shoot fire arrows at your foes. Simply touch the tip of the arrow to fire.

- In Seleucid, take advantage of the oil jars that litter the arena. Hit them with fire to injure nearby enemies.

For each wave, we list every enemy that you must defeat along with the traps and animals that are present in the arenas. Extra strategies are given for each boss.

KROKODILOPOLIS

TERRITORY: Faiyum Oasis

HOW TO UNLOCK: Complete Side Quest: Champions
(suggested level: 23)

Complete the side quest Champions to gain access to the first of
two gladiator arenas in Krokodilopolis. The first of two arenas
presents two bosses, the Brothers and the Slaver.

THE BROTHERS	SUGGESTED LEVEL: 29	ELITE SUGGESTED LEVEL: 34	HOW TO UNLOCK: Unlocked once arena is available

Two brothers, each with a distinctive combat style, share one desire—to bury you in the arena. Show
them that two is not always better than one.

BROTHERS I

BAYEK'S WEAPON: Regular sword and shield

**DESCRIPTION: An easy battle against soldiers
amid spike traps.**

TRAPS: Spiked pillars

WAVE	ENEMIES
1	L27 Soldiers Type A (x4)
2	L27 Soldiers Type A (x4) L25 Soldier Type D
3	L27 Soldier Type A L27 Soldier Type B L23 Soldier Type C L23 Soldier Type D

BROTHERS II

BAYEK'S WEAPON: Regular sword and shield

**DESCRIPTION: A medium-difficulty fight
against soldiers and brutes with spike traps.**

TRAPS: Spiked pillars, ground spikes, fire trap,
caged L27 lion

WAVE	ENEMIES
1	L27 Soldiers Type A (x3) L25 Soldier Type C
2	L27 Soldiers Type A (x2) L27 Brute Type A
3	L27 Soldiers Type C (x2) L27 Brute Type A L27 Lion (if caged lion gone)

BROTHERS III

BAYEK'S WEAPON: Regular sword and shield

**DESCRIPTION: A difficult battle against the
combined forces of soldiers, brutes, and
elite soldiers.**

TRAPS: Spiked pillars, moving spiked pillars,
ground spikes, pit

WAVE	ENEMIES
1	L27 Soldiers Type A (x3) L26 Ptolemic Type B
2	L27 Soldier Type A L25 Soldier Type B L25 Brute Type C
3	L27 Soldiers Type A (x2) L25 Super Type A

BOSS: THE BROTHERS (VIRIDOVIX AND DIOVICOS)

BAYEK'S WEAPON: Regular sword and shield

ENEMY LEVEL: 28

**DESCRIPTION: Two brothers, each wielding their signature weapons with
imposing strength and aggression.**

REWARD ITEM: None

ELITE REWARD ITEM: Leviathan Legendary Heavy Blade

The first arena boss fight is unique in that you face two enemies instead of one.
Viridovix uses a long scythe, while Diovicos whips around a pair of chains. This
makes for a challenging fight, as the pair attempts to team up on their target.

Viridovix has the ability to
grab and throw you with
his scythe, which enables
his partner to follow with
a combo strike. Evade
backward, avoiding the
long-reaching strike.

While Viridovix swings his scythe around, Diovicos jumps in for a strike or goes in for
a melee combo attack. Dodge to the side and go in for a quick strike with your sword.
When he backs up and bangs his chest, get ready for his jump attack and sidestep
the hit. His defenses are minimal, as he has only his bracers to block your sword.

When Diovicos gets close
to Bayek, he attempts to
grab and slam you into
the ground. Depending
on your level, this can be
a devastating blow, so
evade backward when he
moves in.

Viridovix has a charge attack, where he runs at you and swings his scythe. This
allows him to close in from distance, but the strike is still relatively slow. Stay alert
for his combo, dodging backward until he stops. A third attack is his spin attack,
which is highly damaging if he hits you. If he misses, though, he goes down on a
knee to recover—providing a great opportunity to strike.

Attempt to isolate one of the brothers by running to the opposite side of the arena
and fighting the first guy to reach your location. The fire that burns in the middle of

the stadium also allows
you to separate yourself
from a boss. Avoid
attacking when both
brothers are nearby.

THE SLAVER

The Slaver is big, he's brutal, and he wants to put you in chains—permanently. Stop him.

SLAVER I

BAYEK'S WEAPON: Heavy blade and shield

DESCRIPTION: An easy battle against soldiers, brutes, and archers with spike traps.

TRAPS: Spiked pillars, moving spiked pillars, ground spikes

WAVE	ENEMIES
1	L30 Soldier Type A L30 Soldier Type B L28 Archer Type A L28 Brute Type A
2	L30 Soldier Type B L29 Soldier Type C L28 Brutes Type A (x2)
3	L29 Soldier Type C L30 Archer Type C L28 Brute Type A L27 Brute Type B

SLAVER I

BAYEK'S WEAPON: Heavy blade and shield

DESCRIPTION: A medium-difficulty fight against soldiers, brutes, and archers amidst spike traps.

TRAPS: Ground spikes, pit

WAVE	ENEMIES
1	L30 Soldiers Type A (x2) L28 Brute Type A L29 Brute Type B
2	L30 Soldier Type B (x2) L29 Archer Type A L28 Brutes Type A (x2)
3	L29 Brutes Type A (x2) L30 Brute Type B

SLAVER I

BAYEK'S WEAPON: Heavy blade and shield

DESCRIPTION: A difficult fight against soldiers, brutes, and archers while avoiding spike traps.

TRAPS: None

WAVE	ENEMIES
1	L30 Soldiers Type A (x2) L29 Archer Type A L30 Brute Type C (Phylake)
2	L30 Soldier Type C L30 Archer Type A L29 Brute Type A
3	L29 Brute Type A L30 Brute Type B

BOSS—THE SLAVER

BAYEK'S WEAPON: Heavy blade and shield

ENEMY LEVEL: 30

DESCRIPTION: A furious giant with a massive weapon, the Slaver is a man mountain of angry mindless brawn.

REWARD ITEM: 25 drachmas, Dress of the Coastal Realm Legendary Outfit

ELITE REWARD ITEM: 50 drachmas, none

TRAPS: Spiked pillars

Three spiked pillars spin in place on either side of the arena during the Slaver boss fight. Remain aware of these traps as you move around the battlefield, especially when backpedaling

away from your opponent. Place one of these obstacles between you and the boss to recoup health. The Slaver may strike the pillar, destroying your temporary protection.

The Slaver is a beast of a boss who uses a long pole with a claw on the end. He has several moves with the weapon. His big swings are devastating but are fairly slow, giving you a chance to evade back out of his reach.

Worse than his big swing attack is his combos. If he spins around for a really big hit, evade away from him and be ready to repeat this a few times to avoid the entire set of strikes. Learn these strings of attacks and be ready to strike the moment he comes to a stop.

He also has a quick step-stab attack, which you need to be ready for, as he pokes forward with the bottom of his weapon. He may also lunge forward and stab with the claw, which has

can grab his target and toss him forward. This damages Bayek if a spiked pillar stops his momentum.

If he feels confident, the Slaver may rest his weapon on his shoulder in a taunting move. If you're close, go in for a three-hit combo.

If Bayek lies on the ground, the Slaver stabs the claw at you, so ready an evade maneuver to avoid the attack. This gives you an opportunity to get a hit or two in while he is vulnerable.

Continue to wear down the beast until he falls to the ground in defeat.

CYRENE

TERRITORY: Kyrenaika

HOW TO UNLOCK: Complete Side Quest—The Lure of Glory (suggested level: 30)

The owner of the Krokodilopolis arena sends Bayek to Cyrene to meet the owner of the second gladiator arena in the quest, the Lure of Glory. Five arena events are available at Cyrene, with suggested levels between 34 and 40.

SUGGESTED LEVEL: 34	**ELITE SUGGESTED LEVEL: 38**	**HOW TO UNLOCK:** Unlocked once arena is available

THE HAMMER

He's the Hammer, and you're the nail. Avoid the deadly arc of his cudgel, and show him some Siwan justice. Don't get smashed!

HAMMER I

BAYEK'S WEAPON: Regular sword and shield

DESCRIPTION: An easy fight against soldiers, brutes, and archers.

TRAPS: Ground spikes

WAVE	ENEMIES
1	L33 Soldier Type A L34 Soldier Type A L33 Soldier Type D L32 Brute Type A
2	L33 Soldiers Type A (x2) L34 Soldier Type B L32 Brute Type A
3	L33 Soldiers Type A (x2) L34 Archer Type A (x2) L32 Brute Type B

HAMMER II

BAYEK'S WEAPON: Regular sword and shield

DESCRIPTION: A medium-difficulty battle against soldiers and brutes amidst spike traps.

TRAPS: Ground spikes

WAVE	ENEMIES
1	L34 Soldiers Type A (x3) L31 Soldier Type C L32 Brute Type A
2	L34 Soldier Type A L31 Brute Type A L32 Brute Type B
3	L34 Soldiers Type A (x2) L33 Soldiers Type D (x2) L32 Brute Type B

HAMMER III

BAYEK'S WEAPON: Regular sword and shield

DESCRIPTION: A difficult fight against soldiers and brutes while avoiding spike traps and a pit.

TRAPS: Spiked pillars, ground spikes, pit

WAVE	ENEMIES
1	L34 Soldiers Type A (x2) L31 Brute Type A L34 Brute Type C
2	L34 Soldiers Type A (x2) L30 Soldiers Type D (x2)
3	L32 Brutes Type A (x2)

BOSS—THE HAMMER

BAYEK'S WEAPON: Regular sword and shield

ENEMY LEVEL: 34

DESCRIPTION: Brutal warrior who wields his two-handed hammer with the concussive power of a stone block.

REWARD ITEM: Priest of Ma'at Rare Warrior Bow

ELITE REWARD ITEM: Roman Legionary Legendary Outfit

TRAPS: None

Several precarious pillars stand around the perimeter of the arena. You can use these for a temporary reprieve, but one swing of the boss's enormous hammer destroys the obstacle in an instant.

Once healed, move out from behind the pillar to save it for later.

The Raging Hammer is a powerful boss with a massive weapon. He can take quite a bit of punishment before going down, and one swing of his hammer can knock off a good chunk of health. It takes a little time to get his weapon going, though, giving you plenty of time to react to his attacks.

Watch for him to swing his hammer around on the ground; he follows that up with a couple slams. Stay at a safe distance and then go in for a combo after the second ground pound.

When he takes a couple steps forward, he may rear back and slam the hammer to the ground. Sidestep the slow attack and follow up with a strike of your own.

The Hammer may swing his hammer around twice in an attempt to knock you down. Be careful not to jump the gun—wait out both swings before attacking.

Two quicker moves involve the Hammer running toward you and either stabbing with the handle or backhanding you. Backtrack whenever you see him lunge your way. Be careful, as the

big guy can quickly cover a lot of ground when he charges.

Learn the Hammer's moves, evade his big hammer, and strike whenever the opportunities arise. Eventually the giant goes down with a huge thud.

THE AXES

Overcome the Axes and his sadistic strikes. Put an end to his vicious whirling cleavers without losing any body parts.

AXES I

BAYEK'S WEAPON: Sickle sword and shield

DESCRIPTION: An easy fight against soldiers, elite soldiers, and archers.

TRAPS: Ground spikes

WAVE	ENEMIES
1	L34 Soldiers Type A (x4) L27 Super Type A (Phylake)
2	L34 Soldiers Type A (x4)
3	L31 Soldiers Type B (x2) L31 Soldier Type C L34 Archers Type A (x2)

AXES II

BAYEK'S WEAPON: Sickle sword and shield

DESCRIPTION: A medium-difficulty fight against soldiers and elite soldiers amidst spike traps.

TRAPS: Spiked pillars, ground spikes, caged Level 30 hyenas (x4)

WAVE	ENEMIES
1	L34 Soldiers Type A (x3) L28 Soldier Type B
2	L34 Soldiers Type A (x3) L29 Soldiers Type C (x2)
3	L34 Soldiers Type A (x3) L31 Super Type A

AXES III

BAYEK'S WEAPON: Sickle sword and shield

DESCRIPTION: A difficult battle against soldiers and elite soldiers amongst spike traps.

TRAPS: Moving spiked pillars, ground spikes, pit

WAVE	ENEMIES
1	L34 Soldiers Type A (x2)
2	L34 Soldiers Type A (x3) L29 Soldier Type C
3	L31 Soldiers Type A (x3) L31 Soldier Type C L31 Super Type B L28 Hyenas (x2; introduced later in wave)

BOSS—THE AXES

BAYEK'S WEAPON: Sickle sword and shield	
ENEMY LEVEL: 33	
DESCRIPTION: A sadistic psychopath who favors twin axes for the sheer bloody carnage they cause.	
REWARD ITEM: None	
ELITE REWARD ITEM: None	
TRAPS: None	

When he raises his axes, it means he is ready to run at you and release a brutal combo upon you. Stay out of reach of his axes or, at the very least, put up your shield for a chance to withstand the blows. Do not let your defenses down until you are sure he has completed his attacks. If you are feeling confident, you can interrupt his run, especially if you have an Overpower ready.

As his moniker suggests, this boss prefers to fight with a pair of axes, slicing up his opponents with precision. There is not much to hide behind in the arena, besides the wooden wreckage that

sits on one side. That's too bad, as his jump attacks and devastating combos can wreak havoc. His axes are also used for defense—he crosses them in front of his chest to block and disrupt combos.

When in close, the boss can quickly grab you, perform three headbutts, and toss you to the ground. Always be ready to evade since his moves are quick. He may kick you backward in order to create space, though the move does not cause any damage.

Look for him to swing around to his left, signifying a jump attack is imminent. Move back to avoid his lunge. Once he hits the ground, though, let him have it as he pauses for a moment. A second jump maneuver sees the boss cross his axes, leap forward, and swing outward in an attempt to slice you in two. Step out of the way and attack his side as he reorients himself.

Try to keep your health in the middle to upper third of the health bar. The boss's combo can rip through a big chunk if you are not careful. Patiently pick away at his health between his vicious attacks until he finally falls to the ground.

THE HOPLITE

SUGGESTED LEVEL: 35	ELITE SUGGESTED LEVEL: 39	HOW TO UNLOCK: Defeat boss—the Axes

The Hoplite is a battle-ready Greek soldier with the deadly determination of a Spartan warrior. Take him down if you can.

HOPLITE I

BAYEK'S WEAPON: Heavy blunt weapon and shield

DESCRIPTION: An easy fight against soldiers, brutes, and archers amongst spike traps.

TRAPS: Spiked pillars, ground spikes

WAVE	ENEMIES
1	L35 Soldiers Type A (x2) L35 Soldiers Type B (X2) L35 Brute Type C (does not need to be defeated for next wave to enter)
2	L35 Soldiers Type B (x2) L34 Soldiers Type C (x2)
3	L35 Soldiers Type A (x2) L34 Soldiers Type C (x2) L34 Archers Type A (x2)

HOPLITE II

BAYEK'S WEAPON: Heavy blunt weapon and shield

DESCRIPTION: A medium-difficulty battle with soldiers, brutes, and elite soldiers in the midst of spike traps and a pit.

TRAPS: Moving spiked pillars, ground spikes, pit

WAVE	ENEMIES
1	L35 Soldier Type A L34 Soldiers Type C (x2) L33 Brutes Type A (x2)
2	L35 Soldiers Type A (x2) L35 Soldiers Type B (x2) L33 Super Type B
3	L35 Soldiers Type B (x2) L34 Soldiers Type C (x2) L33 Super Type A

HOPLITE III

BAYEK'S WEAPON: Heavy blunt weapon and shield

DESCRIPTION: A difficult fight against soldiers, brutes, and lions amongst spike traps.

TRAPS: Spiked pillars, ground spikes, fire trap, Trojan horse

WAVE	ENEMIES
1	L35 Soldiers Type A (x2) L35 Soldier Type B L33 Brute Type A
2	L34 Soldier Type C L33 Brutes Type A (x2)
3	L35 Soldiers Type B (x2) L34 Soldiers Type C (x2) L33 Brute Type A L33 Predator Type A L30 Lion (x2; emerge from Trojan horse midwave)

BOSS—THE HOPLITE

BAYEK'S WEAPON: Heavy blunt weapon and shield	
ENEMY LEVEL: 35	
DESCRIPTION: A highly trained, battle-hardened Greek soldier who uses his shield as well as he wields his spear.	
REWARD ITEM: None	
ELITE REWARD ITEM: None	
TRAPS: None	

The Hoplite may leap in the air and throw his spear at Bayek. Watch for him to cock his arm back and sidestep the projectile to avoid impact. After releasing the spear, he must switch to the sword.

The skilled Hoplite wields a spear and shield with the option of switching to his sword at any point. His reach is quite impressive as he lunges at his target with the long lance. His skill with the sword and shield are equally impressive as he attacks with both arms. It is best to keep your shield up and always be ready to evade his quick stabs.

When close, he may attempt to grab and throw Bayek over his shoulder, so always keep a bit of distance from him. The Hoplite also has a quick maneuver with either weapon that pushes his target back, though damage is minimal.

When the sword is equipped, be ready for his jump attacks and slicing combos. Use the shield to block the strikes or use evades in order to move behind the boss. He tends to use his shield about as much as his sword, so be ready for attacks to come from either side.

Your mace attacks at a relatively slow speed, allowing the Hoplite to easily disrupt your combos. Time your strikes just as the boss opens his defenses and limit your combos—getting in one or two blows before backing away.

His spear attacks are all about reach. It is possible to deflect some attacks with your shield, but it is typically best to evade them altogether. If he holds the spear up high, be ready for a

quick stab. If he rears back, watch out for a long stab or a circular attack. The stabs can be sidestepped, while you continue to increase your distance from the sweep and swing moves.

If Bayek is knocked to the ground, the boss attempts to stab you, so time your evade during this attack and follow up with a strike of your own.

The boss can switch to his sword at any time, while he must run to one of the weapon racks that line the perimeter of the arena to equip a spear. His attacks between the two setups differ drastically, so be ready for either.

THE SELEUCID

| SUGGESTED LEVEL: 36 | ELITE SUGGESTED LEVEL: 40 | HOW TO UNLOCK: Defeat boss—the Hoplite |

The Seleucid has trained his entire life for the sole purpose of defeating all comers in battle. Show him what a Medjay can do.

SELEUCID I

BAYEK'S WEAPON: Long spear and shield

DESCRIPTION: An easy fight against soldiers, elite soldiers, predators, and archers with the added danger of fire traps.

TRAPS: Ground spikes, fire traps, fire pillars, pit

WAVE	ENEMIES
1	L35 Soldiers Type A (x3) L34 Archer Type A L35 Super Type C (Phylake; does not need to be defeated for next wave to enter)
2	L34 Soldiers Type D (x2) L34 Archers Type A (x2)
3	L35 Soldiers Type A (x2) L34 Archer Type A L33 Brute Type A

SELEUCID II

BAYEK'S WEAPON: Long spear and shield

DESCRIPTION: A medium-difficulty fight against soldiers, brutes, and archers amidst fire traps.

TRAPS: Moving fire pillars, fire traps, archer stands

WAVE	ENEMIES
1	L35 Soldiers Type A (x4) L33 Archer Type C
2	L35 Soldier Type A L34 Soldiers Type D (x2) L34 Archer Type A L33 Archer Type C L33 Brute Type A
3	L34 Archers Type A (x3) L33 Archer Type C L33 Brutes Type A (x2)

SELEUCID III

BAYEK'S WEAPON: Warrior bow

DESCRIPTION: A difficult battle with soldiers, brutes, and archers while avoiding fire traps.

TRAPS: Moving fire pillars, fire traps

WAVE	ENEMIES
1	L34 Soldiers Type A (x2) L33 Soldiers Type D (x2) L33 Archer Type A
2	L34 Soldier Type A L32 Soldiers Type C (x2) L33 Archer Type A L32 Brute Type A
3	L34 Soldiers Type A (X2) L32 Archer Type A (x2) L33 Brute Type A

BOSS—THE SELEUCID

BAYEK'S WEAPON: Long spear and shield
ENEMY LEVEL: 36
DESCRIPTION: A Greek soldier dedicated to the art of systematically dismantling opponents with his long military pike.
REWARD ITEM: Roman Legionary Legendary Outfit
ELITE REWARD ITEM: Roman Marinus Legendary Outfit
TRAPS: Fire traps

The Seleucid wields an extremely long pike and combines it with a leap attack, allowing him to strike from a very long distance. With the ability to add fire throughout the battle, the fight becomes much tougher as it progress.

The boss uses his pike like a pole vault, performing a jump kick, which he combos into a swing attack. Move backward when you see this coming to avoid the wide range of the pike swing.

He may also run after Bayek as he attempts to harpoon you. This attack is easily sidestepped, but you must be ready for it.

When the boss swings the pike around, stand clear throughout the two swings to avoid taking damage. If he lifts the pike up over his head, move backward or sidestep as he slams the blade into the ground.

After eliminating a quarter of his health bar, he becomes slightly enraged and changes up his moves slightly. Watch out for him to combine his run attack with a swing of the pike or perform a jump-stab maneuver.

At half a health bar, the Seleucid sets the end of his pike ablaze, which means successful hits have a chance to set Bayek on fire—providing more incentive to avoid his lengthy strikes.

The Seleucid begins to combine more of his attacks, such as adding a jump-stab after the double-pike swing and an additional swing after the pole-vault move.

Your light attack swings the spear around, while the heavy attack performs a slower, step-stab maneuver. Use the former when in close, while the latter should be used when the boss is left open at a distance. The Seleucid tends not to hang around for more than two hits, so limit your combos.

At three-quarters of a health bar, the boss starts up the smaller, outside fire traps. With half of a health bar, he lights up the middle. Walking over these traps has a chance of igniting Bayek, so steer clear.

THE DUELIST

| SUGGESTED LEVEL: 38 | ELITE SUGGESTED LEVEL: 40 | HOW TO UNLOCK: Defeat boss—the Seleucid |

Defeat the Duelist in single combat. Avoid her rapid, articulated blade and find an answer for her athletic precision.

DUELIST I

BAYEK'S WEAPON: Regular sword and shield

DESCRIPTION: An easy fight with a mix of all enemy types.

TRAPS: Poison pit, cobras

WAVE	ENEMIES
1	L37 Soldiers Type A (x3) L36 Archers Type A (x2) L35 Super Type A
2	L37 Soldier Type A L36 Archer Type A L35 Brute Type A L35 Predator Type A
3	L36 Soldiers Type D (x2) L36 Archers Type A (x2) L35 Predator Type A L35 Super Type A

DUELIST II

BAYEK'S WEAPON: Regular sword and shield

DESCRIPTION: A medium-difficulty fight against a mix of all enemy types.

TRAPS: Fire pit, cobras

WAVE	ENEMIES
1	L37 Soldiers Type A (x2) L36 Archers Type A (x2) L37 Predatory Type B (Phylake)
2	L37 Soldiers Type A (x2) L36 Soldiers Type D (x2) L20 Predator Type A
3	L37 Soldiers Type A (x2) L36 Archer Type B L35 Super Type A

DUELIST III

BAYEK'S WEAPON: Warrior bow

DESCRIPTION: A difficult battle against a mixture of all enemy types.

TRAPS: Ground spikes, cobras

WAVE	ENEMIES
1	L37 Soldiers Type A (x4) L35 Predator Type B
2	L37 Soldiers Type A L36 Soldiers Type D (x2) L35 Predator Type B L35 Super Type A
3	L37 Soldier Type A L35 Predator Type B L35 Supers Type A (x2)

BOSS—THE DUELIST

| **BAYEK'S WEAPON:** Regular sword and shield |

| **ENEMY LEVEL:** 38 |

| **DESCRIPTION:** A disciplined and flawless swordsmith whose skill with her single blade approaches an art form, if art could kill. |

| **REWARD ITEM:** Freeman Sword Regular Sword |

| **ELITE REWARD ITEM:** Roman Venator Legendary Outfit |

| **TRAPS:** None |

The Duelist begins the fight with one sword, but after eliminating about one-quarter of her health, she pulls out a second. This widens her area of attack as she swings two blades instead of one.

At half a health bar, she applies poison to one of her blades. After making contact with the poison, you are unable to regenerate health, making it more urgent to avoid taking damage.

Six pillars offer a little protection for when you need to regenerate health. If you are not directly opposite the boss, she can quickly strike with a jump or lunge attack, so stay on the move until your health has regenerated. The Duelist may also use the pillars or sidewalls to get behind you, so be ready to sidestep when she runs up either one.

While you can block some of her attacks, a flick of her sword can knock your shield to the side, leaving you open for attack. It is best to fight from a distance and move in only when she is open to attack. Try performing quick strikes with an immediate withdrawal to minimize the risk.

An extra danger of fighting up close is her throw, as she flips Bayek over her back onto the ground. She can also slide between your legs and throw you down from behind. Similar to the other bosses, she attempts to strike you when on the ground, so time your evade to just avoid the hit and follow it up with a hit or two against the vulnerable foe.

She can cover a lot of ground with her jump attack. Watch for her to kneel before performing the move, giving you time to move out of the way.

She is the most agile of the bosses, with quick, acrobatic moves, which become more dangerous when she adds the second sword, and even more so with the poison. Stay on your toes and keep moving, since the Duelist can strike extremely fast. Take extra precaution to avoid her poison as you whittle her health down.

HIPPODROME

TERRITORY:	TOTAL:		OBJECTIVE:	XP REWARD:
Kanopos Nome	4 tournaments, 4 time trialst		Win the race	150 per Race

As soon as you reach the village of Kanopos, you gain access to the Lageion Hippodrome, located at the center of the village, where chariot races test your racing ability. Here you compete in a series of tournaments against five rivals and time trials against the clock. Begin by selecting the tutorial from the Tournaments menu to learn drifting, boosting, building stamina, drafting, trampling, climbing back into the chariot, bracing against a rival's hit, and ramming.

HOW TO RACE

The tutorial race leads you through all the basics of racing chariots, but here is a quick rundown of the ins and outs.

- Accelerate by holding the Heavy Attack button. You should hold this for most of the race. Occasionally, you may want to let up to allow an opponent to catch up or for a really tight turn.

- Steer with the left stick. Stick to the dark, well-trodden path on the track, as boost charges faster in this area.

- Boost by holding down the Interaction button. A meter in the middle of the screen indicates available boost; once depleted, you are unable to gain the extra speed. Use this to get up to speed after a turn or after an incident with your rivals. Boost down the straightaways if possible to get the full effect and stick to the dark path to build the meter faster. Drafting also helps build the meter.

- Draft your rivals. The closer you are behind an opponent, the faster your boost charges. It can be a disadvantage to run up front, since a rider can use a good draft to pass at the final turn. Attempt a block if you do lead out of a turn.

- In the turns, hold the Dodge button to drift around the corner. Keep the accelerator down throughout if possible to get a good run out the other side.

- Destroy opponents' chariots. Health bars indicate the "health" of each cart. Once depleted, the racer is eliminated; this includes your own ride, so be careful. If your chariot is destroyed, you do not score in the race and must retry to proceed.

- Trample your foes by riding up on their heels and holding the Grab Ledge button. This damages your opponent's chariot, though it does slow you down significantly.

- Ram rivals by pulling alongside them and pressing the Grab Ledge button. This can damage your opponents but mostly knocks them off course.

- If you are knocked out of the chariot, mash on the Parkour Interaction button to claw back into it.

- You can brace alongside a rival by holding the Shield Mode button. This allows you to take an impact from an opponent's attack.

- Depending on the race, obstacles may litter the course. Horses bust through the objects with ease, but it is best to avoid them altogether.

TIPS

Use the following tips to improve your times in the Hippodrome:

- Avoid obstacles, as there is always a chance of being knocked out of your chariot. This includes the scaffolding that often surrounds a turn or pillar.

- Take the turns as close to the inside as possible without touching the barrier, being careful not to drift too far out. Start a drift just before the turn from the middle of the track and cut the corner.

- Fire is extinguished by boosting. It eats through the "health" of your chariot, so it's best to avoid it, but be ready for an immediate boost when catching on fire seems unavoidable. Place two horses just off the dark path to avoid most damage from the fire that spews from the brazier.

- Watch out for horses that have lost their rider, as they act like additional obstacles. Bumping into them slows your horses down just as any other object.

TIME TRIALS

RACE	UNLOCK CONDITION
Race I	Unlocked from start
Race II	Complete Nike's Winged Victory tournament
Race III	Complete Ramessesses' Divine Justice tournament
Race IV	Complete Sol Indiges' Cursus Magnus tournament

As you complete the tournaments, time trials are unlocked that take place on tracks similar to each tournament. Here the player attempts to get the best time possible equipped with an infinite stamina gauge. Instead of racing against other "physical" chariots, you compete against ghosts that represent the best times of other players. If you play online, you face the best times of your friends and random players. When offline, you go against random opponents. Unlike the tournaments, these races are all about speed and how you handle the turns. Without opposition, you cannot rely on knocking the opposition around or drafting in a rival's slipstream.

Use these races to perfect your turns, drifting throughout the turn while staying on the dark path. Learning how best to take the hairpin turns goes a long way in the tournaments.

RACE I

ROTATION: Clockwise		LAPS: 3
DIFFICULTY	TIME TO BEAT	
Easy	1:44.49	
Medium	1:40.49	
Hard	1:37.34	

The first race is very basic, with only a crashed chariot on the course. The race runs clockwise, so it is all about the right turns.

RACE II

ROTATION: Counterclockwise		LAPS: 3
DIFFICULTY	TIME TO BEAT	
Easy	1:44.08	
Medium	1:41.41	
Hard	1:37.91	

For the second time trial, statues have been added to the course, which runs counterclockwise. While three sit across the halfway point of each straightaway, only the middle gets in the way. Stick as close to it as possible to remain on the dark path. Statues also sit on the outside of the first turn, but as long as you cut the corner well, they are not an issue.

RACE III

ROTATION: Clockwise		LAPS: 4
DIFFICULTY	TIME TO BEAT	
Easy	2:16.45	
Medium	2:13.19	
Hard	2:11.32	

The third time trial returns to the clockwise route, but the race is increased to four laps. It also adds a bunch of pillars and statues to the track. Watch out for an obstacle near the beginning of both straightaways. Keep to the inside track, but

if you do drift to the outside, return to the inside track, as the dark section connects in the middle of each stretch.

RACE IV

ROTATION: Counterclockwise		LAPS: 5
DIFFICULTY	TIME TO BEAT	
Easy	2:50.74	
Medium	2:46.46	
Hard	2:44.56	

Three braziers have been placed along the front and back stretches with the ground on fire between them, creating well-trodden paths to the inside and outside. Each of these braziers shoots fire that alternates between the inside and outside tracks. Remember to boost when your chariot catches on fire to extinguish it. Between the second and third braziers there is a small gap that can be used to switch lanes if you notice the next fire switch to your side.

Don't exit out of the second turn too wide, as a flaming scaffolding provides another opportunity to take on fire. Watch out for a second scaffolding that sits on the outside

middle of the back stretch and a third on the inside, just after turn 1.

This race is increased to five laps, adding to the challenge of the fire. Taking on fire too many times takes its toll, so keep your eyes on the braziers ahead. To limit the damage taken from the fire, take the inside of the inside lane or the outside of the outside lane—keeping two horses in the dark and two in the light areas of the dirt.

INTRODUCTION

THE ESSENTIALS

MAIN QUESTS

SIDE QUESTS

ACTIVITIES

ATLAS

REFERENCE & ANALYSIS

TOURNAMENTS

REWARD: 160 drachmas each tournament won; Pharaoh's Horse Chariot for winning all four tournaments; Roman Warhorse Chariot for winning all four Elite tournaments

POINTS EARNED IN TOURNAMENT RACES

POSITION	POINTS
1st	5
2nd	3
3rd	2
4th	1

Each tournament has three races, with points earned by finishing in the first four positions. Adding the points from the three races determines the finishing order. You must finish in first place to unlock the next tournament.

THE TOURNAMENTS

TOURNAMENT	UNLOCK CONDITION	DESCRIPTION
Nike's Winged Victory	Unlocked from start	A classic Greek-themed race. Can you earn the glory of Nike?
Ramesses' Divine Justice	Win Nike's Winged Victory	A race honoring the Great Ancestor. Can you earn Ramesses' favor?
Sol Indiges' Cursus Magnus	Win Ramesses' Divine Justice	A great race of Kanopos. Can you earn the honor of Sol Indiges?
Darius' Great Battle	Win Sol Indiges' Cursus Magnus	A time-honored race in Persian style. Can you earn the grace of Darius?

Each tournament race has six riders, including Bayek. As you progress through the tournaments, these opponents become faster and tougher to take down.

Win all four tournaments to unlock Elite Event mode, where Bayek can compete in four more tournaments—identical to the first four but with stronger and faster rivals.

NIKE'S WINGED VICTORY

ROTATION: Clockwise	LAPS: 3/3/3

The track for Nike's Winged Victory is clear, besides the rare broken-down chariot. When opportunities arise, take your shots against your rivals. Otherwise, keep the chariot to the inside and on the well-trodden path. Keep some boost in reserve when approaching the final turn and then boost out of the corner to put distance between you and your rivals. Rain adds a little extra challenge in the third race, but it doesn't affect the race too much.

RAMESSES' DIVINE JUSTICE

ROTATION: Counterclockwise	LAPS: 3/3/4

If you have done Time Trial II, you should be familiar with this track. Statues are added to the middle of the front and backstretches, forcing the riders to stick to an inside or outside lane. If possible, use these obstacles to your advantage by ramming rivals into them.

It begins to rain for the second race, making the chariots control a little differently than usual. The third race is extended to four laps, making it more important to avoid damage. Watch out as spectators toss smoke screens onto the track, obscuring vision for a short time. Be aware of who is around you at all times and keep the horses straight as they run through the smoke.

SOL INDIGES' CURSUS MAGNUS

ROTATION: Clockwise	LAPS: 3/4/4

This track is the same as the one used in Time Trial III. Statues and pillars litter the course, with the most dangerous sitting just after each turn. If you are in the lead, stick to the lane you are most comfortable in, whether you prefer turning from the outside or inside. Otherwise, choose your lane based on where the rivals ahead are so that you can benefit from the draft. Use the point in the middle of the stretches, where the dark paths meet, to switch lanes.

If you do get the chance, time your rams so that your target runs into one of the obstacles. When the lane narrows around the statues and pillars, it can get crowded, so be ready with a ram to fend off your rivals. Pay particular attention to the scaffolding that surrounds the pillar on the backstretch. This is a nasty section where you can take serious damage if pushed into the platforms.

For the third race, the crowd becomes a tad nastier as they add firebombs to their arsenal. Now you need to worry about smoke screens and fire. The latter damages your ride if it catches fire, so take defensive measures and steer around the detonation. If you cannot avoid it, boost to extinguish the flame.

DARIUS' GREAT BATTLE

ROTATION: Counterclockwise	LAPS: 4/4/5

The final tournament adds fire down the middle of both stretches. Three statues along both straightaways separate them into two distinct lanes with fire running between them. On top of that, fire arrows and firebombs are launched from the crowd, so be on your toes the entire race. Try to always keep a little boost in reserve in case you catch on fire.

For the second race, the middle statue on each straightaway is turned into a brazier that spews fire that alternates between the inside and outside lanes. Ride with Bayek straddling the outside of the dark path when in the outside lane and the inside of the path in the inner lane. This avoids the brunt of the fire, while still keeping your speed up. Remain alert for incoming fire projectiles from the crowd as they become more and more hostile.

For the final race, the first and third obstacles are braziers that spew fire that alternates between the inside and outside lanes. Now fire runs along most of each straightaway. A small gap between the statue and the end brazier allows you to switch lanes just before the turn. This race is increased from four laps to five, requiring you take on as little fire as possible to survive to the end. Again, stick just outside the reach of the fire to limit the damage.

HUNTING GROUNDS (ANIMAL LAIRS)

| TOTAL: 40 | OBJECTIVE: Kill animal | RELATED QUESTS: *Thick Skin (Suggested Level: 13)* | REWARD: XP per lair |

Animal lairs, found throughout Egypt, house elite wildlife—stronger than normal animals. These creatures are typically found at some kind of den, surrounded by weaker animals of the same species. Kill the alpha animal to earn XP and collect an increased loot value from the corpse.

Keep these tips in mind during hunting trips:

- Scout an area carefully before attacking a lair. Other animals or hostile soldiers may roam nearby. Also note any vantage points that you can fire from or escape to when needed. Be sure to mark the alpha animal beforehand in order to easily track it, especially in case it escapes.

- Some animals are less active at nighttime, giving you the ability to catch your target off guard.

- If available, tame a good fighter and take it into the fight for an added advantage.

- On occasion, animals of opposing species fight it out amongst themselves. Take advantage of this when possible to weaken a pack. Sometimes you can spook a prey toward a pack of predators, causing a nice distraction. You can also carry a corpse to a predator, keeping it busy for a while.

- Use all the tools at your disposal. The elite animals often hang out with weaker members of their species, which can become overwhelming if you are not careful. Sleep darts can be used to reduce numbers, making the fight more manageable. Or, by starting out with a poison dart in your target, you can begin the fight with an added advantage.

COBRA LAIR

| TYPE: Defensive | RESOURCE: 1 Cobra Venom/Cobra |

COBRA LAIR LOCATION

TERRITORY	LEVEL	LOCATION
Saqqara Nome	N/A	Next to pyramid of Djoser, on west side inside small building

Cobras do not vary by level and typically go down within a couple hits or arrows. A sleep dart will take out any cobra in one shot. Fire is also extremely effective against the snakes.

In Saqqara Nome, you must slide through a small opening on the room's north side. Don't move too far inside, as a few cobras are nearby. Grab the treasure while inside the room.

CROCODILE LAIRS

| TYPE: Defensive | RESOURCE: Hard Leather |

CROCODILE LAIR LOCATIONS

TERRITORY	LEVEL	LOCATION
Lake Mareotis	8	Small island, just southeast of the Temple of Sekhmet
Sap-Meh Nome	14	East coast of Lake Mareotis in northwest corner of Sap-Meh Nome
Sap-Meh Nome	14	Near middle of territory, northwest of Anthylla Outpost within a small canyon
Sap-Meh Nome	14	East side of territory, southeast of Apollodorus's estate
Ineb-Hedjet Nome	21	North of the city of Memphis in shallow waters, just off the eastern coast of the territory—directly south of Pr-Hapi-n-Iwnw
Faiyum Oasis	30	On east coast of waterway, between Philadelphia and Krokodilopolis
Im-Khent Nome	32	Far north side of Nome, north of Udjat Apiary
Herakleion Nome	32	Southeast of Thonis and directly west of Yw Huts
Herakleion Nome	33	Far southwest corner of the Nome, southwest of Natho

Each elite crocodile surrounds itself with a bask of younger crocodiles, one level below the target. Typically making their home in shallow water, the reptiles will attack if within range and if you aren't too overpowering. Note that the alpha crocodiles are distinctive with their larger size and black skin.

The group can quickly overwhelm its target if allowed to do so. It is best to attack these creatures from a safe distance, such as from the top of nearby huts, rock formations, or trees.

The elite croc will flee if it feels too threatened. Avoid melee attacks unless you can isolate your target. These animals move quicker than they look, so always be aware of surrounding foes and available escape routes.

HIPPOPOTAMUS LAIRS

TYPE: Defensive | **RESOURCE:** Hard Leather

HIPPO LAIR LOCATIONS

TERRITORY	LEVEL	LOCATION
Lake Mareotis	8	On west shore of lake, between Lakeside Villa Outpost and Temple of Sekhmet
Lake Mareotis	14	Southeast side of lake, southwest of Sais village
Faiyum	27	Northwest corner of the lake
Uab Nome	30	On the east shore of the narrow strip of land that juts out of the northwest corner of Uab Nome, directly west of Krokodilopolis
Uab Nome	31	On northern shore of Nome, southeast of Krokodilopolis, across Tomb of Amenemhat III
Herakleion Nome	33	Southwest section of territory, northwest of Natho

The hippopotamus tends to hang out with other hippos of similar level. Alphas stand out with white spots on their skin. Steer clear of the group of Level 12 hippos on the southeast side of Lake Mareotis, as they are significantly higher level than your target. The lair located in the northwest corner of Uab Nome sits next to a tower with Level 24 soldiers, so keep your distance.

Hippos attack with ferocious bites, though their large size makes them a bit slower. However, watch out for their charge attack, as the mammal can cover a surprising distance with the maneuver.

Its large size makes a hippo an easy target for a sleep dart. Isolate the hippo if possible and keep it inactive with the darts as you pummel it with melee attacks. They do not climb, so pelting the beast with a barrage of arrows is also a good tactic, though it will flee if it feels threatened enough. It also takes a whole lot of arrows to take the large animal down, unless your bow is overpowered compared to the target's level.

HYENA LAIRS

TYPE: Predator | **RESOURCE:** Soft Leather

HYENA LAIR LOCATIONS

TERRITORY	LEVEL	LOCATION
Siwa	3	Northeast side of lake, at small watering hole
Sap-Meh Nome	14	North coast, across water from Alexandria
Giza	19	West side of region at end of path that runs between Tombs of Khafre and Menkaure
Saqqara Nome	25	About 250 meters southwest of Nitria village, directly west of the Bent Pyramid of Djoser
Faiyum	27	Southwest portion of territory, directly west of Dionysias
Uab Nome	31	South of Dioryx Megale Wharf, toward the middle of Uab Nome—west of a world portal.
Isolated Desert	39	Northwest of Theos Elpis Rift, on the south side of a narrow canyon that connects to Qattara Depression

Hyenas travel and snooze in packs that can get quite large. The alphas are distinctive with their white fur and black stripes, surrounded by hyenas that are one or two levels below its level. The predators tend to be less active at nighttime—sometimes finding a more comfortable place to lie with fewer hyenas in the immediate area.

A cackle of hyenas anywhere near Bayek's level can be a huge threat, using sheer numbers to grind away at their target's health. Try to fight from higher vantage points, though they may chase you on easier climbs. Use any tool at your disposal; fire can be very effective against the canines.

Hyenas have the ability to sense Bayek with ease, making it very tough to sneak up on one. Quietly climb to a high vantage point above the hyenas and launch a flurry of arrows at your target. If you can get a sleep dart into it first, more time is gained for the arrow barrage. It will flee the area after a short while, forcing you to pursue on foot.

IBEX LAIR

TYPE: Prey | **RESOURCE:** Soft Leather

IBEX LAIR LOCATION

TERRITORY	LEVEL	LOCATION
Siwa	3	East of city and northeast of big lake, at smaller watering hole

The lone ibex lair is found in Siwa, and since the ibex do not attack, the lair is simpler to complete. Watch out for hyenas nearby, since they may take more interest in the ibex than Bayek. Your target will flee if spooked, making it a slightly tougher target.

LEOPARD LAIRS

TYPE: Predator | **RESOURCE:** Pelts

LEOPARD LAIR LOCATIONS

TERRITORY	LEVEL	LOCATION
Saqqara Nome	20	Directly east of Pyramid of Djoser, in northeast corner of Nome—northwest of Memphis
Faiyum	27	Far southeast portion of territory, between Philadelphia and Kerke villages
Uab Nome	33	East border of Nome, southeast of Etesias' Olive Grove—atop a plateau along with a small ruins
Libue	34	South-central region of territory, near top of mountain, amongst ruins
Green Mountains	34	Near middle of territory, northeast of Necropolis Hideout, southwest of Collis Roman Hunting Camp, and northwest of Aquaeductus Kyrenaike

Leopards are often found in small packs, but if you are lucky, you may catch them down a cat or two as they wander off for some hunting. Leopards are predators and will attack Bayek once detected. Look for the black leopard, which indicates it is the alpha.

Try to keep the fighting from a distance—atop a high vantage point if possible, but if you can isolate your target, the fight is very manageable in Shield mode. Watch out for other felines to join in, though. Use sleep darts to manage smaller groups.

When fighting the leopards on the ground, always have an exit route in mind. Quickly climb to a safe location when things get rough.

At the Faiyum location, if you catch the predator inside the den, you can aim through the hole above and set fire to the brush—blocking their exit and allowing you to pelt them with arrows.

🐾 LION/LIONESS LAIRS

TYPE: Predator	RESOURCE: Hard Leather

LION LAIR LOCATIONS

TERRITORY	LEVEL	LOCATION
Ka-Khem Nome	20	Southern portion of Nome, directly east of Letopolis
Haueris Nome	33	Southern portion of Nome, northwest of Hermopolis and south of limestone quarry
Libue	34	West-central region of territory, at ruins atop mountain northeast of Saragina Camp
Marmarica	40	Top of mountain in middle of territory, west of Livius Roman Tower

Lions and lionesses are ferocious predators and a tough fight for Bayek no matter how many are around. The big males are often fought alone while the lionesses are normally surrounded by younger felines. The alpha lions are denoted by their white fur. Typical for cats, they have their lazier times and it may be worth using the Dawn & Dusk ability to find the best moment for attack.

Try to keep all hunting from a higher, safer vantage point, since the cats are very tough fights in close combat. Sometimes the target may be found inside a den or temple. Do not go in after the lion, unless you are well over its level.

When approaching a lair, be sure to use Senu to spot every predator and keep tabs on their locations. Tall grass may make it tough to spot them all, so be sure to be thorough with your preparations. Tools, such as the sleep dart, come in handy during the fight.

🦅 VULTURE LAIRS

TYPE: Defensive	RESOURCE: None

VULTURE LAIR LOCATIONS

TERRITORY	LEVEL	LOCATION
Siwa	3	Burnt village along the path that leads into the south side of the city of Siwa
Lake Mareotis	8	Just west of the lake, northwest of Temple of Sekhmet
Saqqara Nome	24	East-central portion of region, between Temple of Djoser and Tomb of Sneferu
Faiyum	27	North side of Faiyum, northwest of the lake, near a dome-shaped rock formation
Green Mountains	34	Just north of circular stone ruins, south of Collis Roman Hunting Camp
Isolated Desert	39	West side of desert, east of Pissa Oros Citadel near a partial tower
Isolated Desert	39	West of Remetch Ra village, den sits at base of rock pillars

The vulture lair just south of Siwa is the first hunt found, as it lies along the path that Bayek and Hepzefa take during the Homecoming quest. Look for the white feather that indicates the alpha vulture.

Vultures are defensive animals and will not attack unless provoked. This makes them a fairly simple hunt, compared to the predators. It is best to take out the bird when it has landed, as it becomes a much tougher target once in the air. Use a sleep dart to keep it on the ground longer.

Take advantage of a Warrior Bow's spread when a kettle of vultures takes flight. Showing patience and waiting for your target to land is also a great tactic. Once provoked, the bird may dive-bomb the player, so stay aware.

INTRODUCTION
THE ESSENTIALS
MAIN QUESTS
SIDE QUESTS
ACTIVITIES
ATLAS
REFERENCE & ANALYSIS

PAPYRI PUZZLES

TOTAL: 25	**OBJECTIVE:** Collect the Papyrus and find the treasure	**REWARD FOR COLLECTING PAPYRUS:** 20 XP + XP for completing location (see below)	**REWARD FOR FINDING TREASURE:** 500 XP, 300 drachmas, random piece of gear from a set list

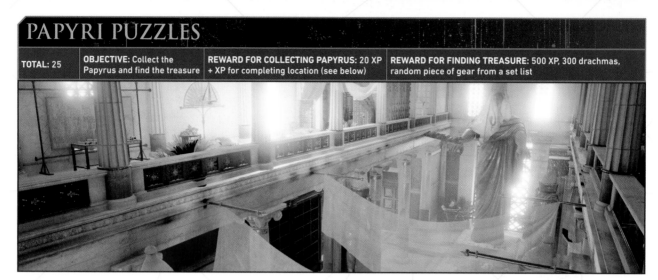

Twenty-five papyrus scrolls can be collected from temples around the country. This alone rewards XP for completing the locations, but the real reward is the hidden treasure that each papyrus describes. Decipher the riddle to learn the locations of all 25 hidden treasures. Once you find the correct site, collect the sparkly treasure to earn 500 XP, 300 drachmas, and a rare or legendary piece of gear—well worth the effort.

In this section, we lead you right to each papyrus. At that point, you can attempt to decipher the riddle yourself or consult the corresponding "Treasure Location" for directions to the loot. Note that the treasure will not show up at its location before you collect the corresponding papyrus, so don't bother skipping a step.

The following table provides a sampling of the weapons and shields that you may receive from the collected treasure.

POSSIBLE GEAR TREASURE

GEAR	RARITY	TYPE OF WEAPON
Aldebaran	Rare	Warrior Bow
Amnhotep's Bow	Legendary	Predator Bow
Antigonus Shield	Rare	Shield
Bitter Bow	Rare	Light Bow
Ceremonial Staff	Legendary	Scepter
Composite Bow	Legendary	Light Bow

GEAR	RARITY	TYPE OF WEAPON
Copper Mace	Legendary	Heavy Blunt
Copper Sword	Rare	Regular Sword
Cutting Axe	Rare	Heavy Blade
Deathstorm	Legendary	Hunter Bow
Djoser's Pride	Legendary	Shield
Fan Axe	Rare	Heavy Blade
Hades	Rare	Predator Bow
Headache Remedy	Legendary	Heavy Blunt
Headsplitter	Legendary	Heavy Blade
Hippopotamus Charge	Rare	Warrior Bow
Mirror Blades	Rare	Dual Sword
Neith	Legendary	Light Bow
Phalangite	Legendary	Shield
Raneb's Hammer	Legendary	Scepter
Reinforced Shield	Legendary	Shield
Skull-Breaker	Rare	Heavy Blunt
Smoke and Mirrors	Legendary	Predator Bow
The Fourth Plague	Legendary	Warrior Bow
Viper's Tooth	Legendary	Sickle Sword
Wolfsbane	Rare	Hunter Bow

APOLLONION OF CYRENE: DEAD OR ALIVE

PAPYRUS TERRITORY: Kyrenaika	
REWARD FOR COMPLETING LOCATION: 450 XP	**HINT:** In the southwest section of the Green Mountains lives a monstrous beast with sharp tusks and tough gray skin. In his deadly arena you can find me, between the edge of the arena and where the beast sates his thirst.
REWARD TERRITORY: Green Mountains	

PAPYRUS LOCATION

Find the papyrus inside the Apollonion of Cyrene, located west of Cyrene Barracks, on the northwest side of the village. It rests on a small table inside the temple, against the left wall.

TREASURE LOCATION

Head to Roman Camp of Surus in southwestern Green Mountains, where the War Elephant Surus resides. On the arena's west side, next to the watering hole, collect the reward off the ground.

ASKLEPIEION: FORSAKEN CITY

PAPYRUS TERRITORY: Green Mountains	
REWARD FOR COMPLETING LOCATION: 450 XP	
REWARD TERRITORY: Paraitonion	

HINT: At the bottom border of Paraitonion is a village of ghosts. I'm in the house of the blasphemous man, who built his house farthest from Ra's, the sun god, dawning grace.

PAPYRUS LOCATION

Travel to Balagrae in eastern Green Mountains and run around to the back of the Asklepieion temple. The scroll sits on a table inside the gazebo.

TREASURE LOCATION

Travel to the Keno point of interest next to the southern border of Paraitonion. While there are two treasures to be found in the ruins, the papyrus treasure sits in the ruin atop the hill.

EASTERN CEMETERY MASTABA: STONE FUNGUS

PAPYRUS TERRITORY: Giza	
REWARD FOR COMPLETING LOCATION: 300 XP	
REWARD TERRITORY: Giza	

HINT: In Giza, three pyramids stand tall. From the top of the smaller one you can see quite a lot, even two mushroom rocks, the smaller of which I lay atop of.

PAPYRUS LOCATION

East of the Great Pyramid and directly north of the Sphinx, in the Eastern Cemetery, find the accessible mastaba with a hole on top and a small opening on the west side. Drop in from above or move one of the blocks on the side and slide inside. Collect the scroll off the table.

TREASURE LOCATION

From the top of the Tomb of Menkaure, you can spot two mushroom rocks to the northwest. They sit at the edge of the mountains, west of the Tomb of Khafre. Climb to the top of the smaller one and collect the reward.

GALENOS'S HOUSE: ROYAL FLORA

PAPYRUS TERRITORY: Herakleion Nome	
REWARD FOR COMPLETING LOCATION: 450 XP	
REWARD TERRITORY: Herakleion Nome	

HINT: In southern Herakleion Nome you can find me beneath the tree who fancies himself king.

PAPYRUS LOCATION

Travel to Natho on the south-central island of Herakleion Nome. Find the two-story Galenos's House on the village's west side and grab the papyrus off the second-floor table.

TREASURE LOCATION

Look for a magnificent tree on a small island south of Neith Cradle Hideout; a narrow footbridge connects it to the bigger island. The treasure is found on the tree's south side.

GREAT LIBRARY: DIVIDED VALLEY

PAPYRUS TERRITORY: Alexandria	
REWARD FOR COMPLETING LOCATION: 150 XP	
REWARD TERRITORY: Sap-Meh Nome	

HINT: In the center of Sap-Meh Nome you can find me hidden in a canyon near Anthylla, in the center of the Western Nile Delta. I'm under a tree that thinks it's unique, but only because the nearby rock bridge is blocking it from seeing the others of its breed.

PAPYRUS LOCATION

In Alexandria, find the Great Library on the city's west side, southeast of Kibotos Arsenal. Enter, turn left and head to the back-left corner of the building. Just before the steps, find the Papyrus sitting on the small table.

TREASURE LOCATION

In the middle of Sap-Meh Nome, look for the narrow canyon that runs horizontally through the territory—a crocodile lair sits within, near the rock bridge. Growing on a ledge on the side of the canyon, next to the lair, is a lone tree unlike the other trees in the area. Find the treasure next to it.

GREAT SYNAGOGUE: NATURE'S WAY

PAPYRUS TERRITORY: Alexandria	
REWARD FOR COMPLETING LOCATION: 150 XP	
REWARD TERRITORY: Kanopos Nome	

HINT: In the east section of the Kanopos Nome is a ravaged land, where many trees fell and lost their home. I'm by the orphan tree whose parents fell down nearby, pointing toward their lonely daughter.

PAPYRUS LOCATION

Find the Great Synagogue in the city's northeast section, southeast of the Royal Palace. It sits on a corner and is inaccessible, but if you move around to the backyard, you will find the scroll lying on a small table under a canopy next to the building.

TREASURE LOCATION

Head east to the next territory and find the trees that have been knocked down on the east-central island. From the main path, find the white tower to the south. Head north past the ruins to find the two big fallen trees. Between them, a small tree stands next to a hay fence. Collect the treasure under the tree.

HOUSE OF IWN: JUST LAWS

PAPYRUS TERRITORY: Faiyum Oasis	
REWARD FOR COMPLETING LOCATION: 450 XP	
REWARD TERRITORY: Atef-Pehu Nome	

HINT: In Atef-Pehu Nome there is a law that states that you can only make pottery on the east side of the road. I'm hidden atop the one illegal clay smoker in the region.

PAPYRUS LOCATION

Toward the middle of Faiyum Oasis, south of Philadelphia, find the fenced-in property that sits on the river's east shore. Enter the workshop on the property's southeast side and grab the papyrus from the central table.

TREASURE LOCATION

Travel to Kerke village and head up the north-south road that runs along the river. About halfway up the territory is a small village with four clay smokers on the right and a fifth on the left. Climb onto the left smoker to find the treasure.

HOUSE OF LIFE: A LONG DRINK

PAPYRUS TERRITORY: Siwa	
REWARD FOR COMPLETING LOCATION: 150 XP	
REWARD TERRITORY: Siwa	

HINT: In Siwa, come find me at the bottom of the only bowl big enough for a god.

PAPYRUS LOCATION

Find the House of Life on the south side of Siwa village and make your way past the guards (if you have completed the side quest, The Healer, you have eliminated the enemy presence) until you reach the tents out front of the temple. The papyrus is found on a table within the right tent.

TREASURE LOCATION

In Siwa, find the big well on the lake's southwest side. It shows up as a small circle on the map. Jump in and collect the reward in the center.

HYPOSTYLE HALL: FERTILE LANDS

PAPYRUS TERRITORY: Lake Mareotis	
REWARD FOR COMPLETING LOCATION: 150 XP	
REWARD TERRITORY: Lake Mareotis	

HINT: A few hundred meters north west of the Temple of Sekhmet, which resides by Lake Mareotis, there is a great place to go for a date. Full of palm trees and surrounded by desert, one rock fence was built and closed off with no exit. Find me there.

PAPYRUS LOCATION

In Temple of Sekhmet, find the two black monuments and proceed inside the Hypostyle Hall. At the pool of water, climb the pillar on the right to reach the walkway above and collect the scroll off the table.

TREASURE LOCATION

Go northwest from the Temple of Sekhmet to find a small settlement, packed full of palm trees. Near the northwest corner, a short stone wall encloses a single palm tree. The treasure lies next to the tree.

ISEION: DEAFENING SILENCE

PAPYRUS TERRITORY: Alexandria	
REWARD FOR COMPLETING LOCATION: 150 XP	
REWARD TERRITORY: Alexandria	

HINT: Alexandria is large and noisy, but one part is quiet, lonely, and surrounded by water. The fallen palm tree points to where I lay, where land meets water.

PAPYRUS LOCATION

Find the Iseion temple on the island in northwestern Alexandria, between Pharos Garrison and Pharos Military Storage. Enter through the front doorway and collect the scroll off the table behind the statue.

TREASURE LOCATION

Just north of the city, a small island sits in the bay and consists of nothing but trees and rocks. Find the fallen tree in the middle of the island and allow the top of the tree to point you to the treasure that rests near the water.

INTRODUCTION

THE ESSENTIALS

MAIN QUESTS

SIDE QUESTS

ACTIVITIES

ATLAS

REFERENCE & ANALYSIS

ORACLE OF APOLLO: WET WORK

PAPYRUS TERRITORY: Green Mountains	
REWARD FOR COMPLETING LOCATION: 450 XP	
REWARD TERRITORY: Green Mountains	

HINT: In the Green Mountains where they're building a great aqueduct, go find its source high up in the mountains. Inside, you can find me sitting at the bottom of the lowest pool, tucked away beside two large jars.

PAPYRUS LOCATION

In northeastern Green Mountains, near the border with Kyrenaika, find the Oracle of Apollo temple atop a hill. Descend into the structure and find the scroll on the right, lying on the ground next to a crate of jugs.

TREASURE LOCATION

In the central Green Mountains, the world portal sits next to Aquaeductus Kyrenaike. Follow the aqueduct northwest into the mountain and dive into the pool of water. At the bottom, in the far back, collect the reward that sits next to a pair of jugs.

PALACE OF APRIES: IN PLAIN SIGHT

PAPYRUS TERRITORY: Memphis	
REWARD FOR COMPLETING LOCATION: 300 XP	
REWARD TERRITORY: Faiyum Oasis	

HINT: On an island southeast of Krokodilopolis, there is a river with unnatural color. Nearby you'll see the cause, and I'll be inside the only one that's unique.

PAPYRUS LOCATION

On the far north side of Memphis, the enormous Palace of Apries sits atop the steps. Make your way to the back of the palace, being sure not to cause any trouble with the guards. Enter the small, luxurious room that is surrounded by lion-headed goddess statues. Climb onto the scroll shelves to find the papyrus.

TREASURE LOCATION

Travel to Krokodilopolis and head to the southeastern island. Find the red and orange splotches in the river that indicates you are at the right place. Workers are busy dying clothes various colors. Look for the rectangular, orange dye and step inside to find your reward.

SARAPEION: THE STONE GAZE

PAPYRUS TERRITORY: Alexandria	
REWARD FOR COMPLETING LOCATION: 150 XP	
REWARD TERRITORY: Lake Mareotis	

HINT: In the south section of Mareotis Lake there is an island full of ruins. A man stares at me all day; it's quite a bother, so I'm hiding behind a column that blocks his sight.

PAPYRUS LOCATION

In southeastern Alexandria, find the huge Sarapeion temple and climb the steps to get inside. Guards are on duty, but as long as you do not provoke them, they will leave you alone. Enter the small room near the southwest corner.

TREASURE LOCATION

Travel to the Temple of Sekhmet in Lake Mareotis and swim or take a felucca out to the Lost Crypt island, east of the village. On the ruins' south side, find the partial column and collect the nearby reward.

SARAPEION OF KARANIS: THE LEANING TOWER

PAPYRUS TERRITORY: Faiyum

REWARD FOR COMPLETING LOCATION: 300 XP

REWARD TERRITORY: Faiyum

HINT: In Faiyum, north of Dionysias Caravanserai, there is a tower with a hole by its feet. It's in need of support, so I sit behind it, but the wooden beams seem more helpful.

PAPYRUS LOCATION

Travel to the village of Karanis in northeast Faiyum and enter the Sarapeion of Karanis temple. Once inside, climb one of the statues on the left to reach the balcony. Find the papyrus in the back room.

TREASURE LOCATION

From Dionysias village, head northwest until you find a lookout tower, north of the Dionysias Caravanserai military installation. Lying on the ground on the tower's north side is the reward.

TOMB OF ALEXANDER THE GREAT: RAY OF HOPE

PAPYRUS TERRITORY: Alexandria

REWARD FOR COMPLETING LOCATION: 150 XP

REWARD TERRITORY: Qattara Depression

HINT: In the Qattara Depression there is only one place that isn't dry and sad. At dawn's first light there is one tree near the valley's entrance whose roots are halfway between Ra's glory and Apophi's shadow. Find me there but make haste, for Ra moves quickly.

PAPYRUS LOCATION

On the northeast side of Alexandria city, find the entrance to the tomb of Alexander the Great on the main east-west road, just east of the theater—look for the open metal gate. At the statue, turn right and enter the structure to find a statue of Alexander. Climb one of the pillars to enter the enclosed area on the roof and collect the Papyrus that sits at the base of one of the statues.

TREASURE LOCATION

In the Qattara Depression, on the desert's west side, a hermit location is located at the only source of water in the territory. A narrow valley leads down to the water from the north. At the entrance to this valley, stop at the first tree in the middle of the path. The treasure lies at its trunk.

TOMB OF BATTOS: UNDERGROUND CURRENTS

PAPYRUS TERRITORY: Kyrenaika

REWARD FOR COMPLETING LOCATION: 450 XP

REWARD TERRITORY: Green Mountains

HINT: South of Cyrene, in the Green Mountains, there is a lake whose water comes from a magical stream. I'll be at the source of that magic, where water flows from nothing.

PAPYRUS LOCATION

Spot the circular temple on the southeast side of Cyrene, between the Roman Akropolis and the gladiator arena. Scale the outside of the temple to the top and then climb through the hole in the ceiling—using one of the pillars for a safe descent. The papyrus sits on the table just right of the statues.

TREASURE LOCATION

Travel directly south from Cyrene into the Green Mountains and spot the Collis Roman Hunting Camp that sits in the middle of a lake near the top of the northern mountain. Avoid the lionesses that inhabit the nearby ruins and the soldiers at the camp. Follow the stream west up the mountain until you reach the end. Collect the treasure that lies in the water.

TEMPLE OF HORUS: SEA OF SAND

PAPYRUS TERRITORY: Sapi-Res Nome	
REWARD FOR COMPLETING LOCATION: 300 XP	
REWARD TERRITORY: Iment Nome	

HINT: In the southeast of Iment Nome lies a broken ship. If you meditate till morning, an X will mark my hiding spot.

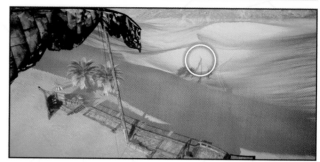

PAPYRUS LOCATION

Travel to Letopolis in southern Sapi-Res Nome and find the Temple of Horus on the southeast side. Step inside and move to the back of the area. The papyrus lies on the ground just beside the farthest Horus statue.

TREASURE LOCATION

To find the ship, locate the world portal in the southeast corner of Iment Nome. Use the Dawn & Dusk ability to change nighttime into day. Now quickly follow the shadow of the ship's mast, before the sun moves too much, to find the treasure where the mast crosses the torn sail.

TEMPLE OF KHONSOU: TWIN DESPAIR

PAPYRUS TERRITORY: Herakleion Nome	
REWARD FOR COMPLETING LOCATION: 450 XP	
REWARD TERRITORY: Herakleion Nome	

HINT: In Herakleion Nome, east of the Temple of Khonsou, is a village that is more water than land. Behind two houses with different problems, one whose feet are always wet and the other who can't cover his head, you can find me sitting under a tree.

PAPYRUS LOCATION

Go to the village of Herakleion, located near the middle of the nome, and approach the big Temple of Khonsou on the town's northern side. Enter the popular temple through the opening on the south side. Against the back wall of the first room, search the desk to find the papyrus scroll.

TREASURE LOCATION

Travel east from the Temple of Khonsou to the small village of Yw Huts. Find the small island on the village's north side that holds a dilapidated home full of hay and a flooded hut. Just behind the former, a tree grows out of the water. Collect the treasure underneath.

TEMPLE OF PTAH: FALLEN FRIEND

PAPYRUS TERRITORY: Memphis	
REWARD FOR COMPLETING LOCATION: 300 XP	
REWARD TERRITORY: Memphis	

HINT: Two men stand guard on the Memphis eastern canal. The south one looks solemnly at his sunken friend. If you follow his gaze, you can find him and me on the river floor.

PAPYRUS LOCATION

Just west of the biggest structure in Memphis, located in the middle of the city, the Temple of Ptah sits atop a hill. There are numerous ways to get inside the temple, even a hidden entrance on the northwest side—just follow the small stream of water, climb the right rock wall, and continue along the path until you emerge from a big well. From here, climb over the south wall and search under the canopy for the scroll.

TREASURE LOCATION

Go east from the temple until you reach the eastern shores and find the central canal as it enters the city, where a statue stands guard on each side of the water. Run east from the southern statue until you reach the water. Jump in and dive to the bottom and continue east until you find the head and body of another statue. Collect the treasure that sits on it.

TEMPLE OF SOBEK: SOBEK'S RAGE

PAPYRUS TERRITORY: Faiyum Oasis

REWARD FOR COMPLETING LOCATION: 450 XP

REWARD TERRITORY: Haueris Nome

HINT: East of Krokodilopolis, south of the shattered pyramid, a large beast of a god stares angrily at a pharaoh who shows him no respect. I'm hidden behind the blasphemer's head.

PAPYRUS LOCATION

In Krokodilopolis enter the Temple of Sobek, found on the city's north side, east of the gladiator arena, through the south entrance. Move into the left room to find the giant Sobek statue. Climb a pillar to reach the balcony above and collect the papyrus off the ground in the southeast corner.

TREASURE LOCATION

Travel east out of Krokodilopolis, following the road south when it splits. Just south of the Tomb of Amenemhat III, find the huge statue of Sobek in the middle of a temple, on the upper level. From there, run south around the hole until you reach the back of a headdress that belongs to a pharaoh statue. Lying on the floor is the treasure.

TEMPLE OF THOTH: THOTH'S SECRET

PAPYRUS TERRITORY: Haueris Nome

REWARD FOR COMPLETING LOCATION: 450 XP

REWARD TERRITORY: Uab Nome

HINT: Southeast of the city Hermopolis is a leopard's den in Uab Nome. At the top of their territory lies a place where birds should live but do not. If you take a leap of faith, you can find me.

PAPYRUS LOCATION

Just west of Hermopolis in south Haueris Nome, the temple of Thoth is located underground; find the entrance on the west side of the village. You can also enter through the Temple Archives, which holds a couple treasures itself. From Hermopolis, head straight west to the back of the temple, where the scroll lies on the floor at the feet of a Thoth statue.

TREASURE LOCATION

Find a leopard's lair near the river in northeastern Uab Nome. The leopards hang out at a small ruin with a Thoth statue at one end. Cautiously climb onto the tree next to the statue and take a leap of faith into a pile of hay hidden in the cave below. Hop out and collect your reward.

TEMPLE OF ZEUS: UNDUE HASTE

PAPYRUS TERRITORY: Kyrenaika

REWARD FOR COMPLETING LOCATION: 450 XP

REWARD TERRITORY: Kyrenaika

HINT: North of Apollonia, I'm next to a lifesaver. It guides in darkness and fog, and I sit beside it under something that did not heed its warning.

PAPYRUS LOCATION

In the city of Cyrene, located in central Kyrenaika, climb the steps to reach the Temple of Zeus, north of the gladiator arena. The papyrus rests on a small table inside the temple, against the right wall.

TREASURE LOCATION

Take a trip to Apollonia and swim out to the lighthouse, north of the hostile Apollonia Roman Barracks. Move around to the north side and locate the wreckage next to the water to find the treasure.

VALLEY MARKET: THE BLASPHEMER

PAPYRUS TERRITORY: Faiyum	
REWARD FOR COMPLETING LOCATION: 450 XP	
REWARD TERRITORY: Haueris Nome	

HINT: There is a place of remembrance for the unfortunate masses in northwest Haueris Nome. While I rest here, immobile, I cannot escape Ra's grace, but at least every dawn I avoid him longer than the others.

PAPYRUS LOCATION

Travel to Euhemeria in southern Faiyum and exit the village out the southern route, turning east when the opportunity arises. This leads to the Valley Market. Climb the steps on the left and collect the scroll from the merchant's table.

TREASURE LOCATION

Several small pyramid tombs have been erected through north-central Haueris Nome. The tomb that sits second from the east, at the base of an upper cliff, gets the last sun during the day. Collect the treasure that lies just in front.

WABET: BURNING BUSH

PAPYRUS TERRITORY: Memphis	
REWARD FOR COMPLETING LOCATION: 300 XP	
REWARD TERRITORY: Memphis	

HINT: If you head to the other side of the Nile in Ineb-Hedjet Nome, you can find a peak with a great view of the Nile. Take a look around, then come find me, hiding under the only tree nearby.

PAPYRUS LOCATION

As you enter Memphis from Ineb-Hedjet Nome by way of the western road, the Wabet is located just ahead on the left. Enter through the opening on the road's left side and then make an immediate left to enter the embalming facility. Once inside, make a right, left, and left again to enter the inner room. The scroll sits on a table just inside.

TREASURE LOCATION

East of Ineb-Hedjet and Memphis, there is a sliver of land on the Nile's east side that is not out of bounds. If you explore too far east, you will be reset near the water. Spot the two palm trees just inside the Memphis region.

ZEPHYROS STABLES: DEAD END

PAPYRUS TERRITORY: Kanopos Nome	
REWARD FOR COMPLETING LOCATION: 300 XP	
REWARD TERRITORY: Sapi-Res Nome	

HINT: In Sapi-Res Nome, north of Letopolis Temple, you can find me in the farmland. I lay where man's creation brings the Nile's water to desert sand.

PAPYRUS LOCATION

Go to the Zephyros Stables east of the Hippodrome in central Kanopos Nome. Find the barn on the property's southeast side and collect the papyrus that sits on the corner table inside.

TREASURE LOCATION

Explore the farmland north of Letopolis in east Sapi-Res Nome. A system is set up to transport water from the Nile up to the sandy farm. Follow the irrigation canals up from the river and then north into the farmland. The treasure sits in the highest canal at the far-north end.

STONE CIRCLES

| TOTAL: 12 | PREREQUISITE: Complete Main Quest—The False Oracle | OBJECTIVE: Align the stars | RELATED QUESTS: BAYEK'S PROMISE (SUGGESTED LEVEL: 5) | REWARD: 150—450 XP each (depending on Stone Circle) |

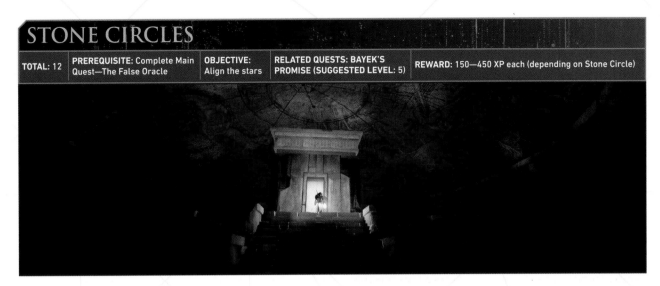

Find any of the 12 Stone Circles around the world to begin the quest "Bayek's Promise." A flashback shows an outing with Bayek's son at the Amun Stone Circle, where Khemu declares he will find every Stone Circle and the Sphinx. Bayek sets out to fulfill this promise.

To complete the quest, you must find all 12 Stone Circles and align each constellation with the stars in the sky, earning XP each time.

Interacting with a Stone Circle will cause the constellation to take shape in the stones. An identical set of stars exists somewhere in the night sky. Move the constellation around with the left stick and rotate with the right stick until you find the stars that match. Move the constellation close enough to allow it to lock in place to complete the stone circle.

Once you've completed all 12 Stone Circles, the quest leads Bayek back to the Amun Stone Circle for the final part of the quest.

THAT'S A WHOLE LOTTA SILICA

Before exploring the final area of this quest, spend some time collecting Silica—that is, if you are a completionist. You can finish the quest without it, but in order to activate the Ancient Mechanism you find along the way, you need 50 Silica.

AMUN

| TERRITORY: Siwa | REWARD: 150 XP |

"Amun, the king of gods, divided in two forms as the great goddess of invisibility Amunet, and master of the wind. He upholds justice. Lord of the shadows and the silence, he comes at the voice of the poor. He hears the confessions of the humble, and forgives them."

Amun is the Stone Circle where Bayek took his son not long before. It is located just south of the village of Siwa.

A simple four-star constellation, there isn't much to look for in the sky. The lone red star sits above the trio of stars. The constellation is placed just left of Pisces.

APIS

| TERRITORY: Isolated Desert | REWARD: 450 XP |

"Apis, the bull god. He is the strength of the Pharaoh. Each year he is born as a calf with special markings. The Pharaoh finds this calf, and worships it."

The second Stone Circle in Isolated Desert is found in the far southeastern portion of the territory, near the border with both Faiyum and Saqqara Nome. It requires a bit of a climb, as it sits on the cliff high above.

The forked side of the constellation forms the bull's body, which points to the left in the night sky. The far left star shines red. Find the spot left of Amun.

DIVINE LION

TERRITORY: Iment Nome	REWARD: 300 XP

"The Divine Lion, the powerful one. Her breath formed the desert. The fiercest of hunters, she leads the armies of the Pharaoh into battle."

Find the Divine Lion Stone Circle in the northeastern section of Iment Nome, west of Temple of Sekhmet.

In the night sky, the lion is tipped onto its hind legs with its nose in the air. Look for the two sets of four stars that form the feline's back and legs. It leaps over Osiris and Apis.

GOAT FISH

TERRITORY: Isolated Desert	REWARD: 450 XP

"The Goat-Fish, called Capricornus by the Greeks. The god has the head of a ram and body of a fish. You see, even the gods do not always make sense."

In the far western Isolated Desert, just beyond the Tomb of the Nomads, look for the steps that lead up to a small, deserted base in the mountain. Turn east to find the Stone Circle on a plateau. You can also just climb the side of the cliff to reach it.

The Goat Fish is found in the sky with its head in the air to the right and its tail up to the left. Look for the lower trio of stars that make up its front legs, while the close pair sits in middle of its body.

THE GREAT TWINS

TERRITORY: White Desert Oasis	REWARD: 450 XP

"Ahhhh, the Great Twins. To the Greeks they are twin brothers. To Egyptians they are he-goats that rise from the underworld, bringing pestilence and protection. Even the gods have two sides."

The Great Twins sits in the northern lake among the rocks near the western shore.

The Great Twins has another very discernible pattern, but it can be tough to find. Look for the six stars along the bottom that form the feet, as the twins stand upright in the sky. It sits between the Divine Lion and Taweret.

HATHOR

TERRITORY: Ka-Khem Nome	REWARD: 300 XP

"Hathor, goddess of motherhood and joy. She is loved by all in Egypt, from the least to the greatest. Mistress of the West, she welcomes the dead to the afterlife."

Hathor is situated in the middle of the eastern coast of Ka-Khem Nome's biggest island.

Hathor lies on her side in the sky with her head facing to the right. It sits above the Divine Lion and just right of the Scales.

HORUS

TERRITORY: Uab Nome (North-Central)	REWARD: 450 XP

"That is Horus, the Falcon. The Great Black One. God of the sky. The sun is his right eye and the moon is his left eye. Forever he flies across the heavens, making night and day."

If available, use the Fast Travel point in north-central Uab Nome. This puts you just southeast of the Horus Stone Circle. Follow the narrow path south to find the stones on the rocky cliff above.

You find the falcon flying upright in the night sky. Look for the trio of stars that sits between a pair to the right and a single to the left. These create the top of its wings and head.

OSIRIS

TERRITORY: Qattara Depression	REWARD: 450 XP

"Osiris was cut into 14 pieces by his jealous brother, who scattered the pieces throughout the land. Osiris' wife Iset searched and found all the pieces except one… It was eaten by a fish. It was his, ah… So Osiris was resurrected and became lord of the underworld."

In the Qattara Depression region, just east of the western mountains, the Osiris Stone Circle sits just west of a path.

Osiris stands up straight in the night sky. Look for the group of five stars that create his head; if you are lower in the sky, spot the three stars that make up his feet. Find him just left of Apis.

PISCES

TERRITORY: Faiyum	REWARD: 300 XP

"Pisces, the two fish. Joined by the thread of this life, they are forever balanced between the afterlife and the underworld."

The Pisces Stone Circle sits in the swampland on the east side of Faiyum, along the lake, east of Philadelphia.

As one of the simpler constellations to decipher, seven stars in a tight circle form the right fish, while a jagged line forms the left. The pair is tilted to the right in the sky so that the right fish is below the left. They are found just right of Amun.

THE SCALES

TERRITORY: Uab Nome	REWARD: 450 XP

"Those are the Scales, called Chonsu. When we die, the goddess Ma'at weighs our hearts on them against her white feather. If our hearts are pure and light, we walk in the Field of Reeds."

The second Stone Circle in Uab Nome sits near the Nile coast in the northeastern portion of the territory, at the south end of a very short branch of the river.

This constellation is fairly small compared to others, so look for a small grouping of stars. The Scales sits upright with the top pointing straight up. It sits left of the Hathor and above Serqet.

SERQET

TERRITORY: Iment Nome	REWARD: 150 XP

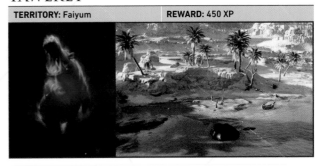

"The scorpion goddess, Serqet. She protected Iset and Horus from jealous Set. She still protects against poisonous animals. But not love. Against that there is no protection, not even the gods can."

Find the Serqet Stone Circle in the narrow, northwestern section of Iment Nome, west of Lake Mareotis.

The scorpion's tail curls upward. Look for the distinct curved body that connects the four stars at the tip of the tail down to the five stars that form the underbody.

TAWERET

TERRITORY: Faiyum	REWARD: 450 XP

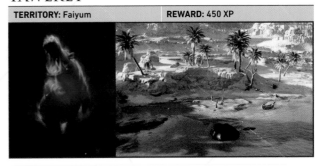

"Oh, Taweret, the hippopotamus who walks. Lady of the Birth House, she is the goddess of fertility and childbirth. Mistress of the Horizon, she brings with her the yearly flood of Ar."

In western Faiyum, sitting on the northern shore of the lake, Taweret is found at the end of a short path that cuts through the rock.

The five stars that make up Taweret form a jagged line that forms a slightly slanted 3 when placed in the sky. This one is hard to see; search in the bluish area of the sky, left of Horus.

When all 12 Stone Circles are complete, you must return to the Amun Stone Circle and approach the objective marker behind the tree to place the final rock. This concludes Bayek's Promise.

THE PLANETARIUM

TERRITORY: Sphinx
ANCIENT MECHANISM: Eesfet Oon-m'Aa Poo
SILICA AVAILABLE: 4
SILICA REQUIRED: 50
SEGMENT: 6
TREASURES: 2 (1 rare treasure)

When all 12 Stone Circles are complete, you must return to the Amun Stone Circle and approach the objective marker behind the tree to place the final rock. To complete the promise, you must travel to the Great Sphinx in Giza.

When The False Oracle main quest is completed, the Great Sphinx in Giza becomes accessible. At the rear of the monument, find a secret entrance and crawl inside. Drop down and follow the path until you reach what seems like a dead end. Spot the opening in the far corner and crouch into the next corridor.

Hop over the hole, collect the two treasures from the room ahead, and then drop into the hole. Descend farther into the tomb until you reach a big doorway. Proceed further into the Planetarium room. Each time a Stone Circle is completed, a corresponding light will be shone onto the diorama from the ceiling.

Once all 12 Stone Circles have been completed, interact with the diorama to raise it, revealing a hidden entrance that leads you to the Esfet Oon-m'Aa Poo Ancient Mechanism.

Once inside the big cavern, collect a Silica to the right and two more to the left of the entrance. A fourth Silica sits on the room's north side. As long as you have 50 Silica in your inventory, you may activate the mechanism in the center of the room. The exit pad sits just beyond the device.

TOMBS AND ANCIENT MECHANISMS

TOTAL: 14 tombs, 6 Ancient Mechanisms	**OBJECTIVE:** Find the Ancient Tablet and activate the Ancient Mechanism	**RELATED QUESTS:** Hideaway (suggested level: 3)	**REWARD:** 1 AP per tomb, 250 XP per Ancient Mechanism

Tombs dating back millennia were constructed throughout the region to honor the dead. Treasures were left with the dead within the structures for their travels to the afterlife. These burial sites have since been targets of thieves and researchers alike.

All 14 tombs contain an Ancient Tablet deep inside, which is the main object for Bayek. Along the way, valuable Silica and treasures are also available to loot. Finding the tablet completes the location and earns an Ability Point, but for a few of the tombs, it doesn't end there.

Farther inside these sites, a mysterious Ancient Mechanism offers a connection to the future, but it requires a set amount of Silica to activate. This triggers a message from and completes another location. The sixth and final Ancient Mechanism is located beneath the Sphinx.

Step-by-step walkthroughs for all 14 tombs and 6 Ancient Mechanisms will help you find the location of every Silica and treasure and will help you complete your main objectives—finding the Ancient Tablets and Mechanisms.

Walkthroughs for the five tombs that also house an Ancient Mechanism are split between, before, and after you find the Ancient Tablet.

LIGHTING THE WAY

A torch is a necessity when exploring the dark tombs of Egypt, but it isn't your only source of light. Keep an eye out for braziers as you search the interiors, touching them with your torch to create another light source. Remember your torch can also be thrown when unsure of what is ahead or down a hole.

Fire is also handy for getting rid of cobwebs throughout the tombs. Two tombs include a light that can lead you to the objective, but often cobwebs keep the light from reaching its final destination. Hold the torch up to the covered mirror or throw the fire out of reach.

LOOT, TREASURE, AND LORE

Use Animus Pulse often as you explore the tombs to find objects hidden throughout. Urns, sacks, and crates provide random loot, such as drachmas, resources, and the occasional trinket. Gear can be found in treasure chests. Interact with lore—left behind on the walls, scrolls, and tablets—to learn of the Egyptian ways. The Animus Pulse also leads you to objects that can be carried and used, which are often necessary to complete the tombs.

BEWARE THE COBRAS!

A few tombs house cobras. There are numerous jugs, urns, and vases that you can destroy as you work toward the Smash! achievement/trophy. Be careful, though, as a cobra may be inside. Get in the habit of dodging backward after hitting the big jugs.

The following tombs are presented in alphabetical order, but this is not the order that you find them. Typically, you complete Mountain of the Dead first as the side quest "Hideaway," which leads you through the tomb just west of the starting village Siwa.

For each tomb, we list the number of Silica and high-value treasure found within, and we note whether there is an Ancient Mechanism. We also list the amount of Silica required to activate the device. Note that the final mechanism needs 50 Silica to complete, so be sure to collect every last one. We also tell you which segment each Ancient Mechanism activates, in case you wish to hear the messages in order.

ADORER OF THOTH TOMB

TERRITORY: Giza	SILICA AVAILABLE: 5	TREASURES: 6	ANCIENT MECHANISM: None

The Adorer of Thoth Tomb sits in the far northwest area of Giza, west of the big pyramids. Look for a camp of thieves, who present an extra challenge for this tomb. The Level 16 hostiles occupy the exterior and interior, so move cautiously and take them down one at a time, if possible. Watch out for snipers who fire from the platforms above, which you can use to your advantage once you've removed the enemies.

Inside the stronghold, you will find several thieves at the first open area. Look for the short, wooden stairs and use them to reach the first Silica. A second Silica sits atop a high platform on the cavern's other side.

Proceed deeper into the enemy base, using the foliage to conceal your attacks. Just inside the next cavern, a treasure is located next to a campfire on the left. Scan often so that you are not caught off guard.

Before continuing up the slope, after the monkey statue drops in the pool behind it, swim underneath to find a hidden room. Behind the tree is a Silica and a rare treasure.

In the next area, you will find several spools lying around, along with an elevator straight ahead and another on the left. By adding weight to one, the other rises and vice versa. The goal is to reach the high ledge above the first elevator.

Begin by grabbing the spool off the elevator ahead and set it on the other one. Add at least three more spools to the left elevator and then use the platform on the left to reach the raised elevator. Follow the dark path into the thieves' treasure room, where a Silica sits on the central platform.

Drop into the final area to find the Ancient Tablet, four treasures, and a fourth Silica on the high ledge left of the tablet. Once you have procured all the loot you can carry, follow a path just beyond the tablet to reach a familiar cavern. Exit the tomb the way you came in.

GOLDEN TOMB

TERRITORY: Isolated Desert	SILICA AVAILABLE: 13	TREASURES: 4	ANCIENT MECHANISM: Oun-mAa Niye Ressoot	SILICA REQUIRED FOR MECHANISM: 5	SEGMENT: 1

Golden Tomb is one of two tombs located in the Isolated Desert. Its entrance is located between the villages of Theos Elpis Rift and Remetch Ra. Find a weak wall on the mountain's north side, surrounded by scarabs. Bust through with a melee weapon to enter the tomb.

The new light enters the tomb and reflects off a couple mirrors, illuminating a doorway ahead. This light, if allowed to continue throughout the interior, leads directly to the tablet. When the light ends prematurely, you must either move another mirror into position or eliminate cobwebs with your torch or fire arrows.

SKIP THE PUZZLE

Though the light reflecting throughout the tomb's corridors leads you directly to the tablet, it is not necessary for completion. If you would rather stumble through the dark toward the objective, do not bother with the mirrors.

Light your torch for better visibility and move through the doorway to allow the light to move into the corridor. Just ahead, it stops on the left wall. Move the nearby mirror back so that it makes contact with the beam. Follow it.

Find the next mirror and clear off the cobwebs before collecting a piece of Silica in the right room. Just ahead, follow the hallway left to find an armory, where another Silica is located. On your way back to the main corridor, there is a under pass on the left side that leads to a small treasure room with one chest inside.

Continue deeper into the tomb, following the light over a barrier of boulders. Clear off the next reflector with a brush of your torch, and then take the first turn to a short dead end. Just on the corner, on your left side, there is another passage underneath that leads to a small treasure room with one chest and one piece of Silica. Go out and take the second left turn into a short dead end. Destroy the containers on the left to find the fourth Silica.

Next, find the nearby moveable object and push/pull it into the path of the light, leading you into a room on the right. Destroy more containers that block the light from its next redirect.

The light now points to some brush on the floor ahead. Toss your torch to reveal a hole and drop down to a lower level. The light now leads into a treasure room that holds the Ancient Tablet, two treasure chests, and a Silica.

Grab the loot and complete the tomb's objective. Follow the corridor to discover Oun-mAa Niye Ressoot.

The right path at the "Y" intersection leads to a moveable object that blocks a narrow exit, leading back out to the Isolated Desert.

ANCIENT MECHANISM: OUN-MAA NIYE RESSOOT

Instead, continue down the left route and descend into an open, well-lit cavern. Before activating the device, search the perimeter to find five Silica—two on the left, one hidden behind two rocks, one on a small platform next to the wall, one on the right, and two more along the back. Now head down the path and hop along the square platforms to score another Silica, before collecting the final one near the mechanism. Place five of your newfound Silica on the device to activate it and retransmit Segment 1.

MOUNTAIN OF THE DEAD

TERRITORY: Siwa	SILICA AVAILABLE: 3	TREASURES: 3	ANCIENT MECHANISM: None

Located just northwest of the village of Siwa, east of the lake, find Fenuku standing outside a tomb. He lost track of his brother, Chenzira, when a cackle of hyenas chased him into the tomb. Talking to Fenuku begins the Side Quest "Hideaway," which introduces the idea of tombs to the player. The first tomb, Mountain of the Dead, is completed as part of the quest. After sending Fenuku home, step inside and move to the T-intersection ahead.

Head left, knock down the wall, and continue down the corridor to find a silica in the right corner near the metal fence. Head back and follow the path to the left and then turn left again to find yourself in a small room with a Silica behind a jar.

Head in the next room to collect the Silica just inside the treasure room to the right, before approaching the moveable objects on the room's other side.

Push the right sled straight until a hidden room is revealed on the right. Collect the treasure that sits among the numerous cat mummies before returning to the previous room. Now destroy the jar in the right corner before moving the second sled into its spot.

This allows you to reach Chenzira, along with the Ancient Tablet and two more treasures. Exit through the corridor opposite from where you entered the room until you reach the outdoors. Beware, as hyenas wait for you outside.

NOMARCH'S TOMB

TERRITORY: Black Desert	SILICA AVAILABLE: 13	TREASURES: 4	ANCIENT MECHANISM: Seshem.eff Er Aat	SILICA REQUIRED FOR MECHANISM: 5	SEGMENT: 2

In southern Black Desert, just west of the Faiyum territory, find a hole in the ground at an excavation site. Drop inside and descend into the tomb. Inside the first chamber, collect a Silica on the left before descending another slope that leads into a vast room with a seesaw mechanism in the middle.

Before solving the puzzle to reach the balcony above, collect a treasure in the far-right corner, a Silica just to its left, and a third Silica in one of the small rooms along the left wall.

Now you must use the boat to reach the ledge above, but running up the vessel causes it to teeter the other way. With it sloped down toward the entrance, tuck the moveable object under the end to create a ramp to the second level. You can also climb the pillars on this side, so you decide how to ascend.

Hop over to the left side of the second floor and bust through the wall to find a rare treasure. Go through the next breakable door to find another chest. Next, drop down and move the moveable object to the other side. Use it to reach the beam above the room entrance. Leap over to the left floor.

Search the first room to find the fourth Silica and then bust through the weakened wall to find another chamber. Inside is a treasure box, a Silica on the left and the Ancient Tablet. Bust through another wall in the back-right corner to find another corridor.

At the "T," intersection head right and collect the sixth Silica. Continue down that route to find an alternate exit. Move the object that blocks the opening to create another way inside the tomb.

ANCIENT MECHANISM: SESHEM.EFF ER AAT

Instead of exiting, head the other way to find the Seshem.eff Er Aat Ancient Mechanism. Before diving into the deep water hole ahead, collect the Silica on the far side. Dive to the bottom, discover six more Silica, and then activate the mechanism. Exit at the nearby circular pad.

SETH-ANAT TOMB

TERRITORY: Desheret Desert	SILICA AVAILABLE: 15	TREASURES: 3	ANCIENT MECHANISM: Qeneb too Kah'Aiye	SILICA REQUIRED FOR MECHANISM: 5	SEGMENT: 5

In the far south, an unnatural-looking, narrow canyon cuts through the middle of the desert. Enter from the west side to find a light bouncing from side to side as it reflects off mirrors that hang from either side of the canyon. When the light stops, you must find the next mirror and either move it into place or burn off the cobwebs to keep the beam going.

In the end, the light leads to both the Ancient Tablet and Ancient Mechanism, though these aren't necessary to complete the site; you can run straight to the objectives.

This walkthrough pinpoints treasure and Silica locations along the way, using the mirrors as reference. Use your Animus Pulse often to find the moveable blocks and loot. Start out climbing the left ledges, enter the first opening on the left, and pull the block out to keep the light moving.

Continue along the same path, drop to the ledge that you are on, shimmy over a mirror, and climb back up on the other side. Search the cubbyhole ahead to find the first Silica.

Exit the room and drop down to the left. Hop diagonally to the canyon's right side, climb to the upper level, and pull out another mirror.

Follow the ledges to the left and enter the opening ahead to find the second Silica. Exit and climb the blocks to the right to find a mirror in need of a cleaning, so clear it off with your torch. Continue ahead, drop down a couple levels, and enter the room on the right to collect the third Silica.

Just ahead on the right side, pull out another block to deflect the light. Farther to the right, drop down a couple levels and spot a cobweb-covered mirror on the left.

Throw a torch or shoot a fire arrow to allow the beam to continue into the temple and find the first objective. Before entering the structure, head back to the left a short distance, and search a ground-level room on the north side to find the fourth Silica.

Head east to the tomb's entrance, but before entering, grab the fifth Silica just across the canyon. Now enter the tomb and interact with the Ancient Tablet. Use fire to clear the mirror on the right wall, leading you deeper into the tomb, where you find the Ancient Mechanism.

ANCIENT MECHANISM: QENEB TOO KAH'AIYE

Collect three Silica scattered around the ramp, as it leads you into the burial room ahead. Collect two treasures on the right and the five Silica scattered about before activating the mechanism. After activating the mechanism, you can use the teleporter to the left of the pedestal and teleport to the entrance of the canyon.

Exit the tomb to the left and search the two rooms in the far corner to find a treasure and Silica. Continue right to the next corner and climb up to an opening to find the last Silica in the area.

TOMB OF AMENEMHAT III

TERRITORY: Haueris Nome	SILICA AVAILABLE: 4	TREASURES: 2	ANCIENT MECHANISM: None

Find the Pyramid of Amenemhat III in west-central Haueris Nome, and squeeze through a crack on the south side. Follow the corridor into the tomb to immediately find the first Silica in the right corner. Climb up through the opening in the ceiling, cut through the next chamber, and descend through another corridor ahead.

Grab the second Silica in the next corner before following the path to the right. In the next chamber, four Level 25 crocodiles emerge from a pool. Fire arrows at them right away—do not become surrounded. Circle around the pool and continue

moving to keep them at a safe distance. Climb onto the railing that blocks the previous hallway and fire arrows at the reptiles from this safe location. Oil jars next to the pool are also available for detonating near the foes.

Once you have defeated them, enter the pool, dive through the opening, and follow the path to find the Ancient Tablet. Rise out of the water to emerge next to a Sobek statue. Grab Silica from the orange bowl and loot the jewelry box before climbing the statue to the upper floor, where another Silica sits on the floor.

In the next room, hieroglyphics cover the far wall just beyond a pit. Two more holes in the floor appear inaccessible, as bamboo poles have been stretched across them.

Throw your torch or fire arrows to bust them open. Drop into each hole and destroy the seal that adorns the far walls, causing sand to pour into the small chambers. Return upstairs and proceed through the new opening.

A moveable sled blocks the exit, so move it aside before exiting the pyramid.

TOMB OF DJOSER

TERRITORY: Saqqara Nome	SILICA AVAILABLE: 4	TREASURES: 5	ANCIENT MECHANISM: None

The pyramid of Djoser is located in northeast Saqqara Nome. Find the tomb entrance just north of the pyramid and follow the path into the first room. Move the sled out from the opening and descend deeper into the tomb. At the intersection, slide straight into a small room and collect the first Silica.

Slip back out and continue down the slope to another intersection. First, squeeze into the room on the right, immediately turn right, and run to the opposite corner. Destroy the urns that block the opening and slide into the adjoining room. Collect a couple treasures and a Silica before sliding back out to the previous room.

Pull the sled away from the far wall, vault into the next chamber, and collect another treasure from inside. Exit back out the narrow crack and follow the corridor into a cavern. Collect another Silica off the floor before busting through the far wall.

After the next left turn, bust open the red jug and immediately evade backward to avoid the cobra that is released. Kill the snake and collect the treasure.

Move through the opening and break the jars so you're able to slide the sled on the left forward to snag a treasure from the chest inside. Exit the room and follow the hallway around the left turn, taking out the cobra along the way. After another left turn, bust through the second wall on the left, but don't go inside just yet. Instead continue through the corridors until you find Silica in the far corner.

Return to the room that you revealed and interact with the Ancient Tablet located inside. Turn right and climb to the corridor above. When you reach another moveable sled, move it to the right. Squeeze through the opening to reach a familiar location. Exit out the way you came in.

TOMB OF KHAFRE

TERRITORY: Giza	SILICA AVAILABLE: 5	TREASURES: 3	ANCIENT MECHANISM: None

Enter the Tomb of Khafre on the north side of the pyramid of Khafre, which sits just southwest of the biggest pyramid. Descend deep into the tomb until the path splits straight ahead and back behind you. Continue forward to the chamber and grab the Silica that lies on the floor. Return to the split and descend deeper into the tomb.

Collect another Silica in the cubbyhole on the right and then follow the corridor to the left. Inside the next chamber, pass through the crack on the left wall.

Another hallway leads you to a contraption, familiar to anyone who has completed Nomarch's Tomb. Pull the sled under the end of the boat to create a ramp to the upper level. At the ledge above, turn around and hop across the beams to find a treasure.

Leap back to the first side and enter the room ahead to find the Ancient Tablet. Circle around the outside to find a Silica and then collect two more treasures and a Silica near the tablet. Complete the tomb before exiting out the chamber's far side. Climb the wall at the dead end to exit the tomb.

TOMB OF KHUFU

TERRITORY: Giza	SILICA AVAILABLE: 12	TREASURES: 3	ANCIENT MECHANISM: Tomb of Khufu	SILICA REQUIRED FOR MECHANISM: 5	SEGMENT: 3

Access the Tomb of Khufu through an opening on the north side of the Great Pyramid at Giza; watch out for the cackle of hyenas that hang just outside. Follow the path straight until it splits. Left leads to the Ancient Tablet, while the narrow slit takes you to the Ancient Mechanism. Go left first.

Follow the trail up and around the right turn until you reach a small opening with ramps on either side. Crawl through the middle tunnel to find a hidden chamber. Grab the Silica and treasure before returning to the split.

Next, run up the walkway on either side of the corridor and duck through another small tunnel. Grab the Silica that sits in the far corner before passing through the crack in the right wall.

In the treasure room, destroy the two seals on the back wall, causing the center portion to lower. Climb into the opening above and run forward to find the Ancient Tablet, along with two treasures and a Silica.

Interact with the tablet before crawling out the back exit. Climb up the side wall in the next room, where you can exit, but before doing so, slide through a narrow opening ahead to find another Silica.

Use the footholds and beams to climb the wall and shimmy to the right to reach the upper level. Follow the long corridor as it makes a right turn. Eventually, after vaulting and sliding, you reach the south side of the pyramid.

ANCIENT MECHANISM: TOMB OF KHUFU

To access the ancient mechanism in this tomb, you must first assassinate the Hyena during the main quest line. Return to the start of the tomb and squeeze through the crack that you passed up earlier. Descend the corridors until you reach a chamber with a hole in the floor. Drop inside and run right until you reach a big cavern. Hop down the big pillars to reach the floor.

Explore the perimeter of the area to find eight Silica and then activate the Ancient Mechanism. You can pass through a crack in the far-west wall or use the nearby teleporter to exit the tomb.

INTRODUCTION

THE ESSENTIALS

MAIN QUESTS

SIDE QUESTS

ACTIVITIES

ATLAS

REFERENCE & ANALYSIS

TOMB OF MENKAURE

TERRITORY: Giza	SILICA AVAILABLE: 3	TREASURES: 3	ANCIENT MECHANISM: None

A smaller pyramid sits along with Khufu and Khafre in Giza. This is the pyramid of Menkaure, which you can explore by entering through an opening on the north side. Descend into the darkness, following the path right at the first room.

Descend the steps in the middle of the room into the treasure room straight ahead, where a chest and Silica are available for your collection.

Return to the corridor and descend left into a room full of gifts for King Menkaure. A second Silica hides inside one of the cubbyholes along the walls, but beware of a cobra that hides inside the neighboring jug.

Return to the first room and climb into an opening above the entrance. Follow the path until you reach a dead end. Use an arrow to bust out the bamboo strips above,

stepping back as the wood comes crashing down, bringing an angry cobra with it.

Climb to the upper floor and move into the final chamber, where the Ancient Tablet rests along with two treasures and Silica. Pass through a crack on the far wall to exit the tomb.

TOMB OF SMENKHKARE

TERRITORY: Haueris Nome	SILICA AVAILABLE: 12	TREASURES: 4	ANCIENT MECHANISM: Eeyoo Sekedoo Aat	SILICA REQUIRED FOR MECHANISM: 5	SEGMENT: 4

Near the southern tip of the main island of Haueris Nome, pillars mark a hidden entrance to the tomb of Smenkhkare. It is best to allow Senu to scout the area first, as lions between Levels 25 and 26 patrol the area. This tomb is explored as part of the side quest "Seven Farmers," so if possible, pick up the quest before attempting it.

Descend the steps and knock down the wall to get inside the tomb. At the top of the steps ahead, enter the small room on the right to find a couple treasure boxes on either side of a sarcophagus.

Run into the next chamber, where a hole in the ground leads to a pool of water below. Another coffin room is located ahead, but only one small-value container makes it of little worth. Once ready, take a leap of faith into the opening and dive underwater.

Look around to find two branches, one that ascends into another room, while the left path leads to a lower level. Follow the latter route and take the next left to find a jewelry box and treasure chest. Follow the main path into the next chamber, ascend out of the water, and step through the doorway to find another split. The right doorway leads back to where you came from, while the second enters a big cavern with two weight puzzles.

On the room's far side, two elevators allow you to reach a balcony in the back left corner. There is a small room to the right with a Silica hidden behind a stone. Two more elevators need to be weighted correctly so that you can leap across them and reach the higher ledge on the right, but there are no weights to use on the platforms. Therefore, this puzzle must be solved with Bayek's weight alone.

Move to the far right corner and quickly run across the left platforms to reach the corner balcony, staying on the move and holding down the Parkour Interaction button to make the jumps. Step into the corner room to find a Silica.

Continue onto the third elevator and allow it to lower all the way. Quickly hop across the next platform onto the hook at the corner, jump when the final elevator is within reach, and immediately run across the platform, leaping to the ledge to complete the room.

The next room holds the Ancient Tablet, but five Ptolemaic bandits guard the area. Lure them out one at a time, if possible, and take them down. Once you've eliminated the threat, collect three pieces of Silica and interact with the tablet to complete the tomb.

ANCIENT MECHANISM: EEYOO SEKEDOO AAT

Squeeze through the narrow opening ahead, collect another Silica on the corridor's right side, and dive into the water ahead. Collect another Silica underwater before climbing out and grabbing two more. In the next room, three more pieces of Silica sit on the floor near the Ancient Mechanism. After activating the device, step onto the circle and exit the tomb.

TOMB OF SNEFERU

TERRITORY: Saqqara Nome	SILICA AVAILABLE: 5	TREASURES: 4	ANCIENT MECHANISM: None

In eastern Saqqara Nome is a pyramid that sits directly east of Nitria village. Enter it via an opening on the north side. Crawl through the small opening into the first room, climb up the far wall, and search the hole on the right to find Silica. Return to the first room and pass through the crack on the left.

Jump over the water, move through the doorway, and descend to the lower level. Slide through the small opening to find an elevator puzzle. Pick up one of the spools located just inside the room, step onto the first elevator on the right, and set it down as you are lowered.

Grab the nearby moveable sled and pull it backward onto the same elevator. Collect the piece of Silica on the room's left side before climbing onto the pair of enclosed statues in the middle of the room. Hop over to the raised platform and continue through the exit.

Destroy the ceramics in the next room to reveal an opening, and continue through to find a second elevator puzzle. Climb atop the big container on the left and step onto the left elevator. Bust open the jug to go flying up to the upper floor. Search the area for another Silica and treasure chest before hopping down to the lowered elevator.

Pick up one of the spools, carry it into the adjacent room, and set it down on yet another elevator on the right. Collect a piece of Silica in the opposite corner and then climb the shelf in the right corner. Run and jump to reach the elevator and climb out through the exit.

In the next room, nab the three treasures on the left and the Silica that sits atop the pedestal. Interact with the Ancient Tablet to complete the tomb before slipping out the opening on the right wall. Now just follow the path down the slope, underwater, and up a wall to arrive just west of the pyramid.

TOMB OF THE CYNIC

TERRITORY: Uab Nome	SILICA AVAILABLE: 2	TREASURES: 2	ANCIENT MECHANISM: None

In northwest Uab Nome, southwest of the water, paths from White Desert Oasis and Uab Nome converge before forking farther to the south. Located just southeast of this

location is the entrance to the Tomb of the Cynic. Vultures are typically found just outside, feeding on animal carcasses.

Once inside, climb the cliff on the right to spot two lionesses napping on the other side. Take them out from the safe location before dropping into their den, where a jewelry box provides valuable resources. A piece of Silica rests on a rock nearby.

Follow the path as it leads southeast past another Silica into a spacious cavern. Ready your bow, as a Level 17 lion hunts inside. A treasure sits near the tree in the far corner.

Continue deeper inside as the cave narrows until you find the Ancient Tablet. Squeeze through the nearby crack to quickly exit the tomb.

TOMB OF THE NOMADS

TERRITORY: Isolated Desert	SILICA AVAILABLE: 4	TREASURES: 3	ANCIENT MECHANISM: None

Located in the northwestern corner of the Isolated Desert, find the entrance to the Tomb of the Nomads in the side of the mountain, among a group of canopies. The entrance immediately opens into a big room with a stairway on the right that leads up

to a second level. A door on the left takes you to a second room that holds only a little loot. Before proceeding upstairs, grab a Silica that lies next to a group of candles on the room's far side.

At the second floor, bust through the weakened wall ahead, ignore the warning on the scroll, and follow the corridor to find a pool of water lit up by the opening above. Immediately jump to a ledge on the right and collect the rare treasure.

Next, dive underwater and collect a second Silica just left of where you entered. Follow the left wall to find a third Silica and then grab a treasure.

Continue underwater, coming up to take a breath if the meter gets low, and search the far side to find a treasure chest and a fourth Silica. Bust through the wood boards and interact with the Ancient Tablet to complete the tomb. Exit the water on the west side and follow the light to find another entrance to the tomb.

GREAT SPHINX

TERRITORY: Giza	SILICA AVAILABLE: 4	TREASURES: 2	ANCIENT MECHANISM: Eesfet Oon-m'Aa Poo	SILICA REQUIRED FOR MECHANISM: 50	SEGMENT: 6

Access the final Ancient Mechanism through a secret entrance behind the Great Sphinx on the east side of Giza. You find this after completing the side quest "Bayek's Promise," so refer to the end of the Stone Circles section of the "Activities" chapter for more details. This final mechanism requires 50 Silica to activate, so be sure to visit all the tombs before accessing this final location.

WAR ELEPHANTS

TOTAL: 4	OBJECTIVE: Kill the elephants	RELATED QUESTS: None	REWARD: 1 AP per War Elephant, piece of Legendary gear (two of the War Elephants)

Located at four camps around Egypt, War Elephants have been trained to kill. Step inside one of these sites to get the attention of the beast, beginning a seemingly unfair fight. Bayek's agility and powerful gear may level the field some, but the mammals are still the most powerful foes in the game. Each battle requires persistence and focus to make it through. Let your guard down for too long and these guys will trample you to death.

Here are a few tips that work for all four War Elephants; more specific strategies are given for each War Elephant next.

◎ The fights get harder as they go on, so conserving a little ammo for the last phase is often a good idea. The elephants tend to be less active early on, so use that time to go in for melee attacks.

◎ Loot bags that partially refill your ammo supply appear around the battlefield. Keep an eye out for them, but be sure you need them before picking them up. Later phases often require more ammunition.

◎ Be ready for opportunities to strike as the elephant moves around the battlefield. When they turn around or strafe, take advantage of the openings and attack.

HERWENNEFER

TERRITORY: Hideout of Herwennefer, White Desert Oasis
LEVEL: 40
REWARD ITEM: Shaman Legendary Outfit

Look for Herwennefer to move out to range as his riders begin firing arrows your way; lift your shield to block them. Afterward, he blows his trunk, which opens up his neck to attack. This is a weak spot, so take advantage of the chance.

After every melee combo, Herwennefer rises up on his back legs. Use this opportunity to shoot his belly for extra damage. At 70 percent health, poison bombs are added to long-range attacks. Lower your shield and run out of range to avoid taking damage. When he hits 30 percent health, arrows and bombs are launched at the same time. Stay on the move to avoid the attacks.

SURUS

TERRITORY: Roman Camp of Surus, Green Mountains
LEVEL: 40
REWARD ITEM: None

The archers on Surus's back occasionally fire arrows at you. Lift your shield when you see the circle at Bayek's feet. Stay on the move to make yourself a tougher target.

When the elephant roars, it is a sign that he is going to run out and charge you. Shoot a volley of arrows at him as he runs away.

At 70 percent health, he enters Phase 2. When the beast heads out for a charge attack, the soldiers begin shooting at you. Block them with your shield while dodging the charge.

Phase 3 begins at 30 percent health. During Surus's charge, arrows and firebombs are sent your way. The elephant also becomes highly aggressive, so be ready to dodge the extra attacks.

INTRODUCTION

THE ESSENTIALS

MAIN QUESTS

SIDE QUESTS

ACTIVITIES

ATLAS

REFERENCE & ANALYSIS

JUMBE

TERRITORY: Roman Camp of Jumbe, Herakleion Nome

LEVEL: 40

REWARD ITEM: None

Look for Jumbe to run out and prepare a charge attack. If you can position yourself near a wall, you can force him to slam into it. This stuns him, opening him up for attack. If caught in the path of his front attack, dash in the opposite direction of his swing to avoid the hit.

At 70 percent health, Jumbe enters Phase 2. When he moves out for a charge attack, his riders toss smoke bombs in an attempt to stun you. Be ready for the incoming projectiles and move out of the vicinity. If you are caught in the blast, you risk becoming vulnerable to the charge.

Once he hits 30 percent health, smoke bombs are thrown while he charges at you. Now you must dodge the smoke screens and his attack. At this point, Jumbe no longer rams into walls and he charges up to three times if he does not make contact.

QETESH & RESHEPH

TERRITORY: Camp of Qetesh & Resheph, Uab Nome

LEVEL: 40

REWARD ITEM: Trophy Hunter Legendary Predator Bow

This pair of elephants takes turns attacking. When one is active, the other one attempts to keep its distance. If you wish to melee, focus on the active elephant.

While Resheph prefers melee attacks, Qetesh likes to leave the work to her riders. She also blows her trunk after their attacks, which opens up a weak spot on her neck. Use that opportunity to attack.

Listen for calls to charge, as this announces Resheph's intention to charge at you. Get ready to dodge away from his melee attack and get in hits of your own.

When an elephant reaches 60 percent health, they start Phase 2 of the fight. During this phase, Qetesh's riders begin shooting you while Resheph runs in for melee attacks. Focus your shield on Qetesh and ready for a dodge when a ground shake proclaims Resheph's charge

Try to keep the two elephants at around the same health, because when one dies, the other enrages, becoming much more aggressive.

HERMIT LOCATIONS

TOTAL: 5	OBJECTIVE: Meditate at each hermit location	REWARD: 1 AP per location

Meditate at five locations around Ancient Egypt to earn one Ability Point each time. These sites are typically located at a high point or guarded by wildlife, so remain alert.

EREMITES HIDEOUT

TERRITORY: Faiyum

Look for ruins on the lake's east side and head up the steps. Watch out for the cobras that often protect loot on each side of the path. At the top, climb the big archway to find the red blanket. Interact with it to get the Ability Point.

RA-HORAKHTY MOUNTAIN TOP

TERRITORY: Black Desert

Climb to the highest point in the Black Desert to find this location. A trail leads all the way up to the destination. You can interact with the red carpet.

OGDAMOS

TERRITORY: Paraitonion

Once you find the deserted village of Ogdamos, built into a mountainside, enter the open house on the far right. Meditate on the blanket that sits on the platform inside. This is a great location to find a house cat as a pet, even though they are unhelpful in a fight.

DEMESNE OF SEKHEM

TERRITORY: Herakleion Nome

Find the hermit location directly east of Herakleion village. Just southeast of the hut, a corpse lies on a blanket, surrounded by candles and flower petals. Watch out for a Level 28 leopard that roams this swampy area. If it gives you trouble, climb the structure and use your bow from the higher vantage point. Interact with the ground at the foot of the body to earn an Ability Point.

AQUIFER OASIS

TERRITORY: Qattara Depression

You may have to clear out a few Level 24 hyenas in the area before proceeding. Keep an eye out for the wild dogs, as you are vulnerable. Look for the trio of torches in the water and you can interact with the point in the middle.

PTOLEMY STATUES

| TOTAL: 19 | OBJECTIVE: Destroy the Ptolemy statues | REWARD: 150, 300, or 450 XP per Ptolemy statue |

Destroy the statues of Ptolemy holding a head in his hand that have been erected in order to instill fear in the public. There are 19 of these monuments around Ancient Egypt. If possible, wait for nearby guards to clear the area or they will attack as soon as you hit the statue.

SIWA

TERRITORY: Siwa

To find the statue, look for the three-way intersection that forms a triangle in the middle of Siwa. It sits just north of Siwa's Nomad's Bazaar.

WEST OF ALEXANDRIA

TERRITORY: Lake Mareotis

Northwest of Lake Mareotis, west of Alexandria, another tribute to Ptolemy sits at a fork in the road just southwest of a narrow bay.

HIPPODROME

TERRITORY: Kanopos Nome

An indoor market sits less than 100 meters north of Lageion Hippodrome. Destroy the statue that sits between the two structures.

SOUTH OF APOLLODORUS' ESTATE

TERRITORY: Kanopos Nome

Follow the main path south from Apollodorus' Estate and take the left route at the fork. The statue sits next to a stable farther south.

SOUTH OF SAIS

TERRITORY: Sapi-Res Nome

Follow the main path south from Sais until you reach the first major intersection, east of a Viewpoint. Destroy the statue at this location.

MEFKAT

TERRITORY: Sapi-Res Nome

A village has been burned at Mefkat, on the region's southwest side. A statue has been erected on the west side of the destruction as a reminder.

HUGROS CROSSING WATCHTOWER

TERRITORY: Ineb-Hedjet Nome

In the northern reaches of the region, next to Hugros Crossing Watchtower, a statue sits at another fork in the road.

KERKASOROS

TERRITORY: Ineb-Hedjet Nome

The statue sits in Kerkasoros, between the waterway and main path. It overlooks a worksite, where bricks are being created.

CASTOFF TEMPLE OF HAPI

TERRITORY: Ineb-Hedjet Nome

Head to the ruin at Castoff Temple of Hapi, south of Kerkasoros. The statue sits between the point of interest and the main path.

NORTHEAST OF PER OUSIR

TERRITORY: Ineb-Hedjet Nome

A little northeast of Per Ousir, a statue sits on the east side of the road.

PHILOTERIS

TERRITORY: Faiyum

Philoteris sits in the southern part of Faiyum, directly west of Euhemeria. A Ptolemy statue has been erected next to the road in front of the property.

NORTHWEST FAIYUM OASIS

TERRITORY: Faiyum Oasis

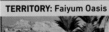

In northwestern Faiyum Oasis, a statue sits directly southwest of a Greek piazza.

INTRODUCTION

THE ESSENTIALS

MAIN QUESTS

SIDE QUESTS

ACTIVITIES

ATLAS

REFERENCE & ANALYSIS

NORTH OF KROKODILOPOLIS

TERRITORY: Faiyum Oasis

A second Greek piazza is being built in the southern portion of the region, north of Krokodilopolis. This statue sits at a fork in the road, just south of the structure.

UDJAT APIARY VIEWPOINT

TERRITORY: Im-Khent Nome

Southwest of Udjat Apiary, a statue sits in the shadow of the nearby Viewpoint, just off the main path.

TEMPLE OF KHONSOU

TERRITORY: Herakleion Nome

Move north through the village of Herakleion, toward the Temple of Khonsou. The statue sits out front of the building.

SOUTH OF MEMPHIS

TERRITORY: Atef-Pehu Nome

Follow the main road south from Memphis into Atef-Pehu, where a statue sits just north of the path.

CENTRAL LIBUE

TERRITORY: Libue

Move up the main path, north from Siwa, until you reach an intersection. The statue sits on the south side of that intersection.

OUAHE

TERRITORY: Isolated Desert

Follow the road west that runs along Giza's southern border, into Isolated Desert. A statue sits next to the Ouahe point of interest.

PISSA OROS CITADEL

TERRITORY: Isolated Desert

The major stronghold of Pissa Oros Citadel sits in the far western portion of the Isolated Desert. Head east about 250 meters to find a statue on the road's north side.

OTHER ACTIVITIES

Beyond the aforementioned activities, there are plenty of events to keep you busy. Reda offers daily quests at any Nomad's Bazaar location, Phylakes hunt Bayek until you eliminate them, and military strongholds offer experience and treasure for completing their objectives.

⬢ REDA'S DAILY QUEST

Reda shows up in the Yamu region (you need to be at least level 9), offering carbon crystals and Heka chests for a hefty price. If you are online, Reda also offers a daily quest.

He asks Bayek to complete tasks, such as rescue certain people, defeat animals, and gather materials. These quests are adapted to your level and reward you with a mystery box once completed.

HEKA CHESTS

Heka chests grant a random item for 3000 Drachma. They guarantee a rare or legendary piece of equipment. If you are lucky you will find a unique or Store item.

⬢ PHYLAKES

| PREREQUISITE: Assassinate the Snake and Gennadios | ENEMY LEVEL: 20-40 | RELATED QUEST: Phylakes' Prey (suggested level 40) | REWARD: 300 XP; Phylake kill, 60-100 drachmas; most kills; piece of Legendary gear; Phylake kill; Black Hood Legendary Outfit (complete Phylakes' Prey) | DETAILS: Assassinate Phylakes before they get Bayek. |

THE PHYLAKES

PHYLAKE	TERRITORY	LEVEL	GEAR	KEY CARRIER	LOOT
The Outsider	Alexandria, west of Alexandria	20	Sword, Small Shield, Bow	No	Golden Wolf
Ptolemy's Fist	Sap-Meh Nome	22	Horse, Heavy Blunt, Bow	No	Copper Mace
The Iron Ram	Ineb-Hedjet Nome	25	Chariot, Sickle Sword, Bow, Smoke Screen	No	Smoke and Mirrors
The Stranger	Memphis	28	Sword, Medium Shield, Bow	Yes	Sarissa
Ra's Mercy	Faiyum	30	Spear, Small Shield, Bow	No	Storm Blades
The Hill	Faiyum Oasis	32	Heavy Blunt, Bow	Yes	Headsplitter
Bane of Hathor	Atef-Pehu Nome	35	Horse, Bow	No	Deathstorm
Half Horn	Im-Khent Nome	38	Chariot, Bow	Yes	Composite Bow
The Iron Bull	Giza, Isolated Desert	40	Camel, Long Sword, Bow, Firebombs	No	Djoser's Pride
The Galatian	Isolated Desert	40	Chariot, Sword, Big Shield, Spears, Firebombs	Yes	The Fourth Plague

KEEP A LOOKOUT FOR PHYLAKES

Phylakes, or bounty hunters, hunt Bayek after completing the Gennadios the Phylakitai Quest. These foes range between Levels 20 and 40, but they are all a challenge as Bayek nears the enemy's level. Look for the red Phylake icons on the world map. They show up above fog in unvisited territories. There are 10 Phylakes in all, and each patrols a separate territory; see the table above for locations. They tend to follow a long path that stretches much of the territory.

ASSASSINATE THE PHYLAKES

A warning appears onscreen when a Phylake is near, so take precaution. Depending on your level, you may be able to assassinate the enemy. Otherwise, you must fight him to the death. If it gets out of hand, flee the scene.

Warning! Phylakes are near!

As you pursue a Phylake, watch out for nearby enemy camps. Any additional soldiers make the fight tougher than it needs to be. Try to pull the Phylake away from the guards before attacking. Likewise, nearby allies may help out in your fight.

Also note that when you infiltrate a stronghold and tip off the enemies to your location, a Phylake may react to a brazier alarm as he roams the nearby area. This gives more incentive to sabotage the fire or keep enemies away from the brazier.

The Phylakes often travel by mount—camel, horse, or chariot—or may be on foot. They vary greatly in fighting style, following many of the same enemy types as the regular guards: soldier, archer, brute, and predator. The gear used by each Phylake is listed in the preceding table.

INTRODUCTION

THE ESSENTIALS

MAIN QUESTS

SIDE QUESTS

ACTIVITIES

ATLAS

REFERENCE & ANALYSIS

Sneak up on the foes and assassinate them if possible. Pull them off their mounts early to keep an archer from simply circling your location as he pelts you with arrows. Limit the fights to just the Phylake and use all tools at your disposal to kill them. Evade their melee attacks, block incoming arrows, and flee from firebombs.

CONFIRM THE KILL

After making a kill, approach the corpse and confirm the kill by holding the Loot button. You are rewarded XP, a Legendary piece of gear, and possibly drachmas.

If this is your first kill or the Phylake is a key carrier, you also receive a quest item(s).

The first Phylake drops an Assassination Contract that explains why the bounty hunters pursue Bayek. Killing the four key-carrying Phylakes gets Bayek Ornamental Keys (refer to the preceding table to see which Phylakes possess the quest items). Collecting all four keys leads Bayek to a fishing village in Herakleion Nome.

INVESTIGATE FISHING VILLAGE

After receiving the letter, head to Yw Huts in Herakleion Nome and find Abar, typically located on the village's north side; use Senu to pinpoint her location. Talk to her and she offers to hand over the final key, if Bayek exterminates the crocodiles found east of the village.

KILL THE CROCODILES NEAR THE FISHING VILLAGE

Scout the island east of the village to find a group of crocodiles. It is the Level 40 reptiles that must be eradicated from the area. Do not pull too many at once as you eliminate the reptiles.

After killing the marked animals, the quest progresses back to the village.

SPEAK TO ABAR AND FIND HER TREASURE

Return to Abar and speak with her to receive the final key and the treasure's location. Head south to the marked area and use Senu to find the treasure, underwater just south of the southern island. Watch out for the enemies (Levels 30 and 31) who occupy the island, though you can avoid them by taking a wide berth. Dive underwater and interact with the chest to receive the Black Hood Legendary Outfit.

If you found the letter before eliminating all 10 Phylakes, the remaining bounty hunters still pursue Bayek within their territories. Assassinate them to receive the legendary gear.

WORLD EVENTS
EXAMPLES OF WORLD EVENTS

EVENT	OBJECTIVE
Assist Rebels	Protect allies (eliminate the enemies they are fighting)
Assist Rebels	Free the prisoners (and assist them out of the enemy stronghold)
Predator Attack	Exterminate threat (kill animal that attacks citizens)
Rogue Animal	Exterminate threat (kill animal that attacks citizens)
Bandit/Roman Attack	Eliminate Bandits/Romans

As you explore Egypt, a "world event" (represented in game by a "!" icon) can appear at almost any time, where Ancient Egyptian citizens need assistance. This

typically requests you to fend off a predator or enemy attack or free prisoners—rewarding you with 100 or 150 XP once you complete the mini-quest.

MILITARY STRONGHOLDS

TOTAL: 🏰 10 Forts, 🏛 16 Medium Military, 🚩 78 Small Military	

POSSIBLE OBJECTIVES: Kill captain, kill commander, find treasure

RELATED QUESTS: See list below

FORT REWARD: 500, 1,000, or 1,500 XP

MEDIUM MILITARY REWARD: 300, 600, or 900 XP

SMALL MILITARY REWARD: 200, 400, or 600 XP

Enemy strongholds are indicated by the three icons shown above on the in-game map as you approach the sites. They come in three basic sizes: full-size forts, medium military installations, and small bases. Enemy level at each base depends on the level range of the territory in which they are found.

Your objectives are as follows:

TYPE	OBJECTIVE
Small Military	Kill the captain. Loot one treasure. Triremes do not have treasure.
Medium Military	Kill the captain and commander. Loot two treasures.
Fort	Kill two captains and the commander. Loot four treasures.

SCOUT THE LOCATION

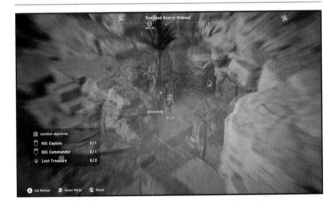

Use Senu to scout each stronghold, marking as many soldiers and as many treasures as you can. Captains and commanders are typically of a higher level and are indicated by the special icon. Items to look out for as you infiltrate strongholds are as follows:

◎ **Ammo rack** Enemy bases are typically well stocked, including plenty of ammo racks. Keep an eye out for their locations and use them when arrows and tools run low.

◎ **Ballistae** These small ballistae fire arrows at a high rate of speed, causing serious harm to anyone that approaches. Man the gun by approaching and interacting with it. These are very useful when the stealth approach is not an option. Nearby soldiers may use these powerful weapons when they detect you, so don't hang out in their line of sight.

◎ **Oil jars** Not the stealthiest tactic, but these jars create an explosion when hit with fire. You can pick up and move them and even throw them.

◎ **Braziers** Enemies can call in reinforcements by lighting a big brazier, typically found near the middle of bigger bases. When you

are detected, a soldier may move to the nearest brazier and attempt to light it. If they light the flame, extra soldiers move into the area, making it tougher for you to complete your objective.

◎ **Vantage points** Use high vantage points, such as cliffs, towers, rooftops, and walkways, to get a good view of an enemy base. Watch out for snipers occupying these positions and assassinate them before they detect you. Clearing out the snipers before taking on a camp can go a long way to securing the location.

◎ **Haystacks and hiding booths** As you infiltrate a stronghold, it is often necessary to hide in order to stay undetected. Use haystacks, hiding booths

booths, and tall grass when the enemy senses you are nearby. Also use these when you're being pursued, but be sure they don't see you enter them!

◎ **Treasure** There is typically at least one treasure chest or jewelry box at these strongholds that are required to complete the locations. Keep an eye out for them and collect the loot.

Here are a few handy tips when taking on an enemy base:

- A white brazier icon above an enemy indicates they are planning to light the alarm. Red indicates that it has been lit and reinforcements are on the way. You can stop him from lighting it in two ways: kill him before he can light the flame or interact with the brazier beforehand. By using the brazier first, you set a trap, causing the device to explode upon use—harming nearby enemies.

- Infiltrating an enemy base at nighttime typically results in less activity, with many guards sleeping inside buildings or on the rooftops. Look for stealthy entrances and assassinate the poor fools while they snooze.

- A cart full of hay can be used to infiltrate an enemy base. If a cart moves toward a stronghold, hide in the hay and ride it deep inside the fortification.

- A vehicle can be set on fire as it moves into a stronghold. This is a great way to spread chaos and cause a nice distraction.

All forts, medium military, and small military strongholds are listed in the following table, along with the territory they are located in and the objectives for each. We also mention if we've covered an enemy base in the quest chapters.

If no quest is listed or if you simply visit it in a quest, we provide an overhead view of the area and pinpoint arrow stands, ballistae, brazier alarms, and treasures. We also use arrows to indicate the hidden entrances. One arrow points to the outside entrance, while the other represents approximately where you enter inside the stronghold. These are typically underground paths into the base, allowing for a stealthier approach.

ENEMY STRONGHOLDS

TERRITORY	TYPE	NAME	OBJECTIVES	QUEST
Alexandria	Fort	Akra Garrison	4 Treasures, 2 Captains, 1 Commander	Main Quest: Gennadios the Phylakitai
Alexandria	Medium Military	Kibotos Arsenal	2 Treasures, 1 Captain, 1 Commander	Side Quest: Serapis Unites
Alexandria	Medium Military	Pharos Garrison	2 Treasures, 1 Captain, 1 Commander	—
Atef-Pehu Nome	Small Military	Kerke Wharf	1 Treasure, 1 Captain	Side Quest: The Matriarch
Atef-Pehu Nome	Small Military	South Nile Trireme	1 Captain, Ship Patrols	—
Faiyum	Medium Military	Dionysias Caravanserai	2 Treasures, 1 Captain, 1 Commander	—
Faiyum	Medium Military	Okteres Blockade	2 Treasures, 1 Captain, 1 Commander	Side Quest: Sobek's Gold
Faiyum	Small Military	Beached Trireme Camp	1 Treasure, 1 Captain	Side Quest: Rebel Strike
Faiyum	Small Military	Dionysias Wharf	1 Treasure, 1 Captain	—
Faiyum	Small Military	East Moeris Trireme	1 Captain, Ship Patrols	—
Faiyum	Small Military	Euhemeria Lighthouse Camp	1 Treasure, 1 Captain	Main Quest: The Crocodile's Scales
Faiyum	Small Military	Ketket Cove Hideout	1 Treasure, 1 Captain	—

TERRITORY	TYPE	NAME	OBJECTIVES	QUEST
Faiyum	Small Military	Pannouki Hideout	1 Treasure, 1 Captain	Side Quest: Curse of Wadjet
Faiyum	Small Military	West Moeris Trireme	1 Captain, Ship Patrols	—
Faiyum Oasis	Fort	Kerkesoucha Granary	4 Treasures, 2 Captains, 1 Commander	Visited during Main Quest: The Crocodile's Jaws, but not covered in full.
Faiyum Oasis	Medium Military	Neorion Naval Arsenal	2 Treasures, 1 Captain, 1 Commander	Side Quest: Sobek's Tears
Faiyum Oasis	Small Military	Psenhyris Trireme Wharf	1 Treasure, 1 Captain	—
Faiyum Oasis	Small Military	South Moeris Trireme	1 Captain	—
Giza	Medium Military	Depleted Quarry Hideout	2 Treasures, 1 Captain, 1 Commander	Main Quest: The Hyena
Giza	Medium Military	Khentkawes Hideout	2 Treasures, 1 Captain, 1 Commander	Side Quest: Precious Bonds
Giza	Small Military	Camp Kataskinono	1 Treasure, 1 Captain	—
Giza	Small Military	Khufu Temple Hideout	1 Treasure, 1 Captain	Side Quest: Precious Bonds
Giza	Small Military	Per-Wsir Hideout	1 Treasure, 1 Captain	—
Great Green Sea	Small Military	East Mediterranean Trireme	1 Captain	—
Green Mountains	Fort	Kyrenaike Roman Citadel	4 Treasures, 2 Captains, 1 Commander	Side Quest: Playing with Fire
Green Mountains	Medium Military	Necropolis Hideout	2 Treasures, 1 Captain, 1 Commander	—
Green Mountains	Medium Military	Prasinos Roman Camp	2 Treasures, 1 Captain, 1 Commander	Side Quest: Carpe Diem
Green Mountains	Small Military	Balagrae Roman Barracks	1 Treasure, 1 Captain	Side Quest: Shadows of Apollo
Green Mountains	Small Military	Akabis Roman Tower	1 Treasure, 1 Captain	—
Green Mountains	Small Military	Auritina Roman Tower	1 Treasure, 1 Captain	—
Green Mountains	Small Military	Bandit Hideout	1 Treasure, 1 Captain	—
Green Mountains	Small Military	Collis Roman Hunting Camp	1 Treasure, 1 Captain	Side Quest: Halo of the Huntress
Green Mountains	Small Military	Desperate Gully Hideout	1 Treasure, 1 Captain	Side Quest: Pax Romana
Green Mountains	Small Military	Kastor High Hideout	1 Treasure, 1 Captain	—
Green Mountains	Small Military	Poludeukes Hideout	1 Treasure, 1 Captain	—
Green Mountains	Small Military	Roman Quarry Camp	1 Treasure, 1 Captain	—
Green Mountains	Small Military	Roman Watchtower	1 Treasure, 1 Captain	—
Haueris Nome	Fort	Fort Boubastos	4 Treasures, 2 Captains, 1 Commander	Side Quest: Fighting for Faiyum
Haueris Nome	Fort	Limestone Quarry	4 Treasures, 2 Captains, 1 Commander	—
Haueris Nome	Small Military	Cleon's Dam	1 Treasure, 1 Captain	Side Quest: Fighting for Faiyum
Haueris Nome	Small Military	Cleon's Wharf	1 Treasure, 1 Captain	—
Herakleion Nome	Small Military	Camp Nisi	1 Treasure, 1 Captain	—

INTRODUCTION

THE ESSENTIALS

MAIN QUESTS

SIDE QUESTS

ACTIVITIES

ATLAS

REFERENCE & ANALYSIS

TERRITORY	TYPE	NAME	OBJECTIVES	QUEST
Herakleion Nome	Small Military	Carcer Roman Compound	1 Treasure, 1 Captain	Side Quest: Reunion
Herakleion Nome	Small Military	Lah Hideout	1 Treasure, 1 Captain	—
Herakleion Nome	Small Military	Mithidrates Roman Camp	1 Treasure, 1 Captain	—
Herakleion Nome	Small Military	Neith Cradle Hideout	1 Treasure, 1 Captain	—
Herakleion Nome	Small Military	Thenessos Hideout	1 Treasure, 1 Captain	—
Iment Nome	Small Military	Eremos Hideout	1 Treasure, 1 Captain	Side Quest: Ulterior Votive
Iment Nome	Small Military	House of Sand Hideout	1 Treasure, 1 Captain	—
Iment Nome	Small Military	Necropolis Bandit Hideout	1 Treasure, 1 Captain	Side Quest: The Book of the Dead
Im-Khent Nome	Medium Military	Saphthis Outpost	2 Treasures, 1 Captain, 1 Commander	—
Ineb-Hedjet Nome	Medium Military	Kerkasoros Outpost	2 Treasures, 1 Captain, 1 Commander	—
Ineb-Hedjet Nome	Small Military	Akronisos Camp	1 Treasure, 1 Captain	—
Ineb-Hedjet Nome	Small Military	Camp Agrophylake	1 Treasure, 1 Captain	—
Ineb-Hedjet Nome	Small Military	Plesionhudor Hideout	1 Treasure, 1 Captain	Main Quest: The Scarab's Lies
Ineb-Hedjet Nome	Small Military	Upper Nile Trireme	1 Captain	—
Isolated Desert	Fort	Pissa Oros Citadel	4 Treasures, 2 Captains, 1 Commander	Side Quest: Plight of the Rebels
Isolated Desert	Small Military	Camp Dory	1 Treasure, 1 Captain	—
Isolated Desert	Small Military	Camp Hetoimazo	1 Treasure, 1 Captain	Side Quest: Plight of the Rebels
Isolated Desert	Small Military	Camp Khoikos	1 Treasure, 1 Captain	—
Isolated Desert	Small Military	Camp Tamaris	1 Treasure, 1 Captain	—
Isolated Desert	Small Military	Camp Xeros	1 Treasure, 1 Captain	—
Ka-Khem Nome	Small Military	Dasos Hideout	1 Treasure, 1 Captain	Side Quest: The Old Library
Kanopos Nome	Small Military	Als Hideout	1 Treasure, 1 Captain	Side Quest: Wild Ride
Kanopos Nome	Small Military	Camp Menouthis	1 Treasure, 1 Captain	—
Kyrenaika	Fort	Roman Akropolis	4 Treasure, 2 Captains, 1 Commander	Visited during Main Quest: The Final Weighing, but not covered in full.
Kyrenaika	Medium Military	Cyrene Barracks	2 Treasures, Captain, Commander	—
Kyrenaika	Small Military	Apollonia Roman Barracks	1 Treasure, 1 Captain	Side Quest: Dead in the Water
Lake Mareotis	Small Military	Abandoned Temple Hideout	1 Treasure, 1 Captain	Visited during Side Quest: Birthright, but not covered in full.
Lake Mareotis	Small Military	Lakeside Villa Outpost	1 Treasure, 1 Captain	Side Quest: Birthright
Lake Mareotis	Small Military	North Mareotis Trireme	1 Captain	—
Lake Mareotis	Small Military	South Mareotis Trireme	1 Captain	—

TERRITORY	TYPE	NAME	OBJECTIVES	QUEST
Libue	Medium Military	Saragina Camp	2 Treasures, 1 Captain, 1 Commander	—
Marmarica	Fort	Chersonesos Roman Fort	4 Treasures, 2 Captains, 1 Commander	—
Marmarica	Small Military	Bemulos Roman Tower	1 Treasure, 1 Captain	Side Quest: His Secret Service
Marmarica	Small Military	Desolated Lookout	1 Treasure, 1 Captain	—
Marmarica	Small Military	Hydrax Roman Camp	1 Treasure, 1 Captain	Side Quest: Shadows of Apollo
Marmarica	Small Military	Kelida Hideout	1 Treasure, 1 Captain	—
Marmarica	Small Military	Legio XXXVII Roman Docks	1 Treasure, 1 Captain	—
Marmarica	Small Military	Livius Roman Tower	1 Treasure, 1 Captain	—
Marmarica	Small Military	Thintis Roman Tower	1 Treasure, 1 Captain	—
Memphis	Medium Military	Memphites Barracks	2 Treasures, 1 Captain, 1 Commander	Side Quest: The Baker's Dilemma
Memphis	Small Military	Apagogeas Hideout	1 Treasure, 1 Captain	Side Quest: Children of the Streets
Memphis	Small Military	Temple of Hathor	1 Treasure, 1 Captain	Main Quest: The Lizard's Mask
Mesogeios Sea	Small Military	West Mediterranean Trireme	1 Captain	—
Sapi-Res Nome	Fort	Nikiou Fort	4 Treasures, 2 Captains, 1 Commander	Side Quest: The Tax Master
Sapi-Res Nome	Small Military	Camp Achlys	1 Treasure, 1 Captain	Main Quest: The Scarab's Lies
Sapi-Res Nome	Small Military	Camp Pyrrhos	1 Treasure, 1 Captain	—
Sapi-Res Nome	Small Military	Camp Shemu	1 Treasure, 1 Captain	Side Quest: The Ostrich
Sapi-Res Nome	Small Military	Nikiou Post	1 Treasure, 1 Captain	—
Sapi-Res Nome	Small Military	Psenemphaia Hideout	1 Treasure, 1 Captain	Side Quest: Lost Happiness
Sap-Meh Nome	Medium Military	Anthylla Outpost	2 Treasures, 1 Captain, 1 Commander	Side Quest: In Protest
Sap-Meh Nome	Small Military	Potamos Hideout	1 Treasure, 1 Captain	Side Quest: The Hungry River
Saqqara Nome	Small Military	Hugros Hideout	1 Treasure, 1 Captain	Side Quest: Secrets of the First Pyramids
Saqqara Nome	Small Military	Psammos Hideout	1 Treasure, 1 Captain	—
Siwa	Small Military	Camp Shetjeh	1 Treasure, 1 Captain	Side Quest: Striking the Anvil
Siwa	Small Military	Coral Escarpment Camp	1 Treasure, 1 Captain	—
Uab Nome	Medium Military	Arsinoites Quarry Hideout	2 Treasures, 1 Captain, 1 Commander	—
Uab Nome	Small Military	Dioryx Megale Wharf	1 Treasure, 1 Captain	—
Uab Nome	Small Military	Trireme Stranding Camp	1 Treasure, 1 Captain	Side Quest: The Jaws of Sobek
White Desert Oasis	Medium Military	Desert Waterfalls Hideout	2 Treasures, 1 Captain, 1 Commander	Side Quest: Demons in the Desert
White Desert Oasis	Small Military	Djbt Jm Hideout	1 Treasure, 1 Captain	—
White Desert Oasis	Small Military	Larder Station Hideout	1 Treasure, 1 Captain	Side Quest: Demons in the Desert

FORTS

CHERSONESOS ROMAN FORT

TERRITORY: Marmarica

Find a hidden entrance on the fort's east side that leads into a shelter. Lions are caged on the camp's north side, so they can be released before immediately climbing to safety. Stop at the brazier on the north side early on to disable enemies' ability to call for reinforcements. The ropes leading to this brazier connect several towers. Three ballistae offer high-power weaponry for you on the west side and in the middle, though you are fairly vulnerable at each one. One captain hangs out on the north side, while the second captain and commander roam around the central area. Work your way south from the north cliff to complete the objectives.

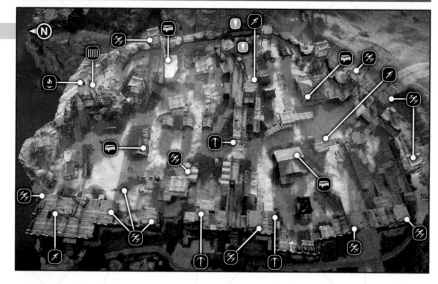

KERKESOUCHA GRANARY

TERRITORY: Faiyum Oasis

The Kerkesoucha Granary is split into two distinct sections: the northern residence that is populated mostly by citizens and the granary portion where guards keep tabs on their commodity. If your business is to the north, sneak through the wall and head through the house. The captains and commander remain in the south, where high vantage points offer a great view of the property. Ammo is in short supply in the stronghold, so use stealth kills when possible. Enter near the south end and use the pigeon towers and connecting wires to reach the brazier. The treasures are concentrated in two locations—a house near the middle and the main residence to the north.

LIMESTONE QUARRY

TERRITORY: Haueris Nomev

The quarry is half surrounded by high cliffs with narrow entrances in the northeast and southeast corners. Approaching from the west allows you to survey the area from the high vantage point and then stealthily descend into the base. If you are on the southeast side, look for a Parkour Up device to reach the path above, which takes you to this same point. This also puts you close to the commander and two treasures. One captain roams the outside on the ground level, while the second guy is typically just inside the opening at the base of the western side. For the third treasure, spot the higher of the two cranes and then access the small room below it. Enter the opening at the base of the west wall, move around the limestone blocks, and bust through the wood door to find the final treasure inside another small room.

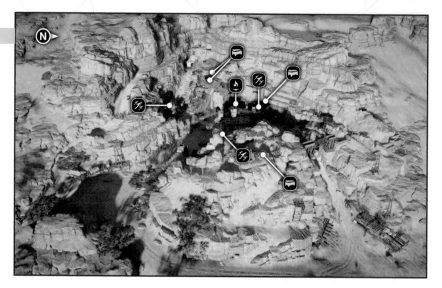

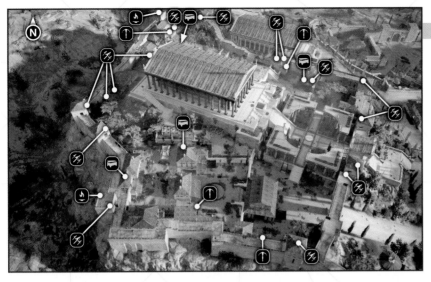

ROMAN AKROPOLIS

TERRITORY: Kyrenaika

The temple on Cyrene's southeast side is walled in and well protected by the military. Ballistae are located on upper platforms on the north and south sides. Two treasures are hidden inside the buildings in the southwest corner, while a third is housed inside a home near the northeast corner. The fourth is a bit harder to find. Enter the buildings against the back wall, northwest of the temple. Find the ladder that leads underground, and follow the tunnel to a hidden room with the final treasure. One captain sticks close to the treasure in the northeast area and the other is typically in the southwest portion. The commander roams across much of the north.

MEDIUM MILITARY

ARSINOÏTES QUARRY HIDEOUT

TERRITORY: Uab Nome

Both treasures are inside the opening on the south side; one is in the southeast corner and the other is in the southwest. Find the hole on the west side. Use it to stealthily drop in from above. This gives you access to the commander, who roams in and out of this area. A Parkour Up device is at that entrance. Use it for a quick getaway when necessary. The captain sticks to the upper level above this interior. Use the wooden fence to hide entry and exit.

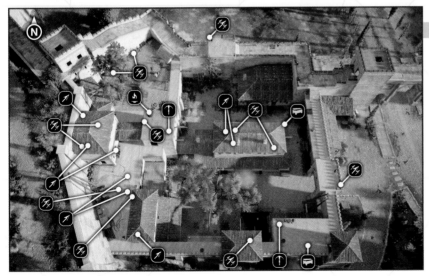

CYRENE BARRACKS

TERRITORY: Kyrenaika

The Cyrene Barracks is well guarded and has enough ammo to take each guard down… and then some. Find a jewelry box inside the lower room in the southeast corner. The second treasure is in the basement of the central barracks. The commander bounces between this central building and the southwest corner. The captain moves in and out of the armory on the west side's upper level.

INTRODUCTION

THE ESSENTIALS

MAIN QUESTS

SIDE QUESTS

ACTIVITIES

ATLAS

REFERENCE & ANALYSIS

DIONYSIAS CARAVANSERAI

TERRITORY: Faiyum

In the base's northern, walled-off area, a captain guards a treasure inside the southern room. The commander spends most of his time in the central office, just east of the statue. A treasure sits on the desk. A small opening on the south side allows you to slide inside the base, not too far from the brazier.

KERKASOROS OUTPOST

TERRITORY: Ineb-Hedjet Nome

The commander works mostly inside the central building, located at the bend in the main road. While there, collect the treasure inside the small box that sits on his table. The captain spends part of his day training just north of this location. At night he sleeps on the northwest rooftop near the ballista. At the base of the west tower, look for a hole in the rock that leads into the stronghold.

NECROPOLIS HIDEOUT

TERRITORY: Green Mountains

This hideout is mostly underground, inside the mountain with several entrances into the hideout. Two entrances are located on the east side, just off the main road. Big holes provide access into the middle of the base. Duck into a small opening just below the ruins on the southwest side to reach the start of Side Quest: Taking Liberty (if available). The commander splits his time between this cavern and outside around the ruins.

At the aqueduct's west end, follow the water into a cavern. Climb the waterfalls on the right, and scale the tall cavern until you reach enemies above. Keep an eye out for the captain along the way. If he isn't near the water below, he may be training at the top of your climb or guarding the east entrance to the right.

One treasure is shown on the map, next to a pillar in the ruins. The other is inside the mountain, near the eastern entrance. From the cavern, just inside the eastern entrance, move into the south corridor. Destroy the clay pot that sits next to the table. Slide into the hidden room to find the second treasure.

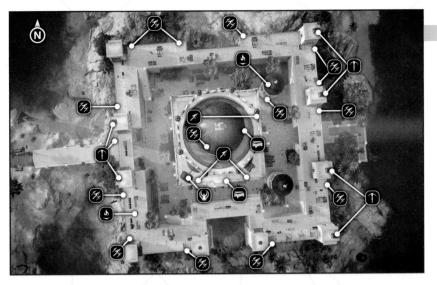

PHAROS GARRISON

TERRITORY: Alexandria

A Viewpoint provides a great view of Pharos Garrison, which is situated at the end of an island, north of Alexandria. You must sneak through the base to reach the high vantage point (once synchronized, you can Fast Travel here).

One treasure is located on the tower's eighth floor, just inside the southern, barred window. Climb up the tower's south side to the platform with the white canopy. Enter the opening. Follow the spiral walkway up a floor to find the treasure. The second treasure is in the tower's top room, just below the fire. Mark the captain and commander early and keep tabs on them. They move all around the area—on the outer wall and below.

PRASINOS ROMAN CAMP

TERRITORY: Green Mountains

Drop in on the Roman camp from the eastern cliffs; one treasure is located in the northern orange tent. The captain is on this side of the road, though he also patrols the camp. The commander spends much of his time on the eastern bridge, while he snoozes part of the night in the elongated tent, just beyond this bridge. The second treasure sits inside this same tent. Try not to draw too much attention, as ballistae surround much of the base.

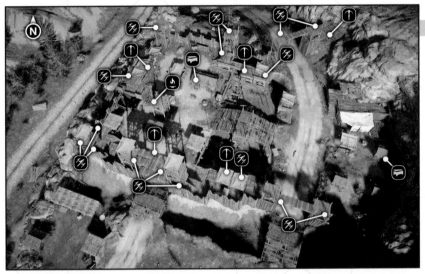

SAPHTHIS OUTPOST

TERRITORY: Im-Khent Nome

Find a cave just outside the southwest corner, and follow it into a storage room inside the base. In the enclosed area in the middle of the stronghold, a treasure sits on the upper ledge against the northern wall. First set a trap at the brazier on this area's south side to avoid adding enemies to the fight. The main building sits on the camp's east side. There are openings on most sides, but you can also slide onto the roof from a zip line that connects to the east tower. Inside this structure you find the second treasure and, usually, the commander. The captain may be near the campfire just south of this location, sleeping on the rooftop to the west, or somewhere in between.

SARAGINA CAMP

TERRITORY: Libue

A central tower dominates the landscape. One of the treasures is atop this structure. The captain spends some time up here, too, though he will also patrol the grounds. At night, he sleeps in the northeast home. Four holes in the ground offer access to an underground maze of rooms with alternate entrances along the south side. Drop into the northern of these holes to find the second treasure. The commander roams throughout much of the base, though he may be found sleeping in the northwest home.

SMALL MILITARY

ABANDONED TEMPLE HIDEOUT

TERRITORY: Lake Mareotis

Find an entrance to an underground room on the temple's north side, just left of the steps. Collect the treasure inside.

AKABIS ROMAN TOWER

TERRITORY: Green Mountains

The treasure sits in an upstairs corner of the building.

AKRONISOS CAMP

TERRITORY: Ineb-Hedjet Nome

At the top of the southern portion of Ineb-Hedjet, this camp has a brazier on the southwest side; easily tinker with this by sneaking through the nearby entrance and hiding in the foliage. The northeastern tent holds the treasure.

AURITINA ROMAN TOWER

TERRITORY: Green Mountains

This outpost consists of a short tower with few amenities. A brazier does allow the enemy to call in help, so avoid being spotted—at least until you have set the trap. The treasure sits against the wall on the top floor.

BANDIT HIDEOUT

TERRITORY: Green Mountains

This modest bandit camp sits against the mountain. Descend down the platforms on the south side for a stealthier approach. Two arrow stands allow you to pick off the bandits with your bow along the way. Enter the tent on that side of the camp, at the base of the cliff, to find the treasure.

CAMP AGROPHYLAKE

TERRITORY: Ineb-Hedjet Nome

This southern Ineb-Hedjet camp is well stocked with arrows, and a brazier allows them to call in reinforcements. Collect the treasure from the central tent before they can do so.

CAMP DORY

TERRITORY: Isolated Desert

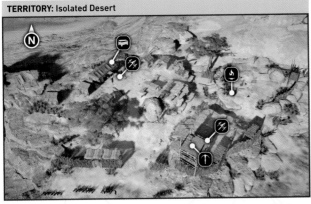

A ballista sits on the tower. Use it for target practice. Find the treasure inside the long tent. Allies may assist you in this region, but watch out for the nearby Phylake, the Galatian.

CAMP KATASKINONO

TERRITORY: Giza

Set on a plateau in southwestern Giza, this camp is fairly wide open. Avoid the southern entrance; instead, scale the plateau's east side, where guard coverage is limited. Watch out for others as you slip through the flap on the back of the central tent and collect the loot.

CAMP MENOUTHIS

TERRITORY: Kanopos Nome

Located on the water border with Herakleion Nome, Camp Menouthis is relatively complex compared to other small military installations—though amenities are more aligned with the smaller strongholds. A ballista looks over the camp on the northeast side, while a brazier is available on the opposite side. Collect the treasure under the wooden shelter that connects a group of buildings in the middle of the camp.

CAMP NISI

TERRITORY: Herakleion Nome

Camp Nisi sits on a northern island of Herakleion Nome with a Viewpoint overlooking the northeast. The location is open on most sides, though much of it is water. Find the treasure inside the main tent in the middle of the camp.

CAMP PYRRHOS

TERRITORY: Sapi-Res Nome

The small camp southeast of Sais is well stocked with arrows, so let them fly. A tower on the north side gives a great vantage point. Collect the treasure from the northern tent; a flap on the back allows a stealthy entry.

CAMP TAMARIS

TERRITORY: Isolated Desert

A ballistae looks over the camp and there's a brazier in case reinforcements are needed. Slip into the northern tent through the flap on the back to find the treasure.

INTRODUCTION

THE ESSENTIALS

MAIN QUESTS

SIDE QUESTS

ACTIVITIES

ATLAS

REFERENCE & ANALYSIS

CAMP XEROS

TERRITORY: Isolated Desert

In south-central Isolated Desert, Camp Xeros sits atop a hill, vulnerable from all sides. Infiltrate from the southeast and slip through the flap in the big tent to find the treasure.

CARCER ROMAN COMPOUND

TERRITORY: Herakleion Nome

The treasure sits out in the open against the central tree. A variety of animals are caged in the compound, if you wish to set them free.

CLEON'S WHARF

TERRITORY: Haueris Nome

Just northwest of Cleon's Dam, the wharf gives the triremes a spot to dock and take on supplies. The East Moeris Trireme and other vessels use the dock during their patrols. Slide through a flap on the main tent's west side to gain access to the treasure and, quite often, the captain.

COLLIS ROMAN HUNTING CAMP

TERRITORY: Green Mountains

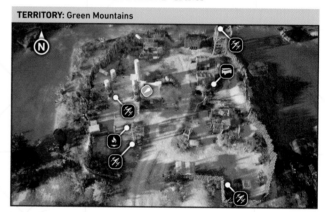

South of Cyrene, near the top of the first mountain in Green Mountains, the hunting camp is tactically placed next to the water. A hole in the west fence and a gap on the east side provide a stealthy entrance into the camp. Find the treasure in the southern tent. Steps lead down to a hidden room underneath the ruins.

CORAL ESCARPMENT CAMP

TERRITORY: Siwa

Low-level guards use the camp on Siwa's north side. The treasure is on an eastern rooftop along with a brazier alarm. The captain is often inside the structure near the northern corner—accessible by a rope stretched from the nearby cliff.

DESOLATED LOOKOUT

TERRITORY: Marmarica

Tents dot this desolated camp. Spot the orange canopy on the north side and destroy the limbs underneath. Descend into the hidden tunnel to find the treasure inside a small cavern.

DIONYSIAS WHARF

TERRITORY: Faiyum

At the tip of a peninsula, north of Euhemeria village, this wharf provides dock access to vessels, including the West Moeris Trireme. A south road leads in from the lone landside. Rocks on the southeast side provide a drier entry point. The captain is often inside the eastern building with the treasure wedged into a corner of the upper room.

DJBT JM HIDEOUT

TERRITORY: White Desert Oasis

Enter the western hole between the two towers or go through the opening next to the southern tower. Turn in toward the center of the hideout and turn northeast to find the treasure. The southern opening is also connected to this underground maze if you want to descend the southwest cliff. Keep an eye out for the Level 40 captain while exploring the area.

EAST MOERIS TRIREME

TERRITORY: Faiyum

This trireme patrols between Psenhyris Trireme Wharf and Cleon's Wharf. This trireme does not hold treasure.

DIORYX MEGALE WHARF

TERRITORY: Uab Nome

Look for a low section of fence at the eastern corner of the wharf and move right toward the nearest tent. Slip through the back and collect the treasure. If you are lucky, the captain will also be inside guarding the loot. Watch for vessels that use the dock to restock their supplies, including the South Moeris Trireme. A ballista on the dock allows you to wipe out the crew with relative ease.

EAST MEDITERRANEAN TRIREME

TERRITORY: Great Green Sea

This trireme patrols between Kanopos village and Alexandria. This trireme does not hold treasure.

HOUSE OF SAND HIDEOUT

TERRITORY: Iment Nome

The hideout is built into the mountainside, its large interior protected from the elements. Inside this area, the treasure sits against a support. The low-level captain spends much of his time in this area as well. Look for an opening around the southeast side for a more stealthy approach.

KASTOR HIGH HIDEOUT

TERRITORY: Green Mountains

This small, open cave on the mountainside has three entrances, with the treasure sitting right in the middle.

KELIDA HIDEOUT

TERRITORY: Marmarica

Just down the mountain from Hydrax Roman Camp is the Kelida Hideout. The hideout is mostly underground with the main entrance protected by a ballista and a hole above. The interior is a loop connected to both entry points. The treasure sits on the higher level in the loop.

KETKET COVE HIDEOUT

TERRITORY: Faiyum

Watch out for vengeful crocodiles at this waterside hideout. The treasure sits inside a small cave on the upper level of the cliff side. The captain patrols between this point and the main gate to the north.

LAH HIDEOUT

TERRITORY: Herakleion Nome

In a dense forest area of northwestern Herakleion, this enemy hideout offers plenty of hiding spots in the tall grass. Sneak in, complete the objectives, and sneak out. Find the treasure under the longer shelter on the south side.

LEGIO XXXVII ROMAN DOCKS

TERRITORY: Marmarica

Watch for triremes that may visit the docks. Collect the treasure inside the long tent just inside the main entrance. The captain often hangs out at this same location.

LIVIUS ROMAN TOWER

TERRITORY: Marmarica

A Roman watchtower is perched on the mountainside in north-central Marmarica. The treasure is inside the tower. Use the Parkour Up device to reach the top and then drop through the hole.

MITHIDRATES ROMAN CAMP

TERRITORY: Herakleion Nome

This Roman camp is located near a war elephant in northeastern Herakleion. A treasure is at the stern of a trireme that is docked just north of camp.

NEITH CRADLE HIDEOUT

TERRITORY: Herakleion Nome

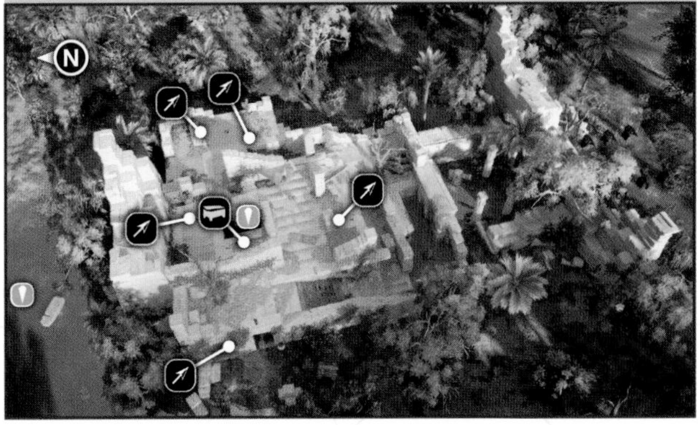

Dive into the water north of the hideout and find the hole in the rocks, as indicated on the map. Follow the tunnel into the structure and swim up until it opens. Just north of the hole, a treasure sits at the foot of a statue.

NIKIOU POST

TERRITORY: Sapi-Res Nome

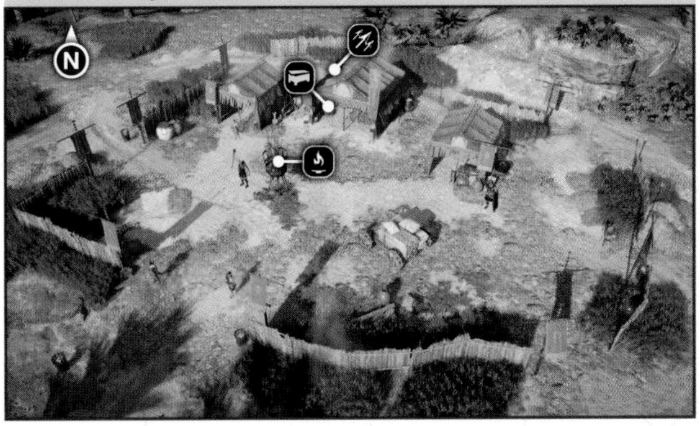

Use the tall grass just north of the camp to access the backside of the tents. Enter the middle one through the flap. Collect the treasure and skedaddle back to the protection of the grass. Hippos inhabit the area, though they may provide a nice distraction, as the guards attack the beast.

NORTH MAREOTIS TRIREME

TERRITORY: Lake Mareotis

This trireme patrols northwestern Lake Mareotis, making stops at Lakeside Villa Outpost and the southern docks of Alexandria. This trireme does not hold treasure.

PER-WSIR HIDEOUT

TERRITORY: Giza

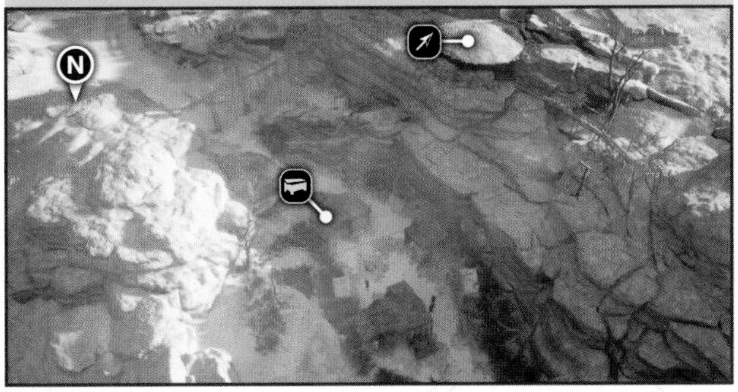

The hideout is erected within a narrow valley on Giza's south side. Approach from either side and scout the area. A bridge on the southeast side and a zip line on the other allow you to move back and forth, depending on which side is safer. Search inside the southernmost canopy to find the treasure. During the captain's patrols, he makes a prolonged stop below the zip line. Take this opportunity to assassinate him from above in spectacular fashion.

POLUDEUKES HIDEOUT

TERRITORY: Green Mountains

The hideout sits on the mountainside, northeast of Kyrenaika Roman Citadel. Sneak down from the east or work your way in from below toward the opening at the back of the camp, near the ladder. The treasure is inside.

PSAMMOS HIDEOUT

TERRITORY: Saqqara Nome

The hideout is fairly well protected from the elements, with three narrow roads leading into the opening. Approach from the west. Use the rope stretched across the canyon for a great view of the area. If you are patient, you can assassinate the captain from above. Climb down to the bottom on the north side and enter the interior at the base of the cliff; turn left and collect the treasure that sits in the far corner.

PSENHYRIS TRIREME WHARF

TERRITORY: Faiyum Oasis

The wharf is located at the northern tip of the western island. It serves as one of the East Moeris Trireme's stops. A well-placed ballista on the dock gives you the opportunity to take down its crew upon arrival.

Sneak around to the base's north side and slip into the tall grass. From there, slide through the flap on the back of the long tent and collect the treasure on the left. The captain spends part of the day working inside the tent, so watch out for him. If you are lucky, you can catch him signing documents at his desk.

ROMAN QUARRY CAMP

TERRITORY: Green Mountains

The quarry is perched just above one of the four war elephants in far western Green Mountains. Head to the back of the quarry, to the long tent on the northwest side. The captain typically spends his time inside; the treasure is here too.

ROMAN WATCHTOWER

TERRITORY: Green Mountains

The watchtower sits atop a hill in southern Green Mountains. Find the treasure on the second floor of the tower's northern portion.

SOUTH MAREOTIS TRIREME

TERRITORY: Lake Mareotis

This trireme patrols southern Lake Mareotis, stopping at the Temple of Sekhmet in Yamu and Camp Shemu. This trireme does not hold treasure.

SOUTH MOERIS TRIREME

TERRITORY: Faiyum Oasis

This trireme patrols between the Trireme Stranding Camp and Dioryx Megale Wharf, with a stop at the Neorion Naval Arsenal in between. This trireme does not hold treasure.

DELTA NILE TRIREME

TERRITORY: Atef-Pehu Nome

This trireme patrols up and down the river east of Atef-Pehu Nome, making a stop at Kerke Wharf. This trireme does not hold treasure.

THENESSOS HIDEOUT

TERRITORY: Herakleion Nome

The treasure sits under the orange canopy, smack in the middle of the hideout. The docked trireme on the west side is equipped with a ballista if you wish to get some target practice.

THINTIS ROMAN TOWER

TERRITORY: Marmarica

A Roman tower is perched atop the mountains due east of Balagrae. Collect the treasure inside the lower room.

UPPER NILE TRIREME

TERRITORY: Ineb-Hedjet Nome

This trireme patrols around the eastern island of Ineb-Hedjet Nome, making a stop at Pyramides Wharf. This trireme does not hold treasure.

WEST MEDITERRANEAN TRIREME

TERRITORY: Mesogeios Sea

This trireme patrols the Mesogeios Sea between Legio XXXVII Roman Docks and Apollonia Roma Barracks. The vessel has a tent that the captain roams in and out of, obstructing your view of the target. This trireme does not hold treasure.

WEST MOERIS TRIREME

TERRITORY: Faiyum

This trireme patrols between Dionysias Wharf and the Beached Trireme Camp, while also making a stop next to the two anchored vessels (Sea of Sobek Anchorage). A tent provides the captain with a strategy room but sometimes restricts your view of him. This trireme does not hold treasure.

INTRODUCTION

THE ESSENTIALS

MAIN QUESTS

SIDE QUESTS

ACTIVITIES

ATLAS

REFERENCE & ANALYSIS

ATLAS OF
ANCIENT EGYPT

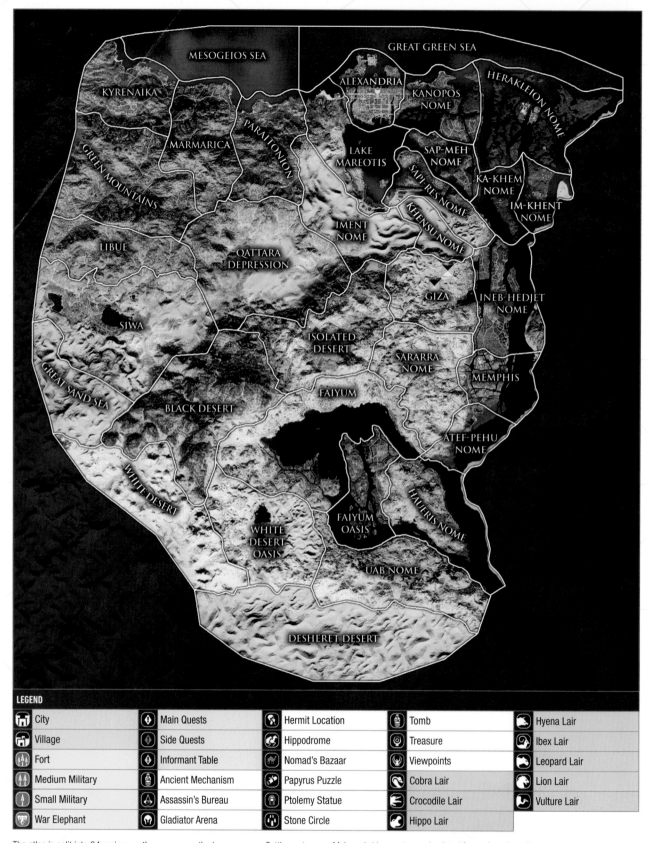

LEGEND

🏠	City	🔶	Main Quests	🎯	Hermit Location	🗿	Tomb	🐺	Hyena Lair
🏠	Village	🔷	Side Quests	🐗	Hippodrome	🌀	Treasure	🐾	Ibex Lair
🏯	Fort	🔶	Informant Table	🐪	Nomad's Bazaar	🕷	Viewpoints	🐆	Leopard Lair
🏯	Medium Military	📜	Ancient Mechanism	🌀	Papyrus Puzzle	🐍	Cobra Lair	🦁	Lion Lair
🗡	Small Military	🔺	Assassin's Bureau	🗿	Ptolemy Statue	🐊	Crocodile Lair	🦅	Vulture Lair
🐘	War Elephant	⚔	Gladiator Arena	🏛	Stone Circle	🦛	Hippo Lair		

The atlas is split into 34 regions as they appear on the in-game map. Settlements, military strongholds, shops, Viewpoints, treasure locations, animal lairs, and activities are pinpointed on the maps with names listed when appropriate. Icons match up with the maps for easy identification.

The treasures locations are the sites noted on the in-game map as they are discovered. Find the treasures at these locations to complete them and earn XP.

Main and side quests are also listed for each territory. Note that the main quests are numbered from the beginning of the story through the end, while side quests start over for each territory. The suggested level for each quest is included in parenthesis.

Approximate enemy levels are given for each region, but you may see other levels in special locations, such as bandit hideouts and near the borders.

ALEXANDRIA

ENEMY LEVEL: 9 - 12

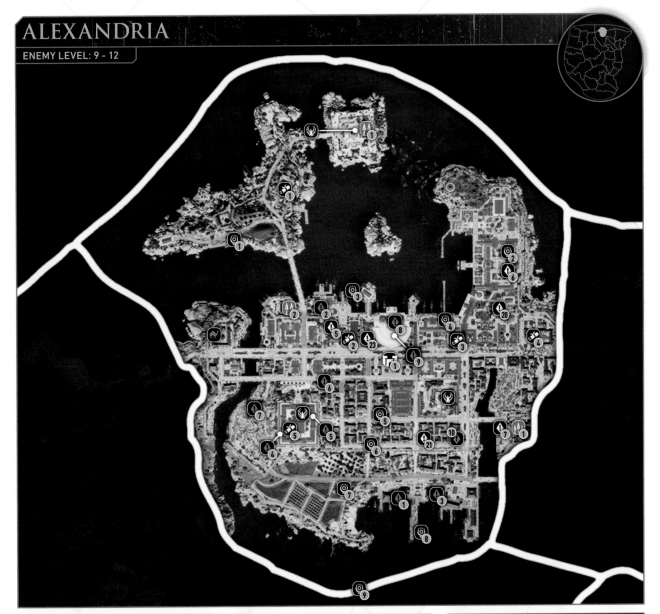

INTRODUCTION

THE ESSENTIALS

MAIN QUESTS

SIDE QUESTS

ACTIVITIES

ATLAS

REFERENCE & ANALYSIS

CITIES

1	Alexandria

FORTS

1	Akra Garrison

MEDIUM MILITARY

1	Pharos Garrison
2	Kibotos Arsenal

TREASURE LOCATIONS

1	Pharos Military Storage
2	Royal Palace
3	Emporion Berthed Trireme
4	Armory
5	Aya's Home
6	South Wall Guard Post
7	Mareia Military Storage
8	Mareia Trireme
9	Narrow Crevice

PAPYRUS LOCATIONS

1	Iseion
2	Great Library
3	Tomb of Alexander the Great
4	Great Synagogue
5	Sarapeion

MAIN QUESTS

5	Aya (9)
6	End of the Snake (unlocked during Aya) (12)
7	Gennadios the Phylakitai (unlocked during Aya) (11)
20	The Battle of the Nile (31)
21	The Aftermath (31)
23	The Last Medjay (35)

SIDE QUESTS

1	The Accidental Philosopher (20)
2	The Last Bodyguard (15)
3	Higher Education (complete The Accidental Philosopher) (21)
4	Serapis Unites (10)
5	A Tithe by Any Other Name (complete Serapis Unites) (10)
6	The Shifty Scribe (11)
7	The Odyssey (complete A Tithe by Any Other Name and meditate to move near Sarapeion) (10)
8	Wrath of the Poets (11)
9	Symposiasts (complete Wrath of the Poets) (21)
10	Phylakitai in the Eye (complete Symposiasts and meditate) (22)

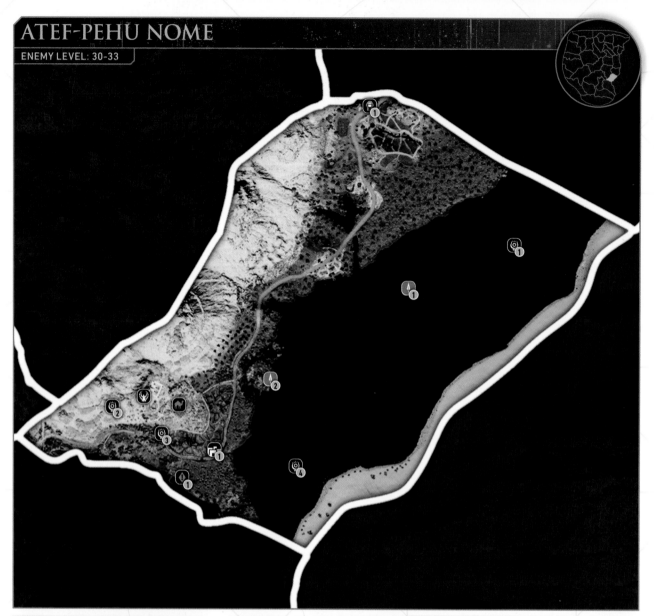

VILLAGES

1	Kerke

SMALL MILITARY

1	South Nile Trireme
2	Kerke Wharf

TREASURE LOCATIONS

1	Aneb-Hetch Anchorage
2	Desecrated Tomb
3	Warehouse of the Toparches
4	Opos Kerkouros Wreck

PTOLEMY STATUES

1	South of Memphis

SIDE QUESTS

1	The Matriarch (31)

BLACK DESERT

ENEMY LEVEL: 27-37

	TOMBS
1	Nomarch's Tomb
2	Ancient Mechanism: Seshem.eff Er Aat

	HERMIT LOCATIONS
1	Ra-Horakhty Mountain Top

INTRODUCTION

THE ESSENTIALS

MAIN QUESTS

SIDE QUESTS

ACTIVITIES

ATLAS

REFERENCE & ANALYSIS

DESHERET DESERT

ENEMY LEVEL: 34-40

	TOMBS
1	Seth-Anat Tomb
2	Ancient Mechanism: Qeneb too Kah'Aiye

FAIYUM

ENEMY LEVEL: 24-29

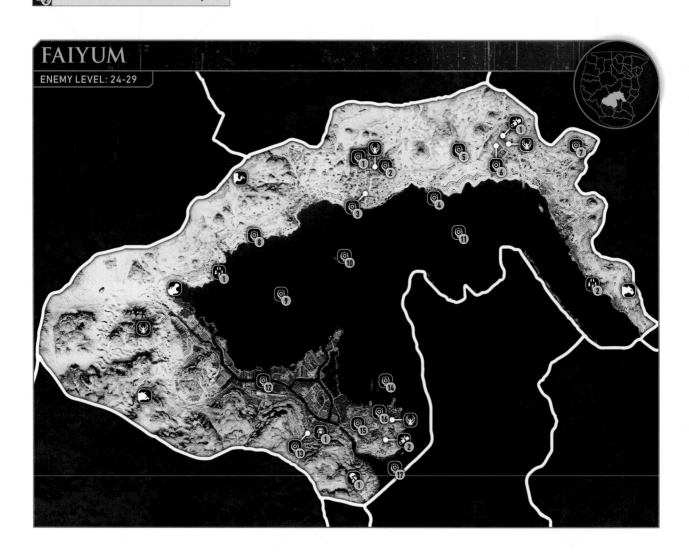

FAIYUM MORE LOCATIONS

ENEMY LEVEL: 24-29

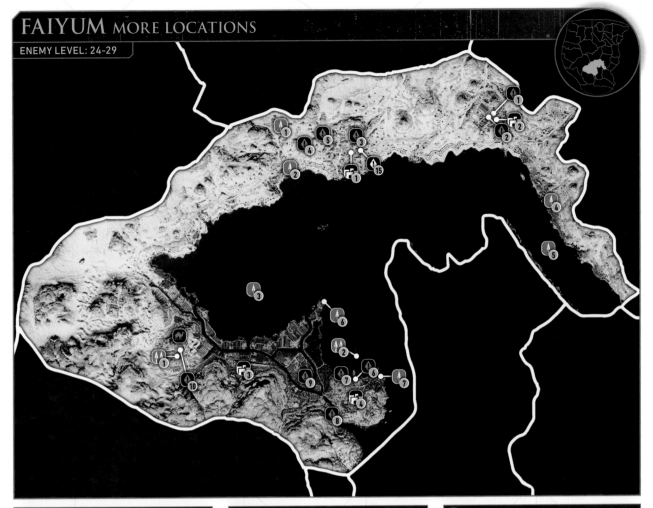

	VILLAGES
1	Soknopaiou Nesos
2	Karanis
3	Dionysias
4	Euhemeria

	MEDIUM MILITARY
1	Dionysias Caravanserai
2	Okteres Blockade

	SMALL MILITARY
1	Pannouki Hideout
2	Beached Trireme Camp
3	West Moeris Trireme (moving in water)
4	Ketket Cove Hideout
5	East Moeris Trireme (moving in water)
6	Dionysias Wharf
7	Euhemeria Lighthouse Camp

	TREASURE LOCATIONS
1	Wadjet's Burrow
2	Vault of Splendors
3	Covert Grain Store
4	Sunken Temple of Pnepheros
5	Senwosret II Temple
6	Underground Stash
7	Bakchias
8	Abandoned Fishing Village
9	Sea of Sobek Anchorage
10	Golden Horn Island
11	Shi-wer Anchorage
12	Requisitioned Dionysias House
13	Philoteris
14	Sunken Trireme
15	Seized Oikos
16	Euhemeria Royal Granary
17	Wrecked Felucca

	PAPYRUS LOCATIONS
1	Sarapeion of Karanis
2	Valley market

	PTOLEMY STATUES
1	Philoteris

	STONE CIRCLES
1	Taweret Stone Circle
2	Pisces Stone Circle

	HERMIT LOCATIONS
1	Eremites Hideout

	MAIN QUESTS
15	The Crocodile's Scales (25)

	SIDE QUESTS
1	Murder in the Temple (24)
2	Feeding Faiyum (complete Murder in the Temple) (24)
3	Curse of Wadjet (25)
4	Rebel Strike (25)
5	The Bride (26)
6	Sorbek's Gold (27)
7	Forging Siwa (28)
8	The Sickness (complete Crocodiles Jaws) (28)
9	Fires of Dionysias (complete Crocodiles Jaws) (37)
10	Demons in the Desert (39)

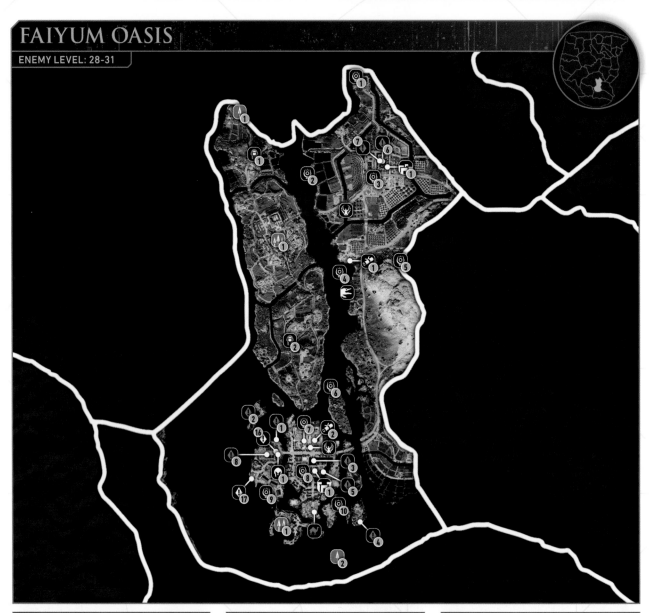

CITIES
1	Krokodilopolis

VILLAGES
1	Philadelphia

FORTS
1	Kerkesoucha Granary

MEDIUM MILITARY
1	Neorion Naval Arsenal

SMALL MILITARY
1	Psenhyris Trireme Wharf
2	South Moeris Trireme (moving in water)

TREASURE LOCATIONS
1	Hephaistias Wharf
2	Sesen Grotto
3	Philadelphia Royal Granary
4	Immersed Reed Pakton
5	Rubbayat Necropolis
6	Piamouei Colossi
7	Schena Wab
8	Faiyum Nomarch Villa
9	Docked Naukleros Ship
10	Confiscated Stathmos

ARENA
1	Krokodilopolis

PAPYRUS LOCATIONS
1	House of Iwn
2	Temple of Sobek

PTOLEMY STATUES
1	Northwest Faiyum Oasis
2	North of Krokodilopolis

MAIN QUESTS
16	The Crocodile's Jaws (29)
17	Ambush at Sea (28)

SIDE QUESTS
1	The Champion (28)
2	The Man Beast (28)
3	Sobek's Tears (29)
4	The Jaws of Sobek (29)
5	Bad Faith (complete The Jaws of Sobek and Sobek's Tears) (29)
6	Shadya's Rest (complete The Crocodile's Jaws) (30)
7	Fighting for Faiyum (complete Shadya's Rest) (30)
8	Lure of Glory (defeat Diovicos and Viridovix during Main Quest: The Crocodile's Jaws) (30)

GIZA

ENEMY LEVEL: 17-20

INTRODUCTION

THE ESSENTIALS

MAIN QUESTS

SIDE QUESTS

ACTIVITIES

ATLAS

REFERENCE & ANALYSIS

VILLAGES

1	Great Sphinx

MEDIUM MILITARY

1	Khentkawes Hideout
2	Depleted Quarry Hideout

SMALL MILITARY

1	Khufu Temple Hideout
2	Camp Kataskinono
3	Per-Wsir Hideout

TREASURE LOCATIONS

1	Hemon Mastaba
2	Sphinx Passageway
3	Lost Village
4	Mausoleion of Crow

PAPYRUS LOCATIONS

1	Eastern Cemetery Mastaba

TOMBS

1	Adorer of Thoth Tomb
2	Tomb of Khufu
3	Tomb of Khafre
4	Tomb of Menkaure
5	Ancient Mechanism: Eesfet Oon-m'Aa Poo
2	Ancient Mechanism: Khufu

MAIN QUESTS

12	The Hyena (20)

SIDE QUESTS

1	Precious Bonds (18)
2	What's Yours Is Mine (19)

GREAT GREEN SEA

ENEMY LEVEL: N/A

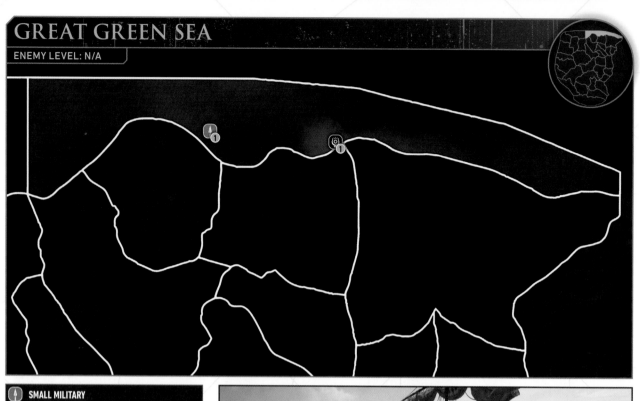

SMALL MILITARY

East Mediterranean Trireme

TREASURE LOCATIONS

Ahment Anchorage

GREAT SAND SEA

ENEMY LEVEL: 36-40

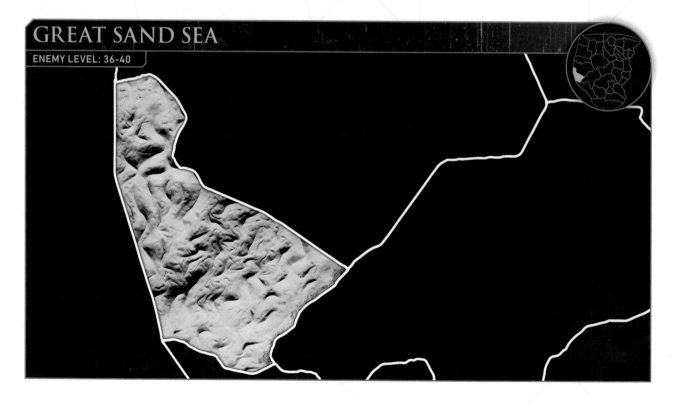

GREEN MOUNTAINS

ENEMY LEVEL: 32-35

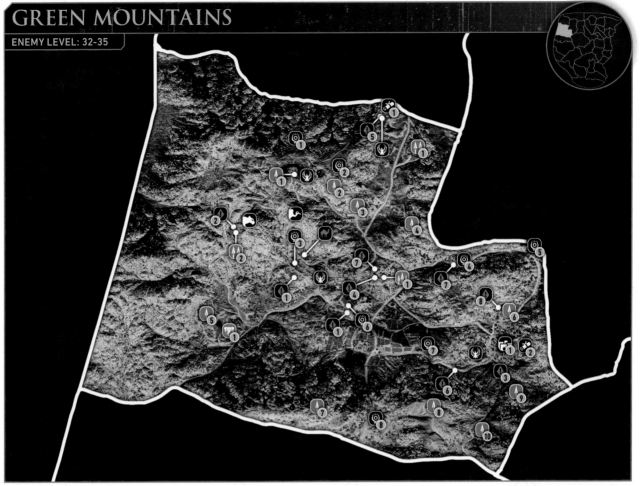

INTRODUCTION

THE ESSENTIALS

MAIN QUESTS

SIDE QUESTS

ACTIVITIES

ATLAS

REFERENCE & ANALYSIS

	VILLAGES
1	Balagrae

	FORTS
1	Kyrenaike Roman Citadel

	MEDIUM MILITARY
1	Prasinos Roman Camp
2	Necropolis Hideout

	SMALL MILITARY
1	Collis Roman Hunting Camp
2	Desperate Gully Hideout
3	Kastor High Hideout
4	Poludeukes Hideout
5	Roman Quarry Camp
6	Balagrae Barracks
7	Roman Watchtower

	(continued)
8	Auritina Roman Tower
9	Bandit Hideout
10	Akabis Roman Tower

	TREASURE LOCATIONS
1	Lake of the Clouds Ruins
2	Forsaken Sanctuary
3	Aquaeductus Kyrenaike
4	Poimen Relay
5	Shrine to Hygieia
6	Lumber Depots
7	Theras Ampelos
8	Refugee Haven

	PAPYRUS LOCATIONS
1	Oracle of Apollo
2	Asklepieion

	WAR ELEPHANT
1	Camp of Surus

	SIDE QUESTS
1	The Good Roman (33)
2	Taking Liberty (33)
3	One Bad Apple (complete Main Quest: The Final Weighing) (35)
4	Playing with Fire (appears after world event) (33)
5	Halo of the Huntress (34)
6	Unseeing Eyes (35)
7	Carpe Diem (35)
8	Shadows of Apollo (38)

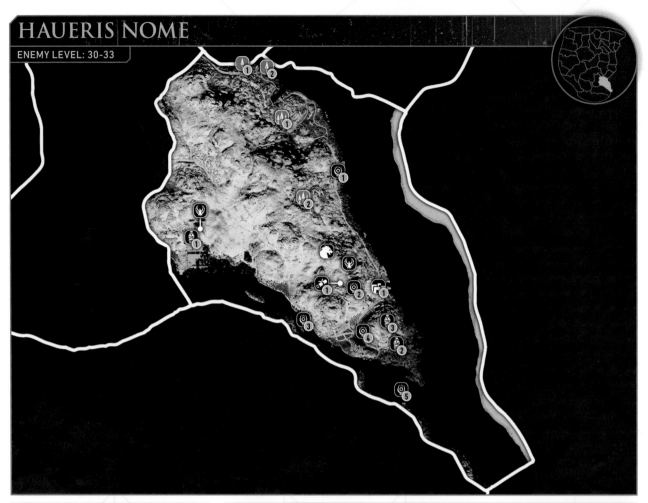

HAUERIS NOME

ENEMY LEVEL: 30-33

	VILLAGES
1	Hermopolis

	FORTS
1	Fort Boubastos
2	Limestone Quarry

	SMALL MILITARY
1	Cleon's Wharf
2	Cleon's Dam

	TREASURE LOCATIONS
1	Metallon Docks
2	Temple Archives
3	Kleithra Dam
4	Etesias' Olive Grove
5	Iw Forgotten Cache

	TOMBS
1	Tomb of Amenemhat III
2	Tomb of Smenkhkare
3	Ancient Mechanism: Eeyoo Sekedoo Aat

	PAPYRUS LOCATIONS
1	Temple of Thoth

HERAKLEION NOME

ENEMY LEVEL: 30-33

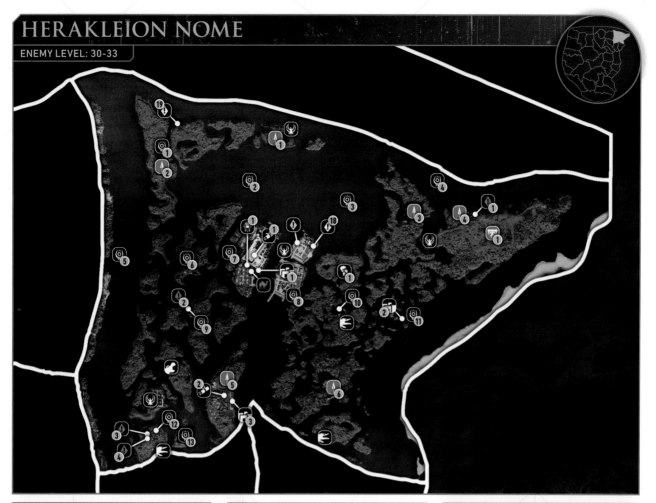

INTRODUCTION

THE ESSENTIALS

MAIN QUESTS

SIDE QUESTS

ACTIVITIES

ATLAS

REFERENCE & ANALYSIS

	VILLAGES
1	Herakleion
2	Yw Huts
3	Natho

	SMALL MILITARY
1	Camp Nisi
2	Lah Hideout
3	Thenessos Hideout
4	Mithridates Roman Camp
5	Carcer Roman Compound
6	Neith Cradle Hideout

	TREASURE LOCATIONS
1	Irsu's Huts
2	Liontari Debacle
3	Sap-Meh Anchorage
4	Wdj-ur Wreck
5	Elephas Remains
6	Chata Pond
7	Home of Nehi
8	Outskirts of Herakleion
9	Zoiontegoi Shipwreck
10	Dismal Tree

11	Meketre's Cache
12	Huntress Cave
13	Desher Bluff

	PAPYRUS LOCATIONS
1	Temple of Khonsou
2	Galenos' House

	PTOLEMY STATUES
1	Ptolemy Statues

	HERMIT LOCATIONS
1	Demesne of Sekhem

	WAR ELEPHANT
1	Camp of Jumbe

	MAIN QUESTS
18	Way of the Gabiniani (31)
19	Aya: Blade of the Goddess (31)

	SIDE QUESTS
1	Recon Work (after collecting from informant table) (31)
2	Loose Cargo (31)
3	Reunion (31)
4	Predator to Prey (Complete Reunion) (31)

	INFORMANT TABLES
	Informant Table

IM-KHENT NOME

ENEMY LEVEL: 30-33

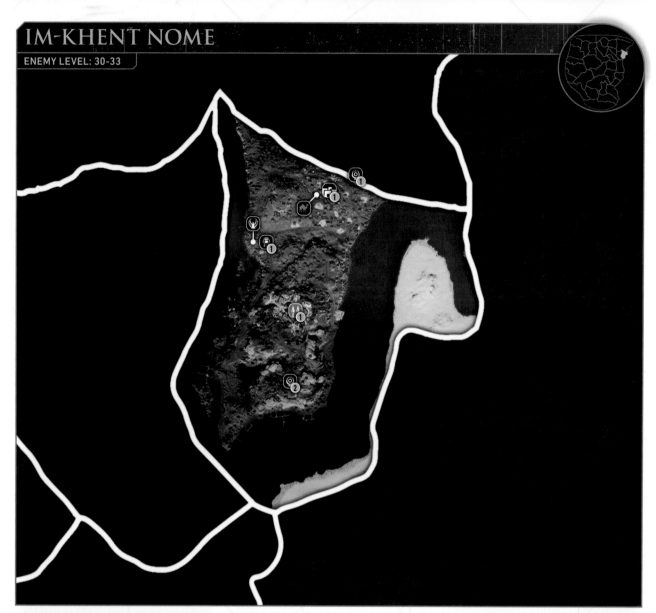

VILLAGES

1	Udjat Apiary

MEDIUM MILITARY

1	Saphthis Outpost

TREASURE LOCATIONS

1	Leirion Apiary
2	Ranos Hamlet

PTOLEMY STATUES

1	Udjat Apiary Viewpoint

INEB-HED

ENEMY LEVEL

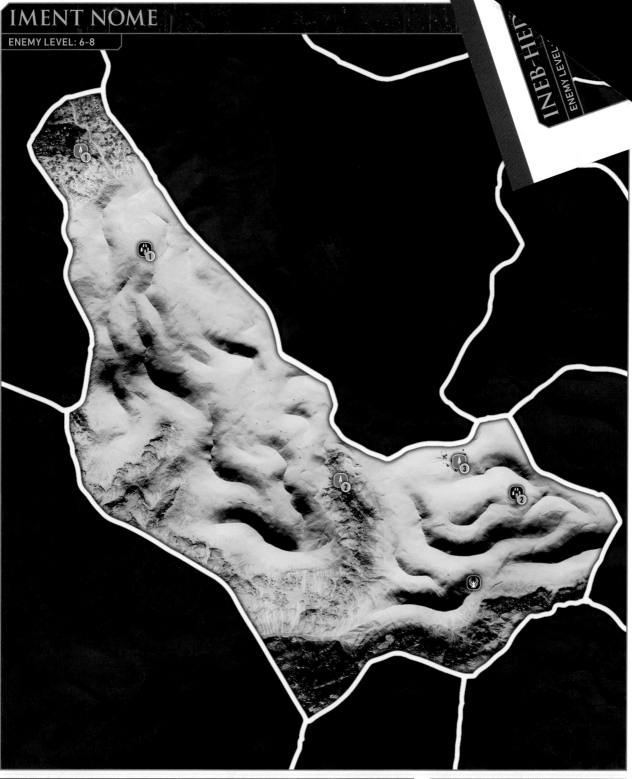

THE ESSENTIALS

MAIN QUESTS

SIDE QUESTS

ACTIVITIES

ATLAS

REFERENCE & ANALYSIS

	SMALL MILITARY
1	House of Sand Hideout
2	Necropolis Bandit Hideout
3	Eremos Hideout

	STONE CIRCLES
1	Serqet Stone Circle
2	Divine Lion Stone Circle

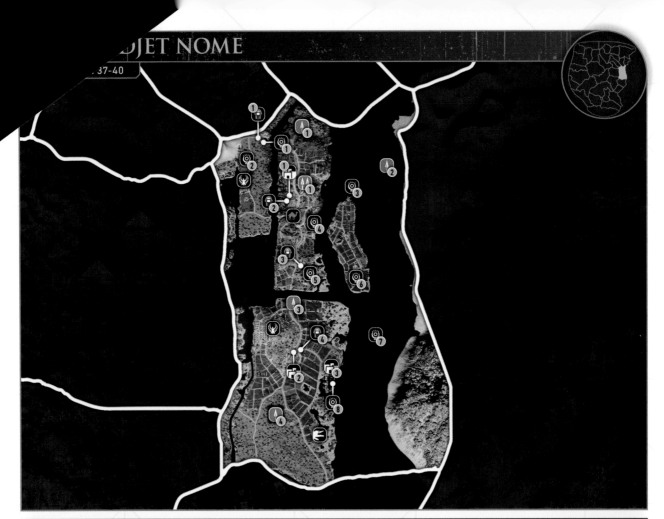

VILLAGES	
1	Kerkasoros
2	Per Ousir
3	Pr-Hapi-n-Iwnw

MEDIUM MILITARY	
1	Kerkasoros Outpost

SMALL MILITARY	
1	Plesionhudor Hideout
2	Upper Nile Trireme
3	Akronisos Camp
4	Camp Agrophylake

TREASURE LOCATIONS	
1	Hugros Crossing Watchtower
2	Abandoned Temple of Kherty
3	Altar to Hapi
4	Pyramides Wharf
5	Castoff Temple of Hapi
6	Winbe
7	Anchorage
8	Akhet's Crown

PTOLEMY STATUES	
1	Hugros Crossing Watchtower
2	Kerkasoros
3	Castoff Temple of Hapi
4	Northeast of Per Ousir

ISOLATED DESERT

ENEMY LEVEL: 37-40

INTRODUCTION

THE ESSENTIALS

MAIN QUESTS

SIDE QUESTS

ACTIVITIES

ATLAS

REFERENCE & ANALYSIS

VILLAGES

1	Theos Elpis Rift
2	Remetch Ra

FORTS

1	Pissa Oros Citadel

SMALL MILITARY

1	Camp Dory
2	Camp Tamaris
3	Camp Hetoimazo
4	Camp Khoikos
5	Camp Xeros

TREASURE LOCATIONS

1	Bathoslythos Ridge
2	Alexander's Temple
3	Ouahe
4	Hmat Oasis
5	Burial Delving
6	Demiourgos Altar
7	Kaminada Stairwell

TOMBS

1	Tomb of the Nomads
2	Golden Tomb
3	Ancient Mechanism: Oun-mAa Niye Ressoot

PTOLEMY STATUES

1	Ouahe
2	Pissa Oros Citadel

STONE CIRCLES

1	Goat Fish Stone Circle
2	Apis Stone Circle

SIDE QUESTS

1	Plight of the Rebels (40)

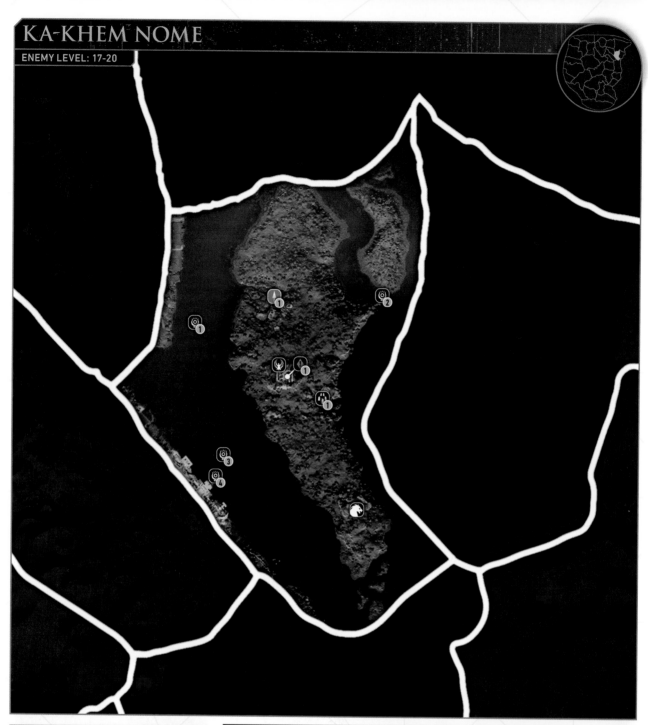

KA-KHEM NOME

 SMALL MILITARY

1	Dasos Hideout

 TREASURE LOCATIONS

1	Sebennytos Shipwreck
2	Abandoned Trireme
3	Khensu Anchorage
4	Khem Trireme

STONE CIRCLES

1	Hathor Stone Circle

SIDE QUESTS

1	Taste of Her Sting Part V Completion (17)

KANOPOS NOME

ENEMY LEVEL: 11-13

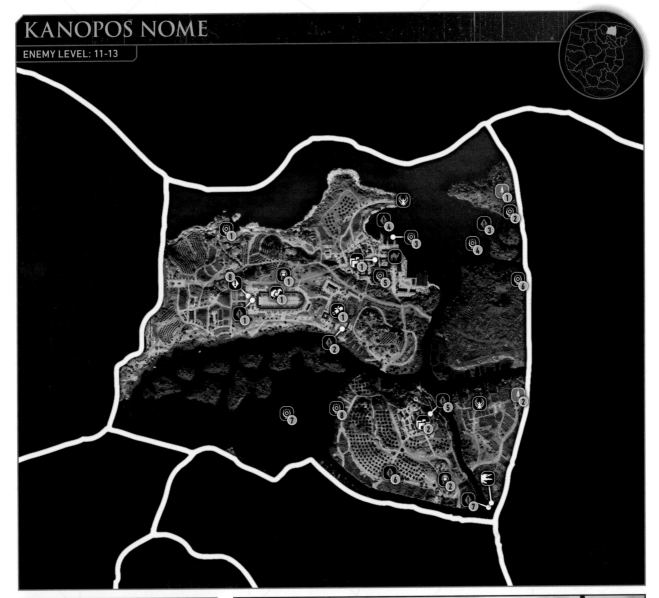

VILLAGES

1	Kanopos
2	Apollodorus' Estate

SMALL MILITARY

1	Als Hideout
2	Camp Menouthis

TREASURE LOCATIONS

1	Aristoteles Shrine
2	Shrine of Serapis
3	Menelaite Trireme
4	Sunken Temple of Sarapeion
5	Requisitioned Tavern
6	Zheruef's Shelter
7	Heket Beer Cache
8	Hamew Hut

HIPPODROME

1	Lageion Hippodrome

PAPYRUS LOCATIONS

1	Zephyros Stables

PTOLEMY STATUES

1	Hippodrome
2	South of Apollodorus' Estate

MAIN QUESTS

8	Egypt's Medjay (12)

SIDE QUESTS

1	Old Times (12)
2	Wild Ride (12)
3	Taste of Her Sting Part II Shrine of Serapis (17)
4	Blue Hooligans (12)
5	The Weasel (14)
6	The Hungry River (14)
7	Taste of Her Sting Part III Croc Lair (17)

INTRODUCTION

THE ESSENTIALS

MAIN QUESTS

SIDE QUESTS

ACTIVITIES

ATLAS

REFERENCE & ANALYSIS

TREASURE LOCATIONS

1	Kleptes End
2	Hathor of Mefkat

KYRENAIKA

ENEMY LEVEL: 34-38

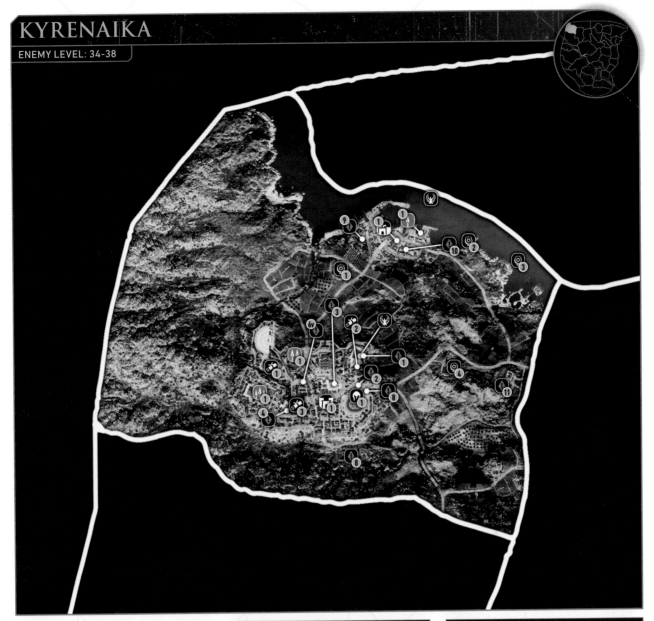

INTRODUCTION

THE ESSENTIALS

MAIN QUESTS

SIDE QUESTS

ACTIVITIES

ATLAS

REFERENCE & ANALYSIS

🏛	**CITIES**
1	Cyrene

🏛	**VILLAGES**
1	Apollonia

🛡	**FORTS**
1	Roman Akropolis

⚔	**MEDIUM MILITARY**
1	Cyrene Barracks

⚔	**SMALL MILITARY**
1	Apollonia Roman Barracks

🏺	**TREASURE LOCATIONS**
1	Apollonia Fields
2	Thibron Expedition Shipwreck
3	Sunken Shrine of Aristoteles
4	Silphion Farm

📜	**PAPYRUS LOCATIONS**
1	Apollonion of Cyrene
2	Temple of Zeus
3	Tomb of Battos

◈	**SIDE QUESTS**
1	The Flea of Cyrene (34)
2	The Lure of Glory (receive in Krokodilopolis) (35)
3	The Mousetrap (35)
4	Founding Father (35)
5	Pax Romana (complete Absolute Power) (35)
6	Cat and Mouse (complete The Mousetrap) (36)
7	Absolute Power (36)
8	Are You Not Entertained? (37)
9	The Smugglers of Cyrene (37)
10	Dead in the Water (38)
11	My Brother for a Horse (38)

LAKE MAREOTIS

	VILLAGES
1	Temple of Sekhmet in Yamu

	SMALL MILITARY
1	Abandoned Temple Hideout
2	Lakeside Villa Outpost
3	North Mareotis Trireme
4	South Mareotis Trireme

	TREASURE LOCATIONS
1	Anoia Cave
2	Dead Men Tell No Tales
3	Mareia Anchorage
4	Adexios Naftis Shipwreck
5	Sunken Desmoterion Ship
6	Lost Crypt

	PAPYRUS LOCATIONS
1	Hypostyle Hall

	PTOLEMY STATUES
1	West of Alexandria

	SIDE QUESTS
1	Hidden Tax (6)
2	The Book of the Dead (8)
3	Ambush in the Temple (6)
4	Ulterior Votive (complete Ambush in the Temple) (7)
5	Lady of Slaughter (complete Ulterior Votive) (8)
6	Birthright (complete Lady of Slaughter) (9)
7	Taste of Her Sting (ongoing quest) (17)

LIBUE

ENEMY LEVEL: 31-34

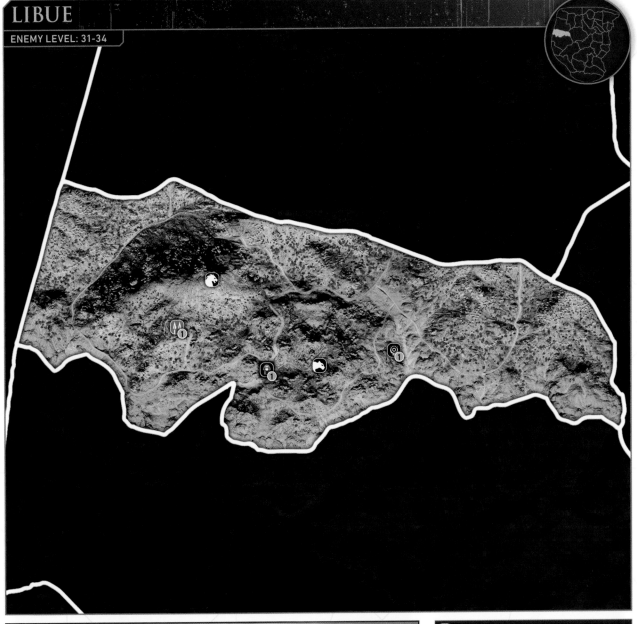

INTRODUCTION

THE ESSENTIALS

MAIN QUESTS

SIDE QUESTS

ACTIVITIES

ATLAS

REFERENCE & ANALYSIS

MEDIUM MILITARY

1	Saragina Camp

TREASURE LOCATIONS

1	Bewail Mountain Cave

PTOLEMY STATUES

1	Central Libue

MARMARICA

FORTS

1	Chersonesos Roman Fort

SMALL MILITARY

1	Legio XXXVII Roman Docks
2	Desolated Lookout
3	Bemulos Roman Tower
4	Livius Roman Tower
5	Kelida Hideout
6	Hydrax Roman Camp
7	Thintis Roman Tower

TREASURE LOCATIONS

1	Erythron Dye Workshops
2	Cape Chersonesos Settlement
3	Hudor Fountain
4	Archile Pandocheion
5	Leander's Villa
6	Theodoros Roadside Camp
7	Endumion's Nemein

SIDE QUESTS

1	His Secret Service (38)

MEMPHIS

ENEMY LEVEL: 20-23

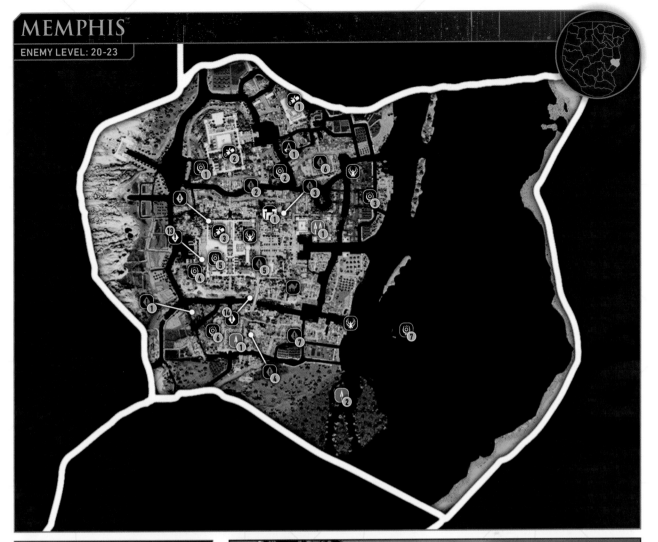

CITIES

1	Memphis

MEDIUM MILITARY

1	Memphites Barracks

SMALL MILITARY

1	Temple of Hathor
2	Apagogeas Hideout

TREASURE LOCATIONS

1	Yuny's Beset Villa
2	Sunken Crypt
3	Corrupted Soldiers Cache
4	Omorfi Villa
5	Fai-Jon Lamentu Crypt
6	Hathor Cistern
7	Sunken Temple of Ramses

PAPYRUS LOCATIONS

1	Wabet
2	Palace of Apries
3	Temple of Ptah

ASSASSINS BUREAU

1	Bureau of the Hidden Ones

MAIN QUESTS

13	The Lizard's Mask (21)
14	The Lizard's Face (23)

SIDE QUESTS

1	A Dream of Ashes (complete Main Quest: The Lizard's Mask) (21)
2	Blood in the Water (20)

3	Odor Most Foul (20)
4	Children of the Streets (23)
5	Taimhotep's Song (complete Main Quest: The Lizard's Mask) (22)
6	The Baker's Dilemma (23)
7	Mortem Romanum (complete Children of the Streets) (30)

INFORMANT TABLES

	Informant Table

285

MESOGEIOS SEA

ENEMY LEVEL: N/A

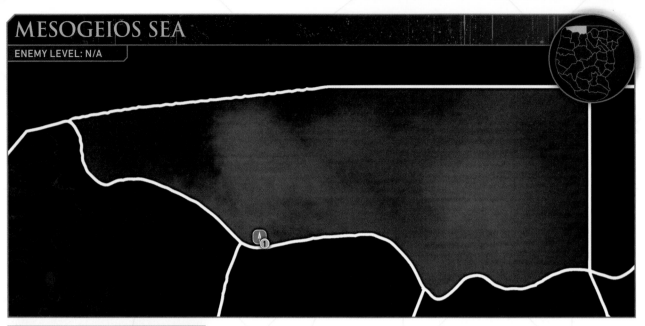

SMALL MILITARY

1	West Mediterranean Trireme

PARAITONION

ENEMY LEVEL: 37-40

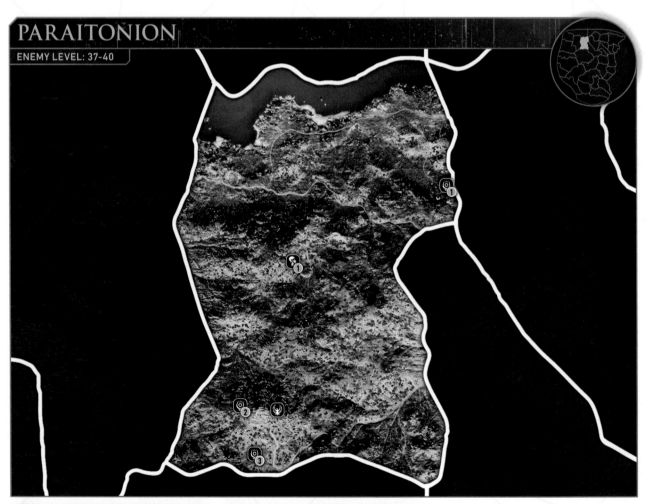

TREASURE LOCATIONS

1	Kalliergeia
2	Keno Hideout
3	Keno

HERMIT LOCATIONS

1	Ogdamos

QATTARA DEPRESSION

ENEMY LEVEL: 37-40

TREASURE LOCATIONS

| 1 | Hotep Cavern |

STONE CIRCLES

| 1 | Osiris Stone Circle |

HERMIT LOCATIONS

| 1 | Aquifer Oasis |

INTRODUCTION

THE ESSENTIALS

MAIN QUESTS

SIDE QUESTS

ACTIVITIES

ATLAS

REFERENCE & ANALYSIS

SAP-MEH NOME

ENEMY LEVEL: 12-15

VILLAGES

1	Sau Village

MEDIUM MILITARY

1	Anthylla Outpost

SMALL MILITARY

1	Potamos Hideout

TREASURE LOCATIONS

1	Smuggler's Dock
2	Hypodoros Hamlet
3	Peristerion Town
4	Mareia Port
5	Taua

SIDE QUESTS

1	In Protest (13)
2	Thick Skin (13)
3	Fair Trade (13)

SAPI-RES NOME

ENEMY LEVEL: 15-18

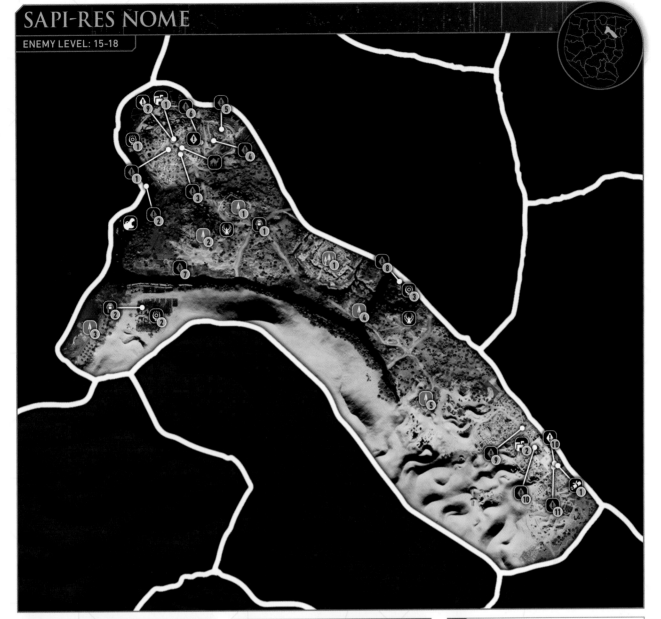

INTRODUCTION
THE ESSENTIALS
MAIN QUESTS
SIDE QUESTS
ACTIVITIES
ATLAS
REFERENCE & ANALYSIS

VILLAGES

| 1 | Sais |
| 2 | Letopolis |

FORTS

| 1 | Nikiou Fort |

SMALL MILITARY

1	Camp Pyrrhos
2	Psenemphaia Hideout
3	Camp Shemu
4	Nikiou Post
5	Camp Achlys

TREASURE LOCATIONS

1	Sap-Meh Warehouse
2	Mefkat
3	Sapi-Res Ruins

PAPYRUS LOCATIONS

| 1 | Temple of Horus |

PTOLEMY STATUES

| 1 | South of Sais |
| 2 | Mefkat |

MAIN QUESTS

9	The Scarab's Sting (15)
10	The Scarab's Lies (18)
11	Pompeius Magnus (in the Aegean Sea) (12)

SIDE QUESTS

1	Conflicts of Interest (after collecting from Informant Table) (15)
2	Smoke Over Water (after collecting from Informant Table) (15)
3	All Eyes on Us (after collecting from Informant Table) (16)
4	Lost Happiness (after collecting from Informant Table) (16)

5	Abuse of Power (17)
6	The Tax Master (17)
7	The Ostrich (17)
8	Taste of Her Sting Part IV Sapi-Res Ruins (17)
9	New Kid in Town (18)
10	Workers' Lament (18)
11	The Old Library (discovered during Workers' Lament) (18)

INFORMANT TABLES

Informant Table (complete Main Quest: The Scarab's Sting to access Conflicts of Interest, Smoke Over Water, All Eyes on Us, Lost Happiness)

289

ENEMY LEVEL: 22-25

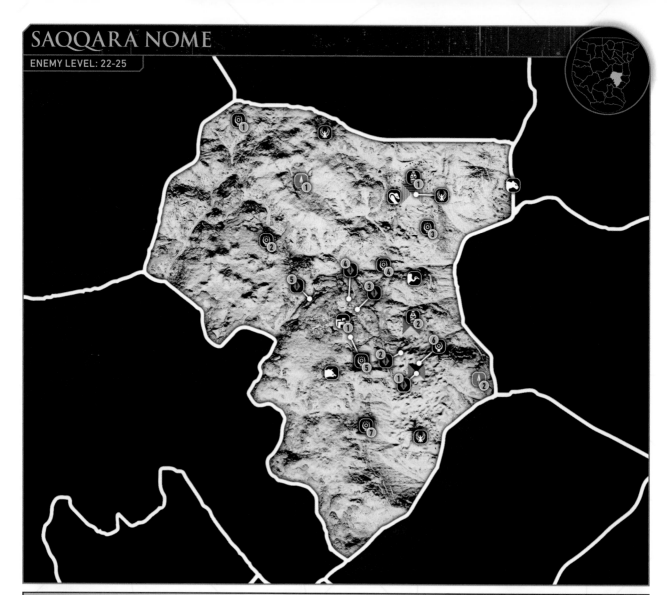

VILLAGES

1	Nitria

SMALL MILITARY

1	Psammos Hideout
2	Hugros Hideout

TREASURE LOCATIONS

1	Ruined Temple of Mafdet
2	Ekdikesis Outpost
3	Per Our Hideout
4	Stranded Natron Caravan
5	Unfortunate Stash
6	Bent Pyramid of Sneferu
7	Mryitmw High

TOMBS

1	Tomb of Djoser
2	Tomb of Sneferu

SIDE QUESTS

1	First Blood (18)
2	Secrets of the First Pyramids (23)
3	Rites of Anubis (23)
4	When Night Falls (complete Rites of Anubis) (23)
5	A Rebel Alliance (24)

SIWA

ENEMY LEVEL: 1-5

CITIES

1	Siwa

SMALL MILITARY

1	Coral Escarpment Camp
2	Camp Shetjeh

TREASURE LOCATIONS

1	Amanai Cave
2	Home
3	Halma Point
4	Temple of Amun
5	Lysandros' Oracle Offerings

TOMBS

1	Mountain of the Dead Tomb

PAPYRUS LOCATIONS

1	House of Life

PTOLEMY STATUES

1	Siwa

STONE CIRCLES

1	Amun Stone Circle

MAIN QUESTS

1	Homecoming (0)
2	The Oasis (1)
3	The False Oracle (1)
4	May Amun Walk Beside You (5)
22	The Final Weighing (32)

SIDE QUESTS

1	Gear Up (2)
2	Family Reunion (2)
3	Water Rats (3)
4	Hideaway (3)
5	Striking the Anvil (3)
6	The Healer (3)
7	Prisoners in the Temple (4)
8	Bayek's Promise (5)

INFORMANT TABLES

	Informant Table

UAB NOME

ENEMY LEVEL: 29-33

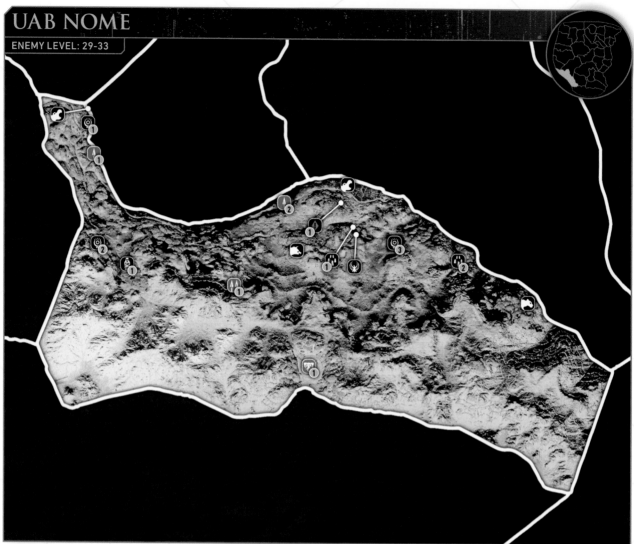

MEDIUM MILITARY

1	Arsinoites Quarry Hideout

SMALL MILITARY

1	Trireme Stranding Camp
2	Dioryx Megale Wharf

TREASURE LOCATIONS

1	Overwatch Tower
2	Ravaged Outpost
3	Senehem Depths

TOMBS

1	Tomb of the Cynic

STONE CIRCLES

1	Horus Stone Circle
2	The Scales Stone Circle

WAR ELEPHANT

1	Camp of Qetesh and Resheph

SIDE QUESTS

1	Seven Farmers (30)

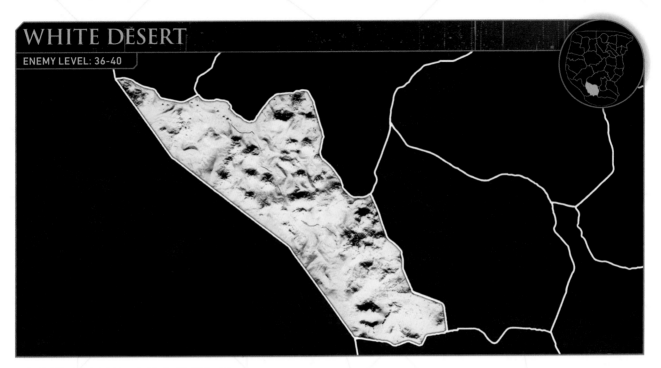

WHITE DESERT

ENEMY LEVEL: 36-40

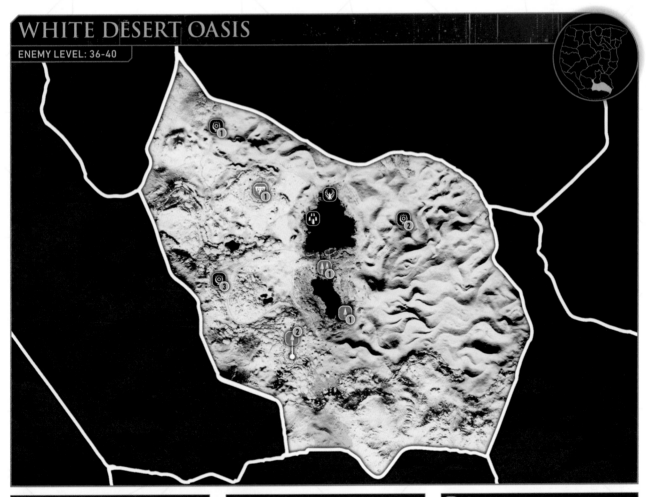

WHITE DESERT OASIS

ENEMY LEVEL: 36-40

🏃🏃 MEDIUM MILITARY	
1	Desert Waterfalls Hideout

🏃 SMALL MILITARY	
1	Larder Station Hideout
2	Djbt Jm Hideout

🔘 TREASURE LOCATIONS	
1	Desheret Dewu
2	White Desert Sobek Ruins
3	Whymhty Vault

🏛 STONE CIRCLES	
1	The Great Twins Stone Circle

🐘 WAR ELEPHANT	
1	Camp of Herwennefer

INTRODUCTION

THE ESSENTIALS

MAIN QUESTS

SIDE QUESTS

ACTIVITIES

ATLAS

REFERENCE & ANALYSIS

REFERENCE
AND ANALYSIS

THE HEROES

AYA

Ethnicity: Greco-Egyptian
Born: Siwa, Egypt
Age: 30
Sex: Female

A Greco-Egyptian who moved to Siwa later in life, Aya was one of the most respected members of her community in Alexandria before she left it behind. A hunter and a peacekeeper, she has dedicated her life to her family and to the honorable cause of helping others. She is a passionate adventurer caught between two cultures of origin, and personifies Egypt's state of flux at the time our story is set.

Unable to cope with the loss of her child nor her husband's thirst for revenge, Aya went to Alexandria where her cousin Phanos lives. There she studied at the great library, learning about ancient history, philosophy, mathematics, and mastering various languages and also becoming a cold-hearted killer, dead set on destroying those who work for Ptolemy, whom she views as the one responsible for killing her son. Her brilliant mind and quick wit brought her to the attention of Apollodorus, who eventually introduced her to Cleopatra.

She is now one of Cleopatra's most trusted allies, and the exiled queen considers her a friend and a bodyguard.

BAYEK

Ethnicity: Egyptian
Born: Siwa, Egypt
Age: 30
Sex: Male

An Egyptian born and raised in Siwa, a remote oasis near the Egyptian-Libyan border, Bayek took on the ancient role of protector, or "Medjay" of his village as he grew to adulthood. This duty instilled in him the values of a peacekeeper, upholding the law and protecting the people. A wise soul and a man of few words, Bayek is steadfast in adhering to his personal code.

When Ptolemaic soldiers came to the oasis demanding access to the sacred Temple of the Oracle of Amun, Bayek refused to cooperate. A fight ensued and they quickly found themselves on the losing side. Their son was mortally wounded and eventually died in their arms.

Bayek survived, but was cast out and lost everything: His son, his home, and eventually Aya, the woman he loved. He has crossed the desert searching for those responsible for the murder of his son. Tattooed on his forearm are the murderers' names, some scratched off by thick scars.

LAYLA HASSAN

Ethnicity: Egyptian
Born: Cairo, Egypt
Age: 33
Sex: Female

Layla Hassan was born to a wealthy Muslim family in Cairo, Egypt, in 1984. Two years later, she immigrated to New York City with her family. As a child, she drove her parents crazy by disassembling her toys rather than playing with them. She was always very practical-minded, and disliked both surprises and objects that seemed to work by magic.

Showing a penchant for rule breaking early on, Layla disliked the regimented nature of formal schooling... with the exception of shop class, of course. She had an unpleasant childhood experience of being punished for playing by the rules, which cemented her existing tendency to buck authority.

After high school, she had no plans to continue her studies, but her father pressured her into post-secondary enrolment. Though her marks were generally poor, her early promise in engineering was such that with the help of a few strings pulled by her father, she was able to enroll in Berkeley's electrical engineering program.

Though she thrived in the highly politicized atmosphere on campus, she remained uncommitted to her studies, preferring her own projects to her courses. She also feuded with university administration, and was on her way to flaming out of school when she met Sophia Rikkin, who was part of a delegation of Abstergo employees touring campuses with the company's "young innovators" recruitment program.

Sophia, prompted by Layla's intense interest in technology, offered her a job with Abstergo where she could work her way up to the Animus lab. Leila leaped at the chance to drop out of school and gain early access to the high-tech world. With the promise of work on the animus project to come, Sophia placed Layla in the R&D division of Abstergo Athletics.

At Abstergo, Layla's disinclination for teamwork did not endear her to her colleagues, though her engineering brilliance continued to shine. She hit her stride once she was removed from the lab and put into the field on behalf of Abstergo's Historical Research Division. From 2006 to 2010, Layla became a valued employee. She turned into a one-woman toolbox—taking on difficult jobs in remote locations without complaint, as long as she was allowed to do things her way. Occasionally and without notice, Sophia would reach out to Layla for what seemed to be a friendly conversation, but Layla began to suspect that she was being used for her ideas. She pressed to join the Animus team in Madrid; Sophia's promises of "one day" were beginning to wear thin.

When Egypt's people took to the streets in protest against their government, Layla felt a corresponding revolution build inside her. She asked for a leave of absence, and took her sketchy childhood grasp of Arabic to Cairo's Tahir square, alongside demonstrators calling for the resignation of President Hosni Mubarak. There, she became deeply involved in the country's revolutionary youth culture, helping her new friends to communicate through social media and hacked digital devices in the face of widespread government censorship. She was in Cairo when William miles,

After the coup d'état that installed Abdel Fattah el-Sisi as the Egyptian President in 2013, Layla decided to leave the country. Reluctantly, she returned to Abstergo where she was issued a portable animus unit, but her job had lost its savor. Contact with Sophia had grown almost non-existent, and Layla—angry over the withdrawal of the professional opportunity—decided to show Abstergo where she belonged.

Secretly, she began work on an ambitious personal project: modding her portable Animus so that it would allow users to experience the unmodified, unsanitized genetic memories not just of their ancestors, but of anyone in the world. Her modifications would also allow for reading of DNA samples too damaged for the ordinary Animus to handle. She felt confident that once she presented a successful prototype to Abstergo, they would give her the opportunity to join the Animus team that she had coveted for so many years. The destruction of Abstergo's Madrid facility in 2016 resulted in a complete withdrawal of contact by Sophia, but Layla knew that the team was regrouping and would soon be looking to expand.

When work on her Animus was almost complete, Layla received an assignment to return to Egypt, this time to investigate a burial chamber that was believed to contain an Isu relic. What she found instead was even better: the mummy of a man who seemed to have some connection to the early Assassins. Layla, with medical officer Deanna Geary in tow, decided that this was the perfect opportunity to test her Animus. Though this approach went against standard procedure, that was nothing new for Layla, and she felt that Abstergo would condone this more significant breach of protocol in exchange for the valuable information her findings would provide. This assignment represents Layla's chance to prove herself.

APOLLODORUS THE SICILIAN

Ethnicity: Greek
Born: Sicilia
Age: 40ish
Sex: Male

Apollodorus is an imposing figure in Cleopatra's entourage, due to both his physical prowess and mental acuity. He has the stocky, weathered demeanor of a man used to long weeks of rough travel when the need calls for it, even though his natural home is prim and proper at Cleopatra's side tending to affairs of state. His hair is dark black and his eyes are solid brown. He has created a network of informants across Egypt to keep him apprised of the comings and goings of local Ptolemies, mostly commoners and merchants under oppression from the official regime under Cleopatra's brother Ptolemy XIII.

Though born in Sicily, his people are ethnically Greek and he came to Alexandria as a young adult to serve the court of King Ptolemy XIII. The epithet "The Sicilian" is therefore a nickname given by his adopted countrymen.

HOTEPHRES

Ethnicity: Greek
Born: Krokodilopolis
Age: 35
Sex: Male

Hotephres is a former Adventurer and a skilled warrior. Although Greek, has settled down and married an Egyptian woman. He is saddened by the Ptolemaic rule and feels partially responsible for the land re-appropriation by Berenike and other Greek officials. His job now is less "sexy" than adventurer is and he is constantly forced to take the high road, however he will quickly regret this when his daughter is callously murdered by Berenike.

Hotephres is charming and gregarious, but following the loss of his daughter, deeply troubled. He blames himself and his wife for her death, and is initially riddled with grief, guilt, and self-loathing. As a father he failed to protect his daughter, inadvertently putting her in harm's way.

He normally speaks easily, with a friendly, cultured tone of voice. After his daughter's death, his voice flattened and betrayed his depression. Once resolved, however, he returns to his normal easy-going, quietly quipping self, albeit with an edge of sadness.

Hotephres is inspired by Bayek, as they share a common bond on having both lived a deep tragedy involving their only child. This links him to the Creed's formation in the end. Being thrown back into the midst of the ongoing battle against the Ptolemaics, he re-discovers himself.

KHENUT

Ethnicity: Egyptian
Born: Memphis, Egypt
Age: Mid 40s
Sex: Female

Khenut is a well-educated Egyptian woman in her late 30s who rose to moderate wealth through her talent as an administrator, officially in charge of land distribution in the Faiyum. She is clear headed, pragmatic, and determined. Despite her position, she does not wear lavish clothes and spends a lot of time as a local activist, advocating for and helping the poor.

She met Hotephres during his younger years when he was an adventuring rogue. They fell in love, married, and settled down. They had a child, Shadya, upon whom they both dote.

Khenut has a strong sense of duty and justice. In contrast to her husband, she does not often show humor (though she has a dry wit) and can be mistaken for being humorless. She has a motherly nature, however, and is gentle and empathetic to those in need. She drives Hotephres to 'do the right thing' when Apollodorus asks him to be his contact in the region. She has a flaw—hubris. She believes she is untouchable as a government official. When 'The Crocodile' begins to lean on her to distribute land unfairly, she thinks the worst that can happen is "mere" intimidation. This is the point where Bayek meets her in the game.

She is wrong. They could not touch her, but her family was fair game, and they drown her daughter.

Khenut begins as someone who thinks herself invincible and her position as unassailably "right." She suffers a grave loss, and for a time is a completely broken person. However, emerges from her tragedy determined, and ready to do whatever is necessary to ensure no other mother in Faiyum has to suffer as she did.

PHOXIDAS

Ethnicity: Greek
Born: Athens
Age: 40
Sex: Male

A Nauarchos (admiral) in Cleopatra's navy, Phoxidas is a wealthy owner of a fleet of ships and its crew, who has pledged his loyalty to Cleopatra. He was loyal to Cleopatra's father, although he found Ptolemy Auletes to be a rather boorish man. He hates how the politicians who seem to manipulate the court of young Ptolemy have dominated the affairs of Egypt and its people.

A strong and rugged man in his forties, Phoxidas prefers the outdoors and the open ocean to the backroom dealings of court. He was a soldier in his youth, but retired into great wealth and used this money to fund his fleet of ships. Despite being a man of means, Phoxidas prefers to dress in practical garb, even if he allows himself the occasional flourish of luxury.

THE HISTORICAL FIGURES

INTRODUCTION

THE ESSENTIALS

MAIN QUESTS

SIDE QUESTS

ACTIVITIES

ATLAS

REFERENCE & ANALYSIS

CLEOPATRA VII THEA PHILOPATOR

Ethnicity: Greek	**Age:** 19
Born: Alexandria, Egypt	**Sex:** Female

Cleopatra was raised as royalty from birth, becoming one of the most intelligent and educated women of her time—speaking nine languages by the time she was 20. At the young age of 18, she ascended to Egypt's throne following the sudden death of her father, Ptolemy XII—a position that she must share with her younger brother Ptolemy XIII.

As a shrewd politician and extremely charming temptress, she has the unsettling ability to persuade almost any opponent into coming around to her point of view. Cleopatra was the last in a long line of Ptolomaic rulers.

PTOLEMY XIII THEOS PHILOPATOR

Ethnicity: Greek	**Age:** 12
Born: Alexandria, Egypt	**Sex:** Male

While Cleopatra is a woman assured of her power and skill, her younger brother Ptolemy is a curious and wide eyed boy who believes everything his elders tell him. He is a mere pawn in an international game, the rules of which he does not understand. He is by turns curious and petulant, wide-eyed and fussy. He does not seem to understand the full weight of the position he is in as King, and tends to focus on petty details rather than the big picture.

GAIUS JULIUS CAESAR

Ethnicity: Roman	**Age:** 52
Born: Roman Republic	**Sex:** Male

Caesar was an impossibly ambitious man, and often checked his own successes against the accomplishments against those of the Alexander the Great. Yet he always found himself falling short of that great man's triumphs, a source of great bitterness. This ingrained insecurity was the engine that propelled him through his greatest military and political battles.

In person he had the charm of a successful entrepreneur—focused, engaged, and never frivolous. He was intelligent without being pedantic, and his vast knowledge of the world and his experience as a priest, a soldier, and a Roman consul gave him an advantage in all political and military affairs. In the field he was a serious man with the weight of his immense legacy always on his shoulders.

BERENIKE—THE CROCODILE

ETHNICITY: Greek
BORN: Faiyum
AGE: 60s
SEX: Female

Berenike is the Nomarch of Faiyum, the Governor of the region.

She is an idealist who has the means to effect change on a sweeping scale, but her wealth and power are largely inherited. She has a vision for peace and order that comes from the Greek aphorism "A society grows great when old men plants trees in whose shade they shall never sit". While her father was content to reap the personal fruits of wealth and power, Berenike is driven to create a better world, a philosophical ideal inspired by her childhood tutor.

It was this agent who engineered conflict after conflict between Berenike's ideals and her father's personal greed, until she was forced to choose whether to kill her father for the sake of the land or to abandon her ideals to save her father. She was inducted as a member of the Order of Ancients on the day she slipped poison into his wine. Ever since then her obsessive pursuit of order and control has been her only means to justify in her own mind her horrific act of patricide.

Berenike's Order of Ancients mission is to use her control of Faiyum to fund their operations. She maximizes this revenue by enacting taxes and regulations that force the consolidation of landholdings into the hands of the Hellenic ruling class.

EUDOROS OF ALEXANDRIA—THE HIPPO

ETHNICITY: Greek
BORN: Greece
AGE: 60s
SEX: Male

A proud and regal man, Eudoros is a shining light of the Peripatetic schools of philosophy, and one of the most respected intellectuals in Alexandria. He is tall and regal, slightly overweight but very healthy looking. He is also quite handsome and enjoys the finest pleasures life has to offer. He is also a respected and accomplished philosopher, having written many books on a number of scientific topics.

He is detached and aloof and has no interest in the affairs of the common people of Egypt, but he is not a misanthrope. He is merely an intellectual enamored with the operation of his own thoughts and opinions. When he does relax, he does so lavishly, firmly believing that his intelligence and charisma are proof of his importance. A firm believer in the idea of inherent nobility, he naturally feels he is one of the most inherently noble.

As a philosopher, scribe, and historian, Eudoros has given himself the task of creating propaganda that proves the inarguable superiority of men like him (Nobles, etc.). He therefore has a vested interest in all things that tell his story "the right way"... legends, myths, political pronouncements, etc.

He has also been given the task of executing all those in opposition to King Ptolemy XIII's rule.

FLAVIUS METELLUS—THE LION

ETHNICITY: Roman
BORN: Rome
AGE: 40s
SEX: Male

Flavius is a powerful and far-reaching Roman soldier with a distinguished military career. He is an ally of Caesar's. He came from an older patrician family that had lost much of its wealth, but he married a wealthy woman Porcia Orestilla to restore his family's treasuries. This was his second marriage, and certain enemies whispered that he had murdered his first wife and son to be able to marry into money.

Flavius came to prominence as proconsul (governor) in the Roman province of Cyrenaica, and spent time in Cyrene, the capital of that region and the oldest and most important of the five Greek cities on the north African coast of the Mediterranean city (modern day Libya). He has been hungrily eyeing the wealth of Egypt for as long as he has been in the region.

Although one of Caesar's allies, it is an alliance built on Flavius' wealth and military strength rather than trust, or honesty, or respect. Flavius knows Caesar needs him, and in return, Flavius uses Caesar to increase his position. Flavius is extremely ambitious—personally and politically—and will use any opportunity to improve his lot. Although he has a reputation for ruthlessness and brutality when it comes to his enemies, he can be obsequious or servile in regards to his superiors—like Caesar—until he is certain he has an advantage over them.

Flavius believes Caesar is too lenient and accepting of his enemies, and in particular looks upon the Egyptians as a resource to be exploited for Rome's—and his own—gain.

HETEPI – THE LIZARD

ETHNICITY: Egyptian
BORN: Unknown
AGE: 40s
SEX: Male

Hetepi is a Second Priest of Ptah, under Pasherenptah, the High Priest of Ptah in Memphis. Working as a member of the Order of Ancients in a city predominantly in support of Cleopatra, Hetepi's attempts to change the identity of Memphis are continuously thwarted by his status. A quiet and reserved fellow, Hetepi draws little attention to himself, facilitating his bid to usurp the High Priest and take his spot.

Hetepi oversees a massive fraudulent operation of "curses" in his bid to manipulate the minds of the people and dethrone the High Priest. He poisons his wife to prevent childbirth, sabotages mummification, and is responsible for the slow and imminent death of the Apis bull. As long as these problems exist, the finger will continue to be pointed at Pasherenptah, and it is only a matter of time before Hetepi benefits from the High Priest's inability to find a solution.

Once nominated to take over for Pasherenptah, Hetepi will "banish" all curses, gain the support of the people, and establish a clear alignment to Ptolemy XIII.

KHALISET—THE HYENA

ETHNICITY: Kushite or Nubian
BORN: Thebes, Egypt
AGE: Mid 30s
SEX: Female

A skilled thief and tomb-raider from Thebes. She dresses in the manner of a hunter and tracker well accustomed to the arid climate of the desert. She has few —only weapons, water, and a reasonable amount of food. The colors and roughness of her outfit allows her to blend with the colors of the desert (for proper coloring, see mission design for the region she will inhabit.) Her primary weapon is a bow, but she is equally good with short blades too. Due to her particular skillset, she has been given the task of locating rare deposits of silica and ancient technology artifacts hidden in tombs and throughout the deserts. This silica, is the primary power source for ancient technology.

Now, with a firm belief entrenched in the spiritual properties of these ancient artifacts, Khaliset holds out hope that she can one day return her daughter's (ESHE) soul to her body, and bring her back from the dead. Seeing the Order of Ancients's obsession with ancient technology and having recently discovered an ancient technology room beneath the great pyramid, Khaliset feels that if there is any hope left for her daughter, it would be through the wonders of this great ancient civilization.

LUCIUS SEPTIMIUS—THE JACKAL

ETHNICITY: Roman
BORN: Roman Republic
AGE: 40s
SEX: Male

A Roman Military Tribune stationed in Alexandria, killer of Pompey the Great, and master manipulator. He is a member of the Gabiniani faction of Roman Soldiers, a group of Roman soldiers who are permanently stationed in Alexandria to protect the Ptolemaic kings and queens.

In 55 BC, Septimius accompanied the General Aulus Gabinius to Egypt to serve as one of Ptolemy XII's protectors. He fell in love with the city almost immediately and married a local Egyptian named Nebetia, vowing to spend the rest of his life there. Around this time he also fell in with members of the Ptolemy's court, men like Pothinus, Achillas, and Ganymedes, a move that solidified his position in the upper echelons of Egyptian society. When Ptolemy XII died of a sudden illness, his advisors Pothinus, Ganymedes, and Theodotus promote Septimius to their inner circle. It was under the orders of Pothinus that Septimius killed Pompey as he came ashore in Pelusium, thus landing the first blow of what would become the Battle of Alexandria.

Septimius is a strong and hearty man who can be friendly in times of calm, but who may also explode in bouts of irrepressible rage at the slightest provocation. Oppressed by the feeling that someone is always taking advantage of him he is twitchy and quick to brand associates as enemies. When agitated he stalks about like a panther searching for prey. He only feels at ease when he is in the company of those he knows are his allies and co-conspirators; otherwise can be brooding, sarcastic, and aloof.

MEDUNAMUN, THE HIGH PRIEST OF AMUN—THE IBIS

ETHNICITY: Egyptian
BORN: Thebes, Egypt
AGE: 55
SEX: Male

Medunamun has replaced the old Oracle as the new brutal spiritual overseer of Siwa. He has very close ties with the Pharaoh and his handlers. He is an intelligent but embittered man who hides great doubts about his role behind a veneer of excessive piety. He pretends to be religious but in reality has a deep insecurity about his understanding of the Gods and the world around him. He has a slightly sadistic side and cares nothing for the feelings of other people when they get in the way of his personal goals.

He has come to Siwa in search of the secrets beneath the Temple of the Oracle.

POTHINUS—THE SCORPION

ETHNICITY: Greek
BORN: Pelusium
AGE: 40s
SEX: Male

Pothinus, Ptolemy XIII's Advisor, is a rather deceptive character. Outwardly gentle and well-mannered, he is in fact Alexandria's central member of the Order of Ancients. Given the task five years before of guiding Ptolemaic Egypt into a position more suitable for the Romans, Pothinus has carefully influenced and shaped the actions and decisions of two generations of Ptolemys, Father and Son. Unfortunately for grander plans, Queen Cleopatra has been a thorn in his side since the day she ascended the throne, sidelining him almost immediately after her father's untimely death.

Since 51 BC, Pothinus has worked tirelessly to manipulate young Ptolemy XIII and his court to do the bidding of the Order of Ancients—transforming Egypt into a vassal of the Roman Empire.

He is loyal to Cleopatra's brother Ptolemy, and wants to see him restored to his place on Egypt's throne. His fight, therefore, is against Caesar and Cleopatra.

INTRODUCTION

THE ESSENTIALS

MAIN QUESTS

SIDE QUESTS

ACTIVITIES

ATLAS

REFERENCE & ANALYSIS

RUDJEK—THE HERON

ETHNICITY: Egyptian
BORN: Unknown
AGE: 33
SEX: Male

Rudjek is a member of the Order of Ancients. And he was there when Bayek and Aya's son died.

An Egyptian who lives in Giza, around Saqqara, Rudjek is a strong warrior who helped in the corrupt natron trade around the mines of Giza.

He received a lot of wealth from the Order, and enjoyed his life, which explains his Wife and his ability to have a mistress. He is very Pro-Ptolemy and does not understand those who are not. His connection to the Order has given him benefits he never dreamed of and he considers himself lucky, he even at times masquerades with the title of Prefect.

A normal person who has been sucked into a crazy situation. "Just accept the Order. They are there. You can't avoid them."

TAHARQA—THE SCARAB

ETHNICITY: Nubian (Kush Kingdom)
BORN: Unknown
AGE: 33
SEX: Male

Taharqa is a lively personality, fond of excitement and heightened stimuli. He's a man of the people, and a real crowd pleaser who knows how to earn the support of the people. As busy as he is, he never lacks for time with his family. His two children adore him to death, and his wife is his biggest supporter. He treats them with respect and often travels with city with them, occasionally teaching them the street tips of a man who has seen a lot.

Taharqa's great intolerance is to those who try to impede his progress. He cannot align with those who are passive or non-action oriented, and believes anyone who does not believe in his work is defying the will of the gods.

ENEMY TYPES

Enemies throughout Ancient Egypt may belong to a number of factions, but they all fit into five types: soldiers, archers, brutes, predators, and supers. Each of these has variations that differ slightly, based on equipment and fighting style.

SOLDIERS

SOLDIER VARIATIONS

TYPE	EQUIPMENT	OVERVIEW	BEHAVIOR
A	• Main weapon: sword • Secondary weapon: short bow • Shield/tool: none	Most basic enemy, performing only simple attacks with no real defensive actions.	• Pursues a fleeing target. • Shoots at a target, who rides a mount. • Attacks a target when approached. • All soldiers may pull out the bow from long range.
B	• Main weapon: sword • Secondary weapon: short bow • Shield/tool: small shield	A Type B soldier carries a small shield that is used to defend against basic attacks, driving the player to evade to the side or use an attack that creates an opening, such as a Shield Charge.	Within close to medium range of his target, he raises his shield. The soldier can perform two basic attacks in succession, which can be interrupted if the first strike misses or the target moves away.
C	• Main weapon: spear • Secondary weapon: short bow • Shield/Tool: small shield	A Type C soldier can perform circular attacks, forcing the player to defend with the shield.	When target flees from soldier, he pursues with shield raised. Raises shield when attacked. Sidestep or evade attack to get around his defense.
D	• Main weapon: spear • Secondary weapon: short bow • Shield/tool: none	A Type D soldier can perform circular attacks, forcing the player to defend with the shield.	Within a close to medium range of his target, the soldier may perform a basic attack or double charge attack. Be ready to evade to the side to avoid the piercing.

ARCHERS

ARCHER VARIATIONS

TYPE	EQUIPMENT	OVERVIEW	REACTIONS
A	• Main weapon: long bow • Secondary weapon: none • Shield/tool: none	A Type A archer occasionally sets up for a single shot from his bow. Use the shield or dodge to the side to defend against the attacks.	When he reaches cover or a ranged position, he aims and performs a basic shot. Strike at him with a melee attack and he pushes back with bow and attempts a shot.
B	• Main weapon: long bow • Secondary weapon: none • Shield/tool: none	A Type B archer encourages the use of the shield to defend against his light bow.	When he reaches cover or a ranged position, he aims and performs a set of three light shots. When his target approaches at less than 10 meters, he strafes away while firing light shots.
C	• Main weapon: long bow • Secondary weapon: none • Shield/tool: none	A Type C archer uses fire arrows, encouraging his target to dodge or roll away.	When he reaches cover or a ranged position, he aims and performs a fire shot. When his target approaches at less than 10 meters, he strafes away while firing light shots. Strike at him with a melee attack and he pushes back with bow and attempts a shot.

BRUTES

BRUTE VARIATIONS

TYPE	EQUIPMENT	OVERVIEW	REACTIONS
A	• Main weapon: heavy weapon • Secondary weapon: short bow • Shield/tool: none	A Type A brute should be kept at a distance to avoid its deadly shield breaker attacks.	The Type A brute simply blocks straight-on attacks, not even reacting to the blow. Within 3 meters of a target, he can perform a sequence of two heavy attacks, a fast fury attack, or a push attack.
B	• Main weapon: heavy weapon • Secondary weapon: javelin • Shield/tool: big shield	A Type B brute carries a big shield that he can use to stun his target, putting the player on the ground. Sidestep his attacks or keep him at a distance.	When he has line of sight on his target, he jogs toward the target, with shield raised. Within 4 meters of a target, the brute can perform a shield stun. With a successful shield charge, he chains the hit with a sequence of two heavy attacks.
C	• Main weapon: heavy long weapon • Secondary weapon: javelin • Shield/tool: big shield	A Type C brute should be kept at an even greater distance since he can put his target on the ground from even farther away with his shield charge, which also inflicts critical damage.	When he has line of sight on his target, he jogs toward the target, with shield raised. Within 10 meters of a target, the brute may perform a shield charge by running at the target. With a successful shield charge, he chains the hit with a sequence of two heavy attacks.

INTRODUCTION

THE ESSENTIALS

MAIN QUESTS

SIDE QUESTS

ACTIVITIES

ATLAS

REFERENCE & ANALYSIS

PREDATORS

PREDATOR VARIATIONS

TYPE	EQUIPMENT	OVERVIEW	REACTIONS
A	• Main weapon: dual sickle sword • Secondary weapon: small bow • Shield/tool: none	A Type A predator encourages the player to use stun actions before attacking since predators have the ability to dodge an attack by dashing backward or to the side.	When he reaches medium range, he may perform a running melee attack or aim a heavy shot. When his target comes within 5 meters, he performs a set of three light attacks, before returning to medium position.
B	• Main weapon: dual sickle sword • Secondary weapon: small bow • Shield/tool: smoke bombs	A Type B predator's purpose is to break the tempo of the fight by disrupting visibility.	When he has a wide-open line of sight on his target, he runs to the stalking zone (such as tall grass) around the target. If there is no stalking zone, he searches for cover, and if there is no cover, he goes to a ranged position. At a ranged position, he aims and tosses a smoke bomb or fires a heavy shot. With a successful heavy shot, he runs at his target and performs a running attack, before returning to medium range. If his target gets within 5 meters, he performs a set of three light attacks and moves back to a medium range or stalking zone.
C	• Main weapon: dual sickle sword • Secondary weapon: small bow • Shield/tool: firebombs	A Type C predator has a deadly ranged attack, which can only be avoided by rolling quickly out of its area of effect.	When he reaches a ranged position, he aims and tosses a firebomb or shoots a heavy shot. Evade to a safe area to avoid fire damage. With a successful heavy shot, he runs at his target and performs a set of four light attacks, before returning to medium range or stalking zone. From a stalking zone position, he throws a firebomb. If his target gets within 5 meters, he performs a set of four light attacks and moves back to medium range or cover.

SUPERS

SUPER VARIATIONS

TYPE	EQUIPMENT	OVERVIEW	REACTIONS
A	• Main weapon: long sword • Secondary weapon: short bow • Shield/tool: medium shield	The super is an archetype, which challenges players' reflexes, since the windows of opportunity are short and errors have stiff consequences. Stay on the move against supers, as they can close in on their targets quickly, catching you off guard.	He raises his shield when the target is within close to medium range. From a ranged position, less than 20 meters away, he may let a heavy shot go at his target. He may perform a jump heavy attack, or a dash plus dash attack, or a fast heavy attack.
B	• Main weapon: long sword • Secondary weapon: javelin • Shield/tool: big shield	The super is an archetype, which challenges players' reflexes, since the windows of opportunity are short and errors have stiff consequences.	From a ranged position, less than 20 meters away, he may toss a javelin at his target. Within close to medium range, he may perform a paired attack or a dash plus dash attack.

ABILITIES

Bayek begins the game with three abilities: Eagle Tagging, Overpower, and Call Mount. As Ability Points (AP) are earned, skills may be purchased at the Abilities screen. Here, each ability is represented by an icon, which is connected to other abilities. In order to acquire an ability, you must own (indicated by yellow icon) at least one connecting ability. Abilities cost between 1 and 3 AP.

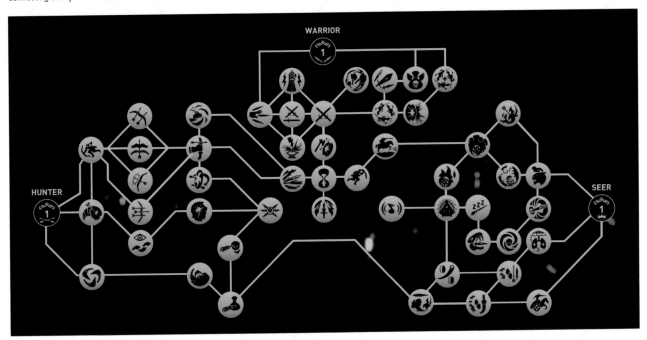

APs are awarded each time you complete the following actions:

HOW TO EARN AP

ACTION	NUMBER AVAILABLE
Level up	39
Earn 20,000 XP after reaching Level 40	Infinite
Meditate at a hermit location	5
Complete a tomb	14
Defeat a War Elephant	4

To acquire all of the abilities, you must spend 85 AP. In addition, each of the master abilities can be purchased multiple times at 1 AP per upgrade. You can earn 62 AP by reaching Level 40 and completing all tombs, War Elephants, and hermit locations. Once Bayek reaches Level 40, you receive an AP each time you earn 20,000 XP.

THE ABILITIES

ABILITY		PASSIVE	COST (AP)	REQUIRED ABILITIES	EFFECT
	Eagle Tagging	—	N/A	Given at start	Tag enemies from the Eagle Hover mode by holding the Aim button and moving the cursor across the foes
	Eagle Harass	Passive	2	Charge Heavy Attack or Bow Bearer	The Eagle can help the hero by harassing nearby enemies. While in Eagle Hover mode, press the button indicated on your HUD to have Senu stun enemies. Also during combat, Senu will harass enemies from time to time.
	Bow Bearer	—	1	Charge Heavy Attack, Eagle Harass, Arrow Retriever, Enhanced light bow, Enhanced Predator Bow, Enhanced hunter bow, or Enhanced Warrior Bow	With this ability, the player can equip a second bow in the Gear menu. While in game, press the D-pad left to switch between the two bows.
	Arrow Retriever	Passive	1	Available from start	Unlocks the possibility to retrieve arrows that have been blocked with your shield.
	Headshot XP	Passive	1	Available from start	Earn bonus XP upon killing with a headshot.
	Assassination XP	Passive	1	Available from start	Earn bonus XP upon killing with an assassination.
	Assassination loot	Passive	2	Headshot XP, Stealth Kill Streak, or Tool Kill XP	Automatically loot an enemy after an assassination.
	Stealth Kill Streak	—	2	Assassination Loot or Chain Assassination	Gain extra XP if you perform a stealth kill immediately after another stealth kill.
	Enhanced Light Bow	Passive	2	Bow Bearer or Elite Ranger	Increases the number of arrows you can fire before needing to reload.
	Enhanced Predator Bow	—	2	Bow Bearer or Elite Ranger	Allows the player to control the arrow when shooting with any predator bow. Hold the shoot button and use the left analog stick to control the arrow in the air.

INTRODUCTION
THE ESSENTIALS
MAIN QUESTS
SIDE QUESTS
ACTIVITIES
ATLAS
REFERENCE & ANALYSIS

ABILITY		PASSIVE	COST (AP)	REQUIRED ABILITIES	EFFECT
	Enhanced Hunter Bow	—	2	Bow Bearer or Elite Ranger	Allows the player to break a shield defense by charging a shot from any hunter bow. Hold the shoot button to perform the attack.
	Enhanced Warrior Bow	—	2	Bow Bearer or Elite Ranger	Reduce the dispersion zone by charging any warrior bow with the shoot button. This concentrates the damage on a single target.
	Hunter's Instinct	—	2	Bow Fury or Assassination XP	Allows the player to see the paths of enemies. While in hover mode with Senu, mark an enemy to see his current activity and destination. Enables the player to set an ambush along the enemy's path.
	Elite Ranger	—	3	Enhanced Light Bow, Enhanced Predator Bow, Enhanced Hunter Bow, Enhanced Warrior Bow, Bow Fury, or Master Hunter	As an Elite Ranger, Bayek enters slow motion when aiming his bow while in the air (hold the Aim button). Perform a headshot during the maneuver to score an achievement/trophy.
	Bow Fury	—	3	Elite Ranger, Hunter's Instinct, Chain Assassination, or Master Hunter	Using a bow to perform a stealth kill activates slow motion for 3 seconds, giving the player an opportunity to perform another quick stealth kill. This only happens outside of conflict, so once detected, this is not an option.
	Chain Assassination	—	3	Stealth Kill Streak, Bow Fury, or Master Hunter	Allows the player to use his knife to stealthly kill another target after an assassination by pressing the button shown on screen.
	Master Hunter	Passive	1*	Elite Ranger, Bow Fury, or Chain Assassination	Increase bow damage by +1%. This ability can be acquired multiple times. This becomes extremely handy when attempting the toughest challenges in the game, such as War Elephants and Phylakes.
	Overpower	—	N/A	Given at start	Given at the start of the game, this allows for an Overpower attack once the adrenaline bar is filled. Unleash the special attack by pressing the two buttons shown on the adrenaline meter. Swords, spears, heavy blades, and dual swords trigger an Overpower attack, a high-damage attack on a single enemy. The sickle sword, scepter, and heavy blunt trigger Fury mode, which gives increased damage and speed for a few seconds.
	Charge Heavy Attack	—	1	Regeneration, Eagle Harass, or Bow Bearer	Allows the player to charge a Heavy Attack by holding down the Heavy Attack button. A fully charged Heavy Attack will shield break tower shields and knock enemies to the ground. Use this move carefully as you are vulnerable to attack, during the charge.
	Regeneration	Passive	1	Available from start	The player's health regenerates during a fight.
	Air Attack	—	1	Regeneration or Hijack	Allows the player to perform an Air Attack against an enemy located below the player. When above an aware target, a Leap Attack option appears above the foe's head. Press the indicated button to attack from this position. Assassinations are still possible when undetected.
	Overpower Ultra	Passive	1	Weapon Bearer	Doubles the damage done by Overpower attacks.
	Parry	—	1	Regeneration	Allows the player to deflect an incoming attack by tapping the parry button while in Shield mode. Hold Shield Lock to enter Shield mode and then press the Parry button just as an opponent attacks. This staggers the enemy, providing the opportunity to perform a counterattack.
	Hijack	—	2	Air Attack or Smoke Screen	Allows players to hijack guards on vehicles and take control of their mount/vehicle.
	Overpower Chain Throw	—	3	Overpower XP, Overpower Combo, Overpower Ultra, or Master Warrior	After an Overpower attack, press the Light Attack button to chain with a combo of light attacks.
	Overpower Combo	—	2	Weapon Bearer	Allows the player to chain an Overpower attack with additional attacks. The type of attack added to the Overpower attack varies, depending on the weapon equipped. With dual swords, chain light attacks after the Overpower. With the spear, chain a throw attack after the Overpower. With the sword, chain a stun attack after the Overpower.
	Weapon Bearer	—	1	Parry	Allows the player to equip a second melee weapon. Press D-pad right to switch between the two melee weapons.
	Adrenaline 1	Passive	1	Weapon Bearer	Always start a conflict with a half-filled adrenaline gauge.
	Shield Charge	—	2	Adrenaline 1 or Adrenaline 2	When in shield mode, hold the parry button to run at your target and bash enemies in your way. This consumes adrenaline and thus requires adrenaline to perform. Use the maneuver to close in on a target, being careful of incoming attacks.
	Overpower XP	Passive	1	Weapon Bearer	Earn additional XP upon killing with the Overpower attack.
	Attack & Push	—	1	Weapon Bearer	Unlocks the ability to charge the light attack by holding the Light Attack button after a light attack, pushing the enemy away.
	Extend Combo	—	2	Adrenaline 1 or Kill Loot	Allows the player to deal an additional attack against an enemy before entering recovery.

ABILITY		PASSIVE	COST (AP)	REQUIRED ABILITIES	EFFECT
	Kill Loot	Passive	3	Extend Combo or Master Warrior	Automatically loots an enemy after killing with a melee attack.
	Adrenaline 2	Passive	3	Shield Charge or Master Warrior	Always start a conflict with a full adrenaline gauge.
	Master Warrior	Passive	1*	Overpower Chain Throw or Adrenaline 2	Increase melee damage by +1%. This ability can be acquired multiple times. Good for those who prefer combat close up.
	Call Mount	—	N/A	Given at start	Given to Bayek at the start of the game, this ability allows Bayek to call his mount by holding D-Pad down.
	Fire bomb	—	1	Dawn & Dusk or Smoke Screen	Unlocks the ability to use firebombs. Equip the tool at the Gear screen and hold D-pad left to equip it. Hold Aim to aim and Heavy Attack to throw it. Sets enemies and certain flammable objects on fire.
	Dawn & Dusk	—	1	Available from start	With this ability, hold the world map button to sit and make time speed forward. Changes night to day and vice versa. This is useful when nighttime is too dark, a quest requires you meet someone at a certain time of day, or you wish to change NPCs' positions and actions. Some enemy strongholds and animal dens tend to be less active at night. Assassinations can be performed against sleeping soldiers.
	Salesman	Passive	1	Dawn & Dusk, Tool Kill XP, or Buy Materials	Allows the player to sell animal goods and trinkets at +25% the price.
	Tool Kill XP	Passive	1	Backstore, Salesman, or Assassination Loot	Rewards player with XP upon killing with a tool. For fire weapons (firebomb, fire arrow, and torch), XP is only given with a kill that results from the hit, not from the burning effect. Same holds true for the poison dart. XP is awarded for killing with an exploding oil jar and Smoke Screen attack.
	Smoke Screen	—	1	Hijack, Pyromaniac, Smoke Screen Damage, or Fire bomb	Press the interact button after melee attacking or rolling to drop this powder. It stuns nearby enemies and creates a smoke screen. Smoke screens can break line of sight. Use to flee trouble or get the jump on an enemy.
	Sleep Darts	—	1	Dawn & Dusk or Flesh Decay	Unlocks Sleep Darts in the inventory. Equip the tool at the Gear screen and hold D-pad left to equip them. Hold Aim to aim and Heavy Attack to throw it. Enemies or animals at your level or lower will fall asleep when hit with a sleep dart. Great for handling multiple foes, taking one or more out of the action.
	Flesh Decay	—	1	Sleep Darts or Berserk	Unlocks Flesh Decay tool, which is used after a kill by holding the indicated button. Poisoned corpses contaminate nearby NPCs.
	Backstore	Passive	2	Tool Kill XP, Buy Materials, or Chariot Owner	Bayek can now acquire rare gear at shops.
	Pyromaniac	Passive	1	Smoke Screen or Animal Taming	The fire produced by fire weapons (fire bomb, fire arrow, and torch) causes 50% greater damage.
	Smoke Screen Damage	Passive	2	Smoke Screen or Animal Taming	Enemies caught within the radius of a smoke screen now take damage and are knocked to the ground.
	Berserk	—	2	Flesh Decay or Poison Darts	Unlocks the ability to inflict Berserk on an unaware enemy. Approach an enemy undetected and hold the indicated button to turn him berserk instead of assassinating him. This causes the foe to attack his nearest target.
	Buy Materials	—	2	Salesman, Backstore, or Breath Holding Champion	Unlocks the ability to buy resources at shops. Very useful for completing upgrades on your gear when materials are in short supply.
	Animal Taming	—	3	Pyromaniac, Smoke Screen Damage, Poison Darts, or Master Seer	(Prerequisite: Sleep Darts) Allows the player to interact with sleeping animals and tame them. When tamed, an animal follows the player around. Predator and defensive animals will assist in fights. Hit an animal with a Sleep Dart, approach it, and hold the indicated button to tame it. The animal can be untamed by holding the same button when next to it.
	Poison Darts	—	2	Berserk or Animal Taming	Unlocks the ability to equip and throw poison darts. Poison deals damage to the inflicted enemy, while also contaminating nearby foes. Equip the tool at the Gear screen and hold D-pad left to equip it. Hold Aim to aim and Heavy Attack to throw it.
	Breath Holding Champion	Passive	3	Buy Materials or Master Seer	Increases underwater breath, so the player can stay underwater for a longer period of time.
	Chariot Owner	—	3	Backstore or Master Seer	Chariots become available for purchase at shops, allowing the player to travel Ancient Egypt in a chariot. Equip the vehicle at the Gear screen.
	Master Seer	Passive	1*	Animal Taming, Breath Holding Champion, or Chariot Owner	Increase tool damage (poison darts, firebombs, smoke bombs, and fire) by +1%. This ability can be acquired multiple times.

*Can be acquired multiple times.

INTRODUCTION

THE ESSENTIALS

MAIN QUESTS

SIDE QUESTS

ACTIVITIES

ATLAS

REFERENCE & ANALYSIS

Gear is found throughout the world and is available for purchase from shops. It is important to continue to acquire new gear as Bayek increases in level. Using equipment too far below your level may result in trouble when fighting enemies around your level.

When collecting equipment from a chest or from a defeated captain/commander, a random weapon or shield is generated. The items come in three rarities: Common, Rare, and Legendary. The level of items found in chests is based on the player's level. Items looted from enemies reflects the enemy's level. This means that you can get higher-level weapons by defeating a tougher opponent.

Both melee and long-range weapons come in a variety of styles. Each style has advantages and disadvantages, making each ideal for certain situations. Also note that each type of weapon has a mutual attribute that is always present within that category. Find your favorite or learn to use them all to be well prepared for whatever the enemy throws your way.

You receive many items by completing a quest or activity (refer to our "Quest" and "Activities" chapters for more information). Buying a Heka Chest from Reda at a Nomad's Bazaar location rewards the player with a random Rare or Legendary gear item. Gear that can be found from these chests is noted in the How to Acquire column.

Killing Phylakes rewards the player with a Legendary piece of gear, which is often randomly selected from a set of items. These are not noted in the tables below but are noted in the "Phylakes" section of the Activities chapter.

The following tables list the weapons, shields, mounts, and outfits available in the game.

MELEE WEAPONS
REGULAR SWORD

DISMANTLE RESOURCES: Bronze, Iron   **MUTUAL ATTRIBUTE:** Critical Hit Rate

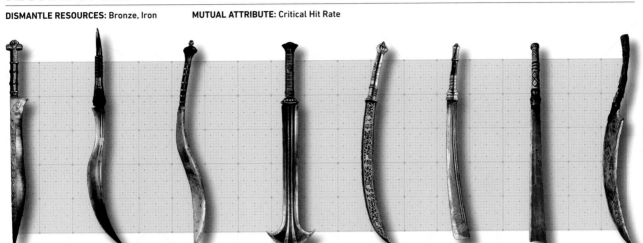

AVAILABLE REGULAR SWORDS

NAME	DESCRIPTION	RARITY	HOW TO ACQUIRE	DAMAGE	UNIQUE ATTRIBUTE	RARE ATTRIBUTE	LEGENDARY ATTRIBUTE
Amun's Blade	Found in the Siwa oasis, at the oracle of Zeus Amun. Intricate details of the life of Amun are sculpted onto the blade.	Common	Blacksmith, Loot	Medium	Critical Hit Rate II	None	None
Bronze Sword	A rudimentary stabbing weapon used by Philistine mercenaries.	Common	Blacksmith, Loot	Medium	Critical Hit Rate I	None	None
Coast of Russicada	This blade fed on the blood of both a Numidian king and a Roman general and hungers for more.	Legendary	Nomad's Bazaar	Medium	Critical Hit Rate II	Adrenaline on Hurt II	Health on Hit
Copper Sword	While the beauty of this sword is masked by a patina of verdegris, it's as sharp as the day it was forged.	Rare	Blacksmith, Loot	Low	Critical Hit Rate II	Combo Multiplier I	None
The Falcata	Wielded by Carthaginian heavy infantry, this short sword is powerful enough to pierce shields and helmets.	Legendary	Nomad's Bazaar	Medium	Critical Hit Rate I	Critical Hit Damage III	Health for Damage
Freeman Sword	This wooden sword is awarded to gladiators when they earn their freedom.	Common	Defeat Boss—the Duelist in Cyrene Gladiator Arena	Low	Critical Hit Rate I	None	None
Golden Wolf	Follow the Golden Wolf's trail, and he will lead you to the afterlife.	Legendary	Blacksmith, Loot	Low	Critical Hit Rate IV	Critical Hit Damage II	Health on Kill
Gudbrand Blade	A warrior with honor would have been heroic with this weapon.	Common	Blacksmith, Loot	Low	Critical Hit Rate I	None	None
Hepzefa's Sword	A mysterious weapon with unique attributes. Whispers of its magical properties have spread to the bounds of the known world.	Legendary	Complete Main Quest—Meet Aya at Siwa	High	Critical Hit Rate III	Adrenaline on Hurt II	On Fire
Humbaba's Fang	Gilgamesh is said to have carved this sword from the tooth of Humbaba the Terrible, a monstrous giant, after slaying him in combat.	Legendary	Nomad's Bazaar	High	Critical Hit Rate IV	Combo Multiplier I	Sleep on Hit
Khamudid Lost Blade	The defenses of Haat-wurat held fast because of courageous Hyksos fighters, prolonging Khamudi's reign for many years until its inevitable fall.	Common	Blacksmith, Loot	Low	Critical Hit Rate III	None	None
Mustapha's Blade	Forged in Mauretania, this blade unerringly slices through whatever meets its edge.	Legendary	Blacksmith, Loot	Extreme	Critical Hit Rate II	Bleeding on Hit II	Instant Charging
Rusted Blade	Lockjaw will finish what blood loss starts.	Common	Blacksmith, Loot	Low	Critical Hit Rate II	None	None
Sea People's Blade	A powerful weapon originating from the Mediterranean raider tribes. It carries a faint tang of the sea.	Rare	Blacksmith, Loot, Nomad's Bazaar	High	Critical Hit Rate I	Adrenaline Regeneration I	None
Shamshir	The scimitar's deadly predecessor.	Rare	Uplay	Medium	Critical Hit Rate II	Adrenaline Regeneration I	None
Silver Wind	Its beautiful engravings belie its dangerous nature.	Legendary	E-Store, Nomad's Bazaar	High	Critical Hit Rate II	Adrenaline Regeneration III	Low Health Critical
Sword of the Free	The crowd gasped as Julius Caesar held the sword aloft. With one flick of his wrist, he could have cut off the Champion's head. Instead, he held the pommel toward the bloodied man. Gave the Champion this weapon and with it, his freedom.	Rare	Complete Side Quest—Are You Not Entertained?	Medium	Critical Hit Rate II	Bleeding on Hit II	None
Thutmosid Sword	Very reliable swords made the fortune of Thutmose Manahpirya's common troops.	Common	Blacksmith, Loot	High	Critical Hit Rate I	None	None

INTRODUCTION

THE ESSENTIALS

MAIN QUESTS

SIDE QUESTS

ACTIVITIES

ATLAS

REFERENCE & ANALYSIS

SICKLE SWORD

DISMANTLE RESOURCES: Bronze, Iron   **MUTUAL ATTRIBUTE:** Bleeding on Hit

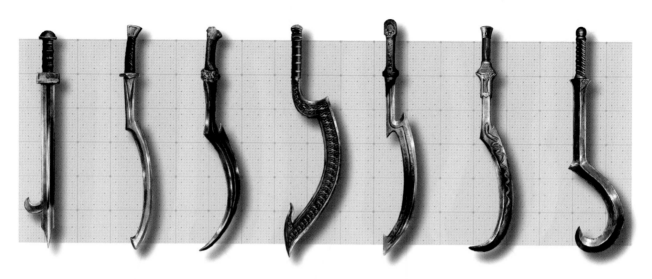

AVAILABLE SICKLE SWORDS

NAME	DESCRIPTION	RARITY	HOW TO ACQUIRE	DAMAGE	UNIQUE ATTRIBUTE	RARE ATTRIBUTE	LEGENDARY ATTRIBUTE
Aruna	A relic from Thutmose III's campaign against the city of Megiddo.	Legendary	E-Store, Nomad's Bazaar	High	Bleeding on Hit III	Adrenaline on Hurt II	Low health Critical
Battle of Gibeon Blade	An evolution of the agricultural sickle, the Khopesh was used by pharaoh Shoshenq's infantry in Gibeon.	Common	Blacksmith, Loot	High	Bleeding on Hit I	None	None
Berserker Blade	Legends say this sword saps the life of its wielder, though it offers them great power in exchange.	Legendary	Blacksmith, Loot	Extreme	Bleeding on Hit I	Adrenaline on Hurt I	Low Health Critical
Bronze Khopesh	A sword trusty enough for both the lowliest peasant and the loftiest pharaoh.	Common	Blacksmith, Loot	Low	Bleeding on Hit II	None	None
Canaanite Blade	This blade embodies the ferocity in battle for which the Canaanites are known.	Rare	Blacksmith, Loot, Nomad's Bazaar	High	Bleeding on Hit I	Adrenaline Regeneration I	None
Devotee of Montu	Any sons of Montu's warrior ideal was to become one of the Mighty Bulls or to die protecting the temple at Karnak.	Common	Blacksmith, Loot	Low	Bleeding on Hit I	None	None
Harpe of Perseus	Whether you find yourself beset by men or monsters, this weapon's sharp hook is perfect for catching your enemies off guard.	Rare	Blacksmith, Loot, Nomad's Bazaar	Low	Critical Hit Rate II	Bleeding on Hit II	None
Imitation Siwan Khopesh	A fake Khopesh that's not even from Siwa. Every effort was spared in its cheap, indifferent construction. However, the damage it does is remarkably genuine.	Legendary	Complete Side Quest—the Nomad's Bazaar	High	Bleeding on Hit II	Critical Hit Damage I	Health for Damage
Iron Shotel	This wickedly curved blade is used to hook shields and rip away enemy defenses.	Common	Blacksmith, Loot	Medium	Bleeding on Hit I	None	None
Khopesh sword	Adapted from the Canaanites, this cruelly curved sword is the symbol of Ptolemaic infantry weapon.	Common	Blacksmith, Loot	Medium	Bleeding on Hit III	None	None
Nilotic Khopesh	The annual flooding of the Nile brought life. This simple Khopesh from a follower of Khnum brings death.	Common	Blacksmith, Loot	Medium	Bleeding on Hit II	None	None
Pearl of Dur-Jakin	King Sargon II received this sword from the hands of King Marduk-apla-iddina when he conquered Babylonia.	Legendary	Nomad's Bazaar	High	Bleeding on Hit II	Critical Hit Damage I	Health on Hit
Sanaa Khopesh	This sword was given to Bayek by his father at the age of 13 after saving a caravan lost in the desert.	Common	Complete Side Quest—Bayek's House	Medium	Bleeding on Hit II	None	None
Sword of Ptah	A beautiful sickle sword, once said to be sacred to both Sekhmet and Serqet.	Rare	Complete Side Quest—Song of the Desert	Low	Bleeding on Hit III	Combo Multiplier I	None
Thorn	For those who like to play with their food before they eat it.	Legendary	E-Store, Nomad's Bazaar	High	Bleeding on Hit III	Critical Hit Rate II	Sleep on Hit
Viper's Tooth	Those who disturb the viper's nest will see how quickly it bites back.	Legendary	Blacksmith, Loot	Low	Bleeding on Hit IV	Combo Multiplier I	Poison on Hit

DUAL SWORDS

DISMANTLE RESOURCES: Bronze, Iron   **MUTUAL ATTRIBUTE:** Adrenaline Regeneration

INTRODUCTION

THE ESSENTIALS

MAIN QUESTS

SIDE QUESTS

ACTIVITIES

ATLAS

REFERENCE & ANALYSIS

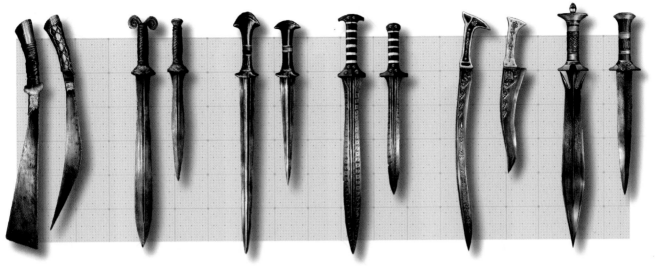

AVAILABLE DUAL SWORDS

NAME	DESCRIPTION	RARITY	HOW TO ACQUIRE	DAMAGE	UNIQUE ATTRIBUTE	RARE ATTRIBUTE	LEGENDARY ATTRIBUTE
Eyes of Horus	When "an eye for an eye" represents the spirit of the times, you need one blade for each.	Legendary	E-Store, Nomad's Bazaar	High	Adrenaline Regeneration II	Critical Hit Rate IV	Health on Kill
Fatal Duet	They'll sing in perfect unison until opening a throat, upon which their voices are joined by a discordant third.	Legendary	Blacksmith, Loot	Extreme	Adrenaline Regeneration III	Adrenaline on Kill I	Health on Kill
Hash and Slash	The only tale these blades tell is one of countless bodies sliced to bloody pulp.	Rare	Blacksmith, Loot	Medium	Adrenaline Regeneration II	Critical Hit Damage II	None
Jutes & Cimbri	Mercenaries from Jutland gave them their home names.	Common	Blacksmith, Loot	Damage Low	Adrenaline Regeneration III	None	None
Mirror Blades	These two blades bear an unnerving similarity, right down to their corresponding nicks and dents. It's almost as though they share a spiritual link.	Rare	Blacksmith, Loot	Low	Adrenaline Regeneration I	Combo Multiplier I	None
Motivational Duet	These blades work relentlessly so you don't have to.	Common	Blacksmith, Loot	High	Adrenaline Regeneration I	None	None
Scissor Blades	Chop chop, slash slash, slash, chop, slice, cut!	Common	Blacksmith, Loot	Low	Adrenaline Regeneration II	None	None
Storm Blades	Light as air, solid as hailstones, fast as the wind, and deadly as lightning.	Legendary	Blacksmith, Loot	High	Adrenaline Regeneration III	Critical Hit Rate II	Instant Charging
Wadjet's Knives	A sting to the neck and a stab to the gut. Your offering pleases the Cobra Goddess.	Legendary	E-Store, Nomad's Bazaar	High	Adrenaline Regeneration IV	Critical Hit Damage I	Poison on Hit

DISMANTLE RESOURCES: Bronze, Iron   **MUTUAL ATTRIBUTE:** Adrenaline on Kill

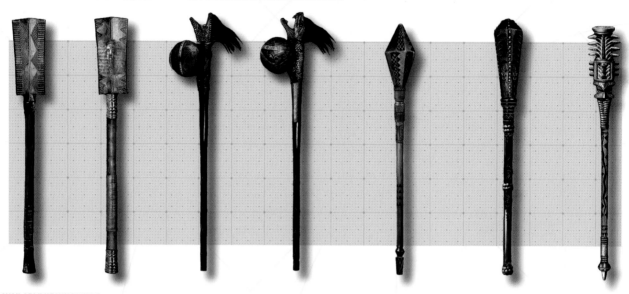

AVAILABLE HEAVY BLUNTS

NAME	DESCRIPTION	RARITY	HOW TO ACQUIRE	DAMAGE	UNIQUE ATTRIBUTE	RARE ATTRIBUTE	LEGENDARY ATTRIBUTE
Boredom Bane	Nicely crafted by worshippers of Ptah in Memphis.	Common	Blacksmith, Loot	Low	Adrenaline on Kill I	None	None
Bronze Bludgeon	Great care has been invested in the maintenance of this well-used club.	Common	Blacksmith, Loot	Low	Adrenaline on Kill II	None	None
Copper Mace	The weight of this weapon requires considerable strength from its wielder.	Legendary	Blacksmith, Loot	High	Adrenaline on Kill IV	Combo Multiplier I	Health on Hit
Diamond Exchange	This mace is as beautiful as it is vicious.	Common	Blacksmith, Loot	Medium	Adrenaline on Kill II	None	None
Eye of Ra	Ra created all forms of life; as their maker, he can also destroy them.	Legendary	E-Store, Nomad's Bazaar	High	Adrenaline on Kill III	Adrenaline on Hurt II	On Fire
Gruesome Mattock	Your enemies would do well to avoid the path of this weapon's swing.	Rare	Blacksmith, Loot	High	Adrenaline on Kill II	Bleeding on Hit I	None
Headache Remedy	This weapon causes headaches…and then cures them permanently.	Legendary	Blacksmith, Loot	Extreme	Adrenaline on Kill III	Adrenaline on Hurt II	Sleep on Hit
Mace	Do not be fooled by its commonplace appearance; this is a powerful weapon.	Common	Blacksmith, Loot	Medium	Adrenaline on Kill I	None	None
Marcus's Thunder Ball	With it, you will not be lied to, be afraid, or remain silent.	Common	Blacksmith, Loot	Low	Adrenaline on Kill III	None	None
Minoan Poppy Pin	This Cretan mace from the Kaphti kingdom made its way into Egypt to replicate what it did home; breaking skulls.	Common	Blacksmith, Loot	High	Adrenaline on Kill I	None	None
No Borders	Carved to commemorate the founding of the Kingdom of Numidia, it was left behind by Juba II along with a record of the land's customs.	Legendary	Nomad's Bazaar	High	Adrenaline on Kill II	Adrenaline on Hurt III	Health for Damage
Sharur	This enchanted mace, whose name means "Smasher of Thousands," was once wielded by Ninurta, a Mesopotamian god.	Rare	Complete Side Quest—Mound of Grain and Gold	High	Adrenaline on Kill III	Critical Hit Rate I	None
Skull-Breaker	An ancient Mesopotamian weapon fashioned from a thick tree branch.	Rare	Blacksmith, Loot	Medium	Adrenaline on Kill III	Adrenaline Regeneration I	None
Spade of All Trades	Some might dismiss this as a gardening implement, but it serves just as well in a fight.	Common	Blacksmith, Loot	Medium	Adrenaline on Kill I	None	None
Sycamore	Carved from the bough of a giant sycamore tree, this weapon is as solid as it gets.	Rare	Uplay	Medium	Adrenaline on Kill I	Critical Hit Rate II	None
The Uab Block	A very convenient and bellicose way to carry a big metal block to the next forge.	Common	Blacksmith, Loot	Medium	Adrenaline on Kill II	None	None

HEAVY BLADES

DISMANTLE RESOURCES: Bronze, Iron   **MUTUAL ATTRIBUTE:** Adrenaline on Hurt

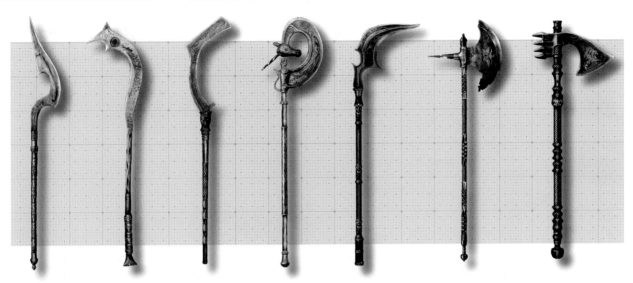

AVAILABLE HEAVY BLADES

NAME	DESCRIPTION	RARITY	HOW TO ACQUIRE	DAMAGE	UNIQUE ATTRIBUTE	RARE ATTRIBUTE	LEGENDARY ATTRIBUTE
Battleaxe	What it lacks in elegance it makes up for in destructive force and intimidation.	Common	Blacksmith, Loot	Low	Adrenaline on Hurt II	None	None
Bronze Axe	More suited for cutting down trees, but it'll protect you in a pinch.	Common	Blacksmith, Loot	Medium	Adrenaline on Hurt I	None	None
Bronze Epsilon Axe	This three-hole blade fixed to the shaft is all about cutting and slashing.	Common	Blacksmith, Loot	High	Adrenaline on Hurt I	None	None
Crescent Axe	This pernicious weapon has a unique look. Its creator was skilled and produced an efficient yet unrestrained weapon.	Common	Blacksmith, Loot	Low	Adrenaline on Hurt III	None	None
Cutting Axe	A simple blade designed for maximum power in each swing.	Rare	Blacksmith, Loot	High	Adrenaline on Hurt II	Critical Hit Damage II	None
Fan Axe	This ornate axe appears to be a ceremonial weapon but still holds a keen edge.	Rare	Blacksmith, Loot	Low	Adrenaline on Hurt III	Combo Multiplier I	None
Headsplitter	Your own personal problem-solver.	Legendary	Blacksmith, Loot	Extreme	Adrenaline on Hurt III	Adrenaline on Kill II	Low Health Critical
Leviathan	Perhaps not powerful enough to defeat the eponymous sea monster, but more than sufficient to capsize your enemies.	Legendary	Defeat Elite Boss—the Brothers in Krokodilopolis Gladiator Arena	Extreme	Adrenaline on Hurt II	Adrenaline Regeneration I	Health Gain on kill
Medusa	The carven head that adorns this weapon is the last thing your foes will ever see.	Rare	Complete Side Quest—Grand Theft Cargo	Medium	Adrenaline on Hurt IV	Adrenaline On Kill I	None
Mushussu	The mythological beast for which this blade is named might be lost to time, but its power still rings true.	Legendary	E-Store, Nomad's Bazaar	High	Adrenaline on Hurt III	Critical Hit Damage III	Sleep on Hit
Nebuchadnezzar's Wrath	The axe used by King Nebuchadnezzar to execute his enemies is now yours to wield.	Legendary	Nomad's Bazaar	High	Adrenaline on Hurt IV	Critical Hit Rate II	Low Health Critical
Scalloped Head Axe	Works at best on bare, armor-free bones.	Common	Blacksmith, Loot	Low	Adrenaline on Hurt I	None	None
Serpent Axe	This axe's unusual shape will slither right past your opponent's guard.	Legendary	Blacksmith, Loot	High	Adrenaline on Hurt IV	Bleeding on Hit II	Poison on Hit
Shark Fin	If you've seen it, it's already too late.	Legendary	E-Store, Nomad's Bazaar	High	Adrenaline on Hurt II	Critical Hit Rate III	On Fire
Sharp Cut	The weighty head of this weapon will help you cleave through your enemies.	Common	Blacksmith, Loot	Medium	Adrenaline on Hurt II	None	None

INTRODUCTION

THE ESSENTIALS

MAIN QUESTS

SIDE QUESTS

ACTIVITIES

ATLAS

REFERENCE & ANALYSIS

SCEPTERS

DISMANTLE RESOURCES: Bronze, Iron   **MUTUAL ATTRIBUTE:** Combo Multiplier

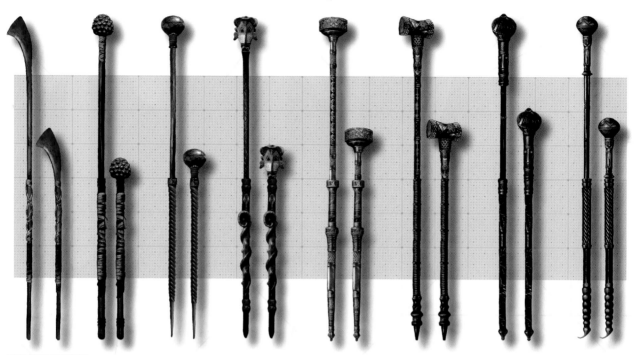

AVAILABLE SCEPTERS

NAME	DESCRIPTION	RARITY	HOW TO ACQUIRE	DAMAGE	UNIQUE ATTRIBUTE	RARE ATTRIBUTE	LEGENDARY ATTRIBUTE
Acacia Rod	Perfect for bludgeoning your opponents, this weapon's water-resistant nature makes it easy to wash off the blood.	Rare	Blacksmith, Loot, Nomad's Bazaar	Medium	Combo Multiplier III	Critical Hit Rate I	None
Alexandria's Light	This scepter belonged to the Commander assigned to the defense of the Great Pharos.	Legendary	E-Store, Nomad's Bazaar	High	Combo Multiplier II	Critical Hit Rate III	On Fire
Apep's Staff	The giant serpent's own personal scepter. You'd swear you've heard it emitting a faint hiss.	Legendary	E-Store, Nomad's Bazaar	High	Combo Multiplier III	Adrenaline on Hurt III	Poison on Hit
Bladed Scepter	A thin steel blade adds a savage bite to this ferocious weapon.	Rare	Blacksmith, Loot	High	Combo Multiplier II	Bleeding on Hit I	None
Bringer of Chaos	Some detest chaos; others revel in it. This weapon is for the latter type.	Common	Blacksmith, Loot	Medium	Combo Multiplier II	None	None
Ceremonial Staff	This sturdy brass staff is strangely warm to the touch.	Legendary	Blacksmith, Loot	High	Combo Multiplier IV	Adrenaline on Kill I	On Fire
Cypriot Gabbro Head	Probably made its way from Kypros, the possession of Cleopatra's ancestors.	Common	Blacksmith, Loot	Low	Combo Multiplier III	None	None
Hasanlu Skeptron	This baton found in Sais was forgotten centuries ago by a Persian warrior in this former capital.	Common	Blacksmith, Loot	Medium	Combo Multiplier II	None	None
Nubian Scepter	Long ago, the Nubians reigned over the whole of Egypt. This scepter was their symbol of power.	Legendary	Nomad's Bazaar	High	Combo Multiplier II	Adrenaline Regeneration III	Sleep on Hit
Peasant's Scepter	A robust stick wrapped in leather cords. Its flat head whistles through the air to jab at your enemies.	Common	Blacksmith, Loot	Medium	Combo Multiplier I	None	None
Pharoah's Mace	Strike down all who oppose your rule. With every hit, a more grievous wound appears.	Common	Blacksmith, Loot	Low	Combo Multiplier II	None	None
Raneb's Hammer	One solid hit from this weapon will knock the light from your enemy's eyes.	Legendary	Blacksmith, Loot	Extreme	Combo Multiplier III	Adrenaline Regeneration I	Low Health Critical
Scepter of Amun	Rumored to be the scepter given to Alexander by the Oracle of Siwa after he was pronounced son of the god Amun.	Rare	Complete Side Quest— Making History	High	Combo Multiplier II	Critical Hit Damage II	None
Scorpion Sting	Head or tail—you'll suffer regardless of which end hits you.	Legendary	E-Store, Nomad's Bazaar	High	Combo Multiplier III	Adrenaline on Hurt II	Poison on Hit
Siwan Scepter	This long weapon is made of a single sycamore tree core, harvested at the oasis of Siwa.	Common	Blacksmith, Loot	High	Combo Multiplier I	None	None
Staff of Sehetep	This holy staff of Sobek seems to emit a pungent smell of incense and blood.	Legendary	Complete Side Quest—All in Bad Faith	Medium	Combo Multiplier II	Bleeding on Hit I	Health on Kill

SPEAR

INTRODUCTION

THE ESSENTIALS

MAIN QUESTS

SIDE QUESTS

ACTIVITIES

ATLAS

REFERENCE & ANALYSIS

DISMANTLE RESOURCES: Bronze, Cedarwood, Iron   **MUTUAL ATTRIBUTE:** Critical Hit Damage

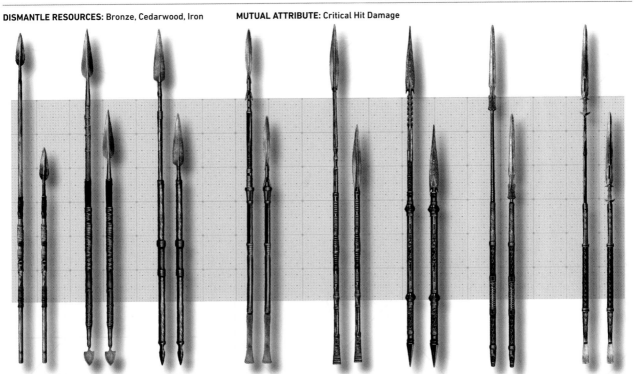

AVAILABLE SPEARS

NAME	DESCRIPTION	RARITY	HOW TO ACQUIRE	DAMAGE	UNIQUE ATTRIBUTE	RARE ATTRIBUTE	LEGENDARY ATTRIBUTE
Cyrene's Spear	A spear whose origins date back at least 400 years. Found in the Cyrene mountains, it was most likely forged for Battus, the founder of Cyraenica.	Legendary	Complete Side Quest—Loose Lips	High	Critical Hit Damage III	Adrenaline on Kill II	Low Health Critical
Golden Feather	Light as a feather but solid as gold, its thrust can pierce any material.	Legendary	E-Store, Nomad's Bazaar	High	Critical Hit Damage III	Critical Hit Rate II	Sleep on Hit
Handy Spear	A convenient tool to get rid of foes.	Common	Blacksmith, Loot	High	Critical Hit Damage I	None	None
Iron Spear	A sharp blade on the end of a long pole. The perfect poking stick.	Common	Blacksmith, Loot	Medium	Critical Hit Damage I	None	None
Lance of Anhur	Nothing can stay the hand of Anhur, Slayer of Enemies.	Legendary	E-Store, Nomad's Bazaar	High	Critical Hit Damage II	Adrenaline Regeneration III	Health on Hit
Leaf-Shaped Impaler	Quite possibly made in Ta-senet to do just what seems right.	Common	Blacksmith, Loot	Low	Critical Hit Damage III	None	None
Light Spear	Most often used from horseback to pierce enemies from afar and then draw them in close.	Common	Blacksmith, Loot	Low	Critical Hit Damage II	None	None
Needle	Stick 'em with the pointy end.	Rare	Blacksmith, Loot, Nomad's Bazaar	Low	Critical Hit Damage IV	Bleeding on Hit II	None
The Phoenix	Like its namesake, this sarissa rises from the ashes of the most unlikely circumstances.	Legendary	Nomad's Bazaar	High	Critical Hit Damage III	Critical Hit Rate I	Health on Kill
Pilum	A rugged javelin commonly used by Roman troops.	Rare	Blacksmith, Loot	High	Critical Hit Damage II	Adrenaline on Hurt I	None
Sarissa	Massive spear equipped by Ptolemaic guards. The Macedonian army used this weapon's long-range capabilities to get the drop on opposing forces.	Legendary	Blacksmith, Loot	High	Critical Hit Damage III	Adrenaline on Kill I	Health for Damage
Sekhmet's Spear	Once this spear tastes the blood of your enemies, it can only be sated by their destruction.	Legendary	Blacksmith, Loot	Extreme	Critical Hit Damage II	Critical Hit Rate I	Health on Kill
Shooting Star	Among the names suggested for this magnificent weapon was "Lung-Puncturer," but strangely, "Shooting Star" proved more popular.	Rare	Complete Side Quest—Fair Trade	Medium	Critical Hit Damage II	Critical Hit Rate II	None
The Trial	Give a man a stick and he'll walk. Give a man a spear and he'll hunt.	Rare	Uplay	Medium	Critical Hit Damage II	Adrenaline on Hurt I	None

BOWS
HUNTER BOWS

DISMANTLE RESOURCE: Cedarwood   **MUTUAL ATTRIBUTE:** Charging Speed

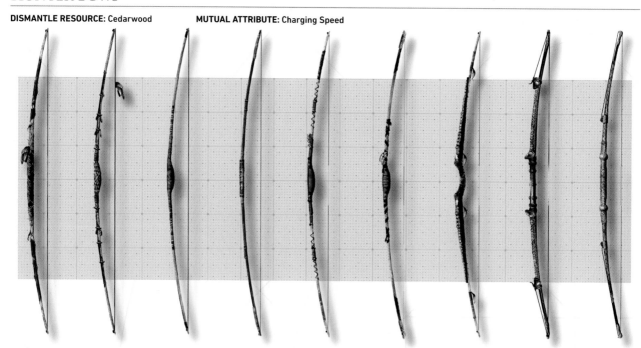

AVAILABLE HUNTER BOWS

NAME	DESCRIPTION	RARITY	HOW TO ACQUIRE	HEALTH	UNIQUE ATTRIBUTE	RARE ATTRIBUTE	LEGENDARY ATTRIBUTE
Achilles Heel Seeker	The design of this bow is said to have derived from the one wielded by Paris.	Common	Blacksmith, Loot	High	Charging Speed I	None	None
Alchemist's Dream	The limbs of this elegant bow are fashioned of coal dust and ashes encased in gold, making it nimble and easy to deploy.	Rare	Complete Side Quest—Predator to Prey	Medium	Charging Speed II	Critical Hit Rate I	None
Ash Bow	A strong, steady weapon that keeps you calm in even the most trying situations.	Legendary	Blacksmith, Loot	Extreme	Charging Speed III	Bleeding on Hit I	Ranged Hit Multiplier
Big Game Bow	Just like pharaohs of old, you too can hunt large game of Kemet.	Common	Blacksmith, Loot	Medium	Charging Speed III	None	None
Bow of Arash	An arrow loosed from this bow can travel from dawn to noon.	Rare	Complete Side Quest—Pax Romana	High	Charging Speed II	Critical Hit Damage I	None
Cobra Royale	Twin cobras guarding the gates of the underworld help the hunter to strike true.	Legendary	E-Store, Nomad's Bazaar	High	Charging Speed III	Bleeding on Hit III	Poison on Hit
Combat Bow	Suitable for hunting animals, but ideal for use on human targets.	Common	Blacksmith, Loot	Low	Charging Speed II	None	None
Deathstorm	Even the bravest warrior weeps to see this bow unslung on the battlefield.	Legendary	Blacksmith, Loot	Medium	Adrenaline on Kill II	On Fire	Charging Speed IV
Desheret Patrol Bow	Desert patrollers would use this bow to chase invaders, criminals, and fugitives in the dunes.	Common	Blacksmith, Loot	Low	Charging Speed III	None	None
Gazelle Bow	Carefully constructed from gazelle horn and acacia wood, this bow has a strong draw and true aim.	Common	Blacksmith, Loot	High	Charging Speed I	None	None
Hunting Bow	Ideal for hunting animals, but suitable for human prey as well.	Common	Blacksmith, Loot	Medium	Charging Speed I	None	None
Im-Khent Bow	Inhabitants of the Im-Khent Nome will prefer to communicate with ranged tools rather than risking the dangerous crocodile-infested Nile.	Common	Blacksmith, Loot	Low	Charging Speed I	None	None
Lion's Mane	Forged by Vulcan himself, this bow displays the god's mastery of metalsmithing.	Legendary	E-Store, Nomad's Bazaar	High	Charging Speed III	Critical Hit Damage III	Health on Kill
Longbow	Accurate at long range. Sometimes used to send messages by affixing a rolled-up papyrus to an arrow shaft.	Common	Blacksmith, Loot	High	Charging Speed I	None	None
Nubian Bow	Deployed by Nubian archers for decades, this is a basic but effective weapon.	Common	Blacksmith, Loot	Medium	Charging Speed III	None	None
Obsidian Bow	Every twang of this bow's string marks a union of stygian glass and crimson blood.	Rare	Blacksmith, Loot	High	Charging Speed II	Critical Hit Damage II	None
Overseer of All Disputes	Sometimes you simply need the right tool for the right task.	Common	Blacksmith, Loot	Medium	Charging Speed II	None	None
Self-Help Remedy	The gift of getting things done.	Common	Blacksmith, Loot			None	None
Serpent's Scourge	Aim it high, aim it true, pull the string, and follow through.	Common	Blacksmith, Loot	Medium	Charging Speed II	None	None
Ta-Sety Bow	Ta-Sety means "Land of the Bow," and no other bow could serve as a better representative.	Legendary	Nomad's Bazaar	High	Charging Speed II	Critical Hit Rate II	Low Health Critical
Wolfsbane	Determination, patience, focus. Death's spread is gradual, but relentless.	Rare	Blacksmith, Loot	Medium	Charging Speed IV	Critical Hit Rate II	None

LIGHT BOWS

DISMANTLE RESOURCE: Cedarwood   **MUTUAL ATTRIBUTE:** Rate of Fire

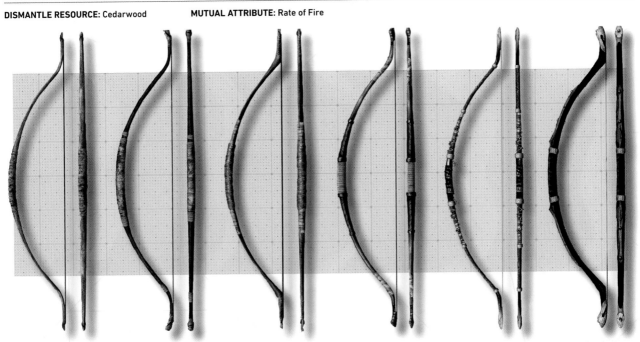

AVAILABLE LIGHT BOWS

NAME	DESCRIPTION	RARITY	HOW TO ACQUIRE	HEALTH	UNIQUE ATTRIBUTE	RARE ATTRIBUTE	LEGENDARY ATTRIBUTE
Apedemak	All Nubian warriors acknowledge the power of Apedemak, the lion-headed god of war worshipped throughout Upper Egypt.	Legendary	Nomad's Bazaar	Medium	Rate of Fire IV	Critical Hit Damage II	On Fire
Arc Bow	A light weapon used to target enemies in quick succession.	Common	Blacksmith, Loot	Medium	Rate of Fire I	None	None
Bitter Bow	This bow's envenomed arrows bring a devious end to an honorable battle.	Rare	Blacksmith, Loot	Low	Rate of Fire II	Combo Multiplier II	None
Bow of Wadjet	A bow crafted in the image of Wadjet, patron of Lower Egypt. Its shaft is adorned with cobra skin and feels cold to the touch.	Legendary	Complete Side Quest—Sleepless Nights	High	Rate of Fire III	Critical Hit Damage II	Poison on Hit
Composite Bow	Light, costly weapon favored by charioteers. The ideal hunting bow.	Legendary	Blacksmith, Loot	High	Rate of Fire IV	Adrenaline on Kill II	Health on Hit
Corrupted Soul	This bow's use might consume the life of a warrior lesser than yourself.	Legendary	Uplay	High	Rate of Fire III	Bleeding on Hit II	Low Health Critical
Griffin	If the lion is the king of beasts and the eagle king of birds, the Griffin is the ruler of them all.	Legendary	E-Store, Nomad's Bazaar	High	Rate of Fire III	Combo Multiplier II	Elevation Multiplier
Hunger of the Underworld	Once the weighing of hearts is complete, the firstborn son of Osiris devours those of the unrighteous.	Legendary	E-Store, Nomad's Bazaar	High	Rate of Fire IV	Bleeding on Hit II	Health on Kill
Hyperion	This gilded Grecian bow is beautiful enough to delight the gods. Its sturdy construction allows the nocking of arrows at high speed.	Rare	Complete Side Quest—The Heart of Faiyum	Medium	Rate of Fire III	Critical Hit Rate II	None
Neith	With the blessing of Neith, goddess of war and the hunt, any arrow loosed from this bow will strike true.	Legendary	Blacksmith, Loot	Extreme	Rate of Fire III	Bleeding on Hit I	Extra Arrow
Ousirmaatre Setepenre	Funny that someone would name their light bow after pharaoh Ramses the Great.	Common	Blacksmith, Loot	High	Rate of Fire I	None	None
The Parthian	This weapon was popularized by the Parthian cataphract, a heavily armored horse archer.	Rare	Blacksmith, Loot	High	Rate of Fire I	Critical Hit Damage II	None
Quick Bow	Fires faster than you can say "hippopotamus."	Common	Blacksmith, Loot	Low	Rate of Fire II	None	None
Toxotai Bow	Scythians carry this kind of bow, along a whip and a small sword.	Common	Blacksmith, Loot	Low	Rate of Fire III	None	None

INTRODUCTION

THE ESSENTIALS

MAIN QUESTS

SIDE QUESTS

ACTIVITIES

ATLAS

REFERENCE & ANALYSIS

DISMANTLE RESOURCE: Cedarwood   **MUTUAL ATTRIBUTE:** Precision

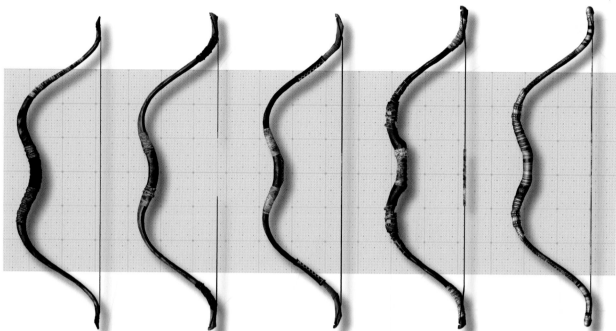

AVAILABLE WARRIOR BOWS

NAME	DESCRIPTION	RARITY	HOW TO ACQUIRE	HEALTH	UNIQUE ATTRIBUTE	RARE ATTRIBUTE	LEGENDARY ATTRIBUTE
Aldebaran	The Follower hits hard, toppling even the most powerful of enemies.	Rare	Blacksmith, Loot	Medium	Precision II	Bleeding on Hit I	None
Battos' Bow	Apollo bade the great Battos I of Cyrene to build a shining city by the sacred spring. Legend says the king fired an arrow that pierced the heavens on that day.	Rare	Complete Side Quest—Founding Father	Medium	Precision II	Critical Hit Damage II	None
The Crimson Death	Another exquisite offering from the Numidian cavalry, demonstrating their prowess in mounted archery.	Legendary	Nomad's Bazaar	Medium	Precision II	Combo Multiplier III	Low Health Critical
Crown Jewel	Don't be fooled by its elaborate ornamentation; this weapon is a deadly one.	Rare	Uplay	Medium	Precision II	Adrenaline on Kill II	None
The Fourth Plague	A thousand tiny stings sap the vitality of any target.	Legendary	Blacksmith, Loot	High	Precision IV	Combo Multiplier II	Health on Hit
Hippopotamus Charge	Why shoot one arrow at a time when you can shoot five?	Rare	Blacksmith, Loot	High	Precision I	Critical Hit Rate I	None
Khryselakatos	Artemis protects you while raining down arrows upon your enemies.	Legendary	Blacksmith, Loot	Extreme	Precision II	Adrenaline on Kill II	Elevation Multiplier
Priest of Ma'at	Shoot first, ask questions later... What? Everyone needs a philosophy.	Rare	Defeat Boss—Hammer in Cyrene Gladiator Arena	High	Precision II	Bleeding on Hit II	None
Rain of Arrows	Deploys five arrows simultaneously. Use at close range to inflict maximum damage.	Common	Blacksmith, Loot	Medium	Precision I	None	None
Sty	The favored multi-arrowed Nubian bow, simply.	Common	Blacksmith, Loot	Low	Precision III	None	None
Til-Tuba Bow	This Assyrian bow was quite useful in the battle at Til-Tuba for foot archers.	Common	Blacksmith, Loot	High	Precision I	None	None
Wall of Sand	The perfect bow for getting out of tight corners. Its arrows sting like a grain of sand in the eye.	Common	Blacksmith, Loot	Low	Precision II	None	None
Wings of Ashur	Arrows shall fall endlessly from the heavens onto the heads of Ashur's enemies.	Legendary	E-Store, Nomad's Bazaar	High	Precision III	Combo Multiplier III	Elevation Multiplier

Predator Bows

DISMANTLE RESOURCE: Cedarwood   **MUTUAL ATTRIBUTE:** Stealth Damage

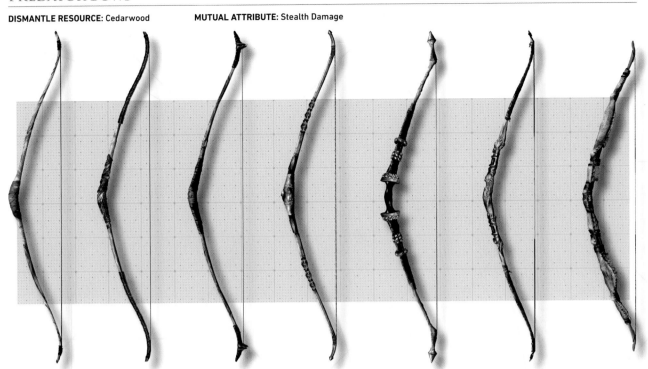

AVAILABLE PREDATOR BOWS

NAME	DESCRIPTION	RARITY	HOW TO ACQUIRE	HEALTH	UNIQUE ATTRIBUTE	RARE ATTRIBUTE	LEGENDARY ATTRIBUTE
Amenhotep's Bow	In skilled hands, this bow carries on the martial tradition of "he who inspires great terror."	Legendary	Blacksmith, Loot	High	Stealth Damage IV	Combo Multiplier II	Health on Kill
Ancestral Bow	A humble-looking bow made from surprisingly sturdy materials, optimized for long-range use. Passed down over many generations, the bow's crude appearance belies its almost unnatural precision.	Rare	Complete Side Quest—Seven Farmers	Medium	Stealth Damage II	Bleeding on Hit II	None
Concealed Garment	This weapon is devoted to Neith, the concealed goddess of Sais. It shall be worn during the Feast of Lamps.	Common	Blacksmith, Loot	High	Stealth Damage I	None	None
Copper Arc	This classic Hyksos weapon may look antiquated but remains as deadly as the day it was made.	Common	Blacksmith, Loot	Medium	Stealth Damage I	None	None
Desert Companion	Hiding from an enemy in the dunes isn't as hard with this bow. It gives a little more confidence but does not prevent exhaustion and haze.	Common	Blacksmith, Loot	Medium	Stealth Damage II	None	None
Hades	Ushering souls across the Styx, one arrow at a time.	Rare	Blacksmith, Loot	High	Stealth Damage I	Adrenaline on Kill II	None
Jebel Barkal	Under King Piye's command, each Nubian General received a gift of this bow on the occasion of a victorious campaign.	Legendary	Nomad's Bazaar	Medium	Stealth Damage III	Combo Multiplier II	Ranged Hit Multiplier
Lord of Bones	This bow inflicts the creeping chill of death on its targets, moments before they come face-to-face with Anubis.	Legendary	E-Store, Nomad's Bazaar	High	Stealth Damage III	Bleeding on Hit III	Poison on Hit
Mute Bow	The arrow cleaves a voiceless path; mute, yet louder than any spoken word.	Rare	Blacksmith, Loot	Medium	Stealth Damage II	Critical Hit Damage II	None
Smoke and Mirrors	You can rest easy so long as this bow never leaves your side.	Legendary	Blacksmith, Loot	Extreme	Stealth Damage III	Critical Hit Rate II	On Fire
Trophy Hunter	With this bow to hand, you are the apex predator.	Legendary	Defeat War Elephant—Qetesh & Resheph	High	Stealth Damage II	Critical Hit Damage II	Elevation Multiplier
Valkyrie Operator	This bow can strike from afar but can also be used as an observation tool.	Common	Blacksmith, Loot	Low	Stealth Damage III	None	None
Victoria	A harmonious heart is a victorious one.	Common	Blacksmith, Loot	Medium	Stealth Damage II	None	None
Whisper of Death	With a gentle hiss and a punctured skull, the Whisper comes and claims its toll.	Common	Blacksmith, Loot	Low	Stealth Damage II	None	None
Wildland Bow	Despite its fragile appearance, this bow fires with surgical precision.	Common	Blacksmith, Loot	Medium	Stealth Damage I	None	None

SHIELDS

DISMANTLE RESOURCES: Bronze, Iron   **MUTUAL ATTRIBUTE:** Melee/Ranged Resistance

AVAILABLE SHIELDS

NAME	DESCRIPTION	RARITY	HOW TO ACQUIRE	HEALTH	UNIQUE ATTRIBUTE	RARE ATTRIBUTE	LEGENDARY ATTRIBUTE
Aegean Prince	Once belonging to an Aegean prince, this bronze shield sports an intriguing metalwork design.	Rare	Blacksmith, Loot	Health: High	Ranged Resistance I	Adrenaline Absorption on Block II	None
Alexander's Shield	Rumored to be the Shield of Achilles, forged by Hephaestus himself. Seemingly flimsy as a parade shield, it has proven itself much more than that.	Rare	Complete Side Quest—Plight of the Rebels	Health: High	Melee Resistance I	Fire Resistance II	None
Antigonus Shield	A light shield, designed by a Macedonian general, that allows for fast troop movement.	Rare	Complete Side Quest—Conflicts of Interest	Health: Medium	Ranged Resistance II	Fire Resistance II	None
Bird of Prey	This shield sits so lightly on your arm that it seems to glide on wings.	Rare	Uplay	Health: High	Melee Resistance II	Fire Resistance II	None
Bronze Shield	The closest thing to a guardian spirit. Bronze and leather combine to produce an item both substantial and supple.	Common	Blacksmith, Loot	Health: Medium	Ranged Resistance I	None	None
Compendium	Wearing this shield sends a tingle up your arm. Memories of foes long dead flood into your mind. A lion's roar echoes in your ears. Must be your imagination…	Legendary	Complete Side Quest—General Issue	Health: High	Bleeding on Block	Ranged Resistance IV	Damage Absorption on Block III
Djoser's Pride	Even future god-kings need sturdy, well-balanced protection.	Legendary	Blacksmith, Loot	Health: Extreme	Sleep on Block	Melee Resistance II	Damage Absorption on Parry III
Kush Shield	A typical Kush warrior's shield.	Rare	Uplay	Health: Medium	Melee Resistance I	Ranged Resistance III	None
Madu's Shield	A beautiful shield made by the skilled hands of Master Blacksmith Madu himself.	Common	Blacksmith, Loot	Health: Medium	Melee Resistance I	None	None
Medjay Shield	A trusty shield. Light, mobile, and good-looking too.	Common	Bayek's default shield, Blacksmith, Loot	Health: Medium	Melee Resistance I	None	None
Medusa's Gaze	Stare at this shield too long and it might petrify you in the blink of an eye.	Legendary	Nomad's Bazaar	Health: High	Ranged Resistance III	Damage Absorption on Block III	Sleep on Block
Metal Shield	Not exactly shiny new, but reliable and sturdy.	Common	Blacksmith, Loot	Health: Low	Melee Resistance III	None	None
Phalangite Shield	A large, yet lightweight phalanx shield, usually paired with a spear or scepter. This one was the property of a high-ranking general.	Legendary	Blacksmith, Loot	Health: Extreme	Poison on Block	Ranged Resistance II	Adrenaline Absorption on Block III
Phalanx Shield	A classic defensive weapon used by Ptolemaic infantry units.	Rare	Blacksmith, Loot	Health: Medium	Melee Resistance II	Damage Absorption on Block II	None
Reinforced Shield	This shield has fended off death more times than its bearer has fingers.	Legendary	Blacksmith, Loot	Health: High	Melee Resistance IV	Ranged Resistance II	Damage Absorption on Parry I
Remission	This piece was commissioned by Pompey as a gift to Ptolemy XII Auletes.	Rare	Complete Side Quest—Farms of Dionysias	Health: Medium	Melee Resistance III	Ranged Resistance III	None
Scorpio	A warning to malicious souls.	Legendary	E-Store, Nomad's Bazaar	Health: High	Ranged Resistance III	Damage Absorption on Parry II	Poison on Block
Shield of Hilarus	A variety of metals were used in the creation of this masterwork by Alexandria's finest blacksmith. The pride and joy of its owner, Hilarus Maximus.	Rare	Complete Side Quest—The Champion	Health: Medium	Melee Resistance III	Damage Absorption on Parry III	None
SPQR	A symbol of the Roman Republic, representing the Senate and the people of Rome.	Legendary	E-Store or Nomad's Bazaar	Health: Medium	Ranged Resistance III	Damage Absorption on Parry II	Bleeding on Block
Wooden Shield	Padded with two layers of coarse fabric, this shield can soften blows without breaking into splinters.	Common	Blacksmith, Loot	Health: Low	Melee Resistance II	None	None
Worn Shield	One rarely imagines tools of war as relatives, but in this case, the name "Grandpa" seems appropriate.	Common	Blacksmith, Loot	Health: Low	Ranged Resistance II	None	None

LIST OF ATTRIBUTES

Common weapons and shields have only one attribute, Rare holds two attributes, while Legendary equipment possesses three attributes. The following table explains the effects of each attribute.

ATTRIBUTE	DESCRIPTION
Bleeding on Block	Blocking attacks have a 20% chance to inflict Bleeding on the attacker
Cursed	Bayek gains 200% damage output but his health is capped at 33%
Elevation Multiplier	Shots taken from 3 meters higher than the target deal double damage
Extra Arrow	Bayek can load two extra arrows
Health for Critical	While below 20% health, all attacks do critical damage
Health on Hit	Bayek recovers 1% of his health each time he hits an enemy
Health on Kill	Bayek recovers 15% of his health each time he kills an enemy
Health on Parry	After a successful parry, Bayek recovers 50% of the incoming damage
Instant Charging	Charged Heavy Attacks are instant
On Fire	Attacks have a chance to set enemies on fire
Poison on Block	Blocking attacks have a 20% chance to inflict Poison on the attacker
Poison on Hit	Attacks have a 20% chance to poison enemies
Ranged Hit Multiplier	Shots taken at more than 20 meters from the target deal double damage
Sleep on Block	Blocking attacks have a 10% chance to inflict Sleep on the attacker
Sleep on Hit	Attacks have a 10% chance to put enemies to sleep

ATTRIBUTE	DESCRIPTION	X VALUE FOR LEVEL			
		I	II	III	IV
Adrenaline on Hurt	Upon receiving damage, Bayek gains [X] Adrenaline Points	10	15	20	25
Adrenaline on Kill	When Bayek kills an enemy, he gains [X] Adrenaline Points	20	30	40	50
Adrenaline on Parry	When Bayek parries an attack, he gains [X] Adrenaline Points	20	30	40	50
Adrenaline Regeneration	While holding this weapon, Bayek regenerates [X] Adrenaline Points per second	1	2	3	4
Bleeding on Hit	Attacks have a [X]% chance to inflict Bleeding	10	20	30	40
Charging Speed	Bow Charge Duration is reduced by [X]%	10	20	30	40
Combo Multiplier	With each consecutive hit, damage is multiplied by [X]%	110	115	120	125
Critical Hit Damage	Bayek's Critical Hits inflict [X]% more damage	180	220	260	300
Critical Hit Rate	When Bayek attacks, he has [X]% chance to inflict Critical Damage	20	30	40	50
Damage Absorption Rate	Bayek has a [X]% chance to absorb 30% of the incoming damage	20	30	40	50
Damage Absorption Value	Bayek has a 10% chance to abosrb [X]% of the incoming damage	50	65	80	95
Fire Resistance	Fire Damage is reduced by [X]%	20	30	40	50
Melee Resistance	Melee Damage is reduced by [X]%	20	30	40	50
Precision	Arrow Dispersion is reduced by [X]%	10	20	30	40
Ranged Resistence	Ranged Damage is reduced by [X]%	20	30	40	50
Rate of Fire	Bow's Rate of Fire is increased by [X]%	20	30	40	50
Stealth Damage	While undetected, Shots inflict [X]% more damage	115	130	145	160

MOUNTS

AVAILABLE MOUNTS

CAMELS

NAME	DESCRIPTION	RARITY	HOW TO ACQUIRE
Basus	This sacred camel is so revered that legend has it, if killed, a war would break out in its honor.	Rare	Complete Side Quest—Striking Back
Bone Cracker	He loves eating bones. If you hunt a lot, you might have to be a bit careful with him.	Rare	Stables
Desert's Pilgrim	The pilgrim's steps echoed across the dunes under the watchful eye of great Amun Ra, each mile a tribute to his glorious eternity.	Rare	Stables
Fidget	This restless dromedary is in constant motion.	Common	Stables
Guardian	This camel would do a great job guarding your stable. It's not that he doesn't like to move; it's more that he really likes to sit.	Common	Stables
Inspiration	A certain artist in Memphis considers this camel as his muse.	Rare	Complete Side Quest—When Night Falls
Khamsin	His last owner had a lively sense of humor, and it seems to have worn off on the camel, who can spit at astonishing range.	Common	Stables
Majesty	Majesty is a quick and reliable mount. However, due to lavish treatment by his previous owners, he needs constant grooming and attention.	Rare	Stables
Meri Heka	Named after the god of magic, good fortune follows her owner as long as they treat her well. Her last owner left her out in the sun on a hot day, and here we are.	Legendary	Stables
Pataikos Herti	Bandits attacked this camel's village, but any who approached her family home were bitten and fought off. After that they named her Pataikos, for the god of protection.	Legendary	Stables
Sand-Dweller	Intricate patterns sheared into this camel's fur tell the history of the gods in pictorial form.	Legendary	E-Store
Wanderer	The Wanderer is said to have walked the length and breadth of Egypt. No corner of the civilized world was too far away to visit.	Common	Stables

INTRODUCTION
THE ESSENTIALS
MAIN QUESTS
SIDE QUESTS
ACTIVITIES
ATLAS
REFERENCE & ANALYSIS

HORSES

NAME	DESCRIPTION	RARITY	HOW TO ACQUIRE
Aa Nekhtou	Named for her great strength, this horse is a veteran of many battles. Her unblemished coat is a testament to her martial skill.	Legendary	Stables
Annapolis	"Ah yes, the Greek mare. Good condition. Well bred. You have the air of a fine horseman. You would like her, yes?"	Common	Stables
Black Arrow	Steady, fast, and responsive to the lightest touch, this horse is an arrow in animal form.	Rare	Complete Side Quest—Go for Green
Blazing Glory	A fiery steed, her temper is well known throughout Egypt. No rider can remain astride her for long, but you seem capable. Care to try her paces?	Rare	Stables
The False Camel	A hardy and powerful mount, known for long journeys through the desert.	Common	Stables
Egyptian Mare	An unremarkable horse. Loyal, though.	Common	Stables
Eternal Glory	Many legendary warriors have ridden this mare in battle. She is unmatched by other horses in experience and in age.	Common	Stables
Kaa	Originating from the ancient kingdom of Nubia, this stallion has a calm temperament, making him a solid ally in the face of danger.	Rare	Stables
Kku	Found covered in soot among the ruins of a burnt village. Washing him caused no change in the color of his coat.	Common	Stables
Menes	He who endures. Snatches you from the fire when things get dangerous.	Common	Stables
Meri Amun	His name translates to "Beloved of Amun." Some believe this stallion was gifted with exceptional endurance and stamina by the god himself.	Legendary	Stables
Morning Mist	This stallion comes from the mountains. They say that on the morning he was born, a white mist descended from nowhere to enshroud his stable. I don't believe a word of it.	Rare	Complete Side Quest—Horse Whispering
Pharaoh's Horse	Horse of kings and king among horses, this beast is considered one of the finest in all of Egypt.	Legendary	Win all four tournaments at the Hippodrome
Roman Warhorse	Tall Andalusian horse with great stamina.	Legendary	Win all four elite tournaments at the Hippodrome
Rusty	Found abandoned in a rickety cage on the bank of the Nile. He might have been imprisoned there for too long, as his legs are prone to cramping.	Common	Stables
Soft Breeze	Mostly used for desert travel, she's a solid mount, albeit lacking in combat experience.	Common	Stables
Stranger	He wandered into town a few weeks back. No one knows where he came from.	Common	Stables
Thunder	When Thunder gallops, people scatter. Her hoofbeats evoke the din of an entire herd.	Common	Stables
True Friend	After his owner sickened and fell limp from the saddle, this stallion stood by for two days until a passing farmer stopped to help.	Rare	Stables
Unicorn	Unicorns are said to originate from faraway lands, though we've never been able to determine which. What we do know is that they are fabulous.	Legendary	E-Store

CHARIOTS

NAME	DESCRIPTION	RARITY	HOW TO ACQUIRE
Royal Chariot	Royal chariots are reserved for the greatest of the elite. Reinforced with shields, they offer sturdy protection to their riders, and their intimidating presence saps enemy morale.	Legendary	Stables
Scout Chariot	Light and versatile, this vehicle is used for scouting missions and for chasing down fleet-footed enemies. Though its price is fair, it is nevertheless too expensive for all but noblemen and the richest of merchants.	Common	Stables
War Chariot	The durable war chariot is the most common in Egypt. Quivers attached to its sides hold extra ammo.	Rare	Stables

OUTFITS

AVAILABLE OUTFITS

NAME	DESCRIPTION	RARITY	HOW TO ACQUIRE
Altaïr's Outfit	The outfit worn by the legendary Assassin Altaïr Ibn-La'ahad	Legendary	Uplay
Bathhouse Towel	This outfit leaves little to the imagination.	Common	Complete Main Quest—Assassinate Eudoros
Bayek's Outfit	The perfect outfit for a wanderer who doesn't want to attract too much attention.	Common	Default equipment
Black Hood	Anyone can kill; few do it with such style.	Legendary	Complete Side Quest—Phylakes' Prey
Dress of the Coastal Realm	Life at sea can be hard, and it's even harder without the right clothes.	Legendary	Defeat boss—The Slaver in Krokodilopolis Gladiator Arena
Dress of the Northern Realm	Northerners are said to value practicality over beauty.	Legendary	Tailor
Egyptian Hedj	A rather distinguished outfit, though still suitable for the demands of everyday life.	Common	Tailor
Egyptian Irtyu	Blue, the color of the heavens, is favored by nobles.	Common	Tailor
Egyptian Wahid	You'll travel unnoticed on the road in this humble outfit.	Common	Tailor
Engai Na-nyokie	A Maasai warrior garbed in red is one in pursuit of vengeance.	Rare	Tailor
Engai Narok	Elder Maasai warriors don this robe as a sign of their power.	Rare	Tailor
Ezio's Outfit	The outfit worn by the Master Assassin Ezio Auditore da Firenze	Legendary	Uplay
Isu Armor	Experience the absolute power of the First Civilization.	Legendary	Complete all Stone Circles and activate final Ancient Mechanism
Maasai Warrior	An outfit traditionally worn by the fierce warriors of the Maasai people.	Rare	Tailor
Marauder Chief	Red evokes power and passion, and a good leader needs both.	Common	Tailor
Marauder's Garb	The desert is under constant assault by the harsh wind and the unforgiving sun. Even the most seasoned of bandits needs protection from the elements.	Common	Tailor
Mummy	A great fashion choice on the occasion of your resurrection.	Legendary	E-Store
Persian Commander	Purple is the color of leaders, feared by their enemies.	Rare	Tailor
Persian Guard	The basic uniform for a soldier in the Persian army's elite guard.	Rare	Tailor
Persian Prince	A remnant of Persian history, worn by a prince as fleet as the wind.	Rare	Tailor
Pharaoh Armor	Step into the light and be recognized as a true Pharaoh.	Legendary	E-Store
Protector	Worn by those who protect the people.	Common	Complete the Main Quest—Narrowing the List
Roman Legionary	The costume of an elite Roman soldier, respected across the Mediterranean.	Legendary	Defeat Elite Boss—The Hammer in Cyrene Gladiator Arena
Roman Marinus	The uniform of a Roman sailor well versed in naval warfare.	Legendary	Defeat Elite Boss—The Seleucid in Cyrene Gladiator Arena
Roman Venator	Worn by Roman hunters who provided for the legion while on campaign.	Legendary	Defeat Elite Boss—The Duelist in Cyrene Gladiator Arena
Savannah Marauder	Skinning your last kill and making it into an outfit demonstrates both your prowess as a hunter and your braggadocio.	Common	Tailor
Scarab Soldier	Elite Egyptian soldiers were inspired by the diligence of the sacred beetle in crafting this outfit.	Legendary	E-Store
Sekhmet Costume	A costume worn during the reenactment of the battle between Sekhmet and Isfet held as part of Yamu's festival.	Legendary	Complete Side Quest—The Festival
Shaman	This outfit may allow you to communicate with the spirits of nature, and thereby improve your hunting skills.	Legendary	Defeat War Elephant—Herwennefer

INVENTORY

Your Inventory screen displays the resources, arrows, tools, quest items, Papyri, animal goods, and trinkets that you currently possess. Highlight an item for more information. Quest items are covered in the quest chapters of the guide, while the Papyri are discussed in the Activities chapter. The rest are listed below with pertinent information. Nomad's Bazaar is covered at the end of this section with details on his valuable goods.

RESOURCES

HOW TO ACQUIRE: Available in various locations

Resources are gathered in the wild or swiped from military convoys. Scout an area with Senu to find the resource that you need. Most materials are used to upgrade gear; see the Crafting section for more information. Silica is used to activate Ancient Mechanisms found inside several tombs.

Obtain the Buy Materials ability to purchase most resources from blacksmiths and weavers—handy for finishing up remaining upgrades. Hard Leather, Pelts, and Soft Leather can be bought from Weavers. Bronze, cedarwood, and iron become available at blacksmiths. Note that shops have a limited supply of each resource that varies between merchants. These six resources can also be sold for a few drachmas, but make sure you do not need them for any upgrades first.

RESOURCES

ITEM	WHERE FOUND	RARITY	PRICE (DRACHMAS)	VALUE (DRACHMAS)	DESCRIPTION
Bronze	Military Convoy	Common	75	6	Ptolemy's soldiers carry this metal in convoys; it's probably too heavy for their delicate hands.
Carbon Crystal	Small Treasure Box	Legendary	N/A	N/A	Mainly found in military camps, these crystals resemble precious gems and thus are often found in jewelry boxes. A limited supply is available for purchase from Nomad's Bazaar. Used in highest levels of equipment upgrades.
Cedarwood	Military Convoy	Common	50	4	Use your eagle to spot military convoys carrying dried wood. It is a common but useful resource.
Hard Leather	Loot Hippopotamus, Crocodile	Common	75	6	Some hippopotamus or crocodile died to offer you the protective skin off its back.
Iron	Military Convoy	Rare	90	7	A rare material. If you need large quantities, use your eagle to track them down.
Pelt	Loot Lion, Leopard	Rare	90	7	Nothing compares to lion or leopard fur when a cold night approaches!
Silica	Tombs	Legendary	N/A	N/A	A unique glass fragment found in tombs and used as a decorative ornament. This strange substance has an eerie feeling. The number of Silica available is limited to 80, with most found inside the tombs. A few are scattered throughout deserts. Once the maximum number has been found, you can no longer collect more.
Soft Leather	Loot gazelle, hyena, ibex	Common	50	4	A supple material suitable for light armor. Harvested from animals with thin and delicate skin, such as the gazelle.

ARROWS

HOW TO ACQUIRE: Loot enemy, refill at blacksmith for 1 drachma/arrow, refill at ammo rack for free, collect from own shield with Arrow Retriever ability

Arrows are invaluable for long-range attacks. Each of the four types of bows requires a unique arrow. Predator bows, which allow the player to snipe enemies from afar, allow up to only nine arrows at a time—requiring frequent trips to arrow supplies. Always refill your supply whenever you come across an ammo rack. Upgrade your quiver to carry more of each arrow type.

The maximum arrows that you can carry for each quiver level is indicated in the Max column. The first number indicates the maximum without any upgrades, while the last number is the most arrows that you can possess when the quiver if fully upgraded.

ARROWS

ITEM		MAX (LEVEL 0/1/2/3/4/5)	DESCRIPTION
	Hunter Arrows	15/18/22/26/30/33	Arrows for the Hunter Bow.
	Light Arrows	15/18/22/26/30/33	Arrows for the Light Bow.
	Predator Arrows	4/5/6/7/8/9	Arrows for the Predator Bow.
	Warrior Arrows	15/18/22/26/30/33	Arrows for the Warrior Bow.

TOOLS

HOW TO ACQUIRE: Loot enemy, refill at blacksmith for 1 drachma/tool, or refill at ammo rack for free

Tools come in six varying types: Berserk, Firebomb, Flesh Decay Toxin, Poison Darts, Sleep Darts, and Smoke Screen. You must obtain the ability of the same name in order to use that tool. See the table below for each tool's purpose and the maximum number of each that can be carried as the Tool Pouch is upgraded.

The maximum number of each tool that you can carry for each tool pouch level is indicated in the Max column. The first number indicates the maximum without any upgrades, while the last number represents the maximum that you can possess when the tool pouch if fully upgraded.

TOOLS

ITEM		MAX (LEVEL 0/1/2/3/4/5)	DESCRIPTION
	Berserk	3/4/6/7/9/10	Use this substance on careless enemies to turn them against their allies. Approach an unaware foe and press the indicated button to cause him to attack nearby targets.
	Firebomb	3/4/6/7/9/10	Throw this bomb to set your enemies ablaze. While in game, Hold Left on D-pad to equip the tool. Hold the Aim button and press Heavy Attack to toss the bomb. This also sets off oil jars and catches flammable materials on fire.
	Flesh Decay Toxin	6/7/10/12/15/17	Use this substance to infect a dead body and allow it to contaminate nearby enemies. After killing a foe, press the indicated button to poison the corpse.
	Poison Darts	3/4/6/7/9/10	Launch these darts to disable an enemy and spread poison to nearby enemies. While in game, Hold Left on D-pad to equip this tool.
	Sleep Darts	3/4/6/7/9/10	Launch these darts to put lower-ranked enemies or animals to sleep and move past them without being detected. While in game, Hold Left on D-pad to equip the tool. Putting an animal to sleep also allows you to tame it once you own the Animal Taming ability.
	Smoke Screen	3/4/6/7/9/10	Use this powder in combat to blind nearby enemies. Press the Loot button after a melee attack or dodge to drop the powder—great for fleeing trouble or getting the jump on an enemy.

INTRODUCTION

THE ESSENTIALS

MAIN QUESTS

SIDE QUESTS

ACTIVITIES

ATLAS

REFERENCE & ANALYSIS

ANIMAL GOODS

HOW TO ACQUIRE: Loot a dead animal

Loot Animal Goods from animal corpses. Sell them to a merchant by pressing down on the D-pad at the Shop menu. Earn an extra 25 percent per item with the Salesman ability. Keep an eye out for animals killed by predators and hunters for free loot.

ANIMAL GOODS

ITEM	ANIMAL TO LOOT	RARITY	VALUE (DRACHMAS)	DESCRIPTION
Cobra Venom	Cobra	Common	7	Even in antiquity, shamans would make antidotes and medicines out of venom.
Crocodile Egg	Crocodile	Rare	12	Can be used to treat a number of ailments and conditions.
Flamingo Tongue	Flamingo	Common	5	The flamingo's meat is succulent, but its tongue is a delicacy fit for kings and queens.
Gazelle Hooves	Gazelle	Common	5	You know it's trading in the market but you have absolutely no idea why.
Heron Feathers	Heron	Common	5	Heron feathers lead the spirits of the dead through the Duat.
Hippopotamus Meat	Hippopotamus	Rare	10	A rare delicacy also known as "lake cow bacon."
Hyena Ears	Hyena	Rare	12	A hunter's trophy and proof of courage.
Ibex Horns	Ibex	Common	5	An ever-popular sculpting material.
Ibis Beak	Ibis	Common	5	Symbol of the crescent moon. Used to represent Thoth in rituals.
Leopard Fur	Leopard	Legendary	50	For cold nights and windy weather.
Lion Claw	Lion	Rare	35	Popularly worn as a pendant by commoners. Not a bad look, really.
Vulture Skull	Vulture	Common	7	When the scavenger becomes the scavenged.

TRINKETS

HOW TO ACQUIRE: Small-value containers

Find trinkets in small-value containers and sell them to shops for money by pressing down on the D-pad. Earn an extra 25 percent per item (rounded to the nearest drachma) with the Salesman ability. Much like the Animal Goods, these items are useless besides earning a small amount of drachmas from a vendor.

TRINKETS

TRINKET	RARITY	VALUE (DRACHMAS)	DESCRIPTION
Animal Flesh	Common	8	Don't keep this in your inventory too long.
Ball	Common	17	Made of leather. Hippos like them a lot.
Broken Pot	Common	8	Who doesn't shave with a sharp shard? This pot bears its owner's name, and that person's probably in a vengeful mood.
Bronze Cup	Rare	25	Where's the cupbearer? This thing needs filling.
Butcher's Cleaver	Common	8	Sometimes the fastest way out of a misunderstanding is to brandish a cleaver.
Cat Amulet	Legendary	80	Twenty-two centuries ago, cats were the bee's knees.
Diadem	Legendary	80	Was probably stolen from a princess. Best sell it before someone traces the theft to you.
Flute	Rare	25	Make no mistake—even in ancient Egypt, parents plugged their ears while their children practiced the flute.
Golden Bolt	Legendary	40	All that's gold does not glitter, unless polished.
Golden Plate	Common	8	It's a plate made of gold. Useful if you ever need to serve appetizers.
Grapes	Common	8	Ah, grapes! The smooth resistance against your teeth, the pleasant rupture of the skin as you bite down, the rush of sweet juice onto your tongue…truly a food fit for the gods.

TRINKET	RARITY	VALUE (DRACHMAS)	DESCRIPTION
Hand of the God	Common	8	Used for religious purposes. No high fives, please.
Hatchet	Common	17	Trees quiver in the shadow of this mighty blade.
Headrest	Common	25	A simple wooden headrest, essential for a good night's sleep. Guaranteed bedbug-free.
Honeycomb	Common	8	The first person in history to taste honey must have been quite courageous. Carefully wrapped in oiled papyrus. Take a bit and relish the sweet taste.
Incense Burner	Rare	40	It wouldn't be a ceremony without incense, would it?
Iron Hammer	Rare	25	All that's missing is a bell and a song.
Jade Scarab	Rare	25	Used as a paperweight, a seal, an amulet, and sometimes even as a murder weapon.
Large Paintbrush	Common	8	You've got a lot to do today, but why not paint a picture instead?
Leather Bag	Common	17	Recursion at its finest.
Leather Belt	Common	8	An essential accessory.
Lute	Rare	40	You're not even going to try your hand at this. Especially not after the lyre incident…
Lyre	Rare	40	Imagining a stirring solo, you grab the lyre and pluck a few chords. But you don't know how to play it, so instead, you return it to your bag with a melancholy sigh.
Manuscript	Rare	25	After quite a lot of time on the road, you've perfected the art of folding this sheet into a cunning little bird. Now what should you call this art?
Necklace	Legendary	80	The quintessential fashion statement, dating from time immemorial.
Opium Pipe	Rare	25	Let the good times roll…
Pestle	Common	8	Coriander, a dash of cumin…add a pinch of sesame seeds, and you've got the best dukkah this side of the Nile.
Salt	Common	8	Keeps away the evil eye. Also tasty on boiled eggs.
Sistrum	Legendary	40	This ancient musical instrument looks like a handheld metal abacus. Used primarily in religious ceremonies.
Small Knife	Common	17	When you think about it, knives are basically fun-sized swords.
Small Statue	Common	8	This statue gives the impression that the gods never smile.
Spearhead	Common	8	Rusty, but worth salvaging for the iron.
Stone Pitcher	Common	17	When empty, fill it. When full, empty it.
Stonemason's Chisel	Common	17	The sturdy, reliable chisel is one of the most important tools known to civilization.
Tambourine	Rare	40	You can't mess up the tambourine. Or can you?
Toy Horse	Common	17	Your father carved you a toy horse like this when you were young. You remember being disappointed that it wasn't life-sized. The disappointment never went away.
Unfinished Sword	Common	8	It's best when people finish what they start.
Wooden Log	Common	8	Examining the cracks of this log reveals a small colony of resident spiders.
Wooden Mallet	Common	8	Mallets are a chisel's best friend.

NOMAD'S BAZAAR

NOMAD'S BAZAAR GOODS

ITEM	COST (DRACHMAS)	NUMBER AVAILABLE	DESCRIPTION
Carbon Crystal	3,000	20	Mainly found in military camps, these crystals resemble precious gems, and thus are often found in jewelry boxes.
Heka Chest	3,000	Infinite	Contains one random weapon or shield. Opens automatically on purchase.

A young man named Reda runs a traveling bazaar as he moves between 15 locations around Egypt. He always spawns to the closest location to Bayek, so there usually isn't a need to go very far. Plus, his camel icon always appears on the map even on top of the fog when a territory has not been discovered. Refer to our Atlas to find all 15 sites.

He possesses 20 carbon crystals, which are invaluable when upgrading your gear to the highest levels. Once this supply is gone, though, it is gone forever. Therefore, remaining carbon crystals must be found in jewelry boxes around the world.

He also sells a Heka Chest that opens automatically upon purchase (for 3,000 drachmas). Inside, a rare or legendary weapon or shield is generated from a set supply. The weapons and shields available change weekly, so be sure to come back often for new gear.

Reda offers a quest for Bayek that changes daily. Complete the objective each day to earn XP.

INTRODUCTION

THE ESSENTIALS

MAIN QUESTS

SIDE QUESTS

ACTIVITIES

ATLAS

REFERENCE & ANALYSIS

CRAFTING

Use resources to upgrade Bayek's gear. The bracer, breastplate, stabilizer, hidden blade, quiver, and tool pouch can be improved with select resources. Upgrading the quiver and tool pouch allows Bayek to carry more arrows and tools. Upgrading the remaining items boosts Bayek's health as well as his melee, ranged, and hidden blade damage. These stats are not dependent on only the gear, though. Here is a rundown of each stat and its modifiers:

Note that you cannot increase an item's level beyond Bayek's level. Therefore, you are unable to max out any gear until Bayek reaches Level 10.

BAYEK'S STATS

STAT	MODIFIERS
Health	Character level, breastplate crafting level, and HP from equipped shield
Melee Damage	Character level, bracer crafting level, and damage of equipped melee weapon
Ranged Damage	Character level, stabilizer crafting level, and damage of equipped bow
Hidden Blade Damage	Upgrading hidden blade increases stealth attack damage

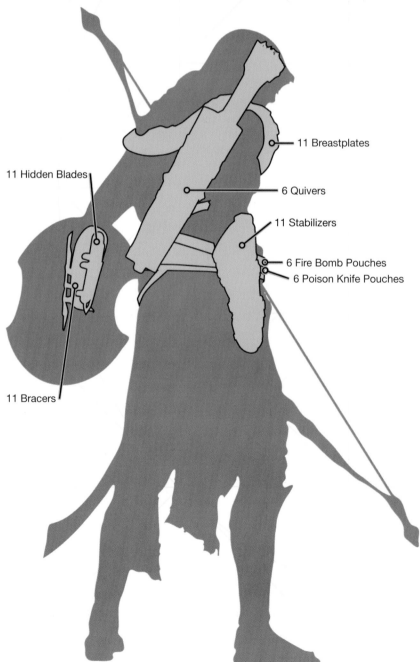

11 Hidden Blades

11 Bracers

11 Breastplates

6 Quivers

11 Stabilizers

6 Fire Bomb Pouches

6 Poison Knife Pouches

BRACER

UPGRADE EFFECT: Increase melee damage

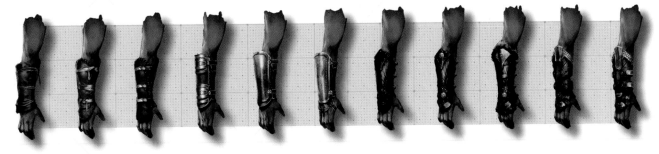

BRACER UPGRADES

LEVEL	RESOURCES REQUIRED	MELEE DAMAGE MULTIPLIER
1	11 Cedarwood	1.2
2	7 Hard Leather + 12 Cedarwood	1.4
3	8 Hard Leather + 13 Cedarwood	1.6
4	9 Hard Leather + 15 Cedarwood	1.8
5	11 Hard Leather + 17 Cedarwood	2.0
6	13 Hard Leather + 19 Cedarwood + 12 Pelts	2.2
7	15 Hard Leather + 21 Cedarwood + 13 Pelts	2.4
8	17 Hard Leather + 24 Cedarwood + 14 Pelts	2.6
9	20 Hard Leather + 28 Cedarwood + 16 Pelts + 3 Carbon Crystal	2.8
10	24 Hard Leather + 38 Cedarwood + 18 Pelts + 5 Carbon Crystal	3.0

Boosting your melee damage allows Bayek to be a fighting machine when taking on enemy soldiers up close. All melee weapons see a boost in their damage.

STABILIZER GLOVE

UPGRADE EFFECT: Increase ranged damage

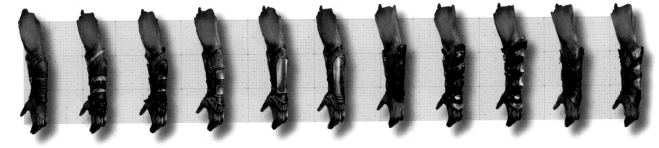

STABILIZER UPGRADES

LEVEL	RESOURCES REQUIRED	RANGED DAMAGE MULTIPLIER
1	11 Soft Leather	1.2
2	12 Soft Leather + 7 Bronze	1.4
3	13 Soft Leather + 8 Bronze	1.6
4	15 Soft Leather + 9 Bronze	1.8
5	17 Soft Leather + 11 Bronze	2.0
6	19 Soft Leather + 13 Bronze + 12 Iron	2.2
7	21 Soft Leather + 15 Bronze + 13 Iron	2.4
8	24 Soft Leather + 17 Bronze + 14 Iron	2.6
9	28 Soft Leather + 20 Bronze + 16 Iron + 3 Carbon Crystal	2.8
10	38 Soft Leather + 24 Bronze + 18 Iron + 5 Carbon Crystal	3.0

Boost Bayek's ranged damage if you prefer fighting with a bow and arrow. Bows are great for taking out the opposition from a safe location. All bows see a boost in damage.

INTRODUCTION

THE ESSENTIALS

MAIN QUESTS

SIDE QUESTS

ACTIVITIES

ATLAS

REFERENCE & ANALYSIS

HIDDEN BLADE

UPGRADE EFFECT: Increase Hidden Blade damage

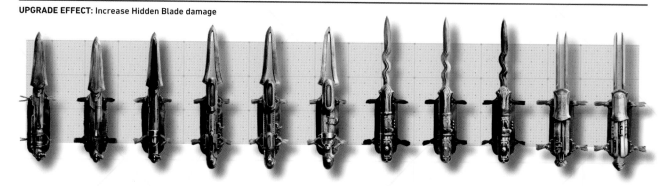

HIDDEN BLADE UPGRADES

LEVEL	RESOURCES REQUIRED	ASSASSINATION DAMAGE MULTIPLIER
1	13 Bronze	1.6
2	14 Bronze + 9 Iron	2.2
3	15 Bronze + 10 Iron	2.7
4	17 Bronze + 11 Iron	3.3
5	19 Bronze + 13 Iron	3.9
6	21 Bronze + 15 Iron + 14 Hard Leather	4.4
7	23 Bronze + 17 Iron + 15 Hard Leather	5
8	26 Bronze + 19 Iron + 16 Hard Leather	5.6
9	30 Bronze + 22 Iron + 18 Hard Leather + 5 Carbon Crystal	6.2
10	42 Bronze + 26 Iron + 20 Hard Leather + 5 Carbon Crystal	6.8

Once the Hidden Blade is received, assassinations come much easier. Boost the damage to take down tougher foes with one stab from your knife.

BREASTPLATE

UPGRADE EFFECT: Increase Health

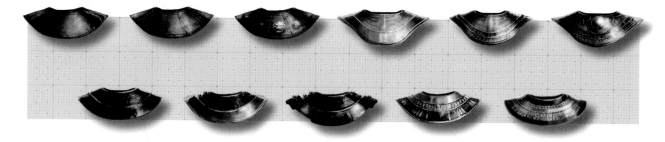

BREASTPLATE UPGRADES

LEVEL	RESOURCES REQUIRED	HEALTH MULTIPLIER
1	5 Soft Leather	1.3
2	7 Soft Leather + 5 Hard Leather	1.6
3	8 Soft Leather + 6 Hard Leather	1.9
4	10 Soft Leather + 7 Hard Leather	2.2
5	12 Soft Leather + 9 Hard Leather	2.5
6	14 Soft Leather + 11 Hard Leather + 7 Pelts	2.8
7	16 Soft Leather + 13 Hard Leather + 8 Pelts	3.1
8	19 Soft Leather + 15 Hard Leather + 9 Pelts	3.4
9	23 Soft Leather + 18 Hard Leather + 11 Pelts + 3 Carbon Crystal	3.7
10	28 Soft Leather + 22 Hard Leather + 13 Pelts + 5 Carbon Crystal	4.0

A boost in health is always a good idea, allowing Bayek to last longer in fights and withstand hits easier.

QUIVER

UPGRADE EFFECT: Increase arrow storage for all bows

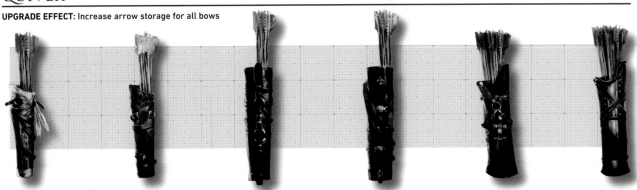

QUIVER UPGRADES

LEVEL	RESOURCES REQUIRED	MAX ARROWS (HUNTER, LIGHT, WARRIOR/PREDATOR)
1	10 Cedarwood	18/5
2	11 Cedarwood	22/6
3	13 Cedarwood + 10 Pelts	26/7
4	15 Cedarwood + 11 Pelts	30/8
5	17 Cedarwood + 13 Pelts + 3 Carbon Crystal	33/9

If you prefer fighting from a distance with your favorite bow, it is well worth the resources to increase your arrow storage. When fully upgraded to Level 5, the quiver can hold a total of 33 arrows for hunter, light, and warrior bows and 9 arrows for the predator bows.

TOOL POUCH

UPGRADE EFFECT: Increase tool storage for all tools

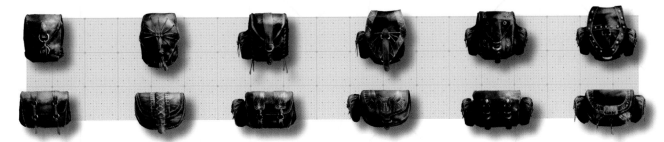

TOOL POUCH UPGRADES

LEVEL	RESOURCES REQUIRED	MAX TOOLS (BERSERK, FIREBOMB, POISON DARTS, SLEEP DARTS, SMOKE SCREEN/FLESH DECAY TOXIN)
1	10 Pelts	3/6
2	11 Pelts	4/7
3	13 Pelts + 10 Hard Leather	5/8
4	15 Pelts + 11 Hard Leather	6/10
5	17 Pelts + 13 Hard Leather + 3 Carbon Crystal	9/15

Tools are extremely valuable when infiltrating an enemy stronghold. Take advantage of their abilities whenever possible. Sleep darts are especially handy against multiple or tough enemies, though their effectiveness decreases as your target's level increases over Bayek's level. Upgrade the tool pouch in order to carry more of each tool. It can carry a maximum of 15 flesh decay toxin and 9 smoke screens, firebombs, berserk, poison darts, and sleep darts.

INTRODUCTION

THE ESSENTIALS

MAIN QUESTS

SIDE QUESTS

ACTIVITIES

ATLAS

REFERENCE & ANALYSIS

ACHIEVEMENTS & TROPHIES

The achievements and trophies in *Assassin's Creed Origins* vary greatly from simply playing through the main quests to completing the numerous side activities to killing enemies in spectacular fashion to experiencing a hallucination, where scarabs fall from the sky.

Complete the main quests and the mentioned side quests, and reach Level 20 to receive the following:

NAME	DESCRIPTION	PS4 TROPHY	XBOX ONE POINTS
First Steps	Complete the Prologue.	Bronze	10
I'm Just Getting Started	Complete Main Quest: Aya (suggested level 12).	Bronze	10
The Sea	Complete Main Quest: Pompeius Magnus (suggested level 12).	Bronze	20
The Scarab	Complete Main Quest: The Scarab's Sting (suggested level 15).	Silver	20
The Hyena	Complete Main Quest: The Hyena (suggested level 20).	Bronze	20
The Lizard	Complete Main Quest: The Lizard's Face (suggested level 20).	Silver	20
The Crocodile	Complete Main Quest: The Crocodile's Jaws (suggested level 25).	Bronze	20
The Siege	Complete Main Quest: The Battle of the Nile (suggested level 31).	Silver	30
Wake Up!	Complete Main Quest: Dream Sequence (suggested level 31).	Silver	30
Almost There	Complete Main Quest: The Final Weighing (suggested level 32).	Silver	30
The End	Complete the last main quest. To finish the main quest, complete Birth of the Creed.	Gold	50
The Festival	Complete Side Quest: Lady of Slaughter. The quest is found in Lake Mareotis near the Temple of Sekhmet (suggested level 8).	Bronze	20
Seven Farmers	Complete Side Quest: Seven Farmers. The quest is found in north-central Uab Nome (suggested level 30).	Bronze	10
You still need 8880…	Reach Level 20.	Bronze	10

ACTIVITIES

The following achievements are earned by completing the various activities around Ancient Egypt. Refer to our Activities chapter for further details.

NAME	DESCRIPTION	PS4 TROPHY	XBOX ONE POINTS
For those about to die…	Complete all arena events in the Krokodilopolis Arena. Only requires defeating The Brothers and the Slaver on Normal mode; defeating elite events is not necessary.	Silver	20
Fatality!	Finish an arena boss with an Overpower attack. Whittle a boss's health down, but once you get down to about one-quarter health, save your next special power until little health is left.	Silver	30
Ben-Hur	Win the first Hippodrome tournament. Finish in first in Nike's Winged Victory tournament.	Bronze	20
Road Rage	Destroy an opponent in a Hippodrome race. Trample and ram an opponent until the rival's chariot is destroyed to earn Road Rage.	Bronze	20
Elementary, My Dear Bayek	Solve a Papyrus mystery. Find a Papyrus and read its clue. Use this information to hunt down the treasure and score this reward. Refer to the Papyri section of the Activities chapter for more information.	Bronze	30
Stargazer	Complete all 12 Stone Circles. Visit all 12 Stone Circles and align the stars to complete each one. Refer to the Stone Circles section of the Activities chapter for details on each Stone Circle.	Silver	20
Raider of the Lost Tomb	Complete a tomb. Any tomb will do, though the early side quest "Hideaway" takes you through the simplest tomb, Mountain of the Dead, as you complete the quest. Refer to the Tombs section of the Activities chapter for information on each tomb.	Bronze	20
The Harder They Fall	Defeat the War Elephants Qetesh & Resheph. War Elephants are the toughest opponents in the game and require great perseverance. Concentrate arrows at its eyes for extra damage, though ammo should be saved, since the beast gets tougher as the fight goes along. Loot bags pop up around the battlefield when ammo runs low. Watch for it to strafe for a good opportunity to strike. Refer to the War Elephants section of the Activities chapter for more information.	Silver	50
Words of Wisdom	Complete all hermit locations. Meditate at all five hermit locations to score 5 Ability Points. Refer to the Atlas for all five locations.	Bronze	5
Defy Authority	Defeat a Phylake. After assassinating Gennadios, Phylake (Bounty Hunters) come after Bayek . with red icons indicating their locations on the map. Be careful when these guys appear; they are some of the toughest enemies in the game—ranking just below the War Elephants. Kill one to score this award.	Bronze	10

THE COMPLETIONIST

A number of awards require upgrading Bayek and making your way around the entire map. Destroy objects whenever possible and sell the trinkets found inside small-value containers.

NAME	DESCRIPTION	PS4 TROPHY	XBOX ONE POINTS
I Know My Land	Defog the whole map. The map unfogs as you travel to new areas. Once you have visited the entire overworld, I Know My Land is awarded.	Bronze	30
I'm Done Learning	Activate a Master ability. Make your way through the skill tree to Master Hunter, Master Warrior, or Master Seer and spend a point on the ability.	Silver	30
I'm a Legend	Be equipped with only Legendary equipment. Requires two melee weapons, two bows, a shield, an outfit, and a Legendary vehicle.	Bronze	20

INTRODUCTION

THE ESSENTIALS

MAIN QUESTS

SIDE QUESTS

ACTIVITIES

ATLAS

REFERENCE & ANALYSIS

NAME	DESCRIPTION	PS4 TROPHY	XBOX ONE POINTS
Handy Man	Craft 20 items. Gather resources whenever the opportunity arises and put them to good use by improving your gear.	Bronze	20
Old Habits	Complete all locations. Complete all world portals, points of interest, tombs, Ancient Mechanisms, lairs, forts, Papyrus locations, Stone Circles, and War Elephants. Refer to our Atlas for all locations and the Activities chapter for further details.	Silver	40
Namaste	Use Dawn & Dusk to make time speed forward 30 times. Purchase the Dawn & Dusk ability and use it to change between night and day. Hold the world map button to perform this action.	Bronze	20
Master Diver	Complete 15 underwater locations. A number of points of interest found in the waterways are actually underwater; dive to find the lost treasure. Watch out for crocodiles in the Nile.	Silver	20
Free as a Bird	Use the eagle for a total of 30 minutes. Senu is very helpful when scouting enemy strongholds and searching for resources, so use him often.	Bronze	10
Triathlete	Swim for 1,500 m, ride for 40km, and run for 10 km. Spend time not only running around the map, but also swimming the seas and riding the various vehicles.	Bronze	10
Rider's License	Use all types of vehicle at least once. This requires using a horse, camel, cart, chariot, and felucca. Chariots can be raced at the Hippodrome or purchased from merchants once the Chariot Owner ability is owned. "Borrow" any felucca from any waterway and take it for a ride.	Bronze	10
Smash!	Destroy 100 breakable objects. There are numerous objects that can be busted with your weapons, such as urns, vases, and wooden benches. Watch out, as a cobra may hide inside or behind the bigger ones. Oil jars are also useful when broken open with a fire arrow, damaging hostiles in the immediate area.	Bronze	10
Reduce, Reuse, Recycle	Sell 100 trinkets at once. Find trinkets inside small-value containers and sell them to vendors. Use the Animus Pulse to find all nearby container locations.	Bronze	10

KILL ACHIEVEMENTS

Kill enemies in spectacular fashion to score the following. Be sure to take down the captains aboard the vessels found in the various waterways.

NAME	DESCRIPTION	PS4 TROPHY	XBOX ONE POINTS
Slasher	Kill three enemies with one hit. A long weapon, such as a heavy blade, works well for the Slasher achievement. The simplest method may be to return to Siwa at a much higher level, and head to an enemy base, such as the Temple of Amun. Run through the stronghold, getting the attention of as many guards as possible. Once surrounded, hit them with a heavy attack. This swings the axe in a circle, hitting all who stands too close.	Bronze	10
Shadow of Egypt	Kill 10 enemies in a row without being detected. Fully scan an area with Senu and stay aware of everyone's positions. Sneak up on one enemy at a time and stealthily take each one down. If the white detection arc appears, quickly take cover and stay away until they return to normal.	Silver	30
BOOM!	Kill 30 enemies by shooting a fire arrow at oil jars. Fire arrow plus oil jar equals spectacular damage. Allow enemies to get close to these red jars and light them up.	Bronze	10
The Arrow Whisperer	Kill an enemy with the predator bow from more than 60 meters while controlling the arrow. You must acquire the Enhanced Predator Bow ability in order to control the arrow. Aim for a stationary, unaware soldier at a distance and go for the head. If you go for an enemy far enough below your level, you could get a kill with an easier body shot.	Silver	20
Overdesign	Kill a poisoned Level 35+ enemy with the torch in less than 30 seconds. Hit a Level 40 enemy with a poison dart, toss a torch on him, and quickly go in for the kill by pummeling him with another torch. Attempting at Level 40 and upgrading the bracer makes this a tad easier.	Bronze	30
Archer of the Month	Headshot kill an enemy with the bow while in the air. The Elite Ranger ability allows the player to enter slow motion when aiming the bow in the air. Dropping from a high point gives you plenty of time to acquire a headshot on an unsuspecting foe.	Silver	20
Where's My Black Flag?	Defeat eight ship captains. Look for vessels in the northern seas, Lake Mareotis, and the Nile marked as points of interest or small military. Each one has a captain aboard. Board a ship and cautiously wipe out the crew, including the captain.	Bronze	30

THE WILDLIFE

The wildlife in the game varies greatly from the tame gazelle to the ferocious predators, such as the lion. These four awards involve handling these animals.

NAME	DESCRIPTION	PS4 TROPHY	XBOX ONE POINTS
Circle of Life	Feed a predator with a corpse. Kill a soldier and carry his body to any predator. It will devour the body, making for a nice distraction. Predators include hyenas, leopard, lion, or lioness.	Bronze	20
Set-up Date	Bring a tamed lion to a crocodile. Find a lion, preferably a sleeping one, and hit it with a dart. With the animal taming ability, make it your companion. Now simply find a crocodile and let them do their thing.	Bronze	10
Run for Your Life!	Run away from three fights with a hippo. Hippos are fairly slow animals, but beware of their charge attack, which allows them to close in on their target surprisingly quickly. They are unable to climb, so this is often the best route when fleeing from the beast.	Bronze	10
RRoooaaarrrrr!	Tame a lion. Try to sneak up on an unsuspecting lion and hit it with a sleep dart. If alerted to your presence, it gets more difficult to get the dart into the predator.	Bronze	5

OTHER ACHIEVEMENTS & TROPHIES

Three awards require you to become overheated in the desert, climb the highest peak, and snap a photo in 5 different territories. Earn every trophy on the PlayStation 4 to earn the platinum.

NAME	DESCRIPTION	PS4 TROPHY	XBOX ONE POINTS
Overheating	Witness raining bugs in the desert. Hallucinations are triggered after spending a short time in the desert. A specific hallucination involves frogs falling from the sky at the end of the vision.	Bronze	20
I Can See My House from Here!	Reach the "Top of the World" in the Black Desert territory. Find the Ra-Hrakhty Mountaintop hermit location at the high peak in eastern Black Desert. Meditate to score an AP as well as this achievement.	Bronze	10
Reporter	Take one photo in in 5 different territories. By clicking the two control sticks, you can snap pictures of anything that looks interesting. These photos are viewed on the map screen. Every time you enter a new territory (34 in all), take a picture.	Bronze	20
Earn Them All!	Win every trophy. Only available on PlayStation 4; acquire all of the above trophies to score the platinum.	Platinum	N/A

INTRODUCTION

THE ESSENTIALS

MAIN QUESTS

SIDE QUESTS

ACTIVITIES

ATLAS

REFERENCE & ANALYSIS

ASSASSIN'S CREED ORIGINS

Written by Tim Bogenn and Michael Owen

DK/Prima Games, a division of Penguin Random House LLC
6081 East 82nd Street, Suite #400
Indianapolis, IN 46250

Based on a game rated by the ESRB:

ISBN: Collector's Edition 9780744018615

Standard Edition 9780744018608

Printing Code: The rightmost double-digit number is the year of the book's printing; the rightmost single-digit number is the number of the book's printing. For example, 17-1 shows that the first printing of the book occurred in 2017.

20 19 18 17   4 3 2 1

001-309169-Oct/2017

Printed in the USA.

CREDITS

Title Manager
Chris Hausermann

Book Designer
Dan Caparo

Production Designer
Justin Lucas

Production
Beth Guzman

Copy Editor
Carrie Andrews

PRIMA GAMES STAFF

VP & Publisher
Mike Degler

Editorial Manager
Tim Fitzpatrick

Design and Layout Manager
Tracy Wehmeyer

Licensing
Paul Giacomotto

Digital Publishing
Julie Asbury

Shaida Boroumand

Operations Manager
Stacey Ginther

ACKNOWLEDGMENTS

TIM BOGENN

A big thank you to Matthieu Bagna, Anthony Marcantonio, Antoine Ceszynski, Pierre Laliberte, and everyone at Ubisoft for their unyielding support in the creation of this guide and for making the latest Assassin's Creed game so immersive and entertaining. A special thanks to everyone at Prima Games for turning my words, screen shots, and maps into a work of art. Thank you Michael Owen for teaming up with me once again to take a massive project from overwhelming, to manageable, to enjoyable. Thanks to Jennifer, Ashlee, Michael, Brianna, and Nicholas for their support while I was in Egypt.

MICHAEL OWEN

First, I would like to give a special thanks to Matthieu Bagna, Antoine Ceszynski, Pierre Laliberte, Anthony Marcantonio, and everyone at Ubisoft for keeping us up to date with new game builds and providing excellent assistance with the guide. Thanks to Chris Hausermann, Dan Caparo, and everyone at Prima Games for the incredible job of putting this stellar guide together. Big thanks to Tim Bogenn for his utmost professionalism and hard work tackling the multitude of quests. Lastly, I would like to thank Michelle for once again showing great patience and taking care of everything around the house while I toiled away on this project.